September 2003

THE POLITICS OF TRADE

The Politics of Trade

The Overseas Merchant
in State and Society,
1660–1720

PERRY GAUCI

OXFORD
UNIVERSITY PRESS

*This book has been printed digitally and produced in a standard specification
in order to ensure its continuing availability*

OXFORD
UNIVERSITY PRESS

Great Clarendon Street, Oxford OX2 6DP

Oxford University Press is a department of the University of Oxford.
It furthers the University's objective of excellence in research, scholarship,
and education by publishing worldwide in

Oxford New York

Auckland Bangkok Buenos Aires Cape Town Chennai
Dar es Salaam Delhi Hong Kong Istanbul Karachi Kolkata
Kuala Lumpur Madrid Melbourne Mexico City Mumbai Nairobi
São Paulo Shanghai Taipei Tokyo Toronto

Oxford is a registered trade mark of Oxford University Press
in the UK and in certain other countries

Published in the United States
by Oxford University Press Inc., New York

© Perry Gauci

The moral rights of the author have been asserted
Database right Oxford University Press (maker)

Reprinted 2003

ISBN 0-19-924193-7

For Christina

Preface

IN COMMON with the early modern merchant, I find myself at the centre of a huge network of supportive friends and colleagues, whose contribution to this book merits more than a simple thank you. My first debt of gratitude must be paid to the Leverhulme Trust, whose three-year award enabled me to undertake the research for this book while based at the Centre for Metropolitan History. At the Centre I was fortunate in having the most supportive associates one could wish for. Derek Keene was crucial in developing the proposal submitted to the Trust, and maintained a steady hand on the tiller through to the completion of the project. Henry Roseveare and Paul Langford also proved invaluable advisers for the three years of this study, and Henry acted as a most prescient reader of the final version. My thanks also go to my colleagues at the Centre who shared in the travails of this study, and provided the ideal circumstances in which to further my historical interests. Not only did they put up with the most incompetent official in trade union history, but they ensured that my single-person project never felt like a lonely furrow to plough. Olwen Myhill, whose administrational, technical, and interpersonal skills do so much to ensure the success of the Centre, was the most complete of bricks, as anyone there will testify.

Many friends of the Centre were instrumental in making the scope of this project possible. Henry Horwitz ensured that I enjoyed a flying start by providing his enormous personal archive of Augustan materials, and has remained a most positive critic, having read the entire book in draft. James Alexander and Craig Spence deserve enduring praise and thanks for compiling the database which determined the City sample used here. Michael Power also provided immense aid by supplying me with his own research materials, and by availing me of his unrivalled knowledge of early modern Liverpool. Gary De Krey also kindly gave permission for me to cite important sources from his unpublished work, while Peter Earle was equally generous with his unpublished data. The anonymous readers for the Oxford University Press also deserve thanks for their helpful critique of this work. I sincerely hope that all these scholars will regard the finished project as a useful expenditure of their time and patience.

Many other fine historians have contributed to this project. Susan Whyman and Maria Fusaro also read the whole draft in full, and Susan has been a source of encouragement throughout. Clyve Jones, Stuart Handley, and Natasha Glaisyer also lent their expertise to several sections of this book, while David Hayton was instrumental in directing my thoughts towards the politics of trade. I am also indebted to Richard Harrison, Chris Kyle, and Julian Hoppit for their specialist knowledge. A happy former workplace, the History of Parliament Trust, both inspired and significantly advanced this project, and I would like to acknowledge the Trustees for granting permission to cite extracts from their unpublished articles and transcripts. Over the last five years, I have been extremely fortunate in the welcome which greeted me at Wadham and Lincoln Colleges, both from inestimable colleagues and their impressive students. In Oxford and London I have mixed with the most stimulating of company, and I thank all those who have reminded me that history should be a joyous road to discovery.

That this particular journey was ever finished owes much to the efficiency and expertise of a very large numbers of archivists and librarians. Great thanks go to the staff of the Guildhall Library of London, and their counterparts at the Institute of Historical Research merit great admiration for providing such service in ever more difficult circumstances. Mike White and Juliet Montgomery also did much to smooth the final stages of composition in Oxford. Due acknowledgement must also be made to the professional and personal support of Tony Morris, Ruth Parr, Michael Watson, Edwin Pritchard, and all those OUP staff who have worked on this book.

I continue to express wonderment at the support provided by friends. Lucy and Charlie Hedgcock ensured that I had the warmest welcome in London, and their hospitality was mirrored by that of Jeremy Eng and Melissa O'Neil, Jerry Chubb, Susan Harris, David Buy, Nick Leapman, Jaimie McHugo, and the Bethell clan of York. I am determined one day to settle on a research project which will not inconvenience such long-suffering allies, but I am sure that they will not be holding their breadth.

However, as with the merchant, my family have been the rock on which any professional progress has been founded. I only hope that the current absence of Great Yarmouth from familial table-talk offers them some compensation for their time and interest. My father did not live to see the completion of this study, but his support for my studies will never dim. The dedication goes out to a lady who has made uxoriousness my abiding pasttime and passion.

P. G.

Lincoln College, Oxford

Acknowledgements

To the Museum of London, for the painting by Egbert van Heemskerk the Younger reproduced on the jacket cover.

To Craig Spence, for the City ward map (Map 1.1).

To the Parish Register Section of the Yorkshire Archaeological Society, for use of their map of York parishes (Map 1.2).

To the Board of the Lancashire and Cheshire Record Series, and especially Philip Morgan, for use of the map of Liverpool (Map 1.3).

Contents

List of Maps

List of Tables

Abbreviations

Add. MSS	Additional Manuscripts, British Library
BIHR	*Bulletin of the Institute of Historical Research*
BL	British Library, London
Bodl.	Bodleian Library, Oxford
CJ	*Journals of the House of Commons*
CLRO	Corporation of London Records Office
CMH	Centre for Metropolitan History
CSP Col.	*Calendar of the State Papers, Colonial*
CSPD	*Calendar of the State Papers, Domestic*
CTB	*Calendar of Treasury Books*
CTP	*Calendar of Treasury Papers*
DNB	*Dictionary of National Biography*
EcHR	*Economic History Review*
EHR	*English Historical Review*
HJ	*Historical Journal*
HMC	Historical Manuscripts Commission
JBS	*Journal of British Studies*
JMH	*Journal of Modern History*
LJ	*Journals of the House of Lords*
MA	Merchant Adventurers
PCC	Prerogative Court of Canterbury
PRO	Public Records Office, London
RCHM	Royal Commission on Historical Monuments
RO	Record Office
TRHS	*Transactions of the Royal Historical Society*
VCH	*Victoria County History*

Author's Note

All dates are given in old style, but with the year taken to have started on
1 January. Spelling has been modernized where it is possible to do so without
affecting the meaning of the quotation.

Introduction

FOR a busy civil servant, an upriver commute from the City to Chelsea provided an ideal opportunity to catch up on some reading. Samuel Pepys, a commissioner of the Navy, chose the morning of 27 May 1663 to leaf through 'a little book' on the 'improvement of trade'. The precise identity of this tract unfortunately went unrecorded, but Pepys enthused that it was a 'pretty book and many things useful in it'. A fairly unremarkable entry for the great diarist, especially when compared to his colourful and dramatic account of Restoration London, but it serves as a rare, and beautifully mundane glimpse of the impact of commerce on the minds of England's governors, the most important theme of this present work. In the months leading up to this boat trip, Pepys had taken an increasing interest in commercial matters, motivated by his appointment to the committee to oversee the government of Tangier, the North African territory recently ceded to the Crown. Not content with some background reading, Pepys had been in touch with John Bland, merchant and author of several treatises on trade. Initially he was sceptical of the importance of Bland's work, pronouncing that there was little value therein, and was especially cutting concerning the limitations of Bland's style. More positively, he later commended one of his pieces as 'very good', and his ruminations on his Chelsea boat trip confirmed a growing fascination with commercial debate. However, he remained cool to Bland in person, worrying to his diary that as a civil servant he might 'confess my ignorance to him, which is not so fit for me to do'. Pepys was ready to acknowledge the singular experience of Bland, a former resident of Spain in the course of an extensive Mediterranean trade, but he could not concede that the merchant might possess greater powers of judgement in a matter of state.[1]

This equivocal response to the edification of the commercial classes can be taken as a common perspective of the nation's governors at that time. Although only of modest birth, Pepys was merely betraying all the classic symptoms of mild distaste which characterized the attitude of the landed classes towards commercial practitioners in the early modern period, a reaction to the world of business which still retains a faint resonance in modern-day suspicion towards the machinations of the City. Such was the prevailing gentlemanly ethos of British society, that until the rise of large-scale industrialization in the nineteenth century it was the merchant–gentry relationship which constituted one of the more obvious front lines of domestic social tension. A huge literature survives detailing this fundamental conflict between

[1] S. Pepys, *The Diary*, ed. R. Latham and W. Matthews (London, 1983), iii. 255, 291; iv. 10, 160.

the competing claims of money against birth, and although historians have regarded this rift to be of only periodic significance in political terms, none have doubted its existence.[2] As a sign of this, scholars have eagerly sought to determine the consequences of such lingering divisions, whose impact was held to have widespread economic, social, and cultural implications. In a society dominated by the authority of the landed estate, trade could arouse the mixture of fear, suspicion, and contempt exhibited by Pepys in his relationship with Bland. Most significantly, Pepys's prejudices were maintained despite an intimate and productive relationship with leading mercantile figures, conducted in the convivial surroundings of the City's coffee-houses and taverns. If a figure of Pepys's metropolitan background could retain these misgivings, then traders could expect even less sympathy from the real powers of the land.[3]

Fortunately for modern readers, it is the fascination of Pepys for commercial practice that has been exhibited by historians, rather than his withering sense of superiority. Of course, economic analysts have never doubted the significance of merchants such as Bland for Britain's development as a commercial power, but more conventional political studies have also paid significant attention to the overseas trader. In particular, the wealth and international connections of the merchant classes have been the subject of much debate, and have been credited as important agencies of political and social changes of profound significance for the development of the early modern British state, most notably with respect to the Reformation and the Civil War. Whether as the chief beneficiaries of the Protestant work ethic, or as the backbone of the rebellious Parliament's support, merchants have attracted much scholarly attention from generations of the country's foremost historians. Many of these studies remain highly controversial, but the notorious attachment of Marxist teleology to the entrepreneurial classes should not obscure the general contribution made by mercantile studies to the historiography of early modern Britain. Inspired by their example, this present study examines the merchant in another era of significant national upheaval, and will highlight the importance of the commercial sector for our understanding of Britain's domestic and international development in the early modern period. Whether damned as the self-centred arriviste, or lauded as the industrious

---

[2] See in particular J. Raven, *Judging New Wealth* (Oxford, 1992) and J. McVeagh, *Tradefull Merchants: The Portrayal of the Capitalist in Literature* (London, 1981). For a review of the debate on social mobility in the early modern period, giving a balanced view on the controversy stirred up by the work of L. Stone and J. C. F. Stone, *An Open Elite? England, 1540–1880* (Oxford, 1984), see Richard Grassby's major synthesis, *The Business Community of Seventeenth-Century England* (Cambridge, 1995), esp. ch. 12. For a useful summary of debate on the interaction of business and land in the nineteenth century, see W. D. Rubinstein, 'Businessmen into Landowners', in N. Harte and R. Quinault (eds.), *Land and Society in Britain, 1700–1914* (Manchester, 1996), 90–118.

[3] Pepys, *Diary*, iv. 412–14. For evidence of Pepys's cordial relationship with the mercantile Houblon family, see *The Private Correspondence and Miscellaneous Papers of Samuel Pepys*, ed. J. R. Tanner (London, 1926), vols. i and ii.

citizen, there can be no mistaking the dynamic contribution of the merchant to the early modern state.[4]

Even though consensus on the particular significance of the overseas trader has been most elusive, recent historiography has suggested that mercantile studies promise much further enlightenment across a wide range of historical interests. In particular, analysts of the seventeenth- and eighteenth-century state have begun to assess the contribution of overseas trade to the country's rise to major power status. It has become abundantly clear that the establishment of an extensive empire owed more to the efforts of thousands of entrepreneurs than to those of successive governments, and thus it is no surprise to see scholars attracted by this energetic and innovative sector of early modern society.[5] Analysis of the intermediary role played by mercantile groups in the development of the colonies has highlighted their value to national aggrandisement, particularly in the absence of consistent state support. Moreover, such studies have also paid tribute to their contribution to domestic innovations within the mother country itself, which were indispensable to the maintenance of the empire. Most notably, the perceived rise of a 'fiscal-military state' at the turn of the seventeenth century, capable of sustaining and protecting such far-flung territories, was closely related to developments within the commercial sector.[6] Further magnifying the significance of economic growth at this time, leading authorities regard the country as experiencing an era of commercial and financial 'revolution', with a significant advance in transoceanic trade, and the establishment of the City as a national stock market. Several studies have questioned the character and scale of these innovations, but there can be no doubt that the overseas trader was at the heart of important changes in the late seventeenth and early eighteenth centuries.[7]

Recognition of such importance has naturally promoted the reappraisal of the merchant within Augustan society. Assisted by burgeoning interest in urban history and by discussion of the emergence of a distinctive culture of

[4] For a survey of the often-fervent historiographic debate over the social and political impact of sixteenth- and seventeenth-century capitalism, see R. C. Richardson, *The Debate on the English Revolution* (London, 1977), 85–112. For more informed studies of the association of City business with parliamentarian politics, see R. Ashton, *The City and the Court, 1603–43* (Cambridge, 1979), and R. Brenner, *Merchants and Revolution* (Princeton, 1993).

[5] K. Andrews, *Trade, Plunder, and Settlement: Maritime Enterprise and the Genesis of the British Empire, 1480–1630* (Cambridge, 1984); P. O'Brien, 'Inseparable Connections: Trade, Economy, Fiscal State, and the Expansion of Empire, 1688–1815', in P. J. Marshall (ed.), *The Oxford History of the British Empire: The Eighteenth Century* (Oxford, 1998), 53–77.

[6] See in particular M. V. Bowen, *Elites, Enterprise, and the Making of the British Overseas Empire, 1688–1775* (London, 1996); A. G. Olson, *Making the Empire Work: London and American Interest Groups, 1690–1790* (Cambridge, Mass., 1992); J. Brewer, *The Sinews of Power: War, Money, and the English State, 1688–1783* (Oxford, 1989).

[7] R. Davis, *A Commercial Revolution* (London, 1967); P. G. M. Dickson, *The Financial Revolution in England*, 2nd edn. (Oxford, 1993). For accounts of general commercial development, see W. E. Minchington (ed.), *The Growth of English Overseas Trade in the Seventeenth and Eighteenth Centuries* (London, 1969); C. Wilson, *England's Apprenticeship 1603–1763*, 2nd edn. (London, 1984).

middle-class England, recent studies have been instrumental in advancing understanding of the domestic role of the merchant. In particular, increasing emphasis on the commercial character of Georgian society has stimulated further debate concerning the impact of the business world on the nation at large, concentrating on the longer-term consequences of the commercial and financial 'revolutions' for state and society.[8] A spirited defence of the aristo-cratic dominance of eighteenth-century society has ensured that much ink has been spilt on defining the exact legacy of commercial expansion, but all this work has significantly advanced the particular claims of the overseas trader to special attention. Some of the most exciting scholarship on the development of eighteenth-century Britain now centres on the relationship between imperial-commercial growth and domestic change. Even scholars who regard Georgian Britain as an *ancien régime* would concede that the world of trade can tell us much about the problems encountered by a state undergoing a very real transformation in its international status.[9]

This current study seeks to aid these investigations by analysis of the politi-cal and social impact of the overseas trader from the reign of Charles II to that of George I. The period was one of immense ferment for all English subjects, not just the commercial classes, but the research for this book was undertaken with the belief that examination of the merchant would not only illuminate the development of a socio-economic group, but also the profound changes which the state was experiencing. Historians have begun to acknowledge the wide-ranging importance of commercial change in this period, but relatively little thought has been given to the mercantile perspective. As a result, we still know far more about attitudes towards the trader, rather than his outlook per se, a situation which led a recent review of the historiography of the middling classes to remark that 'surprisingly little work has been done on the leading mercantile and retailing groups'.[10] In terms of political development, historical accounts are still peopled largely by aristocrats and gentlemen, with the commercial sector as a whole relegated to the sidelines. The need for further research concerning the political role of the trader has been highlighted by recent work emphasizing the interdependence of the fortunes of the merchant and the state in Britain and other countries, which has demonstrated that

---

[8] P. Earle, *The Making of the English Middle Class* (London, 1989).

[9] For the contrasting opinions on the nature of eighteenth-century society, see P. Langford, *A Polite and Commercial People* (Oxford, 1989), and J. C. D. Clarke, *English Society, 1688–1832* (Cambridge, 1985). For recent studies of the eighteenth-century impact of commerce, see D. Hancock, *Citizens of the World* (Cambridge, 1995); N. Koehn, *The Power of Commerce* (Ithaca, NY, 1994); and K. Wilson, *The Sense of the People: Politics, Culture, and Imperialism in England, 1715–1785* (Cambridge, 1995).

[10] J. Barry and C. Brooks (eds.), *The Middling Sort of People: Culture, Society, and Politics in England, 1550–1800* (London, 1994), introduction, 211. Nuala Zahedieh recently noted how transatlantic merchants remained 'shadowy figures'—'Making Mercantilism Work: London Merchants and Atlantic Trade in the Seventeenth Century', *TRHS* 6th ser., 9 (1999),143–58. Keith Wrightson's major survey also noted the relative imbalance between gentry and business studies—*English Society, 1580–1680* (London, 1982), 27–8.

there often existed an uneasy relationship of mutual obligation between commercial and governmental leaders. Governments may have merely regarded traders as a productive fiscal resource, while merchants only turned to the state in their hour of need, but their differing priorities could not mask common objectives. These bonds of mutual interest extended far down the economic order, but at the apex of commercial society the merchant was unavoidably concerned in the political process, even if largely excluded from the real corridors of power.[11]

The connections between the overseas trader and the state will be probed from a variety of perspectives, but not with a view to providing a history of economic policy in the 1660–1720 period. The main outlines of governmental activity in the commercial sphere will be familiar to any student of the period, and there also has been growing interest concerning the impact of trade in the diplomatic field.[12] Building on these foundations, this study will concentrate on the associational culture of the mercantile world, and its research has been designed to establish how these networks responded to the political and commercial challenges of the Augustan period. In turn, the relationship between merchant and state must be squared with contemporary and historiographic perceptions of the role of the overseas trader within society. There already exist several excellent histories of British overseas commerce in this period, but there remain few works which have investigated the links between mercantile, social, and political change. Its approach thus remains socio-political rather than political per se, and even while focusing much attention on Whitehall and Westminster, it will acknowledge the 'political' character of the everyday working and social lives of overseas traders. The novel party affiliations of this era are a necessary part of this inquiry, but this study will highlight forms of mercantile political activity which were predominantly non-ideological in character. As we shall see, it was not until 1713 that Tories and Whigs used commerce to score points at a national level, and this study will endeavour to reconstruct the politics of trade from a mercantile perspective, rather than that of the party manager. Historians of the early modern period have increasingly recognized that the sphere of political activity extended far beyond courtly cabinets or electoral hustings, and this approach will serve to illuminate the widespread impact of the mercantile classes. The burgeoning scholarship on their world testifies to their importance, and this study lends weight to those historians who view it to be of a profound, quasi-cultural dimension.[13]

[11] For a broader discussion of the relationship between merchants and states, see J. D. Tracey (ed.), *The Political Economy of Merchant Empires* (Cambridge, 1991).

[12] For general analysis of commercial policy, see J. Black, *A System of Ambition? British Foreign Policy, 1660–1793* (London, 1991); Wilson, *England's Apprenticeship.* For more detailed studies of Augustan commercial policy, although restricted to the transatlantic sphere, see I. K. Steele, *Politics of Colonial Policy* (Oxford, 1968); A. P. Thornton, *West India Policy under the Restoration* (Oxford, 1956).

[13] For discussion of this broader conception of 'politics', see P. Langford, *Public Life and the Propertied*

Although conscious of the merchant's extensive influence, historians have in general investigated commercial politics from mutually exclusive academic perspectives. Indeed, one of the few studies to examine the political impact of commerce referred to the 'academic apartheid' existing between economic and political historians in the 1970s, while another referred to these 'separate tribes' a decade later.[14] It is this very divide which can explain the relative dearth of studies on mercantile politics, and the structure of this book has been largely shaped by dissatisfaction with methodological approaches towards the political activity of the Augustan merchant. In the absence of more general surveys, our understanding of mercantile politics has mainly been derived from studies of single companies or individuals. Several excellent examples of both genres exist, and biographies of Sir Dudley North, Sir John Banks, and Micajah Perry in particular have illuminated the understanding to be gained from study of businessmen who transcended the worlds of commerce and government. Furthermore, analysis of the East India, Levant, and Royal African companies has highlighted the formal and informal links between the institutions of state and trade.[15] More ambitiously, ground-breaking studies of the relationship between commerce and political ideology have demonstrated the importance of the Augustan period for developing attitudes towards the economic sector. However, there remain few studies which have attempted to take a general overview of the merchant classes, or to analyse their particular contribution to state and society.[16]

This account owes an especial debt of inspiration to those works which have broached the worlds of commerce and politics in order to understand the development of the state in the Augustan age. Particular acknowledgement must be given to the work of Gary De Krey, whose exhaustive study of London from 1690 to 1715 highlighted the socio-economic tensions behind the political upheavals of the capital. Having illuminated many aspects of metro-

---

Englishman, 1689–1798 (Oxford, 1991). For important recent work on the evolution of middling 'culture', see J. Smail, *The Origins of Middle-Class Culture: Halifax, Yorkshire, 1660–1780* (Ithaca, NY, 1994); M. Hunt, *The Middling Sort: Commerce, Gender, and Family in England, 1680–1780* (Berkeley, Calif., 1996).

[14] D. Coleman, 'Politics and Economics in the Age of Anne: The Case of the Anglo-French Trade Treaty of 1713', in *idem* and A. H. John (eds.), *Trade, Government, and Economy in Pre-Industrial England* (London, 1976); K. Andrews, *Trade, Plunder, and Settlement*, p. vii. For a succinct history of the difficulties faced by students of the economy, see D. C. Coleman, *History and the Economic Past* (Oxford, 1987). The still-prevalent apartheid was noted by Nancy Koehn in 1994—*The Power of Commerce*, p. xi.

[15] D. C. Coleman, *Sir John Banks* (Oxford, 1963); R. Grassby, *The English Gentleman in Trade: The Life and Works of Sir Dudley North, 1641–91* (Oxford, 1994); J. M. Price, *Perry of London: A Family and a Firm on the Seaborne Frontier, 1615–1753* (Cambridge, Mass., 1992). Among the best of the company histories are K. N. Chaudhuri, *The Trading World of Asia and the English East India Company* (Cambridge, 1978); K. G. Davies, *The Royal African Company* (London, 1957); A. C. Wood, *A History of the Levant Company* (Oxford, 1935).

[16] J. G. A. Pocock, *The Machiavellian Moment* (Princeton, 1975), esp. 423–505. Also note the work of Steve Pincus—*Protestantism and Patriotism* (Cambridge, 1994); *idem*, 'Neither Machiavellian Moment nor Possessive Individualism: Commercial Society and the Defenders of the English Commonwealth', *American Historical Review*, 103 (1998), 705–36. My thanks to him for a preview of his forthcoming work on the relationship between political and commercial ideology in the later seventeenth century.

politan development, particularly with regard to the City corporation, he has left an important agenda for the investigation of other arenas of urban politics. In particular, his exposure of the complex structures of commercial life has only left historians with even greater desire to probe the links between the mercantile City and Westminster. Also worthy of special note, Alison Olson's study of the importance of connections between London interest groups and the far-flung Atlantic colonies has raised significant questions concerning the relationship of the state and the merchant. Her transatlantic survey of the processes by which religious, commercial, and social networks evolved into political groupings has reminded historians of the potentially complex charac-ter of contemporary associations, which has been too often overshadowed by the convenient polarities of Whig and Tory. Party affiliations cannot be ignored in this period, but they must be assessed against enduring social and professional ties. Political activity must be seen in this broader context, and we still lack case-studies to assess the importance of the Augustan period for the development of commercial politics.[17]

This important research merely highlights the amount of work still to be completed on English merchants. Although their dynamic role as commercial leaders has ensured them historiographic interest, few analysts have attempted to delineate their particular social or political importance, grouping them instead with a middle-class mass, or bracketing them with a 'big bourgeoisie' of town leaders.[18] Given the importance of their economic and socio-political roles within commercial life, and the fluidity of urban society, it is inevitable that the commercial historian is faced with the dilemma of how to isolate their significance while paying tribute to their role as political and social inter-mediaries. This task is further complicated by the essential heterogeneity of the merchant classes in terms of background or commercial interest, and it would be unwise to use such terms as 'business community' without paying tribute to the diversity of experience within this urban elite.[19] Fortunately for this study, there survive excellent sources with which to study the role of active overseas traders within state and society. Thus this account can directly examine the ways in which economic *function*, rather than the more nebulous concepts of class or wealth, affected contemporary perceptions of commercial leaders. This approach does not presuppose that merchants were exclusively interested

[17] G. S. De Krey, *A Fractured Society: The Politics of London* (Oxford, 1985); Olson, *Making the Empire Work*. Although not primarily political in concern, also note Earle, *Making of the English Middle Class*, 240–68. The 'City' has numerous connotations beyond the municipal jurisdiction of the corporation of London, and this study will endeavour to clarify its application in each context.

[18] H. Horwitz, 'The Mess of the Middle Classes Revisited', *Continuity and Change*, 2 (1987), 263–96; N. Rogers, 'Money, Land, and Lineage: The Big Bourgeoisie of Georgian London', *Social History*, 4 (1979), 437–54.

[19] For an excellent example of the potentially wide-ranging portfolio of the late Stuart merchant, see H. Roseveare, *Markets and Merchants of the Late Seventeenth Century* (Oxford, 1987), esp. 112–20. The perils of straying too far from contemporary social categorization are fully debated in I. R. Christie, *British Non-elite MPs, 1715–1820* (Oxford, 1995).

in overseas trade throughout their career, and the evolution of the stock market in this period clearly saw many overseas traders switch to investment in the public funds. However, although the significance of merchant-financiers will be acknowledged, my prime concern remains their impact while engaged in international commerce. On the other side of the social fence, historians of the gentry have found it difficult to draw the precise boundaries of their status group, but this functional approach permits a more coherent perspective to analysis of important political and social developments.[20]

The identification of the 'merchant' as a businessman whose primary interest lay with overseas trade reflects both contemporary usage and recent research. There is plenty of evidence to suggest that in the late Stuart age a more exclusive definition of the term was reserved for overseas traders, in part as a consequence of their growing stature within the state, and this study is fortunate in having the materials to substantiate these contemporary perceptions. In the later medieval period, the title of merchant might have been accorded to any person involved in wholesaling, or used to denote a high-status urban dweller, such as a senior municipal officer.[21] As Defoe noted as late as 1727, there was still a great deal of variance in the use of the term within Britain, with the Scots and Irish applying it to retailers or even travelling pedlars. However, he insisted that 'in England the word merchant is understood of none but such as carry on foreign correspondences, importing the goods and growth of other countries, and exporting the growth and manufacture of England to other countries . . . these only are called merchants by way of honourable distinction'. Although pronouncing on his favoured subject, Defoe must be regarded with some caution, for it is clear that wholesalers and retailers were still active in overseas trade, particularly in provincial towns.[22] Nevertheless, by the late seventeenth century Defoe's assessment was

---

[20] C. Holmes and F. Heal, *The Gentry in England and Wales* (Basingstoke, 1994), 6–19; P. J. Corfield, 'The Rivals: Landed and Other Gentlemen', in Harte and Quinault, *Land and Society in Britain*, 1–33. Richard Grassby has stressed that businessmen formed 'a functional group' rather than a self-conscious class—'Social Mobility and Business Enterprise in Seventeenth-Century England', in D. Pennington and K. Thomas (eds.), *Puritans and Revolutionaries* (Oxford, 1978), 381. The particular effect of the life-cycle on mercantile trading and status is discussed in Chs. 1 and 2.

[21] S. Thrupp, *The Merchant Class of Medieval London, 1300–1500* (Chicago, 1948), pp. ix–x, 6. At a provincial level it 'simply meant an important tradesman, especially a wholesaler who traded overseas'—D. Palliser, *The Company of Merchant Adventurers of the City of York* (York, 1985), 1; also D. H. Sacks, *The Widening Gate: Bristol and the Atlantic Economy, 1450–1700* (Berkeley, Calif., 1987), 125.

[22] D. Defoe, *The Complete English Tradesman in Familiar Letters* (London, 1726), i. 1–4. Although Lewes Roberts argued for a more exclusive definition of merchant in 1638, this view was only widely published from the 1680s onwards—*The Merchant's Map of Commerce* (1638), 2; *The Character and Qualifications of an Honest, Loyal Merchant* (1686), p. 6; D. Thomas, *An Historical Account of the Rise and Growth of the West India Colonies* (1690), 5–6; *A Brief History of Trade* (1702), 112; C. King, *The British Merchant* (London, 1721), i. p. xxv. For recent evidence of the engagement of mariners in overseas trade, see P. Earle, *Sailors: English Merchant Seamen, 1650–1775* (London, 1998), 59–64. For contemporary French concern that the title of 'marchand' had been sullied through use by lesser traders, see W. C. Scoville, 'The French Economy in 1700–1: An Appraisal by the Deputies of Trade', *Journal of Economic History*, 22 (1962), 246–7.

widely shared, and recent work by commercial historians has suggested that the post-Restoration period saw increasing 'concentration' of mercantile activity in the hands of a smaller cadre of professional operators. This economic process would have helped to establish a more exclusive definition of the merchant, and, as will be argued here, the overall growth in overseas trade helped to raise the public profile of this elite urban group. Thus, although it would be impossible to take merchants in isolation from their wholesaling or retailing colleagues, or to suggest that they monopolized overseas trade completely, contemporary developments argue for their study in their own right.[23]

Evidently, the 'professional' overseas trader accounted for a small proportion of dealers in general. Contemporary estimates suggest that they could only be numbered in their thousands rather than tens of thousands, and thus constituted an elite which was largely determined by the financial backing and the personal skills required by an unforgiving business. Without a substantial amount of capital or credit to embark on ventures overseas, there was little prospect of success. Just as importantly, without the contacts abroad to ensure a fair market in which to purchase or sell his wares, the trader was exposing himself to the very real threat of ruin. These were simply the most obvious difficulties facing the would-be merchant, and although a schooling in accounts, languages, geography, and navigation would help him to minimize the risks inherent to his trade, the ability to establish reliable contacts remained a key to success in business. Connections could bring in the financial support to start up new ventures; they would also provide the information on suppliers and markets so vital to business decision-making; they would also gain him access to the local, regional, and national authorities whose powers could significantly affect his potential for profit. If in difficulty, traders might have to turn to their commercial colleagues to act as arbitrators for the resolution of disputes, or hope that they would be sympathetic creditors or partners. Thus, although they could be portrayed as an urban elite motivated by the all-consuming eagerness for private gain, overseas traders were at the heart of complex networks of mutually-dependent associates, the dimensions of which stretched far beyond the mercantile profession. By dint of their economic calling, merchants were middlemen in commercial, social, and political terms, and thus can provide an excellent insight into the workings of the late Stuart state.[24]

[23] J. M. Price and P. G. E. Clemens, 'A Revolution in Overseas Trade: British Firms in the Chesapeake Trade, 1675–1775', *Journal of Economic History*, 47 (1987), 1–43. Much more work is needed on the timing and scale of this phenomenon, particularly since the general survey of S. Chapman argued that the number of merchants did not increase in line with the dramatic growth in British overseas trade in the eighteenth century—*Merchant Enterprise in Britain from the Industrial Revolution to World War One* (Cambridge, 1992), 21–50.

[24] Earle, *Making of the English Middle Class*, ch. 4; J. Barry, 'Bourgeois Collectivism? Urban Association and the Middling Sort', in *idem* and Brooks, *Middling Sort of People*, 84–112. The significance of personal connection for business success is illustrated most fully by C. Muldrew, *The Economy of Obligation: The Culture of Credit and Social Relations in Early Modern England* (Basingstoke, 1998), esp. ch. 2.

The late seventeenth century appears an ideal point at which to study the overseas trader, for it offered him both increased opportunity and new challenges. In purely economic terms, England had reached a vital point in its apparent 'commercial revolution', with an era of rapid expansion from the 1660s to the 1680s which largely defined the form of its eighteenth-century trade. In particular, the dynamism of the American, Caribbean, and Indian trades confirmed a decisive shift to extra-European commerce earlier in the century, and foreshadowed an even more dramatic period of imperial growth in the Georgian era. Economic historians have cautioned against too teleological a pattern of inexorable expansion, in particular by drawing attention to the dislocation of the great wars of the reigns of William and Anne, but there is general agreement that the post-Restoration merchant witnessed a key shift in overseas commerce. As one historian commented on the relative decline of the once all-powerful cloth trade, 'the Restoration was the economic exit from medievalism'. These changes placed huge demands on the merchant to generate the necessary capital to exploit new markets, and also forced traders to look to the state to provide the requisite protection against the competition of other European powers, who increasingly came to regard overseas trade as an essential source of national economic strength. In such circumstances, it is hardly surprising that contemporaries spent much time discussing the impact of commercial development, the consequences of which were perceived to have resonated far beyond the economic sector. This study will follow their lead, although seeking to prioritize the perspective of the merchants themselves.[25]

In political terms too, historians have suggested that the merchant may have reached an important crossroads in the Restoration era. During the reigns of Elizabeth and the early Stuarts, the state had provided encouragement for the mercantile sector in the form of chartered companies and colonies, but such aid was desultory and strictly limited in scope. Successive monarchs did not view overseas trade as an overwhelming priority, and the infrequent sessions of Parliament offered little in the way of systematic support. The most intensive study of government economic 'policy' in the 1603–42 period concluded that 'disparate official measures were not meaningful and complementary parts of any "plan" greater than a pressing need to maintain the economy on at least an even keel'.[26] However, even if one doubts the broader social significance of mercantile backing for the parliamentary cause in the 1640s, the Interregnum period saw some very interesting develop-

[25] B. Dietz, 'Overseas Trade and Metropolitan Growth', in A. L. Beier and R. Finlay (eds.), *London, 1500–1700* (London, 1986), 115–40; Minchinton, *Growth of English Overseas Trade*, 11. Dietz saw early Stuart change as more decisive than the post-Restoration 'revolution'.

[26] B. Supple, *Commercial Crisis and Change in England, 1600–42* (Cambridge, 1959), 225–53. For the Crown's fluctuating regard for the chartered companies, see Ashton, *The City and the Court*, 106–35. The government's staccato approach to the colonies and colonial trade before 1630 is illustrated by Andrews, *Trade, Plunder, and Settlement*.

ments in the politics of trade. Scholars have eagerly debated whether the wars against the Dutch and the Spanish constituted England's first overtly commercial conflicts, while innovations such as the Navigation Laws and the Council of Trade seemingly bespoke a heightened priority for economic affairs. More intriguingly still, the latest research has suggested that this period saw the first challenge to the view that land was the ultimate source of a society's wealth, with the proponents of trade on the ascendant.[27] In 1660 Charles II returned from exile seemingly convinced of the advantages of overseas trade, setting up a Council of Trade which included many mercantile representatives. Coupled with Parliament's re-enactment of the Navigation Laws, their sponsorship of an aggressively protectionist policy towards the taxation of commerce, and two more Dutch wars, it is indeed tempting to see the period as a critical era of transition towards an imperial phase, as the traditional landed elite finally acknowledged the contribution of the commercial sector to the strength and status of this island nation.[28]

While these signs of increasing respect for trade remain significant, research has questioned the ease with which England advanced to its commercial destiny. As in so many other spheres of the governance of Charles II, the early promise of the Restoration went largely unfulfilled, despite the effusive observations of 'the infinite importance the improvement of trade must be to this kingdom'. Historians have recognized that certain mercantile interests were advanced by state aid, but there still appeared little in the way of systematic support for the aggrandisement of the commercial sector. In particular, leading economic historians have been hard-pressed to discover any commercial mandate in the direction of state policy in our period, especially at the rarefied level of high politics. In the eyes of Ralph Davis, the Walpolean tariff reforms of 1722 were preceded by '32 years of piecemeal, unco-ordinated concessions to protectionism'. Likewise, Charles Wilson saw little consistency but in the 'determination of the government to retain control of economic policy'. He observed that merchants were kept at arm's length by late Stuart governments, who used more experienced officials to act as brokers between themselves and the scrum of trading interests who sought to access royal power.[29]

[27] Pincus, *Protestantism and Patriotism*, esp. 1–12, 195–8; *idem*, in *American Historical Review*, 103 (1998), 705–36. In a forthcoming publication, he will argue for a division between Tory 'land' supporters and Whig 'commerce' allegiance in the 1680s and 1690s. For a survey of broader Interregnum trends, see T. Venning, *Cromwellian Foreign Policy* (Basingstoke, 1995).

[28] N. Canny, 'The Origins of Empire: An Introduction', in *idem* (ed.), *The Oxford History of the British Empire: The Origins of Empire* (Oxford, 1998), 1–33; C. D. Chandaman, *The English Public Revenue* (Oxford, 1975), 9–36. Analysis of the Navy's protection of merchant shipping has suggested that the state rendered more systematic support for English commerce after 1650—S. Hornstein, *The Restoration Navy and English Foreign Trade, 1674–88* (Aldershot, 1991); T. Dickie, 'Commerce and Experience in the Seventeenth-Century Mediterranean: The Market Dynamics, Commercial Culture, and Naval Protection of English Trade to Aleppo', D.Phil. thesis (Oxford, 1997).

[29] *LJ*, xi. 175; C. M. Andrews, *British Committees, Commissions, and Councils of Trade and Plantations, 1622–75* (Baltimore, 1908); R. Davis, 'The Rise of Protection in England, 1669–1786', *EcHR* 2nd ser., 19 (1966), 306–17; Wilson, *England's Apprenticeship*, 167; M. Braddick, 'The English Government, War,

The socio-political order was similarly little troubled by commercial advance, with the nobility and gentry continuing to dominate state institutions, even those concerned with the administration of trade. In the absence of any overt or systematic leadership from the state in the field of overseas commerce, it is little wonder that analysts regard the Georgian period as having 'marked the emergence of trade as a "patriotic" political issue, one that placed commerce at the centre of the national interest'.[30]

The following pages will show that the status of the merchant and his profession had already experienced significant change within the 1660–1720 period, and their development reflected the commercial and political trans-formation of the state. As economic historians have stressed, there was little to differentiate the Augustan merchant from his predecessors in terms of com-mercial technique, but fundamental innovations in the scale and character of international trade forced a reassessment of the relationship between merchant and the state. Throughout Western Europe contemporaries dis-cussed the importance of commerce for national aggrandisement, an endur-ing debate mirrored by academic interest in the perceived 'mercantilism' of France, Brandenburg, Sweden, and other countries in the late seventeenth century.[31] At a domestic level, English political change posed a significant challenge to the accustomed relationship between merchant and governors, most notably the growing importance of Parliament at the expense of the Crown. Once the preserve of the monarch, the regulation of overseas trade increasingly fell within a parliamentary remit after 1688, and merchants had to bow to the new order. Thus, in terms of political organization and argument, merchant groups had to adapt to rapid change, in order to seize the opportunities presented by the fluctuating balances of power within Britain and Europe. At times, both traders and ministers struggled to come to terms with the new politics of trade, but it was vital for both to reach a tolerable accommodation if the country was to develop into a world power. The ability of state institutions to further the objectives of the mercantile sector has been identified as a most significant factor in the rise of the Dutch republic in the seventeenth century, and it is imperative that we understand how the English polity rose to the economic challenges of the age.[32]

While the ensuing chapters will stress the importance of the overseas trader

Trade, and Settlement, 1625–88' in Canny, *The Origins of Empire*, 286–308. For a brief, but illuminating discussion of the state's equivocal relationship with trading interests in the field of foreign affairs, see Black, *A System of Ambition?*, 87–101.

[30] Wilson, *The Sense of the People*, 129–30.

[31] For an excellent discussion of European developments, see B. Supple, 'The Nature of Enterprise', in E. E. Rich and C. H. Wilson (eds.), *The Cambridge Economic History of Europe* (Cambridge, 1977), 394–461. For the fullest case-study, see C. W. Cole, *Colbert and a Century of French Mercantilism* (New York, 1939); *idem*, *French Mercantilism, 1683–1700* (New York, 1965).

[32] J. I. Israel, *Dutch Primacy in World Trade, 1585–1740* (Oxford, 1989). For recent insights concerning the executive control over trade after 1660, see D. Gardiner, 'The Work of the English Privy Council 1660–79', D.Phil. thesis (Oxford, 1992).

in promoting a more productive partnership between merchant and minister, the commercial success of eighteenth-century Britain should not be seen as the fulfilment of a premeditated bourgeois agenda. Although more powerfully expressed in the Augustan period, mercantile objectives remained purely professional and were essentially specific and short-term. The sheer diversity of world trade, and the specialist character of the overseas dealer, ensured that the state rarely had to face a united merchant 'interest'.[33] Thus, although vociferous in the pursuit of state support, merchants did not represent a social or political threat to landed hegemony, and their limited demands for political favour could be accommodated with relatively little difficulty. Pepysian suspicion may have continued to colour social attitudes towards the merchant, and could manifest itself in the public arena in times of especial national difficulty. However, these continuities should not obscure important new developments, most notably the consolidation of a more positive image of the merchant as a patriotic servant of the state. Historians of Augustan literature have already commented upon the increasingly sympathetic treatment of the merchant on the contemporary stage, but the political sphere was the real testing-ground for attitudes towards commercial change. The elevation of the merchant was not merely the result of post-1660 developments, but the inter-action of Augustan political and commercial change raised his profile to a significant degree. This study does not posit yet another 'revolution' to rank alongside those of commerce and finance, but it will argue that this period was vital for establishing the 'commercial' character of the gentrified Georgian century.[34]

The structure of the book has been designed to highlight the complex character of the mercantile world, and to demonstrate the breadth of its potential influence. Therefore, the six chapters are divided into two parts, the first analysing the distinctive form of mercantile society in terms of urban environment, life-cycle, and association. These chapters provide essential background analysis for the second half which considers the broad 'public' impact of the overseas trader. The ordering of discussion is most deliberate, directing attention first of all to the merchants themselves, whose identity and extra-commercial activities remain opaque despite a wealth of historiographic interest. While acknowledging the overwhelming importance of family and profit to the individual, attention will be drawn to the social and political associations which were instrumental to the functioning of commerce, and which remain the essence of a distinctively mercantile way of life. Moreover, these links are the key to understanding the impact of overseas traders in

---

[33] J. M. Price observed that much of the pre-1960 historiography had mistakenly assumed a homogeneous mercantile interest—'The Tobacco Adventure to Russia', *Transactions of the American Philosophical Society*, NS, 51 (1961), 1–120.

[34] McVeagh, *Tradefull Merchants*, 53–82; J. Loftis, *Comedy and Society from Congreve to Fielding* (Stamford, 1959), 77–100.

the wider environment of region and realm, which themes will be explored further in the second half. Chapters 4–6 examine the contemporary profile of the merchant from a variety of perspectives in order to measure his reaction to the great challenges of a changing polity. They show that the overseas trader was alive to the significant political developments of the time, and was far from a passive spectator. In particular, analysis of the great debate over the proposed Anglo-French commercial treaty in 1713 will demonstrate the extent to which the politics of trade had matured by the dawn of Hanoverian rule. More generally, the changing public profile of the merchant will provide further evidence that the period was most significant for determining the eventual character of the British state.[35]

Throughout the work I have attempted a general survey of the development of the English merchant, particularly in terms of geographical distribution. In the first half, study of the merchant within his urban base will principally centre on London, which handled an estimated three-quarters of national overseas trade throughout the period. However, each section will be complemented by a brief comparison with the mercantile communities of Liverpool and York. These two ports exhibit differing responses to the political and socio-economic changes of the Augustan era, and thus are a salutary reminder of the unevenness of contemporary commercial change. Liverpool experienced a tremendous boom after 1660, growing from a mere hamlet to a thriving urban centre on the back of an extensive transatlantic trade. York's commercial economy suffered greatly in the same period, as the remains of its overseas trade was yielded to the superior port facilities of Hull. Such variety in economic development invites investigation of how mercantile leaders coped with commercial change, and of the ways in which success and failure affected their role within society. Furthermore, these chapters will highlight the inextricable bonds between London and provincial merchants, and suggest that the political resonance of these links has been underrated. Recent excellent work on provincial mercantile communities, most notably Bristol, suggests that the local case-study can still yield much instruction about so-called 'national' developments.[36]

Of course, the ambitious agenda set forth here cannot possibly be covered in the space of one monograph, and there remains a great amount of research to be completed. Even after years in the archives, I can readily concur with the informed verdict of mercantile author John Cary, who complained in May 1696 'how difficult it is to comprise so spacious a thing as the trade of England in a few lines'. In particular, this present work hopes that it will encourage others to pursue some of the themes which have only received tangential treat-

---

[35] For discussion of the importance of commerce as a foundation of 'national' identity, see L. Colley, *Britons: Forging the Nation, 1707–1837* (New Haven, 1992).

[36] Sacks, *Widening Gate*; K. Morgan, *Bristol and the Atlantic Trade in the Eighteenth Century* (Cambridge, 1993). Note also J. H. Agnew, *Belfast Merchant Families in the Seventeenth Century* (Blackrock, 1996).

ment in this book. Space has precluded a more searching analysis of provincial developments, and much more research is needed on the workings of commercial politics on a regional basis, especially as channelled through Parliament.[37] Furthermore, although this present study has been unashamedly English in orientation, the excellent work of scholars such as Cullen, Smout, and Devine suggests that there is a rich harvest to be reaped from investigation based upon a truly British perspective, especially as it is becoming increasingly clear that a significant proportion of the transatlantic community were of Scots, Irish, or Welsh origin. More generally, the international dimensions of political-commercial life still require close scrutiny for the pre-1720 period, and more instructive comparisons with mercantile groups in other countries would be highly desirable. Hopefully this study will provide the necessary framework for a more thoroughgoing appreciation of the stature of the British merchant both at home and abroad.[38]

Thus the real priority of this work has been to encourage research and debate, for a great amount of study is still needed on the broader consequences of commercial change, and there remain relatively few workers toiling in that field at present. Compared to the richness of the historiography of the gentry and aristocracy of early modern England, we know little of the response of the commercial classes to the great changes of this era. Commercial developments and social attitudes must be linked more directly to conventional political considerations, which would provide a more holistic account of the early modern state. In common with their predecessors, Britain's Augustan merchants represented a tiny proportion of the populace, and concentration on them may seem too narrow a perspective on society, but their singular role illuminates many aspects of national change. Like Pepys, we must assess the contribution of the merchant with a critical eye, and recognize their private interests as well as their public roles. However, our principal priority must be to assess the merchant by the challenges of his immediate urban environment, and it is to that natural habitat that we first must turn.

---

[37] Add. MSS 5540, fos. 72–3. John Smail has recently highlighted the cultural impact of the market as an agent of economic change, and his focus on the importance of the entrepreneur could be broadened to address other societal issues—*Merchants, Markets, and Manufacture* (Basingstoke, 1999).

[38] T. C. Smout, *Scottish Trade on the Eve of the Union, 1660–1707* (Edinburgh, 1963); T. M. Devine, *The Tobacco Lords: The Merchants of Glasgow, 1740–90* (Edinburgh, 1975); L. M. Cullen, *Anglo-Irish Trade, 1660–1800* (Manchester, 1968).

CHAPTER ONE

The Mercantile City

'Rough seas, rocks and pirates, treacherous factors, and leaking ships affright them. They are strange politicians, for they bring Turkey and Spain into London, and carry London thither.'[1]

DANIEL LUPTON's account of merchant activity at the Royal Exchange in the 1630s encapsulates much of the fascination of the overseas trader, bewitching both to contemporaries and historians. Although merchants were regarded as social parvenus by the landed elite and often ridiculed by the literati, outsiders who actually took the trouble to visit the City were clearly struck by the singularity of the business undertaken by traders. Few visitors attempted to fathom the mysteries of international commerce, but overseas trade retained a distinctive aura to the uninitiated, not least due to its inherent uncertainties, with merchants vulnerable to the whims of weather and war, but also liable to make great fortunes should they master its intricacies. Most interestingly for this study, Lupton's identification of them as 'strange politicians' highlights one of the fundamental preconditions for mercantile success: the ability to construct reliable networks of influential contacts to help them overcome the perils of their profession. Such a basic economic necessity imbued the mercantile world with very sophisticated political mechanisms, designed primarily for commercial success, but which had a dynamic impact on the manner in which the merchant operated in public life. Eighty years after Lupton, outsiders such as Joseph Addison could still come to the heart of the City to marvel at the complexities of commercial interaction, and describe merchants as political animals, being the 'representatives' of their respective trades. Like Lupton and Addison, it is to the square mile that this study will principally turn to understand the character and impact of mercantile life, and seek further instruction in analyses of Liverpool and York.[2]

Lupton's observations clearly demonstrate that the sphere of mercantile politics was far from restricted to the courts of princes or the halls of Westminster, and that the City itself was very much a political arena, in which individuals and groups sought to acquire influence to further their personal

[1] Daniel Lupton, *London and the Countrey Carbonadoed and Quartered*, cited in A. Saunders, *The Royal Exchange* (London, 1991), 16.

[2] J. Addison and R. Steele, *The Spectator*, ed. D. F. Bond (London, 1965), i. 293. Addison also thought that 'factors in the trading world are what ambassadors are in the politick world'. For the latest work on the Exchange, see A. Saunders (ed.), *The Royal Exchange* (London, 1997).

and professional ends. As a reflection of this, historians of London have led the way in furthering our understanding of the political structures which underpinned urban life in the early modern period. From a variety of perspectives, the work of Ian Archer, Stephen Rappaport, Robert Brenner, Henry Roseveare, and Richard Grassby has made historians aware of the ways in which the social, economic, and political structures of the City determined the future of its inhabitants, and how a teeming metropolis could maintain rapid growth without serious instability.[3] All have probed the connection between economic and political change, and raised important questions concerning the nature of their relationship within a state undergoing significant development on both counts. In the field of Augustan politics, Gary De Krey has been foremost in linking the capital's political development to its socio-economic roots, and his exciting findings come closest to connecting the power-broking of the Exchange to that which took place at the Guildhall and Westminster, the relationship being illustrated by an imaginative combination of prosopographical, topographical, and psephological analysis. Most importantly, even while acknowledging the force of ideological division, he has demonstrated that the political life of the early modern City cannot be divorced from its social and economic foundations.[4]

Encouraged by such historiographic rewards, this chapter will examine the socio-economic environment of the overseas trader, as a necessary prelude to concentration on the merchant as a political figure. Taking advantage of an excellent series of City sources, the ensuing sections will outline the organizational structures of London's overseas commerce, seeking thereby to clarify the workings of the complex interrelationships which lay at the heart of mercantile activity. This analysis will provide a realistic portrait of the character of mercantile society, and will also test several recent theories concerning the City's political development. In particular, it will seek to square continuing scholarly emphasis on the political importance of mercantile 'interests' with the findings of economic historians, who suggest that merchants were in general independent traders, a contrast which begs very serious questions concerning the cogency of mercantile political activity. In order to resolve this apparent paradox, commercial political activity will be reconstructed from the 'bottom up', for without establishing an overview of the merchant body it will be impossible to measure how formal and informal networks advanced interaction between individual merchants. In agreement

[3] I. Archer, *In Pursuit of Stability* (Cambridge, 1991); S. Rapparport, *Worlds within Worlds* (Cambridge, 1989); R. Brenner, *Merchants and Revolution* (Princeton, 1993); H. Roseveare, *Markets and Merchants of the Late Seventeenth Century* (Oxford, 1987); R. Grassby, *The Business Community of Seventeenth-Century England* (Cambridge, 1995). All would acknowledge the seminal importance of Valerie Pearl's earlier work on the government and society of London, especially her *London and the Outbreak of the Puritan Revolution* (Oxford, 1961), 9–68.

[4] G. S. De Krey, *A Fractured Society: The Politics of London* (Oxford, 1985); D. W. Jones, *War and Economy in the Age of William III* (Oxford, 1988).

with the aforementioned scholars, great stress will be laid on the importance of the family to business activity, but awareness shown of its weaknesses, which necessarily forced the overseas trader into wider trading associations. Direct focus on the merchant will also clarify uncertainties concerning the personal dynamics of English overseas trade, and help us understand the relationship of big business and politics in this key period of growth.[5]

i. Sampling the London elite

Given the obvious attraction of London as the seat of wealth and power, it is not surprising that several of the most valuable studies of English politics and society have concentrated on the capital's elite, which inevitably included many merchants. A great deal of this pioneering work focused on the early Stuart merchant, as historians tried to define the longer-term origins of London's decisive role in the Civil Wars.[6] However, the Augustan period has been far from neglected, and extensive prosopographical analyses have fired a spirited debate on the relationship between land, business, and social opportunity in the eighteenth century. Most importantly for this study, Henry Horwitz made a telling contribution to the controversy over the so-called 'mess' of the middle classes with his study of 128 City leaders of the 1694–1714 period, which raised important questions concerning the likely social advancement made by big businessmen at the turn of the century. This work has certainly improved our understanding of City aspiration by a detailed critique of surviving indicators of status, and by stressing the importance of individual choice within the business elite. As with all prosopographical studies, concerns must be expressed over the representativeness of his sample, but the scholarly rewards are there for all to see.[7] Dwarfing even Horwitz's impressive field of study, Gary De Krey identified a sample of 1,339 'merchants' active in the 1690s in order to study commercial and constitutional development within the capital, and made many important points concerning political association within the business world. However, his main interest centred on the development of Whig and Tory polarities, and thus focused on merchants on the London livery (559 traders, or under half of his sample) in order to take advantage of surviving London poll books, and more particularly on an elite

---

[5] For discussion of commercial organization and mercantile 'interests', see De Krey, *Fractured Society*, 121–76, and Jones, *War and Economy*, 249–307. Our understanding of merchant politics has been further refined by A. G. Olson's *Making the Empire Work: London and American Interest Groups, 1690–1790* (Cambridge, Mass., 1992). For debate concerning merchant numbers, see Grassby, *Business Community*, 54–60.

[6] See in particular, Brenner, *Merchants and Revolution*, esp. chs. 3 and 4; R. G. Lang, 'The Social Origins and Social Aspirations of Jacobean London Merchants', *EcHR* 2nd ser., 27 (1974), 28–47; R. Ashton, *The City and the Court, 1603–43* (Cambridge, 1979); B. Supple, *Commercial Crisis and Change in England, 1600–42* (Cambridge, 1959); T. Rabb, *Enterprise and Empire* (Cambridge, Mass., 1967).

[7] H. Horwitz, 'The Mess of the Middle Classes Revisited', *Continuity and Change*, 2 (1987), 263–96.

of 198 'City leaders' who held, or were promoted for high civic and commercial office in the period 1688–1714. This study will seek to build on this
work by trying to understand the impact of political associations from a
variety of perspectives, rather than any simple concentration on civic or
parliamentary activity, which were far from the sole concerns of merchant
'politicians'.[8]

In common with the work of Horwitz and De Krey, this study has sought to
construct a meaningful sample with which to direct investigation of 'middling'
London, targeting 850 individuals who can be identified as merchants from
the City assessments for the poll taxes levied in the 1690s. An almost complete
set of returns survives for the poll tax of 1692, and can be complemented with
records from 1694 and 1698 to provide a detailed account of London's
mercantile society at the turn of the century.[9] Of course, even such a large
selection remains open to the familiar criticisms of omission and misrepre-
sentation. However, there can be little doubt that the 850 traders studied here
can provide a realistic impression of mercantile life, for by the terms of their
statutory brief the poll tax assessors had to take special note of overseas
traders.[10] Merchants, along with brokers and gentlemen with estates of over
£300 p.a., were distinguished by their liability to a surtax of £4, and thus
the assessments were sensitive to professional distinctions within the City
hierarchy. About 2,500 City inhabitants paid this highest rate of surtax out of
over 80,000 who contributed to these levies, but one cannot assume that they
were predominantly mercantile on the basis of their residence, even though
four out of five of these surtax payers came from the City within the walls. In
fact, after the ranks of the urban gentleman have been removed, it has been
possible to identify only 848 men and two women as active in overseas trade, a
figure which represents only about a third of the recorded intramural surtax
payers.[11] This finding is in itself most significant, and offers a more certain

---

[8] De Krey, *Fractured Society*, esp. ch. 4. His mercantile sample can be found in the unpublished
appendices in his 'Trade, Religion, and Politics in London in the Reign of William III', Ph.D. thesis
(Princeton, 1978).

[9] All the tax records used here can be found in the assessment boxes at the CLRO; for a detailed
account see C. Spence, *A Social Atlas of London in the 1690s* (CMH publication, forthcoming), appendix 1.
Two wards, Portsoken and Walbrook, lack returns for 1692, but a reliable impression of the
mercantile presence in each ward has been established from other tax records of the 1690s. Thus,
corroborative evidence suggests that supplementary assessments from 1698 (Portsoken) and 1694
(Walbrook) can be used with confidence. The two wards encompass less than 8% of the total sample.

[10] Fortunately, assessors had to make a distinction between overseas traders and factors or packers,
many of whom became directly involved in foreign commerce. For more general analysis of occupational assessment, see J. M. B. Alexander, 'The Economic and Social Structure of the City of London,
c.1700', Ph.D. thesis (London School of Economics, 1989), 73–106, 340–56; P. H. Lindert, 'English
Occupations, 1670–1811', *Journal of Economic History*, 40 (1980), 685–712; D. V. Glass 'Socio-economic
Status and Occupations in the City of London at the End of the Seventeenth Century', in A. E. J.
Hollaender and W. Kellaway, *Studies in London History* (London, 1969), 373–92; L. D. Schwarz, *London in
the Age of Industrialization* (Cambridge, 1992), 241–9.

[11] In the assessments, 807 individuals are specifically denoted as merchants; 43 surtax payers with no
specified occupation have been identified as active merchants (as opposed to gentlemen) from other

benchmark with which to assess contemporary and academic opinion. The most authoritative contemporary account of the national picture remains that of Gregory King, who in his famous *Natural and Political Observations* suggested that in 1688 there were 2,000 'merchants and traders by sea' earning £400 p.a., and 8,000 lesser maritime traders with half that income. Since King was probably aware that the vast majority of greater merchants were to be found in the capital, his calculations appear to be on the high side, although his distinction tacitly acknowledges the problem of distinguishing traders who were predominantly mercantile by profession.[12] Modern historians have in general lamented the lack of precision which can be brought to such an important issue as the numbering of the mercantile profession, but the poll tax returns remain particularly illuminating for the study of the overseas trader. Thus, this sample forms the basis for the succeeding analysis of mercantile activity within the capital, and, although only a snapshot of City life, its reliability and scale provides a fairly comprehensive survey of those individuals most directly involved in overseas trade.[13]

The very fact that the merchants formed a separate category in the eyes of national politicians is in itself significant, since it suggests that overseas trade was regarded as a profession distinct within the economy. Research has highlighted the wide diversity of the investments of the commercial elite, but the design of the tax suggests that the authorities were able to differentiate a class of traders whose predominant interest was in foreign trade.[14] Growing academic recognition of the specialization and concentration of overseas trade in fewer hands accords with this impression, although it would be erroneous to suggest that the boundaries of this group were well defined and impermeable.[15] With more immediate matters in mind, the government was clearly try-

records. Ensuing discussion will continue to regard the overseas trader as masculine, given the overwhelming gender bias of the sample. The two female merchants identified were both widows of naturalized merchants, and were probably maintaining their husbands' trade. For detailed analysis of a trading widow, see Roseveare, *Markets and Merchants*, 121–52.

[12] P. Laslett, *The World We Have Lost: Further Explorations* (New York, 1965), 32–3. Laslett has shown continued respect for King's general reliability—K. Schurer and T. Arkell (eds.), *Surveying the People* (Oxford, 1992), 6–30. In his other unpublished notes King was more conservative in his estimates, suggesting in a journal of early 1696 that London had some 500 merchants and brokers to merchants, 60 merchant strangers, and 30 Jewish merchants—J. Thirsk and J. P. Cooper (eds.), *Seventeenth-Century Economic Documents* (Oxford, 1972), 768.

[13] Judging by the most authoritative guesstimates of active English traders, the London and provincial samples used here are sufficiently large to give a comprehensive impression of mercantile life,— P. Earle, *The Making of the English Middle Class* (London, 1989), 34–5; Grassby, *Business Community*, 54–60. For discussion of the difficulties of analysing settlement in early modern towns, see J. Langton, 'Residential Patterns in Pre-industrial Cities: Some Case-Studies from Seventeenth-Century Britain', *Transactions of the Institute of British Geographers*, 65 (1975), 1–27.

[14] For analysis of other indices of merchant wealth, especially investments, see P. G. M. Dickson, *The Financial Revolution in England*, 2nd edn. (Oxford, 1993); Jones, *War and Economy*, 330–1.

[15] For the concentration debate, see J. M. Price and P. G. E. Clemens, 'A Revolution in Overseas Trade: British Firms in the Chesapeake Trade, 1675–1775', *Journal of Economic History*, 47 (1987), 1–43. London was probably ahead of the provincial outports in terms of mercantile concentration, as

ing to tap the perceived wealth of the mercantile classes, whose evasion of heavy land tax liabilities during wartime was regarded with particular ire by the gentry-dominated Parliament. Since the Restoration parliamentary authorities had been reassessing the occupational status of overseas traders. Under the poll tax of 1660 the only native merchants to be singled out were those who had failed to become free of the City. Mercantile freemen faced surtaxes on account of their status and office-holding, but not because of their business interests. On the other hand, several separate categories of 'merchant strangers' were penalized. Most importantly, differentiation was made between those aliens 'trading to sea' and those trading 'within the land', with the former paying twice the assessment of the latter, while merchant strangers with a knighthood had to pay £40, four times the rate of their sea-trading brethren. The poll tax of 1677–8 was much more specific, only singling out unfree City merchants and alien traders. In addition, investors in overseas trading ventures were targeted by a 1 per cent tax on shareholdings in the East India and Guinea companies. The earliest post-Revolutionary poll levies largely maintained this policy, although in 1689 an additional distinction was made between Jewish merchants and brokers, the latter of whom only had to pay a quarter of the former's assessment. Thus the formula of the 1692 poll tax was a notable departure in targeting native merchants so directly, especially while not seeking to increase the contribution of foreign merchants. It is thus doubly fortunate that it is this assessment which survives, since it provides an insight into an occupational group to which the state had accorded increasing interest since the Restoration.[16]

As with any prosopographical study, acknowledgement must be given to the limitations of the sample. Historians are well aware of the fallibilities of tax assessments, and in this instance consideration must be given to the possible erroneous identification of merchants by assessors, and to the exclusion of some overseas merchants by accident or design. In general, concerns about the fallibility of local officials can be resolved fairly easily by reference to records of mercantile activity, such as the port books and the archives of the overseas trading companies. This evidence overwhelmingly affirms that the assessors were scrupulous in identifying active overseas traders as merchants, and thus accords with the views of the pioneering economist Charles Davenant, who regarded the officials of the Home Counties as more rigorous

suggested by Bristol merchant John Cary's call for greater separation between retailer and merchant in 1695—*An Essay on the State of England in Relation to its Trade* (Bristol, 1695), 41. For evidence of increasing specialization among Bristol traders in the eighteenth century, see K. Morgan, *Bristol and the Atlantic Trade in the Eighteenth Century* (Cambridge, 1993).

[16] *Statutes of the Realm*, v. 207–25, 584, 601, 852; vi. 63, 156–8. In 1660 the authorities still assessed City wealth by livery company, dividing sixty-one companies into five graded tax brackets. However, innovations in the 1690s, such as the 'stocks' assessments of the 1693–4 four-shilling aid, demonstrated that the state was targeting mercantile wealth. For broader discussion of poll taxes in the seventeenth century, see T. Arkell, 'An Examination of the Poll Taxes of the Later Seventeenth Century, the Marriage Duty Act, and Gregory King', in Schurer and Arkell, *Surveying the People*, 142–77.

than their northern and western colleagues concerning 'payment for degrees and qualities of persons'.[17] The problem of omission is more worrying, for it raises several methodological issues which have bedevilled modern analysts. In particular, the attribution of the title of 'gentleman' or 'esquire' to a known participant in overseas trade was not uncommon, and the deference of local assessors might have taken priority over the accurate recording of commercial activity. On the other hand, the attribution of these status titles can be read as a sensitive interpretation of personal circumstances, in that it may signal the retirement of an individual from trade, and perhaps into the rentier status of the urban 'pseudo-gentlemen'.[18] More unpredictably, such identifications may simply reflect the idiosyncrasy of the assessor or assessee. Given such an insuperable difficulty, and our priority of identifying *active* overseas traders, it has been decided not to include gentlemen or esquires within the mercantile sample, although their important contribution to City life has not been ignored.[19]

A potentially greater difficulty exists with regard to underassessment, since it would have been financially advantageous for overseas traders to declare themselves as domestic wholesalers or even retailers. Recent research has stressed the potential diversity in the investments of the upper urban classes, and there are certainly some individuals assessed below the £4 p.a. surtax band who can be identified as prominent in overseas commerce at some stage in their career. However, it does appear that the assessors were scrupulous in determining who were active merchants, for they were prepared to reassess individual claims to mercantile status from quarter to quarter. For example, there was evident concern among the assessors of Bassishaw about the occupation of former Blackwell Hall factor Paris Slaughter junior, which was ultimately resolved by his payment of the surtax as a merchant. There are also several examples of downwards assessment, such as Thomas Merret and John Day of St Dunstan-in-the-East, who were bracketed as merchants in April 1692, but then relegated to substantial 'tradesmen' nine months later. In fact, both their wills styled them as corn-factors, which suggests that they may have switched their commercial interest to domestic trade. Despite their demotion,

[17] Thirsk and Cooper, *Seventeenth-Century Economic Documents*, 806. Davenant's fellow arithmatician, Gregory King, was more concerned with the ignorance of the assessor in London's large parishes, where he 'shall scarce know five families on each side of him'—ibid. 791.

[18] Among those identified as esquires or gentlemen by the poll tax assessors are Thomas Papillon and James Houblon, two of the City's greatest Restoration merchants. However, this categorization brackets them with such figures as Charles Duncombe, a leading banker with no active involvement with overseas trade.

[19] Late Stuart commentators were concerned for the accuracy of status-based assessments— M. Braddick, *The Nerves of State: Taxation and the Financing of the English State, 1558–1714* (Manchester, 1996), 103–6. For scholarly discussion of the definition of the gentleman—see K. Wrightson, 'Estates, Degrees, and Sorts: Changing Perceptions of Society in Tudor and Stuart England', in P. Corfield (ed.), *Language, History, and Class* (Oxford, 1991), 30–52; P. Corfield, 'The Rivals: Landed and Other Gentlemen', in N. Harte and R. Quinault (eds.), *Land and Society in Britain, 1700–1914* (Manchester, 1996), 1–33.

they have been maintained within the sample in order to preserve the diversity of mercantile experience. These examples in fact highlight the fluidity of City life, while also suggesting that contemporaries retained a good idea of what they imagined a merchant to be. Given its size, there can be little doubt that the sample will afford ample coverage of this fast-moving and cosmopolitan merchant world.[20]

Of course, the sample of 850 cannot be regarded as all-inclusive for the metropolitan area, since it is clear that many active merchants based themselves just outside City jurisdiction, particularly in Hackney or Stepney, attracted no doubt by cheaper rentals and an escape from the suffocating bustle of life within the walls. By the late seventeenth century commuting was already regarded as a chore for many Londoners, and the most ready alternative guide to merchant distribution, Samuel Lee's *Directory* of 1677, suggests that some 7 per cent of metropolitan merchants could be found beyond the City. However, doubts have been raised concerning the reliability of this source as a guide to active overseas traders, for it appears to include a number of coastal specialists, which may explain the significant number listed in the peripheral areas of Wapping and Southwark.[21] As we shall see, the merchant was extremely discerning in his choice of domicile, and only a handful of overseas traders dispensed with the perceived necessity of having an inner-City address. Lee's *Directory* acknowledges this centripetal force, with several extramural residents providing an additional intramural address. The greater merchant might indeed have the opportunity to maintain two habitations, in order to relieve the personal and commercial pressures working on all London businessmen. However, it is clear that active traders could not stray far from the nerve-centre of their operations, and the patterns of householding revealed by the poll tax returns suggest that most merchants had at least some lodgings within the City.[22]

[20] CLRO: assessment boxes 35/15, 112/2, 36/7, 33/10, 4/3. Historians have been well aware that wholesalers and retailers could become involved in overseas trade, D. W. Jones remarking on the bewildering number of small-time traders below the 699 he found with a £500 turnover in the port books of 1694–5—*War and Economy*, 262; also see the appendices to his 'London Overseas Merchant Groups at the End of the Seventeenth Century and the Move against the East India Company', D.Phil. thesis (Oxford, 1970), 387–468. The assessors actually ranked a large number of Gary De Krey's 1,172 'confirmed' merchants of the 1690s as retailers—Ph.D. thesis, appendices.

[21] S. Lee, *The Little London Directory* (London, 1677). This directory lists 138 'merchants' with extra-City addresses (and nine with a City and extra-City address) out of a total of 1,829. The only significant mercantile residences beyond the City were Hackney (23), Southwark (12), Wapping (11), and Hoxton (10). There is evidently a problem with Lee's definition of merchant here, which is illustrated by the case of Daniel Allen. In December 1676 the Levant Company refused to admit Allen as a freeman, arguing that as a warehouseman selling goat's wool within the City he did not fit their criteria as a 'mere merchant'—SP105/154, fo. 4ᵛ.

[22] For an excellent study of the extramural activity of Levant merchant John Verney of Hatton Garden, see S. Whyman, *Sociability and Power in Late-Stuart England* (Oxford, 1999). The need for daily attendance at the Exchange has been recently emphasized by N. Zahedieh—'Making Mercantilism Work: London Merchants and Atlantic Trade in the Seventeenth Century', *TRHS* 6th ser., 9 (1999), 143–58.

Further confidence concerning the representativeness of the sample can be taken from contemporary London commentators, in particular the merchant tutor John Vernon, who wondrously observed of the counting-house in 1678, 'so many merchants, so many minds, or fashions', yet went on to conclude that 'although they differ in trivial things, yet in the substantial things they do not disagree much'.[23] Moreover, several other excellent London tax assessments survive to permit analysis of the fluidity of London life. Most importantly, the size of the sample will enable us to cover three generations of merchants, and thus provide some idea of the forces of change and continuity within London's mercantile society across the 1660–1720 period.

ii. Merchant distribution in the City

Breaking down this mass of mercantile experience is not easy, and, as with all prosopographical studies, there is always a danger of mapping patterns which might have meant very little to contemporaries. However, the tie of mercantile activity gives all 850 members of our sample a common purpose, and certain generalizations can be made. The tax itself highlights some very essential points about the status of the overseas merchant. The fact that the merchants were expected to pay a surtax of the same magnitude as the gentlemen shows that they were regarded as an urban elite, an impression subsequently reinforced in the eyes of the government's revenue officials by the calculations of Gregory King, who thought that the average income of greater merchants (at £400 p.a.) exceeded that of the gentlemen by £120 p.a. Indeed, his estimate of £198 p.a. for lesser merchants placed them above 'persons in the law' and 'eminent clergymen'. Further confirmation of the general standing of the overseas trader comes from recent research which concludes that the wealth of the 'merchant-financial' sector was significant even in comparison with the prosperous metropolitan region as a whole.[24]

However, how did such financial muscle transfer into actual social and political influence? Contemporaries were well aware that the City's political subdivisions could affect the course of its affairs, since the wards and precincts possessed electoral powers over the composition of the ruling corporation. Nevertheless, it remains to be seen whether topographical analysis of the elite mercantile group can tell us more about the socio-economic roots of City politics. De Krey's work gives a powerful endorsement to this approach, able as he was to link broad patterns of social zoning to ideological outlook. With the added advantage of excellent occupational records, this study can probe the structures of mercantile life down to precinct level in order to reconstruct

---

[23] J. Vernon, *The Complete Comptinghouse* (London, 1678), 35.
[24] Laslett, *World We Have Lost*, 32–3; Alexander, Ph.D. thesis, 80–92. King also concluded that merchants were more 'productive' than gentlemen, in regard of the latter's propensity to spend.

TABLE 1.1 *Merchant distribution within the City by ward, 1692*

Ward		Number	% of total merchants	% of assessed ward population (heads of household)
1.	Aldersgate Within	3	0.4	0.4
2.	Aldersgate Without	3	0.4	0.5
3.	Aldgate	96	11.3	8.0
4.	Bassishaw	19	2.2	7.7
5.	Billingsgate	44	5.2	7.5
6.	Bishopsgate Within	31	3.6	5.5
7.	Bishopsgate Without	22	2.6	1.8
8.	Bread Street	2	0.2	0.4
9.	Bridge Within	10	1.2	2.1
10.	Broad Street	126	14.8	9.9
11.	Candlewick	51	6.0	11.8
12.	Castle Baynard	7	0.8	0.8
13.	Cheap	30	3.5	4.9
14.	Coleman Street	34	4.0	3.9
15.	Cordwainer	43	5.1	7.7
16.	Cornhill	8	0.9	1.2
17.	Cripplegate Within	14	1.6	1.3
18.	Cripplegate Without	1	0.1	0.1
19.	Dowgate	29	3.4	7.0
20.	Farringdon Within	5	0.6	0.2
21.	Farringdon Without	6	0.7	0.1
22.	Langbourne	77	9.1	9.2
23.	Lime Street	13	1.5	4.6
24.	Portsoken	3	0.4	0.4
25.	Queenhithe	0	0.0	0.0
26.	Tower	102	12.0	9.2
27.	Vintry	14	1.6	2.1
28.	Walbrook	57	6.7	12.6
TOTAL		850	99.9	3.3

Sources: The table is compiled from assessments at the CLRO. The tax was applied broadly on a household basis, but more than one mercantile household could be found at the same address. The numbering of the wards correlates to that displayed in Map 1.1.

the associations which directed commercial life. Our first task is to identify the immediate sphere of mercantile influence, which is represented in Table 1.1 and Map 1.1.[25]

[25] De Krey, *Fractured Society*, esp. 165–76. For published analyses of the topography of the late Stuart city, see M. Power, 'The Social Topography of Restoration London' in A. L. Beier and R. Finlay (eds.), *London, 1500–1700* (London, 1986), 199–223; J. M. B. Alexander, 'The Economic Structure of the City

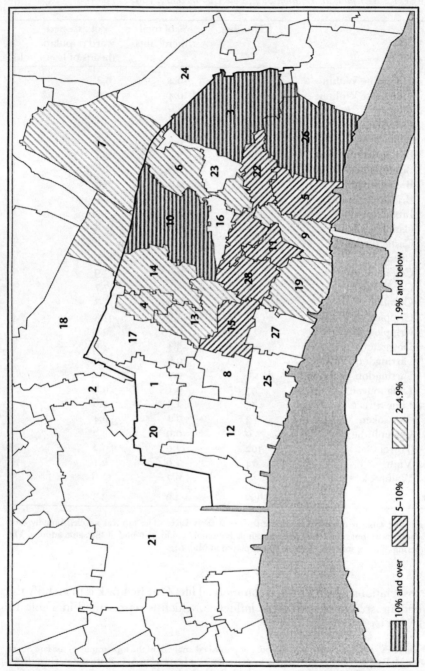

MAP 1.1 Merchant distribution through the City Wards, 1692

The pattern which emerges from the poll tax returns is of a mercantile population condensed into the eastern half of the City, obviously drawn there by the primary sites of overseas commercial activity: the Royal Exchange, the wharves and warehouses of the dockside, the customs house, and the post and insurance offices. Moreover, in this small area were also located some of the key services which linked domestic markets to international trade, such as Blackwell Hall, the conduit for the all-important English cloth industry, and Billingsgate, the hub of the fishery. These services ensured that some 90 per cent of the mercantile population were packed into just half the City wards. Although merchant domination of the eastern City was never a question of pure numbers, the ratio of overseas traders to their fellow ward inhabitants fully demonstrates the degree of concentration. Significantly, this distribution correlates to that of the occupational groups with whom merchants had daily contact, such as factors, packers, brokers, and Exchange men. Thus, the occupational map of the City reveals the unmistakable focus for overseas traders in the capital, and indicates the fundamental importance for merchants to maintain close contact with the services which it provided, and the personnel who manned them. Most importantly of all, this topographical concentration also ensured that merchants could stay in communication with each other, and be ready to seize opportunities for business dealings as they presented themselves. [26]

While the proliferation of overseas traders in the eastern half of the City is clear, there remain idiosyncrasies within this broad pattern which provide a more defined picture of City life. For instance, it appears strange that merchants are so poorly represented in the ward of Cornhill, within which the Royal Exchange partly lay. Their absence must be linked to the magnetism of the Exchange as a concourse of all walks of City society, and it appears that merchants were unprepared to pay the inflated rents within those precincts, thereby leaving the area to be peopled with retailers of luxury goods. Moreover, while the riverside wards of Dowgate, Walbrook, and Tower proved popular with overseas traders, the fact that Queenhithe housed no merchants at all emphasizes how particular merchants could be in their choice of domicile. In the absence of overseas traders, its position above London Bridge had promoted Queenhithe's use as a base for inland and coastal dealers, such as malt-factors and wood-mongers, who jostled for space with watermen, porters, and wharfingers. Contemporaries and historians have noted the development of specialist locales within the capital, and merchants

of London at the End of the Seventeenth Century', *Urban History Yearbook* (1989), 47–62; *idem* in Schurer and Arkell, *Surveying the People*, 181–200.

[26] Alexander, Ph.D. thesis, 90–106. For a contemporary guide to the location of commercial services, see E. Hatton, *The New View of London* (London, 1708). For an important insight into the social and spatial networks which could bind traders and non-traders, see S. Whyman, 'Land and Trade Revisited: The Case of John Verney, London Merchant and Baronet', *London Journal*, 22 (1997), 16–32.

obviously had to compete with their fellow townsmen for the most desirable sites. In general, this survey underlines the point, perhaps a little overlooked by some political analysts, that the City was at root a workplace, providing sophisticated services to a demanding commercial population within a very compact area. As we shall see, this does not minimize the significance of the City's 'political' institutions, but it does alert us to the economic priorities underpinning all activity therein.[27]

Derek Keene has drawn attention to the slow drift eastwards of the financial and mercantile City from the later medieval period onwards, but it is fairly clear that merchant residence in the 1690s closely resembled that of the 1660s.[28] The more imprecise Lee *Directory* of merchants in 1677 portrays a similar picture for the intramural distribution of a preceding generation of 'merchants', with concentrations along the major City arteries east of the Guildhall, most notably Fenchurch Street, Throgmorton Street, Broad Street, and Coleman Street. In a cramped urban environment, which could only be traversed with difficulty during working hours, the demands of business evidently dictated that the merchant be close to the public workplaces, and this can account for the general distribution to the east.[29] Once a merchant had set his mind on a central City base, the determination of its precise coordinates would principally rest with the physical structure of the property and its access to mercantile facilities, rather than any other preoccupation, such as the proximity of traders in his chosen field. By examining the series of City tax records from 1690 to 1695, it is quite clear that there was a brisk and competitive market in 'mercantile' houses, which could boast adequate storage facilities, and a decent office for running the business. Newspaper adverts from the 1690s suggest that vendors were very attuned to the requirements of prospective mercantile buyers, who would obviously prefer to have their goods stored in their own property rather than having to hire expensive warehousing elsewhere.[30]

As if to illustrate the basic introspection of the mercantile business unit, contemporaries such as Edward Hatton emphasized the manner in which the great merchant houses faced away from the street, leaving the more expensive

---

[27] This impression of life on the riverside accords with the findings of M. Power for the 1660s—Beier and Finlay, *London, 1500–1700*, 204.

[28] D. Keene, 'The Setting of the Royal Exchange: Continuity and Change in the Financial District of the City of London, 1300–1871', in Saunders, *Royal Exchange*, 253–71.

[29] Lee, *The Little London Directory*; also see C. W. F. Goss, *The London Directories* (London, 1932), 16–23.

[30] For the 1690s in particular, see John Houghton's *Collection for the Improvement of Husbandry and Trade*. The idiosyncrasies of assessors obscure the identity of specific houses, but it does appear that certain addresses were most attractive to merchants, judging by the succession of overseas traders who took up residence there. For instance, Isiah De Walpergen, a native of Frankfurt, moved house within the parish of St Nicholas Acon in late 1692, taking a property vacated by merchant widow Alida Vandermarch. This move was facilitated by Isiah's recent marriage to Alida's daughter, and other evidence suggests that alien settlers took advantage of such ties to gain a desirable mercantile base— CLRO: assessment boxes 20/17, 36/12.

main thoroughfares to the retailers. Hatton recognized their need for 'courts, offices, and all necessary apartments enclosed to themselves', and 'because of the great quantity of ground they are built on . . . [they are] . . . generally situate backward, and by that means the City appears not to strangers who walk the streets near so stately and beautiful as it really is and would show itself were these ornaments exposed to public view'. Such an assessment was no doubt influenced by the critical observations of foreign travellers to the business capital, who seldom showed much enthusiasm for the physical fabric of the City, even though they could enthuse about the opulence it generated. Plans of the inner City, such as the excellent Ogilby and Morgan map of 1676, reveal that it was a maze of courts, warehouses, and offices, reflecting the merchants' desperate hunt for storage space for their commercial goods, and even a civic patriot such as Hatton could not disguise the commercial mandate for substance over style.[31]

Although it appears that merchants were attracted like moths to the flame of London's commercial hub, it would be premature to portray them as a homogeneous body merely on the basis of their common commercial priorities and their propensity to congregate in a very confined area. In particular, differences in wealth within the merchant class could obviously have a crucial impact on the flexibility of their choice of residence. The housing market of London, then as now, was commercially attuned to the intense demand for business space, and merchants were just as keen as other occupational groupings to secure the properties they needed, thus ensuring fierce competition. Fortunately, the London returns for the four-shilling aid of 1693–4 permit some provisional insights into the wealth of the sample, although such assessments remain a perennial source of difficulty for the historian, and must be treated with care. Even contemporaries jested about the impossibility of judging a merchant's fortune, John Houghton musing in 1701 that 'a timber tree is a merchant adventurer; you shall never know what he worth till he be dead', and fiscal uncertainties were shared by City tax assessors throughout the eighteenth century.[32]

The four-shilling aid provides information on two aspects of merchant wealth; a 20 per cent levy on the annual profits of personal estate in a wide

[31] Hatton, *New View of London*, 627. For a critical German view of Hatton's descriptions, see W. H. Quarrell and M. Mare (eds.), *London in 1710* (London, 1934); the domestic architecture of the pre-fire City had not impressed French royal councillor Monconys in 1663—B. de Monconys, *Journal des voyages de Monsieur de Monconys* (Lyon, 1666), 8–11. For the 1676 Map, see *The A to Z of Restoration London* (London, 1992). For a detailed study of a great merchant house in the City, see B. Cherry, 'John Pollexfen's House in Walbrook', in J. Bold and E. Chaney (eds.), *English Architecture Public and Private* (London, 1993), 89–105.

[32] *Collection for the Improvement of Husbandry and Trade*, issue 478 (19 Sept. 1701); S. Brown, 'Politics, Commerce, and Social Policy in the City of London, 1782–1802', D.Phil. thesis (Oxford, 1992), 23. Also note Sir William Petty, *A Treatise of Taxes and Contributions* (1662), 34, where the credit of an individual in London is seen as a 'mere conceit', as gauged 'without any certain knowledge of his wealth or true estate'.

TABLE 1.2. *Mercantile stocks and rental assessments by City ward, 1693–4*

	Number of merchants	Mean rental in 1693–4 (£)	Mean stocks in 1693–4 (£)
Aldersgate Within	3	86	600
Aldersgate Without	3	39	400
Aldgate	96	38.8	297
Bassishaw	19	44.8	357
Billingsgate	44	52.2	310
Bishopsgate Within	31	69.9	358
Bishopsgate Without	22	55.2	392
Bread Street	2	30	200
Bridge Within	10	44	400
Broad Street	126	53.5	366
Candlewick	51	50.6	326
Castle Baynard	7	29.7	262
Cheap	30	59.1	253
Coleman Street	34	64.6	367
Cordwainer	43	47.4	326
Cornhill	8	0	200
Cripplegate Within	14	35	281
Cripplegate Without	1	20	200
Dowgate	29	60.1	236
Farringdon Within	5	33.7	200
Farringdon Without	6	31.4	240
Langbourne	77	59.4	314
Lime Street	13	52.6	269
Portsoken	3	35	200
Queenhithe	0	—	—
Tower	102	77.8	331
Vintry	14	60.8	513
Walbrook	57	59.3	272
Totals/averages	850	55.4	323

Sources: The table was compiled from assessments at the CLRO.

variety of forms, including cash, debts, goods, and merchandises; together with a 20 per cent exaction on the rack rents of all 'lands, tenements, and hereditaments'. While the assessments for real estate may be regarded as reliable, those for personal 'stocks' are more problematic, and historians, doubtlessly in the same manner as hard-pressed tax officials, have struggled to understand how such a wide-ranging tax could be calculated. In the particular case of mercantile wealth, surviving inventories highlight how difficult it was to evaluate the estate of an overseas trader at any one time, when so much of it would be tied up in adventures around the globe, or in other investments. Nevertheless, comparison with other near-contemporary assessments suggests that the evaluation for stocks can be regarded as a rough guide of the *perceived* wealth of the individual, and, judging by their preference for broad bands of assessment, it appears that local assessors were unable to aspire to any more than the most general estimate of personalty. With these caveats in mind, Table 1.2 is submitted only as a general guide to mercantile wealth, and attempts to relate it to their spatial distribution.[33]

The table demonstrates that in general it would be hard to differentiate any particularly prosperous merchant locales on a ward basis. The most eye-catching of the averages given for stock assessment come from wards in which there were few merchants to be found, and thus their return could be hugely distorted by the presence of a single very wealthy trader. In fact, all the wards with the highest density of merchants were home to a broad spectrum of mercantile wealth, with very substantial and more modest traders living as neighbours. These observations underline the meaningless of ward boundaries for commercial activity, but certain economic factors did promote particular locales above the rest. In particular, the average rental values are a more reliable guide to the strategic value of each ward to individual merchants, since they provide an overall assessment of the value of a site, as linked to the availability of appropriate housing. Note the high mean value of mercantile rents in Tower ward, poised advantageously on the riverside below the bridge, and close to the customs house. Within its precincts lay Mincing Lane, home to some of the foremost figures in City commerce. However, even this precinct could not be represented as Millionaire's Row, since the presence of more modest merchants in the vicinity brought down its mean value. More generally, the table highlights the diversity of merchant experience throughout the wards, and argues for further analysis of the character of the mercantile classes, especially in terms of wealth. Therefore, Table 1.3 employs the returns of the four-shilling aid to assess the correlation between stocks and the rental value of householders.[34]

This table can only be taken as a snapshot of the perceived wealth of the sample, but both valuations serve to illustrate the sharp gradations possible within the mercantile group, even while in general establishing their prosperous credentials within London society. The authors of the poll tax of 1692 were thus fully justified in imposing a surtax on the merchant, even though such blanket coverage meant that they failed to tap the wealth of the greatest of the overseas traders, whose riches would dwarf those of many of their colleagues on the Exchange. The stocks assessment of 1693–4 in fact

---

[33] For an account of the 1693–4 levy, see Spence, *Social Atlas of London in the 1690s*, ch. 1.

[34] CLRO: assessment boxes 33/10, 4/3. In Mincing Lane precinct (Tower ward) there were twenty-five merchants, five of whom were rated at £600 or over, including Sir Edward Desbouverie at £1,000. However, six of their neighbours were rated at under £300, including two lodgers at only £100.

TABLE 1.3. *Comparison of the City sample's stocks, rentals, and householding, 1693–4*

Assessment	Total Number	Number of Householders		Mean value of rental 1693–4 (£)
less than £100	11	6	(54.5%)	26.3
£100–199	85	46	(54.1%)	49.2
£200–99	179	130	(72.6%)	48.9
£300–99	146	115	(78.8%)	49.0
£400–99	96	81	(84.4%)	49.9
£500–99	94	82	(87.2%)	75.6
£600–99	22	21	(95.5%)	67.2
£700–999	16	14	(87.5%)	83.4
£1000 and over	5	5	(100%)	103.8
TOTAL	654	500	(76.4%)	55.4

Sources: The table was compiled from assessments at the CLRO.

demonstrated official determination to ensure that the trading sector paid their way in the midst of the most expensive war which the country had ever fought. As previous analysts have stressed, the assessments for stocks must be regarded as an imperfect gauge of commercial activity, but their broad correlation with other tax returns lends to their creditability as a general estimate of the perceived financial status of a merchant.[35]

At first sight this data appears to endorse the recent arguments of economic historians, who argue for a creeping 'concentration' of commercial control into the hands of a small cadre of supertraders. However, the persuasive concentration of wealth in the uppermost echelons of mercantile society has to be put into the context of the general prosperity of this group as a whole. In particular, it says a great deal for the *common* respect for the overseas trader that some two-thirds of the merchants were assessed at between £200 and £400 (inclusive), which was well above the average for the intramural City. Interestingly, these findings very much accord with the income estimates suggested by Gregory King, and more generally the returns may well have influenced his thinking on the distinction between lesser and eminent merchants.[36] In itself King's analysis might appear an endorsement of mercantile

[35] James Alexander could not correlate the stocks assessments with the trading activity as recorded in the 1694–5 port books—Ph.D. thesis, 96.
[36] Price and Clemens, *Journal of Economic History*, 47 (1987), 1–43. There has been some debate concerning King's access to the poll tax assessments, but his views on mercantile income support those scholars who regard them as indispensable sources for his calculations—Schurer and Arkell, *Surveying the People*, 29–30, 171–6. However, King's estimate of mercantile numbers remains questionable, especially in the case of the greater merchants, since only 233 of our sample had a ranking of £400 or over, and it may be safely presumed that he would have regarded London as the domicile of the majority of the 2,000 eminent merchants he identifies.

THE MERCANTILE CITY   33

'concentration', and it is significant that other observers expressed concern at perceived changes within the mercantile elite, with a pamphleteer of 1707 insisting that there were twice as many substantial merchants in the 1660s than in his day. Contemporaries were also alive to the existence of those traders at the poorer end of the scale, a foreign visitor to early Georgian London warning that 'you must not imagine . . . that all merchants are prosperous; the greater number are not and live like ordinary citizens'. Yet, within the City such distinctions were often blurred, since it is clear that modestly regarded traders were prepared to pay for very expensive residences in order to advance their business, and to secure comfort for their families. In terms of house-rentals, the only sharp disparities between our tax bands remain between those richer and poorer traders who did not fall within the £100–499 stocks bracket. Thus, even while contemporaries could drool at the fabulous wealth of certain super-rich magnates, they were prepared to accord the profession general respect, and it would have been extremely premature to judge the fortunes of a trader merely on the criterion of address, even in the case of an inner-City domicile.[37]

These impressions of mercantile society can be further investigated by reference to the marriage duty returns of 1695, one of the most ambitious schemes of rating attempted in early modern England. This levy differed considerably from the poll tax, by requiring the payment of additional contributions according to a combination of status and wealth categories. Thus, not only were the titled and gentry liable for extra taxes, but anyone with a minimum personal estate of £600 capital value was also targeted. However, although the marriage duty was enforced on different criteria, its returns (illustrated in Table 1.4) endorse the general character of mercantile society provided in the earlier poll and land taxes.[38]

Although the inclusion of status categories introduces further cause for concern regarding the idiosyncrasies of the assessors, the table concurs with the earlier taxes in demonstrating that overseas traders deserved to be ranked among the City's higher echelons, thereby ensuring a certain degree of social homogeneity within the merchant classes.[39] Most importantly, the broad hierarchical distinctions suggested by the marriage duty returns correlate well

[37] J. B., *The Interest of England Considered* (London, 1707); *A Foreign View of England, 1725–9: The Letters of Monsieur Cesar de Saussure to his Family*, ed. Madame Van Muyden (London, 1995), 135. The propensity of modest traders to take expensive dwellings has also been identified in the late eighteenth century— Brown, D.Phil. thesis, 106. In general, it would have been difficult for any contemporary to perceive that 10–20 merchant princes 'dominated' the City's overseas commerce, as suggested by Peter Earle— *Making of the English Middle Class*, 35.

[38] For the administration and rating of the marriage duty, see D. V. Glass (ed.), 'London Inhabitants within the Walls, 1695', *London Record Society*, 2 (1966), pp. ix–xxxix.

[39] The assessors were required to assign individuals to set categories, each of which was liable for the payment of set rates for births, marriages, and deaths within their family. Of the surviving assessments from eighty parishes, about 27% of householders were liable for the payment of surtaxes—*London Record Society* 2 (1966), pp. xx–xxi.

TABLE 1.4. *Comparison of the City sample's stocks of 1693–4 with the marriage duty returns of 1695*

Stocks assessment in 1693–4	(Total)	No surtax	1695 marriage duty returns			
			Surtax (£600)	Gentleman +esquire	Knight +baronet	Total
Under £100	(11)	4	2	0	0	6
£100–99	(85)	11	36	4	0	51
£200–99	(179)	15	73	16	0	104
£300–99	(146)	13	64	23	1	101
£400–99	(96)	4	45	23	0	72
£500–99	(94)	2	21	27	4	54
£600–99	(22)	2	8	5	4	19
£700–999	(16)	1	3	3	4	11
£1,000+	(5)	0	0	3	1	4
TOTALS	(654)	52	252	104	14	422 (65%)
Other rating under marriage duty						11 (2%)
Inhabitant of parish without marriage duty return						112 (17%)
No City address in 1695						109 (17%)

Sources: The estimates for stocks come from the assessments at the CLRO. Marriage duty returns can be found in D. V. Glass (ed.), 'London Inhabitants within the Walls, 1695', *London Record Society*, 2 (1966); Guildhall Library Staff, 'Supplement to the London Inhabitant List of 1695', *Guildhall Studies in London History*, 2 (1976), 77–104, 136–57. For City parishes outside the walls, see transcripts at the Guildhall Library and CLRO.

with those supplied by the stocks assessment. For instance, 14.7 per cent of our sample were assessed at under £200, while 12.3 per cent were not liable for payment of any surtaxes under the marriage duty. Likewise, the solid core of £200–399 merchants (49.7 per cent) in 1693–4 was replicated by the 59.7 per cent who were liable to the £600 surtax in 1695. Thus, both sets of returns suggest that contemporaries could recognize vertical distinctions within the generally prosperous mercantile group.

On the other hand, the marriage duty also shows that it would be hazardous to equate an individual's social status with his perceived wealth. As many a social commentator lamented, the definition of gentleman or esquire was increasingly problematic in the later Stuart period, and the non-correlation of stocks and status assessments suggest that the marriage duty assessors did not judge social rank on the mere criterion of wealth. In accordance with social custom, they would have assessed the gentility of specific traders in terms of lineage, public activity, and perhaps commercial probity as well as personal fortune, and it would be dangerous to delineate a mercantile oligarchy simply on the basis of fortune. Most notably, several of the more modest traders of 1693–4 were recognized as gentlemen under the marriage duty.[40] However, wealth retained an undeniable importance in City circles, and it does not appear that overseas traders could scale the City's upper hierarchy with incredible speed. One of those merchants rated at under £500 could boast the distinction of a baronetcy, but Sir Benjamin Ayloffe had inherited it unexpectedly some two decades before, and thus his title could not be represented as the reward for personal prominence or merit. Even the classification of 'esquire' appears to have been reserved for traders with stocks of over £500, although such a status distinction could never relate to the bare recommendation of wealth. In general, the narrowing apex of the marriage duty returns appears just as pronounced as that suggested by the four-shilling aid, and again suggests that a sharp distinction existed between the greatest traders and their lesser mercantile colleagues. Whether contemporaries would have perceived these differences as clearly as historians remains a moot point. In common with the other taxes, the marriage duty returns reveal no clear pattern of mercantile distribution in terms of fortune or social esteem, and thus topographical diversity would have helped to blur such disparities across the prosperous mercantile body as a whole.[41]

On closer inspection, it is evident that distinctions of wealth or status could vary in line with differentials such as age or marriage, and the basic influences of the life-cycle had an obvious bearing on the residential priorities of merchants. The poll tax returns remain an excellent source on such matters, since the assessors recorded a great deal of information concerning the structure of merchant households. This valuable data helps to pinpoint many of the most important factors which determined the residence of the merchant at particular stages of their careers. Most importantly, the assessors distinguished the relationship of male adults within each property, thereby establishing three broad categories of resident:

Householder	563	(66.2%)
Lodger	186	(21.8%)
Unspecified occupant	101	(11.9%)

The fact that nearly two-thirds of the merchants were full householders is yet further confirmation of their important status within the capital, and closer inspection of this group illustrates the stabilizing force which they represented within City society. Most pertinently, there is a clear link between wealth and householding, as demonstrated by the decreasing number of lodgers and

---

[40] There is a broad, although by no means exact, correlation between the status-ranked merchants in the marriage duty returns and the visitation of the College of Arms of 1687—College of Arms MSS K.9. It is highly unlikely that the forty-three sub-£400 merchants ranked as gentlemen or esquires could have made sufficient fortunes in the space of a year to have risen to a more elevated category. These inconsistencies suggest that citizens based their estimation of gentility beyond the question of wealth.

[41] The pedigree of Sir Benjamin Ayloffe, 4th Bt. can be found in G. E. Cokayne, *Complete Baronetage* (Gloucester, 1983 repr.), i. 93.

unspecified occupants among the richer merchants in Table 1.3. There is also a very close correlation between householding and marriage, with nine in ten married merchants being identified as a householder. Furthermore, the vast majority of those merchants known to be over 50 were householders. The desire for independence in residence thus appears a very real priority for the successful businessman, and the sample suggests that a broad spectrum of the City's merchants were able to enjoy a secure City base for the benefit of their trade and their families. The high rents of the inner City ensured that the decision to set up in business there was not taken lightly, but the vast majority of merchants saw a City address as indispensable for their personal advancement. Many purchased a retiring house beyond the metropolitan suburbs, but a City residence was widely regarded as essential for the maintenance of an active overseas trade.[42]

This priority can also be discerned among the non-householders within the sample, even though their foothold within the City was more uncertain. As already noted, the lodgers and unspecified occupants featured at the lower end of the scale of mercantile wealth, and their tenure can be simply ascribed to a lack of sufficient funds to acquire a more permanent City lease. However, there are other important common factors at play here, which are highlighted by their household structure. Nearly 85 per cent of these merchants had no dependants listed with them, and thus their tenure can be linked to their apparent bachelor status. Furthermore, over half of the unspecified occupants shared the surname of the householder, and thus can be plausibly identified as merchants who were taking advantage of a familial connection to reside in the City. The relationship between lodgers and their landlords/ladies is far more opaque, as one would expect, but there is a most significant clustering of mercantile lodgers in the wards at the heart of the mercantile City. This concentration further suggests the attraction of key sites for overseas traders, even those of more modest fortunes. Lodgers and unspecified occupants also figure prominently among the younger element of the overseas traders, who would be eager to make their name within the capital. With money and reputation behind them, traders could afford to be more choosy in their residence, but it appears that mercantile novices had to be close to the heart of City life. Back in 1672, the 26-year-old Levant trader George Boddington had borne direct testimony to the City's centripetal force, rebuffing his wife's plea for a move from Lothbury on the basis that 'we were young beginners and two houses would be too chargeable for us'. He did relent to permit a family move to the healthier environment of Newington Green, but only as long as he could still 'come to London in the morning to follow my affairs'. In fact, the lure of the City was too much for Boddington himself, and he was back in the com-

---

[42] 107 merchants have been identified as over 50 at the time of their assessment, and 93 (87%) were recorded as householders. For a discussion of mercantile land purchases, see Ch. 2.

mercial hub of St Helen's by 1692, by which time business success had enabled him to attain the status of full householder.[43]

Significantly, nearly a third of these lodgers and unspecified occupants could be found in merchant households, a pattern which again stresses the desirability of certain advantageous sites with direct access to commercial facilities. On closer inspection, there is strong evidence that this cohabitation reflected a strong economic relationship, especially if the lodger/occupant boasted familial ties with the householder. This is not to suggest that it was common for traders to live together to pursue mutual business interests, but it does appear that longer-term partners were happy to take quarters together. For instance, John Schoppen, a Dutch immigrant, can be identified as partner of Samuel Seale in the Northern European trade as early as 1677, and they could be found at the same St Mary Colechurch address from that time until at least 1695. An even closer relationship existed between Levant traders Timothy Lannoy and George Tredway of St Peter Le Poer. They had resided in the parish since at least 1686, but only months after the 1692 assessment moved out to Hammersmith, jointly paying £13,600 for an estate. Helping to cement their partnership was Tredway's recent marriage to Lannoy's sister, and this familial bond proved a solid foundation for a lifelong association. Other small partnerships can be identified by their joint movement within the City, but in many cases it is impossible to be certain of the business connections between residents at the same address. More generally, there appeared no absolute need for partners to live cheek by jowl, although judging by the testimony of Barbary trader William Clarke, who visited his associate Richard Holder 'frequently, two or three times a week', a certain proximity would be desirable.[44]

In conclusion, the distribution of mercantile units was thus a commercial matter at root, and beyond a general concentration to the east of the City, reflected the largely atomized organization of City commerce at that time. Merchants congregated there to secure services and contacts, but one cannot assume a herd mentality across the mercantile spectrum, especially with the diversity of wealth and household structure suggested by the tax returns. Nevertheless, having echoed due caution concerning the diffuse nature of London mercantile society, certain patterns of residence can be espied which are highly illustrative of the requirements for mercantile success. Studies of

[43] Guildhall Lib. MSS 10823, fo. 22. Five central wards (Aldgate, Broad, Langbourne, Tower, and Walbrook) accounted for 161 (56%) of the 287 lodgers and unspecified occupants. Only Aldgate was noticeably cheaper than other wards for mean rental among our sample. The Lyon merchant Peter Lauze is a good example of the temporary lodger. He owned property in London, but was only 'frequently in this city, going and coming from Lyons about the affairs of his trade'—CLRO: MCD38.

[44] C24/1172, case 45. Biographical details: Schoppen-Seale—Lee directory (as Sale and Scopin); Jones, D.Phil. thesis, appendices; *London Record Society*, 2 (1966), 256, 265; Lannoy—*Harleian Society*, 30 (1890), 251; CLRO: CSB inventory 2812, box 42 (June 1703); C. J. Feret, *Fulham Old and New* (London, 1900), iii. 70–1.

certain trading groups, such as David Mitchell on importers of Low Countries linen in the Restoration period, or Ralph Davis on the eighteenth-century Levant traders, have remarked upon the propensity of certain trading groups to reside within close proximity of each other, and the longer-term existence of such settlements would certainly help to see them as recognizable 'communities'. However, as yet no real attempt has been made to trace the importance of such associations across the merchant class as a whole within the particular context of the City.[45]

iii. Topography and City association

From the outset, it should be stressed that it is very difficult to draw precise lines of association which will neatly delineate mercantile society into regimented sectors, determined by particular trading interests or any other commercial criteria. Unlike the retailing industry, and to a lesser extent the domestic wholesaling trades, the various branches of the City's overseas trade cannot be neatly apportioned to particular precincts or even wards.[46] Previous attempts to segregate mercantile society by trading specialism have not discerned any clear overall pattern, which is not surprising given the nature of business ventures at this time, most of which revolved around the family unit, and did not bind large numbers of merchants in any long-term manner.[47] This is a most fundamental problem for analysts wishing to dragoon their mercantile subjects into convenient categories defined by commodity specialization or geographic trading area. The City only served the interest of trading groups on a macro-level, in that it provided the necessary services within a compact and accessible area. Given the mercantile dominance of the eastern City, and the close proximity of the main commercial services therein, it simply was not necessary for merchants to group together in certain streets. It was the Royal Exchange, Blackwell Hall, and other institutions which provided the most vital element of organization in the commercial world, and, given these central hubs, merchants could choose their residence on more direct financial and commercial criteria.

Although these general caveats must be entered, the poll tax returns do throw up certain topographical sub-patterns, which illustrate some of the most

---

[45] D. M. Mitchell, 'It will be Easy to Make Money: Merchant Strangers in London, 1580–1680', in C. Lesger and L. Noordegraaf (eds.), *Entrepreneurs and Entrepreneurship in Early Modern Times* (Haarlem, 1995), 117–45; R. Davis, *Aleppo and Devonshire Square* (London, 1967). Alison Olson noted a 'slight tendency' among American merchants to congregate in certain locales, although a stronger pattern emerged in the early Georgian period—*Making the Empire Work*, 53, 97.

[46] Alexander, Ph.D. thesis, 97–100.

[47] This pattern remains in contrast to the Scottish tobacco merchants, who embarked on large partnerships—T. Devine, *The Tobacco Lords: The Merchants of Glasgow, 1740–90* (Edinburgh, 1975), esp. chs. 4–6.

TABLE 1.5 *Ethnic background of the City sample with identifiable foreign ancestry*

	Number	Mean stocks (£)	Mean rental (£)
First Generation			
Dutch	40	385	50.3
German	18	257	88.0
French	70	249	46.4
Italian	5	450	53.0
Jewish	36	454	42.4
Polish	1	300	60.0
Armenian	1	—	—
Swedish	1	—	—
Swiss	1	—	—
Second Generation			
Dutch	13	336	51.4
German	2	400	70.0
French	28	363	54.5
Italian	1	600	150
Flemish	1	—	—
Unidentified Alien	8	—	—
TOTAL	226	335	48.8

Sources: The major source used here was W. A. Shaw, 'Naturalizations and Denizations of England and Ireland', *Huguenot Society*, 18 (1911), and 27 (1923). Depositions at the High Court of Admiralty were a most useful corrective to assuming nationality on the basis of surname alone.

important factors in determining business success in the Augustan City. The clearest examples concern the settlement of traders of foreign descent, whose propensity to reside in close proximity to each other confirms an enduring immigrational trend. However, the sheer scale of these international groupings is most significant, and economic historians have already remarked on their particular importance for the direction of City trade from the 1690s onwards. The data to be found in Table 1.5 underlines their numerical significance, and delineates the impact of the waves of mercantile settlers who had arrived in England over the previous forty years. It should be stressed that the data has been compiled only from direct evidence of parentage, as the sample has revealed that mere surname analysis is a most inadequate method of discovering national origins.

Although the vast majority of new mercantile immigrants were quick to procure denizen or naturalized status, the sheer size of this 'foreign' presence had led to the creation of several clearly discernible communities of settlers by the 1690s. This in itself was nothing new in the history of such a cosmopolitan city as London, but the influx of the post-Restoration period represented a most significant injection of wealth and entrepreneurial talent, which in the case of the larger groups of French, Dutch, and Jewish traders was heavily focused on certain City areas. The communal patterns of these settlements were clearly influenced by centripetal forces of language, religion, and familial connection. However, they also reflect close business ties which were the source of their disproportionate commercial success. Recent work has stressed the manner in which ethnic groups were able to gain a clear competitive edge by exploiting superior international ties, by providing mutual support, and by instilling religious and familial discipline among their compatriot business associates. To varying extents, all these advantages can be shown by brief analysis of the three main ethnic groups within the capital.[48]

The most tightly-knit community in terms of propinquity, and by any other yardstick of commensality, were the Jewish merchants. Thirty-six merchants can be identified in this group, a very high proportion of the Jews settled in London, and most were of Iberian-Sephadic origin. Recovering from continuing uncertainty about their future in England in the 1660s, they had experienced great success in the bullion and diamond trades, and several of their number were placed high in the 'stocks' assessment of 1693-4. Most of the sample had been in London for at least a decade, and were almost exclusively based in just four contiguous City parishes: St James Duke's Place, St Andrew Undershaft, All Hallows the Wall, and St Katherine Creechurch, the last-named being the site of the London synagogue. In contrast to their neighbourliness, they exhibited the widest set of contacts in the international field, enjoying familial connections all over the world. Their clannishness, based on exclusive religious practices, did not help to eradicate traditional resentments towards them, nor work to assimilate them into English society, whose own barriers debarred closer integration. The perceived wealth of the Jewish community is reflected by the stocks assessments in the table, and the fortunes of several prominent Jews promoted their role as government financiers. However, although the period did see the emergence of a second generation of Anglo-Jewish traders, they remained an international 'nation' in outlook, and a high proportion of them died overseas. This cosmopolitanism could be matched by other individuals, but not on the scale afforded by the Jewish members of this sample.[49]

The growing intolerance of Louis XIV ensured that the largest of the ethnic groups was French Huguenot, and most of these émigrés had arrived since the

---

[48] See in particular S. Chapman, *Merchant Enterprise in Britain from the Industrial Revolution to World War One* (Cambridge, 1992); Jones, *War and Economy*, 253-60; N. Zahedieh, *TRHS* 6th ser., 9 (1999), 143-58.

[49] For general works on English Jewry, see H. Pollins, *Economic History of the Jews in England* (East Brunswick, 1982); C. Roth, *A History of the Jews in England*, 3rd edn. (London, 1964); idem, *The Great Synagogue, London* (London, 1950). For the wider picture, see J. I. Israel, *European Jewry in the Age of Mercantilism, 1550-1750* (Oxford, 1985). Tensions caused by such concentration can be traced in the parish records—Guildhall Lib. MSS 1196/1 (St Katherine Kree), 4118/1 (St Andrew Undershaft).

early 1680s, correctly anticipating the ultimate Revocation of the Edict of Nantes. They joined a Huguenot community of already significant size, although of more diverse Flemish and French origin, reflecting the impetus of earlier Catholic persecutions. The disparity in the mean assessment between first- and second-generation French settlers (£249 against £363) is most striking, highlighting both the difficulties and opportunities facing immigrants when starting afresh in a new country. In all, Frenchmen accounted for over 10 per cent of all City merchants, and thus it is predictable that concentrations of them could be found scattered throughout the eastern City. Although contemporary opinion was usually drawn to the hordes of artisans settling on its eastern fringes, mercantile clusters were important centres of émigré activity, most notably in the parish of St Martin Orgar, which became the site of one of the new French churches which proliferated in the closing years of the century following the Revocation. Despite this diffusion, the major focus of Huguenot merchants remained Threadneedle Street, where they dominated the congregational offices throughout the period. These leaders were also the greatest beneficiaries of the essential openness of City society, integrating rapidly to become leading figures in the commercial and financial innovations of the period.[50]

Numerous, and with influence as powerful as that of the Huguenots, were the merchants of Dutch origin. However, although displaying a high degree of endogamy, there is little pattern to their residence, and many chose not to settle within easy reach of the Dutch church at Austin Friars, even though it was still dominated by mercantile figures. Like the French, a high proportion was first generation, and in general had come over since the mid-1670s, when the Anglo-Dutch wars for naval superiority had come to a halt. In general, these later immigrants were richer than other Christian settlers, and their arrival speaks volumes for London's growing attractiveness as an international business centre.[51] Further evidence of the continuing importance of the Low Countries to English trade came in the form of twenty merchants of German origin. Their residence was equally diffuse in distribution, but at least one of their number maintained the German tradition of residence in the Steelyard, encouraged no doubt by the presence of the new Lutheran church nearby.[52]

[50] A leading authority on Huguenot migration has recently highlighted the failure to recognize the wider significance of these refugees—Robin Gwynn, 'Minutes of the Consistory of the French Church of London, Threadneedle street 1679–92', *Huguenot Society*, 58 (1994); *idem, Huguenot Heritage* (London, 1985).

[51] Little attention has been given to this small community of German mercantile settlers, even by scholars of the Hamburg trade. Paucity of congregational records might well explain their obscurity, although those of the post-Fire Lutheran church in Holy Trinity the Less survive at the Guildhall Library. See P. Norman, 'Notes on the Later History of the Steelyard in London', *Archaelogia*, 61 (1909), 389–426.

[52] W. J. C. Moens (ed.), *The Marriage, Baptismal, and Burial Registers, 1571–1874, . . . of the Dutch Reformed Church, Austin Friars, London* (London, 1884); J. H. Hessels (ed.), *Ecclesiae Londino-Batavae Archivum: Epistulae et Tractatus* (London, 1882), esp. vol. iii. For the best account of the late Stuart Dutch settlers,

Patterns of ethnic settlement highlight the importance of background and religious allegiance to the spatial distribution of merchants, and recent research has increasingly stressed the importance of familial structures to the success of merchant adventurers of both native and foreign origin. Resentful contemporaries were evidently well aware of these advantages, a patriotic observer remarking in 1702 that 'all strangers are like Jews, they herd together and keep a general correspondency, transacting all matters of trade and profit with one another'. However, while this may be true of new immigrants, second-generation settlers did not see as great a necessity to stick close together, and many were both willing and able to assimilate rapidly into mainstream English life. Their successful integration again reflects the essential fluidity of City society, and demonstrates the peculiar flexibility of the institutions therein. It is no coincidence that merchants featured among the most vociferous of supporters of a general naturalization bill. Despite the success of prominent immigrants, London's 'foreign' institutions did not inexorably decline as a focus for ethnic activity. In particular, the foreign churches were still strong in the 1690s, contrary to current historical opinion which ignores their success in securing the support of the richest of immigrant traders. However, new settlers realized that they needed access to the indigenous networks of power if they were to compete successfully in their new environment. Ethnic bonds could prove invaluable, but these courageous immigrants could not exclusively rely upon them to establish themselves in the capital.[53]

By the standards of their alien neighbours, English merchants did not exhibit broad patterns of communal association. As Chapter 3 will demonstrate, it is very difficult to divide native merchants into distinctive mercantile interests, and thus it is even more hazardous to apportion them to particular zones of the City on the basis of trading activity or background. More promisingly, a small group of Scots colonized the parish of St Edmund the King, but it would be extremely difficult to link more than a handful of English merchants in any particular locale according to geographic origin or on any other basis. A major difficulty in this regard remains the paucity of nonconformist records for the capital, which may have thrown up more direct

see O. P. Grell, 'From Persecution to Integration: The Decline of the Anglo-Dutch Communities in England, 1648–1702', in *idem*, J. I. Israel, and N. Tyacke (eds.), *From Persecution to Toleration* (Oxford, 1991), 97–128; and C. Wilson, *Anglo-Dutch Commerce and Finance in the Eighteenth Century* (Cambridge, 1966), esp. ch. 4.

[53] *A Brief History of Trade in England* (London, 1702), 135–6. For a fresh and extensive treatment of the attitudes towards naturalization, see D. Statt, *Foreigners and Englishmen* (Newark, NJ, 1995). For contemporary debate, see Sir F. Brewster, *Essays on Trade and Navigation* (London, 1695), esp. 10–11, where foreign settlers are cited as no threat to English merchants. However, Charles Davenant could support naturalization while still questioning the advisability of enfranchising first-generation settlers. He also expressed concern at the failure of many foreigners to integrate—'An Essay upon the Probable Methods of Making People Gainers in the Balance of Trade', in *The Political and Commercial Works of Charles Davenant*, ed. C. Whitworth (London, 1771), ii. 186–7.

connections between neighbours. However, the finest collection of such records, that of the Quaker meetings, only highlights the polycentric influence of the distribution of dissenting churches within the City. Several small clusters of Quaker merchants existed among the twenty-one merchants identified from this sect, which predictably relate to the site of their meeting-house, and, as significantly, to mutual business ties. Research has shown that the Quakers combined with their overseas co-religionists to dominate certain trades, most notably American commerce, but given the paucity of non-conformist records it is difficult to draw up broader patterns of settlement. The propensity of citizens to attend several different denominations also argues against any rigid classification along religious lines.[54]

In general, it is the English merchants who are the hardest to pin down, but the effort is well worthwhile, for they demonstrate the importance of 'public' (or extra-familial) activity to the functioning of City business. In order to understand the importance of the 'public' sphere, examination must be made of the limitations of the private, and recognition given to how the basic house-hold unit of mercantile activity struggled to combat the dangers of risk and uncertainty so inherent in their profession.[55] The interplay between personal strategies for survival and the existing structures of the City is crucial to our understanding of the patterns of merchant life. In order to achieve a fuller appreciation of this key relationship, a snapshot of the City will not suffice, and thus the next section seeks to trace the development of the sample between 1692 and 1695, taking advantage of the excellent materials to hand.

iv. Fluidity and stability within the City

Amid the bewildering array of mercantile experience featured in our sample, it becomes evident that the essential problem in delineating spatial patterns is the fluidity of commercial society. The merchant princes have to date occupied most historiographic interest, but their success has to be put into per-spective by awareness of the rapid turnover of personnel within the mercantile world. Overseas trade, as the fears of hundreds of mercantile wills testify, was not an easy option as a career, and for every Sir Gilbert Heathcote, reputedly worth £700,000 at death, there were probably a score of broken merchants, whose piteous falls from affluence are recorded in the petitions for brokers'

---

[54] Quakers' Library, London, records of monthly meetings; J. M. Price, 'The Great Quaker Business Families of Eighteenth-Century London', in R. S. Dunn and M. M. Dunn (eds.), *The World of William Penn* (Philadelphia, 1986), 363–99. Research into London nonconformity has been given an even higher priority by the work of Gary De Krey on the importance of the 'dissenting interest' in the City—*Fractured Society*, 74–120.

[55] For fresh discussion of the problematic division between 'public' and 'private' spheres, see R. B. Shoemaker, *Gender in English Society, 1650–1850* (Harlow, 1998), esp. ch. 8.

bonds.[56] As a first defence, the merchant might seek to protect himself through the intimate associations of marriage and kinship. However, the institutions of the City also endeavoured to cushion the blows of misfortune, both formally, for instance the organization of convoys in wartime, and informally through the more elusive bonds established in the course of hectic business-cum-socializing at livery company and coffee-house. Fundamental significance must be accorded to the workings of the City's institutions, which brought much-needed stability to a bewildering thoroughfare of men and their fortunes. The commercial family unit may have been paramount in importance, but it operated within a framework of mutually supporting City structures which helped to carry individuals through the perils of overseas commerce, as well as the basic periodic terrors of the life-cycle. The struggle between dependence and independence remained a dynamic tension within the world of overseas commerce, and it is the inherent instabilities of mercantile life which lies behind the ill-defined picture supplied by the tax returns.[57]

As the previous sections have demonstrated, residence could be determined by a wide variety of personal factors, and the tax records can provide a most sensitive guide to mercantile mobility within the capital, in both a physical and socio-economic sense. A survey of the 825 merchants with identifiable residences in 1692 indicates that by 1693–4 nearly a quarter had departed from the City, a very high turnover of residence. Of this group, another sixth cannot be traced in the marriage duty returns of 1695, thus leaving only 523 (63.4 per cent) with continuous City residence during this three-year period. Specific evidential problems, and the upheaval of war have undoubtedly inflated the usual rate of City resettlement, but its scale is impressive nonetheless and accords with contemporary perceptions of mercantile mobility.[58] Critics of the overseas trader commented on their moveable wealth in order to contrast them unfavourably with the landed gentleman, the latter being unable to 'run away if they should be tempted to' and were thus 'more answerable to the world and to their neighbours'. Even mercantile apologists, such as

---

[56] *The Gentleman's Magazine*, iii (1733), 47. Brokers bonds can be found at CLRO: BR/P. William Leybourn's *Panarithmologia* (London, 1693), 55, notes that brokers were 'persons generally that have had misfortunes in the world, and have been bred merchants (or else they are not capacitated to be brokers)'. Of our sample, at least thirty can be identified as brokers from the (incomplete) remaining brokers' licences. However, there were evidently other avenues to pursue, as witnessed by the newspaper advertisements placed by ex-merchants, offering their potential services as ships' pursers, bookkeepers, land stewards, etc.—see John Houghton's *Collection for the Improvement of Husbandry and Trade*.

[57] For the reality of mercantile failure, see J. Hoppit, *Risk and Failure in English Business 1700–1800* (Cambridge, 1987), esp. 96–103. See Ch. 2 for further discussion of the importance of the life-cycle.

[58] Due to the absence of poll tax returns for Portsoken and Walbrook in 1692, mercantile residence for that year has had to be drawn from other sources, most notably the 1690 poll tax returns. Thirty-five Walbrook residents of 1694 have been confirmed as residents there in 1692, and have thus been added to the other 790 merchants in the original 1692 return. Of these 825, only 630 appear in the City's returns for the four-shilling aid, thus suggesting that 195 (23.6%) had died or removed themselves. Thirty-seven of these 825 are known to have died in the 1692–5 period.

John Cary, observed that overseas traders were 'but temporary residents', in order to warn government authorities to attend to commercial interests. Behind these conflicting opinions was a common recognition of the difficulties of maintaining a business in the City, and the general prosperity of the mercantile classes could not mask the very real dangers facing all overseas traders. Analysts of mercantile 'concentration' have shown that certain traders were able to strengthen their position in the late Stuart period, but closer investigation of the essential fluidity of mercantile society can pinpoint its true dynamism.[59]

As a study of a wartime environment, our sources are more suggestive of the hazards of mercantile life rather than the ability of merchants to weather personal crises. Table 1.4 demonstrates that one in eight of the traders formerly assessed for stocks in 1693–4 did not qualify for surtax payment in 1695, a collective reversal of fortune which illustrates the immense difficulties of the Nine Years' War for London's merchants.[60] Continued military upheaval clearly had a big impact on individual traders, and such reverses could mean a reluctant search for cheaper accommodation within the inner suburbs. For instance, in about July 1693 Ambrose Upton, an experienced Canary and Iberian wine merchant, was forced to move from a central Bishopsgate address to the extramural parish of St Clement Danes after he had 'failed in the world and become insolvent'. His problems are a salutary reminder that a westward move did not necessarily reflect a desire to ascend to the elevated social world situated at the other end of town. The afore-mentioned example of the Lannoy-Tredway move to Hammersmith was obviously a 'betterment' move, but Upton's dilemma appears far more common an experience within the mobile sector of our sample.[61]

Although all was not doom and gloom for the merchant thrown on hard times, such hardship would obviously put traders on their personal mettle if they wished to rebuild their mercantile career. In order to avoid unnecessary risks, many merchants turned to the public funds in search of a safer invest-ment during wartime, but that option was clearly unavailable for the least fortunate of their mercantile colleagues. As the marriage duty assessors were making their rounds in May 1695, the Quaker merchant Joseph Strutt found himself a miserable resident of the Fleet debtors' prison, having in his own words received 'great losses', and he was now incapable of paying the customs on a consignment of tobacco. Not surprisingly, he was one of the several £200

---

[59] *Honest Advice to the Electors of Great Britain on the Present Choice of their Representatives* (London, ?1708), 7–8; Cary, *An Essay on the State of England*, 96. Also see P. Langford, *Public Life and the Propertied Englishman, 1689–1798* (Oxford, 1991), ch. 1.

[60] For the great losses of the Smyrna fleet, and other mercantile catastrophes in the 1690s, see Jones, *War and Economy*, 156–9. The dangers of overseas trade ensured that merchants were among the leading supporters of the new national funds, which represented a more secure investment during wartime.

[61] C24/1173, case 86, 1179, case 68.

merchants of 1693/4 who was deemed below the surtax bracket in 1695, but his desperate straits did not last for long. Once freed from jail he became a shipmaster, following in his father's footsteps, and moved to his native East End. A more common switch of occupation was to that of broker, in which role former merchants put their experience to good use. At least thirty of the sample took out licences to undertake such work, and many of them remained in that position for the rest of their career. However, the fortunate, such as the insolvent Caribbean trader Thomas Hunt, were able to prosper sufficiently as brokers to resume trading, although Hunt himself was only too keen to acknowledge his luck in having understanding creditors. Others found it much more difficult to bounce back. Dean Monteage, the son of a noted merchant accountant, was in financial difficulties in 1695, and, probably by dint of his family's excellent City-court connections, managed to secure himself the post of accountant-general of the Excise. Unfortunately for him, even this opportunity was squandered, and he never resurfaced as a force within City life. As the capital city, London could provide many opportunities for the desperate trader, but ruin was a very real risk for even the greatest of traders. The piteous example of Sir Alexander Rigby, an MP and Mediterranean trader who ended his days in the Fleet, serves as sufficient reminder that success in overseas commerce was no guarantee of a gilded retirement.[62]

Business failure must not be seen as the only cause of a withdrawal from City life. The disappearance of an immigrant merchant may simply have represented a return home, perhaps after acting as factor for an agreed period in the capital, in very much the same way as English merchants travelled abroad. More generally, native merchants, especially lodgers, could be drawn away from the capital by sudden changes in personal circumstance, often for reasons little connected with business.[63] Julius Deed, Bridge Within lodger and the son of the Hythe MP of the same name, departed for good to Exeter in his mid-twenties, after securing a match with a mercantile household in that city. William Beecher, who lodged with a packer in St Peter Le Poer, had returned to England in October 1691, having spent at least four years in the Levant. He appeared set fair for a successful career, but, on the death of his father in 1695, and his own marriage in that same year, he was content to return to his Bedfordshire home and live the life of a Home Counties gentleman. The unspecified occupants were much more stable in their residence than the lodgers in the 1692–5 period, principally because they were in general relatives

---

[62] Biographical details: Strutt—Guildhall Lib. MSS 15860/6 (Sept. 1669); *CTB* x. 1085; HCA13/82, fos. 1–2; Hunt—*London Gazette*, 5–9 Aug. 1697; PCC 1711, fo. 131; Monteage (whose father was a friend of the Houblons and auditor to the Duke of Albermarle)—*CTB* x. 925; xiv. 234; xv. 345; xviii. 267; PCC 1687, fo. 140; C24/1135, case 18; Rigby—History of Parliament trust, draft biographical article, 1690–1715 section. The brokers' bonds can be found at CLRO: BR/P.

[63] Of the 186 lodgers identified in the 1692 sample, 55 (29.6%) could not be found in the City returns of 1695.

of greater merchants, and reflected the stability of their mentors. More generally, comparison between the 1677 directory and the 1695 marriage duty returns shows considerable intramural movement possible even among the 200 merchants identifiable in both sources, whose longevity within the City precincts can be taken as sign of reasonable commercial prosperity. Such movement may only reflect commercial opportunity, or the changing demands of a household, but it certainly reflected the frenetic pace of City life so obvious to visitors to the square mile.[64]

Thus a general survey of 850 City merchants demonstrates many important aspects concerning the workings of commerce, and the relationship of business to its socio-political environment. Although engaged in the same commercial activity and distinguishable as an urban elite, the mercantile 'class' was in fact a very heterogeneous group, within which there could exist a wide variety of wealth and experience. Differentials such as residence, age, marital status, and ethnic origin can be shown to have been key determinants of London's mercantile culture, which probably became even more cosmopolitan in character in the post-Restoration period. The City itself benefited enormously from such diversity, especially by the settlement of a very large number of foreign traders, who, although prone to clannishness, found to their benefit that there were ample opportunities for advancement in their new home. Yet, it would be wrong to underestimate the real dangers of trade, and how they could ruin the individual within a very short space in time, particularly in a competitive business climate. The subsequent two chapters will seek to probe the impact of this socio-economic environment on the merchant, both as an individual and as a member of various City associations. However, for further insight into the anxious, politicized world glimpsed by Lupton, attention will now turn to the provincial examples of Liverpool and York. Both towns were dwarfed in scale by the metropolis, but instructive parallels can be drawn from the structures of their mercantile societies.

v. Provincial parallels

The overwhelming role played by metropolitan merchants in the nation's overseas trade has ensured them the lion's share of historiographic interest, and their dominance and scale of operation necessarily influenced the structures of mercantile life on a nationwide basis. Even London's greatest late seventeenth-century rival, Bristol, could boast less than a twentieth of its

---

[64] Biographical details: Deed—J. E. Cussans, *History of Hertfordshire* (London, 1870–81), ix, 42–3; PCC 1722, fo. 50; PRO: C24/1158, case 82; Beecher—C24/1187, case 75; 1189, cases 42–3; Lee, *Little London Directory*. N. Rogers found that mid-Hanoverian businessmen of gentry background were more likely to return to their roots after a career in trade—'Money, Land, and Lineage: The Big Bourgeoisie of Georgian London', *Social History*, 4 (1979), 437–54.

population, and only about a tenth of its shipping. The examples examined here were even more overshadowed, with York, the nation's traditional second city, mustering about 11,000 inhabitants for most of this period; while even a rapidly expanding Liverpool could only boast about 12,000 souls in 1720. These outports experienced widely fluctuating fortunes during the Augustan age, but even at their most successful, they could only challenge the capital's traders in restricted fields of commercial activity, most notably Liverpool's tobacco imports. Nevertheless, this section and the provincial studies of the next two chapters will demonstrate how the disparities of scale actually masked similar trends in the organization and associations of merchant life, and indicate that in microcosm provincial merchants shared common perceptions and experiences with their London brethren. Inevitably, there are unique characteristics to all these ports, but ensuing analysis will suggest that it would be foolhardy to overlook the provincial contribution to national developments in overseas trade.[65]

It is perhaps most appropriate to begin with York, for even though its Augustan experience has been characterized as one of commercial decline, its development can be directly linked with the fortunes of the capital.[66] Under the guidance of the York residence of the Merchant Adventurers' Company, the town had enjoyed a medieval high-point as a conduit for the export of the region's vital cloth trade, but its merchants were unable to sustain the city's growth in competition with regional and national rivals. Worsening problems with the navigation of the River Ouse, its vital link to the Humber estuary and the North Sea, left them in a shaky position even by 1660. The late Stuart era would confirm this as a terminal trajectory, with the rise of Hull and Leeds as better-connected centres for the export of woollen manufacturers. At the Restoration, town leaders were already bemoaning their fate: 'Leeds is nearer the manufacturers and Hull more commodious for the vending of them, so York is in each respect, furtherest from the profit'. Such ill-fortune has ensured that this period has been largely overlooked by students of the York economy, believing it to be the mere death throes of an ailing commercial centre, which by the Hanoverian age had been reduced to serving the particular needs of a gentry clientele gathering together at York for the purposes

[65] P. Corfield, *The Impact of English Towns* (Oxford, 1982), 36–7. London's continuing commercial domination is demonstrated by C. J. French, 'Crowded with Traders and a Great Commerce: London's Domination of English Overseas Trade, 1700–75', *London Journal*, 17 (1992), 27–35, and by R. Davis, *The Rise of the English Shipping Industry* (London, 1962), 35. For provincial population figures, see *VCH Yorkshire: The City of York* (London, 1961), 162–3, 212; P. G. E. Clemens, 'The Rise of Liverpool 1665–1750', *EcHR* 29 (1976), 211–25.

[66] For general accounts of York commerce in the late seventeenth century, see D. Palliser, *The Company of Merchant Adventurers of the City of York* (York, 1985); M. Sellers, 'The York Mercers and Merchant Adventurers 1356–1917', *Surtees Society*, 129 (1917); B. Johnson, *The Last of the Old Hanse* (York, 1949); *VCH Yorkshire: The City of York*, 166–70, 215–26. For a most illuminating study of York's overseas trade in the fourteenth and fifteenth centuries, see J. Kermode, *Medieval Merchants: York, Beverley, and Hull in the Later Middle Ages* (Cambridge, 1998).

of entertainment rather than business. These broad trends are undoubtedly correct, but analysis of the local merchant body can reveal how the overseas trader coped with fundamental economic difficulties, both within their immediate urban environment, and within the nation at large.[67]

Although the York returns for the 1692 poll tax have not survived, it is relatively easy to delineate the extent of the mercantile classes due to the corporation's strict regulation of the local economy. The guild system was still firmly in place in the late Stuart period, thus leaving resident merchants little option but to seek admission to the freedom and to register their particular trade. Analysis can thus focus on those freemen who declared themselves as merchants on becoming free of the City, or who took the trouble to become a member of one of the town's mercantile societies, which by 1660 included both the Merchant Adventurers' and the Eastland companies. The vast majority of these traders also became members of the town's Company of Merchant Adventurers, but this body also included a number of retailers dealing in merchandises, i.e. mercers, apothecaries, and drapers. Thanks to the keenness of local authorities to differentiate between traders, it is clear that York's overseas merchants were apt to change their occupational status in the course of their career between the mercantile, wholesaling, and retailing sectors. This fluidity must be acknowledged, but admission to the freedom pinpoints the intent to pursue a particular calling, and thus is invaluable in determining local attitudes towards York's declining overseas trade. A survey of the admission trends in Table 1.6 demonstrates how the problems of the town's maritime commerce had a dramatic influence on the composition of the town's mercantile body.[68]

York's post-1660 decline is clear from this table, with dwindling numbers of freemen declaring themselves merchants. Even a relaxation of the admission fees demanded of newcomers to the Eastland and Hamburg trades could not reverse the trend, and by the 1720s the only overseas traders of true stature were concentrated in the wine business, which thrived on local gentry demand. The town's historian of 1736, Francis Drake, was not without hope of an upturn in the town's commerce, but lamented the lethargy of York leaders in allowing such decline to reach so far. In these criticisms he can be shown to have been less than generous to the resourcefulness of the York mercantile elite, but the fact remains that they were unable to attract a sufficient number

[67] T. Widdrington, *Analecta Eboracensia: Some Remains of the Ancient City of York*, ed. C. Caine (London, 1897), p. x. For the physical transformation of eighteenth-century York, see H. Murray, *Scarborough, York, and Leeds: The Town Plans of John Cossins, 1697–1743* (York, 1997), 17–59.

[68] For studies of the merchant companies, see D. M. Smith, 'The Company of Merchant Adventurers in York, Register of Admissions, 1581–1835', *Borthwick Lists and Indexes*, 18 (1996); and A. B. Bisset 'The Eastland Company Residence, Register of Admissions to the Freedom 1646–89', ibid. 17 (1996). For discussion of the problems of separating domestic and international traders at provincial level (Newcastle in particular), see J. Langton, in *Transactions of the Institute of British Geographers*, 65 (1975), 1–27.

TABLE 1.6 *Admission of merchants to the York freedom, 1640–1740*

Decade	Number admitted	Patrimony	Service	Purchase	Gift
1640–9	71	13 (18%)	57 (80%)	1	0
1650–9	52	12 (23%)	40 (77%)	0	0
1660–9	34	9 (26%)	24 (71%)	1	0
1670–9	33	14 (42%)	17 (42%)	1	1
1680–9	43	20 (47%)	22 (51%)	1	0
1690–9	14	7 (50%)	7 (50%)	0	0
1700–9	15	9 (60%)	6 (40%)	0	0
1710–19	12	4 (33%)	8 (67%)	0	0
1720–9	6	4 (67%)	2 (33%)	0	0
1730–9	8	6 (75%)	2 (25%)	0	0
TOTAL	288	98 (34%)	185 (64%)	4	1

Sources: For York freeman admissions, see 'Register of the Freemen of York, 1559–1759', *Surtees Society*, 102 (1900).

of well-heeled merchants to the port, in order to make up for the lack of self-generated investment and expertise. The increasing proportion of merchants with freeman fathers is the surest indicator of ossification, and even within York itself there appears a contraction in numbers seeking a mercantile career. As a reflection of this trend, the freemen of late-Georgian York usually claimed that merchandising was but one of several economic activities, thereby suggesting that there was simply not enough overseas trade to maintain an individual business. A process of 'concentration' thus does appear to have taken place, but in this case the dearth of trade eventually forced the handful of mercantile adventurers to diversify their investments when a specialist interest in overseas commerce could not be sustained.[69]

While Table 1.6 establishes the shrinking size of the mercantile body, and its increasingly oligarchic foundations, they betray little of its general character, or the associations between traders, and their relationship with the rest of the urban community. As civic historians have suggested, the decline of overseas trade had only a delayed impact on the City's social hierarchy, and many indices suggest that merchants were at the forefront of York life well into the Hanoverian era.[70] Their prominence can be traced to basic recommendations such as wealth and familial connection, which evidently had a much more immediate impact than in the case of London, where these influences were

---

[69] F. Drake, *Eboracum, or the History and Antiquities of the City of York* (London, 1736), esp. 225–40. Jenny Kermode has recently shown that a decline in the number of large traders, and a proliferation of smaller operators, were features of York's mercantile decline in the late medieval period—*Medieval Merchants*, 254–65, 318–22.

[70] *VCH Yorkshire: The City of York*, 180.

diffused through twenty-six wards and 110 parishes. Enclosed within an area about a quarter of the size of the City, York boasted only four wards and less than thirty parishes, but it in general exhibited the same degree of topographical concentration among merchants. Table 1.7 employs several contemporary tax sources to identify the location of York merchants in the period 1661–1701, distinguishing the six most popular parishes for mercantile residence. The location of the parishes is identified on Map 1.2.[71]

TABLE 1.7 *York merchant residence, 1661–1701*

Parish	1661 poor rate	1672 hearth tax	1691 poll tax	1701 window tax
All Saints, Pavement	7	6	5	2
St Crux	3	4	7	4
St John Micklegate	7	7	9	8
St Martin-cum-Gregory	12	11	10	3
St Michael-le-Belfry	2	0	7	5
St Michael Spurriergate	2	0	5	0
Other parishes	6	8	10	8
TOTAL	39	36	53	30

Sources: The table was compiled from the York City archives: E73, fos.. 38–51 (poor rate); Ms.30.8–14 (poll tax); K96 (window tax), and PRO: E179/260/21–2 (hearth tax).

The variety of tax liability exhibited here, combined with certain lacunae within the existing sources must condition the representativeness of each of these sample years, and the table cannot be regarded as providing a complete picture of York's mercantile society. Nevertheless, it does indicate that in general overseas traders preferred to live in a handful of parishes which were conveniently situated for the maintenance of their trade. Five of the parishes in fact form a belt across the centre of the town on either side of the only intra-mural bridge across the Ouse, which had been the site of the merchant's 'bourse' since the Reformation, and overlooked the two main 'staithes' for the unloading of goods. The presence of the civic council chamber at Ousebridge was a further magnet for the York elite. The contraction in merchant numbers in the late seventeenth century did not alter this pattern significantly, with overseas traders still concentrated on the riverside parishes. Although the Ouse remained the principal attraction for merchant residents, it is important

[71] For recent analysis of York's topography and society, see C. Galley, *The Demography of Early Modern Towns: York in the Sixteenth and Seventeenth Centuries* (Liverpool, 1998), esp. chs. 2–5; P. Withington, 'Urban Political Culture in Late Seventeenth-Century England: York 1649–88', Ph.D. thesis (Cambridge, 1998), esp. 63–87; D. J. Hibberd, 'Urban Inequalities: Social Geography and Demography in Seventeenth-Century York', Ph.D. thesis (Liverpool, 1981), esp. 87–210.

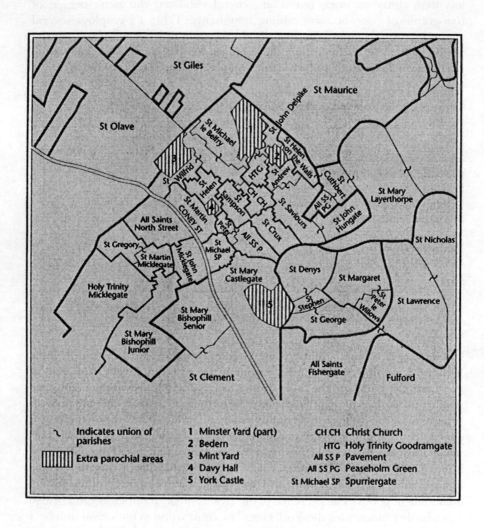

St Giles

St Maurice

St John Delpike

St Olave

St Michael le Belfry

St Helen on the Walls

St Wilfrid

HTG

St Andrew

St Cuthbert

St Helen

St Martin CONEY ST

St Sampson

CH CH

St Saviours

All SS PG

St Mary Layerthorpe

All Saints North Street

St Peter

St Crux

St John Hungate

St Nicholas

St Gregory

St Michael SP

All SS P

St Martin Micklegate

St John Micklegate

St Mary Castlegate

St Denys

St Margaret

St Peter le Willows

St Lawrence

Holy Trinity Micklegate

St Mary Bishophill Senior

St Stephen

St George

St Mary Bishophill Junior

All Saints Fishergate

Fulford

St Clement

∿ Indicates union of parishes	
▥ Extra parochial areas	

1 Minster Yard (part)
2 Bedern
3 Mint Yard
4 Davy Hall
5 York Castle

CH CH   Christ Church
HTG   Holy Trinity Goodramgate
All SS P   Pavement
All SS PG   Peaseholm Green
St Michael SP   Spurriergate

MAP 1.2 Mercantile York in the late seventeenth century

to note that three of the most popular parishes (St Michael Spurriergate, All Saints, Pavement, and St Crux) were also well placed for access to the Merchant Adventurers' Hall in Fossgate.[72] The only real exception to such distribution was the parish of St Michael-Le-Belfry, sited some way from the river but close to the high-status Minster area. However, the more genteel surroundings of the Minster could not tempt the greatest of the town's traders away from Ousebridge, which remained the centre for the wine trade. Enduring commercial practicalities were still manifest at the end of our period, for in 1726 the inhabitants of Bootham ward (which encompassed St Michael-Le-Belfry) successfully petitioned the corporation for the siting of a quay at Lendal, above Ousebridge, having complained of 'the great inconveniences' presented by 'their great distance and remoteness from the King's staithe'. The half-mile carriage of goods from the riverside to their homes was simply too much of a commercial impediment for their business, a fact of economic life that had largely shaped the topographical distribution of merchants throughout our period.[73]

Although lacking some of the richness of detail to be found in the London archives, York's taxation records do suggest that similar influences were working on patterns of householding. Taking the best of the surviving records, the 1691 assessment, it appears that all but seven of the fifty-three merchants were liable to payments for properties, suggesting that the vast majority were householders. All of these seven had taken up their freedoms during the 1680s, and can be identified as among the youngest of the sample, which correlates well with the London findings. Also in accordance with the London evidence, their personal assessments do not put them in the front rank of mercantile society, although several of them went on to play a prominent part in York itself. More generally, the taxation records reveal that York merchants were prepared to move house several times in the course of their careers, although the most successful tended to establish themselves in one parish, particularly in those closest to Ousebridge. Even in the hard times experienced by the port in the early eighteenth century, ambitious wine merchants such as Henry Pawson (1695-1730) were still prepared to invest in the construction of 'noble vaults' in Skeldergate, which ran parallel to the Ouse. The historian Drake admired his resolve, but was more eager to celebrate his family's achievement as wine importers, noting that Henry's 'father and grandfather were of the same business, lived in this street and were all of them in their times the chief traders in that way in this City'. In a contracting economic sector, such con-

---

[72] Kermode noted that St Crux and All Saints, Pavement had been the most popular parishes with her mercantile sample—*Medieval Merchants*, 19–20. More immediately, Philip Withington concluded (from a study of a single year) that York's dealing trades provided the clearest case of occupational zoning in the city—Ph.D. thesis, pp. 80–7. The decline of St Martin-cum-Gregory in Table 1.7 was clearly to the advantage of St John Micklegate, which was closer to the river.

[73] York City archives, B42, fo. 76. For a contemporary account of York's topography, see T. Gent, *The Ancient and Modern History of the Famous City of York* (London, 1730).

tinuity and leadership was deemed crucial, and the importance of these greater traders can be easily gauged by their stability of residence.[74]

The resilience of the Pawsons could only be founded on a sure economic footing, and surviving tax records suggest that the decline of the city's trade was accompanied by a widening gulf between greater and lesser merchants. While the uncertainties of trade were liable to trip up any individual, it does appear that an elite tier of merchants had established itself by the end of the century. The 1691 assessment for personalty suggests a very real divide, with thirteen of the fifty-three merchants rated at over 20 shillings, and thirty-four rated at 10 shillings or below. Although this polarization is not so evident in the 1661 poor rate returns, the hearth taxes of 1665 and 1672 do indicate an oligarchic trend, which is confirmed by the assessments for houses made in 1691. The liabilities for personal wealth in 1691 suggest that the merchants of All Saints Pavement, St Martin-cum-Gregory, and St John Micklegate were noticeably more prosperous than their colleagues elsewhere in the city, although certain individuals could buck this trend. Such clustering in the best commercial sites again underlines the business priorities underpinning mercantile settlement, and this concentration of function and wealth were the key features of the York's truncated mercantile community by the early eighteenth century.[75]

The absence of the ethnic and religious ties which influenced settlement patterns within the capital helped to ensure that wealth remained the most important determinant of York's mercantile topography. Not one of the sample can be identified as a first-generation immigrant, and the non-conformist presence was limited in both scale and prominence.[76] In purely business terms, it appears that several wine traders clustered near Ousebridge, but the overlapping membership of the Eastland and Merchant Adventurers companies make it impossible to isolate specific associations on a residential basis. As in London, it appears that business partners saw it in their interest to live in fairly close proximity, as was the case of the wine-trading families of Dawson and Hilary in St Martin-cum-Gregory. However, port-book evidence once again suggest that the family firm predominated as the essential business unit, and its location was principally conditioned by broader commercial considerations, rather than specific associational ties. Therefore, although a far less complex mercantile society than the capital, in broad outlines York exhibited many features of City life, even in a period of steady decline. Commercial developments would pass the town by, but its merchants leaders

[74] York City archives, MS. 30.8–14; Drake, *Eboracum*, 266. The Pawsons hailed from Leeds, and had established themselves in York in the mid-seventeenth century, but by the mid-eighteenth century were in Newcastle—J. W. Walker (ed.), 'Yorkshire Pedigrees', *Harleian Society*, 94–6 (1942–4), 305–6.

[75] For York tax returns, see footnote to Table 1.7.

[76] For an excellent analysis of York nonconformity, see D. A. Scott, 'Politics, Dissent, and Quakerism in York, 1640–1700', D.Phil. thesis (York, 1990).

tenaciously kept to their traditional working ways, despite the contraction of economic opportunity.[77]

Experiencing a very different late Stuart age, Liverpool saw great expansion, with the town population rising from some 2,000 to 12,000 in the course of our period. The key to this impressive growth was transatlantic trade, as the port took full advantage of the burgeoning markets in West Indian sugar and American tobacco to become one of the leading provincial commercial centres by 1720.[78] Even more astonishingly, the town had more than doubled in size again by 1750, as local merchants managed to usurp Bristol as the leading provincial centre for the slave trade. Victorian civic patriots and economic historians have eagerly chartered the parameters of their commercial success, but it is only recently that analysts have dispassionately studied the men who made Liverpool. Its transformation from a large village to thriving port renders it an excellent case-study of the impact of overseas commerce in this period, and all the structures of Liverpool life were severely tested by such unprecedented growth. In certain key ways, the port was completely unprepared for the commercial blessings of the age, and important decisions concerning the direction of its growth were settled on a very ad hoc basis. Whether unplanned or not, however, Liverpool's rise highlights the characteristic resourcefulness of the early modern merchant, and his determination to form a socio-political environment attuned to his essential mercantile priorities.[79]

Such was the rapidity with which the town changed that it is very difficult to reconstruct the Liverpool merchant body with any exactness. In direct contrast to York, the relative insignificance of the port as a centre for international trade before 1660 had ensured that it had escaped the notice of the great London companies, and thus there was little to stop wholesalers, retailers, and especially sea-captains from investing directly in overseas trade, thereby ensuring great fluidity in local occupational titles. However, during the late Stuart period the ruling corporation was just as keen as York's city fathers to enforce exclusive trading rights for local freemen, and their records demonstrate that a more recognizable cadre of overseas traders emerged in the course of the period. Combined with helpful parish records and the port books, a broad impression of the Liverpool mercantile 'community' can be established from a survey of merchants admitted as freemen, which is represented in Table 1.8.[80]

[77] Dawson and Hilary were recorded as partners in the Hull port books—E190/348/6.

[78] For the most informative histories of Liverpool's late seventeenth-century commerce, see Clemens, *EcHR* 29 (1976), 211–25; J. Longmore, 'The Liverpool Corporation as Landowners and Dock-Builders, 1709–1835', in C. W. Chalklin and J. R. Wordie (eds.), *Town and Countryside* (London, 1989), 116–46; J. Touzeau, *The Rise and Progress of Liverpool from 1551 to 1835* (Liverpool, 1910).

[79] M. Power, 'Councillors and Commerce in Liverpool, 1650–1750', *Urban History*, 24 (1997), 310–23.

[80] Recent research suggests that many merchants in late Stuart Liverpool were likely to have served as mariners, and that many were still engaged in sea-going trade—D. Ascott, 'Wealth and Community: Liverpool, 1660–1760', Ph.D. thesis (Liverpool, 1996), 163–9, 290–9. For further discussion of the use of

TABLE 1.8 *Liverpool merchants admitted as freemen, 1660–1719*

Decade	Total	Method of entrance			
		Service	Patrimony	Purchase	Other/unknown
1660–9	9	1	1	6	1
1670–9	18	2	1	12	3
1680–9	13	1	5	5	2
1690–9	35	15	3	16	1
1700–9	38	14	6	16	2
1710–19	64	40	7	17	0
TOTALS	177	73	23	72	9
%		41.2	13.0	40.7	5.1

Sources: For freeman admissions prior to 1692, merchants have been identified from the corporation minute books and the parish registers—see Liverpool RO, MF2/2–5; *Lancashire Parish Register Society*, 35 (1909), and 101 (1963). A freeman register exists from 1692—Liverpool RO, 352/CLE/REG/2/1.

Even though the table cannot be taken as a comprehensive guide to all the merchants who used the port, it serves as a reliable indicator of those overseas traders who shared more than a passing interest in the future of the town, and demonstrates several of the important changes which accompanied the growth of Liverpool trade. The rising number of merchants taking up the freedom mirrors the increasing volume of town trade, particularly in the 1690s when Liverpool was seen to enjoy a distinct advantage over London as a safer haven for transatlantic traffic during wartime. The method of freeman entry indicates that the town's mercantile body was swollen by locally trained merchants and by new settlers who simply bought access to the port's trading privileges. The increasing competition for Liverpool trade was recognized by a grateful corporation, whose admission fines for freedom purchasers rose from about £10 in the 1660s to as much as £50 in the 1690s. The proportion of immigrant merchants remained significant throughout the period and was a predictable reflection of the lack of home-grown recruits with the capital and connections to take advantage of expanding markets. However, the town did not depend entirely on outsiders, and the rise in the number of freeborn and apprenticed merchants indicated that from the time of the Revolution the port was entering a new phase of development, whereby an increasing number of merchants would have been locally trained. Thus, even though the port still relied upon a large influx of settlers, a growing proportion of new traders learnt to identify their futures with the longer-term success of the port.[81]

occupational titles in Liverpool, see F. Lewis, 'The Demographic and Occupational Structure of Liverpool: A Study of the Parish Registers 1660–1750', Ph.D. thesis (Liverpool, 1993), ch. 3.

[81] For records of freedom purchasers, see Liverpool RO: MF2/2–5. Freemen by patrimony would only pay 3s. 4d. and apprentices 6s. 8d. The origins of these newcomers will be discussed in the next chapter.

While these broad trends in freedom-taking illustrate the causes of the port's growth, the most dramatic evidence of Liverpool's mercantile expansion comes from topographical evidence. In 1660 the town consisted of a mere six streets, as traders huddled together on the banks of the Mersey. By the reign of Queen Anne the number had risen to thirty-four streets, with significant expansion to the south and east of the old town centre (illustrated in Map 1.3).

Major administrative adjustments accompanied these developments, with the creation of a distinct parish of Liverpool in 1699, and the erection of a new church over the Pool by 1704. In commercial terms, the most important innovation was the building of docks in the Pool after 1709, a bold enterprise which helped to secure the port's success, and further encouraged investment away from the town's traditional heart. The period thus saw Liverpool undergo a significant physical transformation, a process which fostered intense competition among merchants for the best sites within this changing environment. The town thus presents a very different predicament for traders compared with the historic strictures of London or York, offering greater opportunity, but also causing uncertainty as to the direction of future development.[82]

A general survey of mercantile residence reveals that Liverpool merchants were acutely aware of the need to adapt to the changes which economic growth had brought to their town. The hearth taxes of 1662–73 indicate a concentration on the four central streets of the old town, all of which lay within easy reach of the Mersey and the customs house on its bank. Predictably, when the town took the decision to erect a 'public exchange for the merchants' in 1673, it was sited at the crossing of these four streets. A generation later, with the numbers of resident merchants having risen from about 20 to over 70, this residential pattern still held true, with about half of the overseas traders condensed into Water Street, Castle Street, and Chapel Street. Such continuity, evident from the town's assessments of 1705–8, was promoted by topographical foci which were not solely commercial in nature, such as the town hall and St Nicholas's church. Moreover, innovatory features such as nonconformist meeting-houses also looked to this central hub, with both Quakers and Presbyterians congregating nearby. However, the building of the new docks and the erection of St Peter's did have an impact on merchant settlement, and even by 1708 it was clear that traders were being drawn to the streets facing the Pool rather than towards the Mersey. This migration was slow at first, but after the transference of the customs house to the new docks in 1722 there were even stronger reasons for relocation, and by the mid-eighteenth century St Peter's could boast several of the tombs of Liverpool's

---

[82] For maps tracing Liverpool's physical growth, see S. Nicholson and A. Black, *The Changing Face of Liverpool, 1207–1727* (Liverpool, 1981). For more specific studies, see W. F. Irvine, *Liverpool in the Reign of Charles II* (Liverpool, 1899); H. Peet, 'Liverpool in the Reign of Queen Anne, 1705 and 1708', *Transactions of the Historical Society of Lancashire and Cheshire*, 59 (1908); *VCH Lancashire*, iv (London, 1911), 2–3. For the development of the dock, see Chalklin and Wordie, *Town and Countryside*, 116–46.

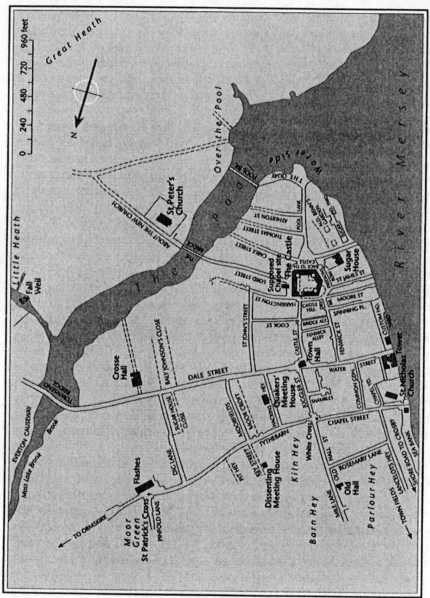

MAP 1.3 Liverpool in 1705

leading magnates. Nevertheless, while this transition was important, the siting of the exchange in the old town was an enduring magnate for mercantile residence, maintaining commercial continuities even in an era of tremendous growth. Recent research has shown that it was not until the 1740s that Liverpool merchants began to withdraw to the town's periphery, and even then they were careful to maintain a central business base. They thus showed attachment to both political and commercial centres of activity in the same manner as their contemporaries at the well-established port of Newcastle.[83]

Overseas traders were responsible for many of the new buildings erected, both residential and commercial. These investments facilitated the mobility of merchants within Liverpool, and it is significant that several prominent Liverpool businessmen could boast pew space at more than one of the town churches. The corporation, with mercantile figures very much to the fore, endeavoured to keep close supervision of this building boom, and by the end of the period there appeared increasing concern for prestige as well as commercial facility within the port. The oft-quoted delight of Celia Fiennes at finding a little London of regular streets and ordered terraces reflects well on those responsible for the town's planned expansion, and it is clear that some mercantile leaders harboured even more ambitious plans. For instance, in April 1707 Thomas Johnson desired that a 'handsome square' be built on the central site of the old castle, which, if populated by mercantile residences rather than retailers, would prove 'a mighty ornament to the town'. His hopes were not realized within his lifetime, but the area was dignified by the building of St George's church by 1762.[84]

Merchants were evidently keen to take advantage of the opportunities fostered by an expanding town centre, as the face of Liverpool was radically transformed. However, the benefits of such growth were far from equally spread among the resident population, and in purely commercial terms, it appears that control of town trade came increasingly under the control of the greater traders. Michael Power has noted a 'concentration' of economic activity among an elite tier of merchants, and credits them with the crucial leadership which sustained the town's expansion over the early Georgian decades.[85] This important thesis helps to explain much of the dynamism of the port at this time, but it is important to consider how that authority was diffused within a domestic urban context. At York 'concentration' was a feature of commercial decline, with a shrinking topographical focus and a commensurate polarization of wealth within the mercantile community. How did Liverpool's experience differ from this?

[83] E179/250/6, 9; E179/132/355; H. Peet, 'Liverpool in the Reign of Queen Anne'; Lewis, Ph.D. thesis, ch. 2; Langton, *Transactions of the Institute of British Geographers*, 65 (1975), 1–27.

[84] *The Journeys of Celia Fiennes*, ed. C. Morris (London, 1949), 183–4; T. Heywood (ed), *Chetham Society*, 9 (1846), 159. Note the town's sanitary problems in Lewis, thesis, ch. 8. A Clayton Square was eventually developed, the town paying tribute to one of Johnson's leading contemporaries.

[85] M. Power, *Urban History*, 24 (1997), 310–23.

Given the shortcomings of Liverpool's existing taxation records, it is difficult to make any categorical statement about the degree of concentration among merchants, particularly at such an early stage of the port's development. Nevertheless, it appears that the growth of the town's trade was accompanied by the emergence of a distinct cadre of overseas merchants, whose prominence reflected increasing commercial specialization in terms of geographic region or commodity. As Power has shown, the number of merchants making ten or more shipments rose from eleven to forty in the course of 1665–1709, and this group clearly helped to raise the commercial profile of the port. Over half of this group of forty made over thirty shipments in 1709, which suggests that there was an elite tier within the upper echelons of the trading fraternity. The influence of these traders can be easily exaggerated, and the likes of the Johnsons, Tarletons, Claytons, and Cunliffes have been duly celebrated as pivotal figures in the rise of Liverpool. However, there is also plenty of evidence to suggest that the benefits of the town's growth were more widely shared. The desultory but continuing involvement of local retailers in international commerce helped to blur professional boundaries, while ship captains still traded on their own account, sometimes on an impressive scale. As many as 365 individuals traded out of the port in 1709, and local magnates could not afford to ignore the views of their more modest mercantile colleagues, many of whom were substantial traders in their own right. Thus, although acknowledgement must be given to the general importance of the new breed of Liverpool merchant, particularly as mutual interest in colonial trade invested them with common priorities, the port should not be represented as a mere commercial oligarchy. Liverpool's trade had yet to advance to the stage where control of the port rested with a handful of dealers, even though the mercantile sector had clearly undergone significant change in an era of unprecedented growth.[86]

In terms of pure wealth there are stronger indications that a small number of merchants were able to distance themselves from their professional colleagues. The hearth taxes of 1662–73, while remaining a crude index of comparative wealth, suggest that there were already wide differences in the personal circumstances of individual traders, with the assessments for merchants ranging from one to seven hearths. Predictably, Water Street boasted some of the larger trade dwellings, but such was the density of mercantile residence that little significance can be attached to this precise concentration. However, the growth of the town by 1705–8 offers more food for thought, particularly as the assessments of that time included estimates for stock-in-trade and local landholdings. These records indicate that the greater

[86] Power, ibid. For an excellent example of the ship captain-turned-merchant, Bryan Blundell, see 'Journal of a Liverpool Merchant', Lancashire Record Office Report 1967–8, pp. 18–25. The most exhaustive analysis of probate evidence in early modern Liverpool concluded that there was a widening spectrum of wealth throughout the town—Ascott, Ph.D. thesis, esp. 452–61.

merchants had drawn even further away from their lesser brethren, with the valuations for 'stocks' ranging from £12 10s. to £350, a twenty-eight-fold difference. As with the London data, such estimates have to be regarded as impressionistic, but the fullest of the Liverpool tax returns, the 1708 poor rate, confirms that the most active traders were strengthening their position within the town. They dominated the central axis of the old port, and had already made extensive landed investments in nearby undeveloped town lands. Lesser traders could be found in the traditional hub, but mainly congregated on its fringes, in which position many were well placed to take advantage of developments towards the Pool. On the whole, however, the fluid environment of early eighteenth-century Liverpool makes it impossible to isolate locales of richer and poorer merchants in the same manner as York, especially since even the greater traders were willing to move as the commercial focus of the town shifted. This mobility also works to obscure the influence of age and geographic origin. The failure of ambitious social zoning, such as Johnson's proposed Castle Square, reflected the fact that the town's social topography was still in state of flux. In particular, the port had yet to reap the genteel rewards of its success, and remained overtly commercial in orientation without a West End or Minister Yard to complement its industrious business district.[87]

Social and topographical evidence indicates that Liverpool, in a very different way from York, underwent significant changes as a consequence of a concentration in the control of overseas trade. In terms of residence economic factors played an overwhelming part, but wealth gave a few individuals much greater opportunity to adapt to the town's changing landscape. By comparison, influences such as religion and ethnicity do not appear to have had a significant impact on residential patterns. Nonconformity was a more prominent feature of town life than at York, but the dissenting churches do not appear to have become foci for distinct communities of merchants.[88] Even traders of Scots and Irish origin do not appear to have stuck closely together, although the limitation of the sources may have obscured important connections between Celtic settlers.[89] However, while patterns of specific mercantile association remain elusive, the increasing professionalization of Liverpool's leading merchants was a trend of longer-term significance. Always at the heart of town development, these men embodied the general interest of the port in its first era of expansion, and maintained a prominence which their

[87] For tax sources, see above; Lewis, Ph.D. thesis, ch. 2.

[88] Due to a paucity of records, Liverpool nonconformity is extremely hard to pinpoint—see B. Nightingale, *Lancashire Nonconformity* (Manchester, 1893); J. Murphy, 'The Old Quaker Meetinghouse in Hackins Hey, Liverpool', *Transactions of the Historical Society of Lancashire and Cheshire*, 106 (1954), 79–98; Ascott, Ph.D. thesis, 169–78.

[89] Proof of origin is often elusive, and the positive identification of certain Celtic settlers only warns of the danger of assuming nationality by surname. Nevertheless, it is clear that such immigrants made a great contribution to Liverpool growth, an impression which accords with increasing historiographic emphasis on the Celtic contribution to transatlantic development—H. V. Bowen, *Elites, Enterprise, and the Making of the British Overseas Empire, 1688–1775* (London, 1996), 157–65.

mercantile counterparts in more traditional ports had always enjoyed. Thus, even in its infancy as an international port Liverpool's mercantile society exhibited many of the features of York and London, although it is clear that the demands of continued expansion would keep its leading traders continually on their toes.

Topographical surveys can reveal a great deal about the associational character of mercantile societies, although a realistic impression of their urban environment must embrace both diversity and fluidity. The extremely cosmopolitan society of London presents the researcher with forbidding problems in terms of scale, but its very complexity ensures that the priorities which invested mercantile choice of business location can be delineated. Beyond the mere question of size, York and Liverpool presented very different arenas in which traders could pursue their fortunes, and the composition of their mercantile groups reflected the peculiar pressures working on their economies. All three examples, however, reveal enduring commercial priorities, and how the individual merchant relied on the locality to provide the services and connections to promote his business. In such a fast-moving and ever-changing profession, the formal and informal structures of urban life offered a semblance of stability in which to conduct their affairs. On a more personal level, residential, and by extension business continuity could turn out to be a forlorn hope, but the broader forces for stability must be recognized, even in Lupton's world of flux and danger.

Recognition of the difficulties faced by individuals amid 'the hurry of business' is vital when assessing the overall impact of the merchant.[90] Lupton's anxious traders clearly had much to be worried about, and would need all their political skills to maintain success throughout their career. Although business was usually organized on an individual or family basis, the merchant could not afford to isolate himself, and he had to be able to count on others. Even the greatest of traders had to recognize such dependency, but for the younger, less wealthy, or immigrant merchant there was an even higher premium on securing useful contacts. This chapter has demonstrated that the life-cycle is often the key to understanding the status of a merchant at any given time, and we must now turn to study the career structure of the trader in business and public life. Traders were busy men, who could not afford to devote valuable reserves of time or effort to urban organizations which could not promote their businesses, and thus the commitments undertaken by our three mercantile samples at various points of their career remain of particular significance. By studying the individual and the strategies which he employed to make his way in an unforgiving trade, and in a challenging urban environment, we can learn much about the feasible impact of overseas commerce in an important era of expansion.

---

[90] Quotation from the epitaph of Isaac Milner (d. 1713)—Guildhall Lib. MSS 2480, p. 789.

CHAPTER TWO

Business and Public Life

A mayor or other chief magistrate's business in a corporation is so intermixt with pageantry, feasting, judicature, and something of his own trade and employment that it is difficult for him to know overnight what part he is to act the next morning, whether a judge on a bench, or guest, a master of a feast, a consul in a triumphal show, or dealing in his private occupation with a man in his shop, or compting-house.[1]

SIR FRANCIS BREWSTER's emphasis on the parallel lives of the leading citizen demonstrates that the modern obsession with 'networking' has a long heritage. As a merchant, he was aware that politicking was not simply a matter for the occasional City poll, and his comments suggest that the quest for influence was almost a daily chore. The preceding survey of the urban environment has outlined the manifold ways in which it was structured to forward business, but tells us less about the challenges facing the individual, and his struggle to succeed within that socio-political framework. If we are to understand the public impact of the merchant, it is imperative that we first acknowledge his business priorities and see how they influenced the multiple relationships which facilitated the achievement of commercial goals and personal status. Through analysis of the 'strange politicians' themselves, attention will be drawn to the great diversity of mercantile experience, but also to the common strategies for advancement employed by a wide range of overseas traders. Some excellent research has been completed on various aspects of the mercantile life-cycle, but rarely has a holistic approach been taken to the career path of the merchant, both in his private and public capacities.[2] Indeed, much of the research into the life of the seventeenth- and eighteenth-century merchant has concentrated on civic and other institutional elites, or has been overtly concerned with the enduring issue of 'social mobility'. Here it will be argued that a more comprehensive approach is essential if an effective perspective is to be gained concerning the role of traders at a national,

[1] F. Brewster, *New Essays on Trade* (London, 1702), 45–6.
[2] For life-cycle studies of the middling orders, see P. Earle, *The Making of the English Middle Class* (London, 1989); *idem*, 'Age and Accumulation in the London Business Community, 1665–1720', in N. McKendrick and R. B. Outhwaite (eds.), *Business Life and Public Policy* (Cambridge, 1986), 38–63. Only a few individuals have been thoroughly studied in their public and private capacities, most notably— R. Grassby, *The English Gentleman in Trade: The Life and Works of Sir Dudley North, 1641–91* (Oxford, 1994); D. C. Coleman, *Sir John Banks* (Oxford, 1963); J. Price, *Perry of London: A Family and a Firm on the Seaborne Frontier, 1615–1753* (Cambridge, Mass., 1992).

regional, and local level. Focus on the practicalities of merchant life will demonstrate that traders shared a basic attachment to their own urban environment, largely because of their dependence on the economic, social, and political mechanisms located therein. This orientation necessarily conditioned the impact of the merchant on a more public stage, but could not obscure the importance of extra-urban agencies to the preservation of both business and status.[3]

For the purposes of studying the merchant in public life, it would have been tempting to start, as so many other historians have, with the most successful of the merchant breed, as defined by wealth, civic office, or eminence within a certain trade. However, such an approach fails to acknowledge the many failures who never achieved the accolades of civic greatness, whose misfortunes can tell us much about the requirements for success in urban society. The previous chapter has highlighted the endemic fears of the merchant, and it is clear that even the greatest figures of the business world could not take their success for granted. This study does take into account the more modest achievers of the entrepreneurial elite, although it must be recognized that many budding overseas traders never even made it into the lower ranks of the samples discussed here. Nonetheless, the diversity of mercantile experience can be represented by this comprehensive survey, which will in turn further illuminate the kinds of associations promoting individual advancement. The career paths of the London and provincial samples will be studied according to the sequence of challenges facing the maturing trader, especially those which historians have deemed especially important for structuring urban associations in the early modern period: background, training, marriage, and civic involvement. In particular, close attention will be paid to any generational changes in the merchant life-cycle, in order to establish the importance of the Augustan period for the social and political advancement of the trader. Although an elite group, the wide-ranging experience of the merchant body can certainly tell us much about the challenges and opportunities facing all Englishmen at that time.[4]

[3] For analysis of London's early modern elites, see G. S. De Krey, *A Fractured Society: The Politics of London* (Oxford, 1985), esp. ch. 4; H. Horwitz, 'The Mess of the Middle Classes Revisited', *Continuity and Change*, 2 (1987), 263–96; N. Rogers, 'Money, Land, and Lineage: The Big Bourgeoisie of Georgian London', *Social History*, 4 (1979), 437–54; R. Lang, 'Social Origins and Aspirations of Jacobean London Merchants', *EcHR* 2nd ser., 27 (1974), 28–47; J. R. Woodhead, 'The Rulers of London: The Composition of the Courts of Aldermen and Common Council of the City of London 1660–89', MA thesis (London, 1961).

[4] For recent emphasis on the need for 'a new approach to public life' in the early modern period, see J. Barry, 'Introduction', in *idem* and C. Brooks (eds.), *The Middling Sort of People: Culture, Society, and Politics in England, 1550–1800* (London, 1994), 1–27.

i. The background and training of the City merchant

The cosmopolitanism and apparent openness of the City, as with so many other facets of London life, inspired contrasting emotions. The wonderment of Addison as he moved among the parliament of nations at the Exchange must be juxtaposed to the xenophobia expressed by vociferous critics of the naturalization of the poor Palatines only a few years before. In fact, beyond these extremes, much of London's appeal rested with the sheer diversity of its social fabric, and there were few visitors or settlers, whether native of foreigner, who could not find the solace of a compatriot's company in the capital. By dint of its business, the City's merchant body was very international in character, and duly received admiration and mistrust in varying measures. However, as yet we have no general guide to the broad make-up of this mercantile elite during the expansion of the late seventeenth century, in order to assess its permeability to various social groups from home and abroad. Given the fluidity of the City, it can be very difficult to trace the way in which newcomers ventured into City commerce, but sufficient evidence survives to demonstrate the dizzying opportunism exhibited by London's merchants. Thus, Table 2.1 examines the geographical origins of the sample, grouping the results into broad categories to trace general patterns of mercantile background.[5]

The table must be recognized as a very general guide to the City's source of mercantile personnel, since the limitations of certain archives have ensured that several regions have been underrepresented, especially the colonial and Celtic peripheries. Nevertheless, the scale of the traceable sample ensures that it faithfully delineates the three main sources of recruitment to merchant ranks: London itself, the English provinces, and the European continent. Historians have been particularly struck by the number of home-grown businessmen who climbed to the top of the City's civic and commercial hierarchies, and the table in general accords with their findings, revealing a sizeable proportion of merchants of London origin, or from its adjoining counties. These figures may not have been as high as those traced for the civic elites of the late Stuart or mid-Hanoverian period, but overall the table serves as an important reminder of the capacity of the City for self-generation.[6] Especially when taken with the recruits from the South-East region, the prominence of native London merchants highlights the presence of stable

---

[5] The obscurity of the commercial classes below the great boardrooms has been lamented by many historians, including those studying them—N. Rogers, 'A Reply to Donna Andrew', *Social History*, 5 (1981), 365–9.

[6] Both Horwitz (50.1% from a sample of 112 City leaders in 1694–1714) and Rogers (45% from a sample of 74 aldermen in 1738–63) suggest significantly higher London background rates. The table is closer to Lang's early Stuart civic sample (23%) and Woodhead's aldermanic figure of 25%. For a convenient comparison of these findings, see Horwitz, *Continuity and Change*, 2 (1987), 270. From a less elite perspective of London church court deponents, Peter Earle notes a 26.2% rate of London-born males in the 1665–1725 period—*A City Full of People* (London, 1994), 47.

TABLE 2.1 *Geographic origins of the City sample*

Region/country of origin	Number	% of total sample (850)	% of traced sample (583)
England			
London	230	27.1	39.5
South-East	50	5.9	8.6
Midlands	40	4.7	6.9
West	31	3.6	5.3
North	17	2.0	2.9
East	14	1.6	2.4
South	9	1.1	1.5
Wales	1	0.1	0.2
Scotland	5	0.6	0.9
Ireland	2	0.2	0.3
Colonies	2	0.2	0.3
Foreign immigrant	181	21.3	31.0
Uncertain/unknown	267	31.4	
TOTAL	849	100	100

Sources: Mercantile origin has been defined here as the settled residence of the trader's parental household. The sources used are too numerous to list, but apprenticeship records at the CLRO, Guildhall Library, and livery halls were particularly useful, supplying 180 indentures (21% of the sample). The counties covered here are: South-East (Bedfordshire, Berkshire, Buckinghamshire, Essex, Hertfordshire, Kent, Middlesex, Surrey, Sussex); Midlands (Derbyshire, Herefordshire, Leicestershire, Northamptonshire, Nottinghamshire, Rutland, Shropshire, Warwickshire, Worcestershire); West (Cornwall, Devon, Gloucestershire, Somerset, Wiltshire); North (Cumberland, Durham, Lancashire, Northumberland, Westmorland, Yorkshire); East (Cambridgeshire, Lincolnshire, Norfolk, Suffolk); South (Dorset, Hampshire).

forces within the fluid metropolitan environment. However, it is clear that the City could not provide all its recruits, and both contemporaries and historians have been impressed by the large numbers of immigrant merchants within the City. Throughout the early modern period hostile social critics liked to portray London as the all-consuming, bloated head of an enervated English state, but the table demonstrates that the City did not lean too heavily on any particular region for a continuing stream of able, and well-funded recruits. Thirty-five English counties are represented within the sample, and testify to the widespread attraction of London as a centre of commercial opportunity, but the capital did not remorselessly gorge itself on provincial talent to maintain its overseas trade. From a generational perspective, there was also little departure from traditional patterns of mercantile recruitment in terms of native traders. Even with the noticeable increase in London's overseas commerce after 1660 there was no significant shift in the recruitment of native merchants, or any other suggestion that the magnetism of the City was increasing for particular regions. Greater concentration of City trade within fewer hands may have acted as a novel deterrent for provincial recruits in the later seventeenth century, but the experience of the three generations within the sample suggests that outsiders encountered difficulties in establishing themselves in an unfamiliar environment throughout the century.[7]

It is clear that the traders of foreign extraction constituted the most dynamic element within the mercantile world of post-Restoration London. An influx of foreign skill and wealth had little immediate impact on the civic elites which have been researched for the late Stuart and Hanoverian periods, but it had obvious consequences for the form and character of mercantile society in this period.[8] The constant absorption of newcomers had always put particular strain on the social and political institutions of the City, but it appears that the scale of late Stuart immigration marked out the period of one of longer-term significance for London's mercantile development. The City fathers could not really claim any credit for commercial foresight, since the decision of settlers to come to England was principally determined by major political events, such as war, religious persecution, or other manifestations of government policy. This was particularly true of Jewish immigration from the 1650s onwards, and that of the Huguenots in the 1680s. Moreover, it is clear that their success as merchants owed a great deal to their continuing links with their former homelands, over which the City had little control. Nevertheless, their long-term presence was an undoubted boon to England's general economic growth, and helped to ensure that London would retain its pre-eminence within national commerce. Their achievement ensured that the capital remained a hybrid City, with nearly a third of merchants of known origin having been born abroad. In addition to this contingent, a further forty-five merchants of London birth (7.7 per cent of the traceable sample) can be identified as the offspring or direct descendants of foreign immigrants. Most of the merchants whose background is uncertain or unknown were probably of English stock, but the overall picture demonstrates that London commerce was heavily influenced by merchants of foreign origin.[9]

The table raises some significant questions concerning the feasible social and political impact of a sizeable sector of the business world. Despite the

---

[7] For emphasis on the restrictive character of London commerce, see M. Kitch, 'Capital and Kingdom: Migration to Later Stuart London', in A. L. Beier and R. Finlay (eds.), *London, 1500–1700* (London, 1986), 224–51. The continuity of City recruitment patterns is highlighted by the combined figures for the London and the South-East, since Woodhead's figures for 1660–88 would rise to 45%, while Rogers's for 1738–63 would be 55%.

[8] Rogers admitted that the absence of foreign-born merchants from his sample cast doubt on its representativeness—*Social History*, 4 (1979), 442. For other criticisms, see D. Andrew, 'The Aldermen and Big Bourgeoisie Reconsidered', *Social History*, 5 (1981), 359–64. Earle's non-elite sample suggested that only 12.1% of London males came from outside England and Wales, although he noted that this proportion rose to 17.5% among those born after 1660—*City Full of People*, 47–8.

[9] For discussion of the longer-term significance of this foreign influx, see S. Chapman, *Mercantile Enterprise in Britain from the Industrial Revolution to World War One* (Cambridge, 1992), esp. 29–34. Significantly, he stresses commercial, rather than political causes for this influx of foreigners. For discussion of the contemporary debate on immigration, see D. Statt, *Foreigners and Englishmen* (Newark, NJ, 1995).

spirited attempt of Defoe and others to alert their countrymen to the mongrel nature of their island race, English prejudice towards foreigners was all too obvious in this period, and posed a potentially serious obstacle to individual advancement. Outspoken attacks on the Jews greeted Charles II on his return, and the Dutch and French were vilified by turns during England's wars in this period. Thus if trade was to prosper, the London environment had to demonstrate greater tolerance to commercial settlers, and cocoon merchants from the most vituperative attacks. The previous chapter has already noted how introspective some of the alien communities were in their working and personal lives, doubtless as a protective instinct forged within an unfamiliar and potentially hostile people. However, it would be wrong to characterize the London merchant world as a series of ghettos, and the successful assimilation of rich, well-connected, and innovative merchants was crucial for England's growth as a commercial nation. Thus, in the ensuing sections these settlers deserve especial attention for the light which they can shine on the permeability of English customs and institutions, as much as their distinctive practices in the workplace and at home.[10]

Of course, the prospects of a young merchant were not exclusively determined by geographic origin, and in terms of advancement a much more crucial question lay with the social and occupational standing of his forebears. Only with the advantages of familial wealth could an adolescent secure the formal route into overseas trade via an apprenticeship, and as yet we have little idea of how many merchants were fortunate enough to enjoy substantial early support. The difficulties encountered by historians when seeking to ascertain paternal status or occupation are considerable, especially since they could change so easily within the space of a lifetime, as Peter Earle has most recently demonstrated for the urban classes.[11] International differences would have even further complicated matters, and thus ensuing discussion will centre on the origins of merchants who have been identified as English-born in Table 2.1. The available data on paternal status and occupation is summarized in Table 2.2, where an important distinction is also made between urban and country origins in order to highlight recruitment patterns. In addition, the mean stocks assessments of 1693–4 are included for each category as a rough guide to the relative standing of mercantile recruits from different backgrounds.

Given the problems inherent in analysing occupation and status, it would be unwise to make too categorical a statement about the origins of the English merchant. Nevertheless, in general the table does not suggest that there was a dramatic interchange between the landed and the urban sectors at a mercan-

---

[10] H. V. Bowen has recently argued that Britain only partially assimilated its foreign settlers—*Elites, Enterprise, and the Making of the British Overseas Empire, 1688–1775* (London, 1996), 149–70. For discussion of English xenophobia, see M. Duffy, *The Englishman and the Foreigner* (Cambridge, 1986).

[11] P. Earle, *City Full of People*, chs. 3 and 4; Beier and Finlay, *London, 1500–1700*, 246–7.

TABLE 2.2 *Status/occupation of the fathers of English-born merchants (City sample)*

	Number	Percentage	Mean stocks in 1693–4
Country			
Baronet	2	0.5	250
Knight	7	1.8	333
Esquire	15	3.8	323
Gentleman	27	6.9	328
Yeoman	7	1.8	325
Cleric	6	1.5	360
Lawyer	3	0.8	400
Others	4	1.0	238
Country subtotal	71	18.2	323
Town			
Baronet	1	0.3	300
Knight	7	1.8	500
Esquire	3	0.8	300
Gentleman	12	3.1	363
Merchant	120	30.6	375
Cleric	5	1.3	220
Lawyer	1	0.3	300
Doctor	1	0.3	200
Ironmonger	4	1.0	350
Mercer	4	1.0	250
Packer	3	0.8	400
Brewer	2	0.5	500
Grocer	2	0.5	400
'Citizen'	48	12.2	332
Others	17	4.3	350
Town subtotal	230	58.8	356
Unknown/uncertain	90	23.0	
TOTAL	391	100	

Sources: Apprenticeship records at the CLRO, Guildhall Library, and livery halls were again most useful in the compilation of this table. The pedigrees listed in the visitation of 1687 were also very illuminating—College of Arms, K.9. Where possible, occupational and status attributions have been
checked against other sources, and uncertain entries have been listed separately. The custom of identifying fathers by their livery company has necessitated the provision of a 'citizen' category.

tile level. Alongside previous analysis of civic and institutional elites, it
indicates that a high proportion of merchants hailed from urban business
backgrounds.[12] Not only does all appear relatively quiet on the sensitive

[12] Lang suggests that 37% of his civic elite were from a provincial or London business background;
.Woodhead 35%; Horwitz 63%; Rogers 53%. The corresponding rates for the 1692 group would be
52.5% of the total sample, and 66.6% of the identifiable sample.

gentry–merchant border, but the figure for business background may even be much higher, since the obscurity of the origins of a significant number of English-born merchants probably hides a more diverse occupational profile than the one outlined in the table, especially regarding men of more humble origins. A cautionary example is the case of Thomas Tryon, a major West Indian merchant, who rose from the household of a provincial tiler-cum-plasterer to become a leading City figure and author. In his early career he held a variety of jobs, including shepherding, and without the testimony of an autobiographical work it would have been impossible to reconstruct his background and early progress. Thanks to his eventual prominence, and that of several other rag-to-riches businessmen such as Arthur Moore and James Craggs, it is clear that resourceful, determined, and fortunate men of low birth could rise quickly within London society. However, it is much more difficult to delineate the early progress of more modest merchants who did not take out an apprenticeship to a freeman, or whose limited success did not merit the attention of contemporaries. Further research may well widen the field of mercantile recruitment in both social and occupational terms.[13]

Despite such lingering uncertainty, the preponderance of merchants of urban origins can be accepted with some confidence, and London itself accounts for the lion's share of town recruits. In fact, provincial urban centres were successful in keeping aspirant merchants at home, and major ports such as Bristol, Newcastle, and Exeter sent few mercantile apprentices to the capital. These patterns highlight the difficulties of setting up as an overseas trader in the City, and in general the table demonstrates the apparent advantage enjoyed by traders whose father was already involved in commerce. Just as importantly, in common with the findings of Henry Horwitz, it suggests that the offspring of overseas traders did not take the first opportunity to abandon the family profession in favour of a leisured gentry world.[14] Not only were mercantile sons a common feature of City trade, but the assessments for stocks suggest that they were perceived to figure among the City's wealthiest inhabitants. Further proof of the benefits of a commercial background can also be drawn from the immigrant merchants, whose former residence in major European ports suggests that the vast majority came from families who had participated in overseas trade.[15] In general, the table counsels caution against too great an emphasis on gentry recruitment into merchant ranks, even though a significant minority of gentle younger sons entered trade and could prove very successful. From a generational perspective, it does not appear that London's commercial expansion had enticed a greater number of gentle offspring to enter mercantile ranks, or that traders

[13] T. Tryon, *Some Memoirs of the Life of Thomas Tryon* (London, 1705).

[14] Horwitz found that 30% of his elite samples of the 1694–1714 period left business and invested a sizeable proportion of their assets in landed estates—*Continuity and Change*, 2 (1987), 278–86.

[15] Probate evidence is particularly suggestive of the international dimensions of the networks of foreign-born City merchants.

with landed backgrounds were playing a more prominent role within City life.[16]

Novice merchants with urban business connections obviously enjoyed a huge advantage as they began their commercial education. Many English merchants tried to ensure the continuity and security of their business through the employment of their own offspring or near relatives, who could be trained in-house, and save the family from the expense and difficult decisions involved in securing the young lad's future. The family unit was not impervious to internal division and many fathers lamented their good intentions to their offspring, but the household in general proved a very fertile breeding-ground for successful traders. Families of overseas origin appear to have enjoyed a distinct advantage in this regard, especially in European-based trade, where the newcomer could enter an international family firm which could safely incorporate his untrained abilities. This pattern of commercial inbreeding was clearly far more common than the employment of a young gentleman in the family company, and could be maintained without a formal apprenticeship. The aspirant merchant from outside the commercial fold, however, could hardly hope to secure rapid commercial advancement without an apprenticeship to a well-connected, prosperous trader. As a result, one of the key criteria for their early progress within the City was financial backing, necessary for persuading successful merchants to take on a young apprentice, and for providing a reasonable starting capital. A gentle household could more easily afford the £500–1,000 sums demanded by London traders to take on their offspring, but there was no guarantee that their sons would stay the course.[17] The Onslows of West Clandon, Surrey, are a good case in point, with two of their younger sons being indentured to London merchants, probably at the recommendation of a mercantile relation. Neither went onto City fame, resting content instead with landed acres and a guaranteed life of influence within the family's Surrey orbit, which in turn led to seats in the House of Commons. Thus, even an apprentice indenture was no guarantee of a successful mercantile career, and complaints were often aired concerning the lack of motivation among gentle sons in trade. In general, the bare recommendations of breeding and fortune were clearly insufficient to ensure advancement within the City.[18]

---

[16] For evidence to cast doubt on the commercial benefits of gentlemen entering trade, see R. Grassby, 'Social Mobility and Business Enterprise in Seventeenth-Century England', in D. Pennington and K. Thomas (eds.), *Puritans and Revolutionaries* (Oxford, 1978), 355–81.

[17] For a useful summary of evidence for apprenticeship premiums, see Grassby, *Business Community*, 65–9. Francis Brewster was concerned that too many merchants were emerging from their apprenticeships with small stocks, thus encouraging them to take greater risks. He wanted gentlemen's sons to be encouraged on account of their greater fortunes—*Essays on Trade and Navigation* (London, 1695), p. vii.

[18] Thomas Onslow was apprenticed in May 1652 with a £1,000 bond to Joseph Ashe, while Denzil Onslow was indentured to William Peake in December 1661. Richard Onslow, Levant trader, may well have helped them secure these places—Drapers' Hall MSS apprentice bindings 1634–55; Clothworkers' Hall MSS, apprentice bindings 1641–62. Note Thomas Manley's contemporary

The training of the embryonic merchant would probably have been enough to sort out the time-servers from the truly committed: painstaking copying of letters, endless repetition of tables of exchange, and attendance at some of the busiest concourses in London all could sap the enthusiasm of the keenest apprentice. Moreover, merchant masters were often criticized for putting their charges through unprofitable drudgeries in order to stop the youngster acquiring the skills which one day might make him an informed rival of his one-time master.[19] Given these considerations, it is less surprising that a great many of our sample were directly related to their masters, who were more likely to offer a protective and supportive environment for their training. Moreover, many of the most successful traders owed their rise to the confidence of kinsmen-masters who trusted one of their own to guard the company secrets. Trust has been recognized by economic historians as a key basis for the growth of early modern commerce, and in microcosm it would clearly have been a pivotal issue in determining the relationship between master and apprentice, especially if the former wished to send the youngster abroad to further his commercial education. The standing of the apprentice's family would help to establish such belief in a youngster's character and prospects, as long as the master's risk in taking on a young gentleman was cushioned by a bond secured on the credit of their name. There were outstanding gentle successes, such as Dudley North, but he should not be regarded as typical. Many merchants would take on gentle apprentices for the money to be made, but it could prove an unwise investment for both parties.[20]

Whether gentle born or not, the apprentice could not fail to recognize the potential importance of the master for his future career in trade. Through the master he would learn the general techniques of merchandising, and also be tutored in the necessary details of his particular trade, especially the goods with which he would be dealing. Recent work has raised questions concerning the value of the seven-year apprenticeship in certain artisan trades, but there can be little doubt that the young merchant would undergo a steep learning curve for the duration of his service.[21] The fact that in general mercantile apprentices were taken on in their mid to late teens suggests that they already needed a good deal of schooling before being taken on an extensive course of further instruction. Furthermore, an extended sojourn abroad, to learn foreign languages and to make vital contacts, singled out the merchant's education as especially challenging. After such experience, and with possession of much hard-earned knowledge and connections, it is not surprising that

concern that men were being pushed into trade through necessity, not their 'proper genius', and consequently mismanaged trade—*Usury at Six Per Cent Examined* (London, 1669), 45–6.

[19] For the potential drudgeries of apprenticeship, see Grassby, *Business Community*, 43–5.

[20] On the key importance of trust for commercial credit, see C. Muldrew, *The Economy of Obligation* (Basingstoke, 1998), esp. chs. 4–7. For North's career, see Grassby, *English Gentleman in Trade*.

[21] Earle, *City Full of People*, 59–66. For evidence of the mercantile success to be won without the formal apprenticeship, see D. Hancock, *Citizens of the World* (Cambridge, 1995).

most apprentices would initially continue in the same sphere of trade as their master's. With additional years of experience, and, vitally, more capital, the successful merchant might seek to broaden his commercial portfolio, but the apprenticeship remained the crucial stepping-stone to becoming an independent man of business.[22]

Even after the formal end of his indentured service, the link between master and apprentice could remain strong, most obviously symbolized by the perceived habit of former apprentices marrying into the families of their masters. Several such alliances were made by our sample, but the tie of matrimony represented not only personal attachment, but also enduring commercial priorities. Given the challenges facing the novice, especially the enormity of the task of establishing oneself in a very competitive, and potentially hazardous profession, the support of his master could be instrumental in maintaining the momentum of his career. Personal connection was so crucial, since it provided access into this difficult and unforgiving world. Josiah Child highlighted the importance of this early connection, and indeed argued that the cost of an apprenticeship should be gauged by 'the condition [of] the master, as to his more or less reputed skill in his calling, thriving or going backward, greater or lesser trade, well or ill government of himself and his family'. If the master did score highly on all these counts, then his reputation could be a very considerable boost to the young merchant, and open doors to various avenues of commercial and social opportunity. The master would not only be a communicator of necessary skills, but a passport to connections in the various organizations which influenced City life. Most significantly of all, it appears that the young merchant's ultimate choice of trade was inextricably linked to this personal contact. Little wonder then that an apprenticeship with a leading merchant was regarded as 'very hard to get at'.[23]

The actual length of apprenticeship is very difficult to gauge, even in the case of merchants with surviving apprentice indentures, which in general required seven or eight years' service. Most merchants took a great deal longer than this specified period to take out their freedoms, and thus formally end their period of servitude. Apprentices who spent significant periods abroad could take over twenty years to formally dissolve their apprenticeship. Levant Company records show that it was common for young merchants who had completed their indentured service to begin to trade on their own account

---

[22] The age of apprenticeship binding has been ascertained for 154 (18%) of the sample, and less than a third were taken on at an age younger than 16. There was no discernible shift in this pattern in the post-Restoration period. For the active contemporary debate on the education of merchants, see Ch. 4.

[23] Child, *A New Discourse of Trade* (London, 1693), 87; Bodl. Rawlinson Letters 63, fo. 46ᵛ. For emphasis on the importance of apprenticeship connections, see R. Brenner, *Merchants and Revolution* (Princeton, 1993), 69–70. The significance of the master's contacts was often made very clear in the apprentice's indenture, and several of the masters within our sample boasted trading links with more than five countries or regions.

without becoming free of the company until their return to England.[24] Many young merchants never became free at all, and without personal business records it is impossible to discover when they became independent of their masters or families, if indeed they chose to do so. Formal partnership agreements reveal that fathers were quite prepared to enter into fixed-term contracts with their own children for a division of the profits of the family trade, and thus a young merchant's business status might alter without any apparent outward change.[25]

However, for the vast majority of the sample, the onset of marriage was an unmistakable sign of their emergence as an independent force within the City. This observation does not suggest that marriage was an absolute precondition for mercantile advancement, since there were plenty of examples of prosperous bachelors, whose finances went unstraitened by the pressures of bringing up a family. Nevertheless, given the responsibilities of marriage, it remained a most important step, and would not be undertaken without serious thought concerning its financial and social consequences.[26] As a potential economic opportunity and an agency of associational influence, marriage was inevitably viewed as one of the crucial turning-points in the young merchant's life. The actual event may have merely confirmed an already existing link, rather than open up a new network, but it in general ensured a long-term connection, the assuredness of which even rivalled other key allegiances such as religion. Broadly speaking, first marriages came in their late twenties or early thirties, precisely at the time when the young merchant also became a full member of various civic and commercial institutions. Indeed, this period was the coming of age for the merchant, during which time he established for himself a more public role away from the protective cocoon of family and master. The marital portion was a welcome boost to his embryonic capital, but the match also could confirm standing within the mercantile world, and thus be of double significance.[27]

The actual identity of the brides again highlights the metropolitan focus of

---

[24] From a miscellany of sources, only 87 (10.2%) of the sample have been identified as foreign residents for a substantial part of their professional career. However, there can be little doubt that trainee merchants would have made foreign trips, and a majority probably spent several years abroad. The Levant Company minute books provide the most accurate account of the time spent abroad by merchants, while the deposition records of the High Court of Admiralty also provide a good deal of information concerning foreign travel—SP105/152-6; HCA 13.

[25] For instance, the will of tobacco trader John Cary (d. 1701) revealed that he had drawn up formal articles of partnership with his son Thomas in January 1695, apportioning a quarter of his £12,000 stock-in-trade to Cary junior—PCC 1701, fo. 58.

[26] For an excellent survey of contemporary views on marriage and courtship, see K. Wrightson, *English Society, 1580–1680* (London, 1982), chs. 3 and 4.

[27] For records of London marriages, see published lists in Harleian Society series, and manuscript records at the Guildhall Library and Lambeth Palace (Faculty Office and Vicar-General). Of 335 first marriages identified, 79% took place between 25 and 35. This figure is close to Earle's findings for his 'middle-class' sample (71.3%) and to national averages—Earle, *Making of the English Middle Class*, 180–5.

mercantile life. The vast majority of the matches made by the sample involved the daughters of families from the London region, and a high proportion of them can be identified as the offspring of families in trade.[28] As already mentioned, there are several examples of the former apprentice marrying the daughter of his master, but in general the young merchant enjoyed a wide catchment area in which to find his future bride. The highest degree of endogamy is predictably to be found within the ethnic groupings, with the Jews remaining particularly introspective due to religious constraints. However, it should be stressed that gentile immigrants did not feel constricted to marrying within their nationality. For instance, French immigrant Peter Renew (1647–1729) married into a London merchant household only two years after arriving in England, and went on to achieve prominence within both the London Huguenot community and the wider City world. His adventurousness was emulated by other settlers, who used a match as the springboard for rapid social progress within their adopted country. In general, the longer-term importance of marriages made within the merchant world is more obvious than the alliances made with gentle families, whose benefits could fall well short of expectations. Once a merchant had made his pile, then young gentlemen and ladies might seek the favour of his offspring to bolster an ailing landed fortune. However, the choice made by the merchants themselves were in general directed towards securing City contacts rather than social cachet. [29]

It was common for marriage to lead to an immediate physical separation from the household of the family or master.[30] However, all merchants knew that they could not afford to dispense with the connections which they had garnered through the early stages of their career, since they would continue to prove vital for the growth of their business. As Francis Brewster intimated at the beginning of this chapter, these connections would not be maintained or extended simply by their presence at the Exchange, and the reputation and influence of the merchant would also rest on his extra-curricular activities. Once into their thirties, merchants reached an important stage of their life, when many were confronted with the decision whether to invest their time and energy in those civic and commercial institutions which still had an important influence on London trade. The political significance of the major

[28] Of the 355 identifiable brides, 55% were from London, and a further 27% from Middlesex, Surrey, Kent, Hertfordshire, or Essex. Over a quarter of the fathers of these London brides can be identified as merchants. These overall figures are broadly in line with those of Lang (66%) and Horwitz (civic sample 66%; second sample 50%). Thus, they further bolster the Rogers argument that the mid-eighteenth century saw a significantly higher proportion of gentry matches among the City elite. Only 9.3% of the 355 brides considered here can be identified as of gentry background.

[29] Peter Renew married Elizabeth, daughter of John Cox, merchant—Vic.-Gen. marriage lic. 1 Sept. 1679 (he aged c.32). At that time he was a deacon of the leading Huguenot congregation at Threadneedle Street.

[30] D. V. Glass's analysis of the 1695 marriage duty returns concluded that the extended family was the exception rather than the rule in the City—*London Record Society*, 2 (1966), pp. xxviii–xxxiv.

commercial associations of City life will be discussed in the next chapter, but as a guide to the continuing importance of other organizations to the overseas trader, the following section will analyse the ways in which office-holding within the City affected the career paths of the sample.

ii. Independence and association: office-holding in the City

The pattern of office-holding within the square mile was heavily conditioned by a complex web of overlapping jurisdictions wielded by a variety of economic, religious, and political authorities. Although this morass of competing loyalties may appear a basis for confusion, it in fact serves notice of the wide-ranging significance of associational ties for any citizen, especially for those within the City's upper hierarchy. Historians have eagerly sought to delineate the careers of prominent individuals by reference to their service in a variety of City bodies, and accorded great political significance to the relative preparedness of traders to take on onerous duties, especially in the field of local government. Most interestingly, analysts of the Augustan and mid-Hanoverian City have detected a decline in the numbers of merchants serving on the corporation, as the trading elite found influence and status via other channels. This development is seen to have mirrored the broad lines of socio-political tension within the eighteenth-century City, as an alliance of greater merchants and financiers distanced itself from the modest artisan and retailer.[31] However, while there can be little doubt that the common council declined as a focus for mercantile politicking under the first two Georges, recent research on the late eighteenth-century City has questioned whether such elite withdrawal was terminal. Furthermore, as yet there has been little consideration of office-holding on the lower rungs of the urban ladder of advancement. At the most basic level of all, it is unclear how the so-called 'flight from the freedom' affected the mercantile class in general. Thus we still have a great deal to learn concerning the activities of the mercantile classes in a public capacity, and of their basic aspirations beyond advancement within the commercial sphere. Most importantly, such office-holding has to be squared with their fundamental priority of making profits, and consideration must be given to the reasons why busy merchants would apportion precious time to duties which had little direct relevance to their trade. In the absence of great caches of personal papers, it is imperative that the priorities of the merchant be discovered by analysis of their voluntary activities outside their immediate

---

[31] See in particular De Krey, *Fractured Society*; H. Horwitz, 'Party in a Civic Context: London from the Exclusion Crisis to the Fall of Walpole', in C. Jones (ed.), *Britain in the First Age of Party* (London, 1987), 173–94; I. Doolittle, 'The Government of the City of London, 1694–1767', D.Phil. thesis (Oxford, 1979), 29–48. By the late 1730s, merchants made up only 15% of the common council, while in the 1660–88 period the figure was 25%.

commercial orbit. Obviously, the public career of any individual will reflect particular aspirations and interests, but a wide-ranging prosopographical survey can reveal the common priorities invested in a range of City associations. The spending of time, as much as that of money, can demonstrate basic ambitions and needs.[32]

From the outset it appears that there were great pressures working on the trader to devote his energies to the commercial, social, and political institutions of the City. The powerful influence of these authorities conditioned the opportunities open to a young merchant, and the City was far from a level playing-field for newcomers. Most importantly, overseas trade was heavily influenced by a combination of commercial and civic structures, whose interdependent connections had been designed to tap the human resources of the City elite. At a purely business level, there were restrictions facing those who wished to engage in commercial areas monopolized by the great chartered companies. For those embarking upon the Levant, Russia, Eastland, and Hamburg trades in the 1660s, there were further obstacles, most notably the minimum commitment to civic life in the form of a compulsory City freedom. The Augustan period saw a successful attack on such a limitation of individual choice, which would ultimately hasten the demise of a fully regulated urban economy, but such requirements represented a very real obligation for many of the merchants of our sample. A City freedom was not a formal requirement for participation in other trading monopolies, such as the East India, Hudson's Bay, or Royal African companies, but the onus on the individual to become a member of these joint-stock companies was just as great.[33] In appearance the unregulated trades offered much greater freedom of action, and there was ample opportunity for retailers, manufacturers, and wholesalers to deal direct with foreign markets, especially with the colonies and continental Europe. However, even though lacking the formal structures of the great City companies, unregulated traders also needed protective associations to preserve their independence. The prevalence of strong networks of ethnic and religious traders in the unregulated spheres of English commerce can in fact be seen to have compensated for the lack of an arbitrational authority to ensure basic coordination amongst fellow merchants. Thus, even though the formal tie between commercial and civic spheres only existed with regard to a

[32] S. E. Brown, 'Politics, Commerce, and Social Policy in the City of London 1782–1802', D.Phil. thesis (Oxford, 1992), esp. 35–46. For discussion of the relationship between individual choice and City association, see J. P. Ward, *Metropolitan Communities* (Stanford, Calif., 1997), esp. 145–6. For a more personalized discussion, see Grassby, *English Gentleman in Trade*, 151–76.

[33] During the great free-trade debates after 1660, the City tried on several occasions to impose a freedom requirement on company charters. They succeeded with respect to the Levant Company, but failed elsewhere, most notably in 1702 on the union of the East India Companies—Horwitz, *Continuity and Change*, 2 (1987), 268, 276. The free merchants also complained to the common council in 1713, citing the evasion of both office and local tolls by the unfree merchants—Doolittle, D.Phil. thesis, 48. In that year the City corporation petitioned Parliament to ensure that free merchants were not disadvantaged at the customs house—*CJ*, xvii. 446.

few trading areas, the operation of English overseas trade did not relieve any merchant of the necessity to maintain connections with their fellow Londoners. Although essentially an independent commercial entity, the overseas trader simply could not afford too splendid an isolation.[34]

Due to the acknowledged independence of the merchant, it is often difficult to track the full range and significance of his associations, whether in relation to another individual, or to a group of mercantile colleagues. However, analysis of office-holding promises some insight into the personal priorities of the overseas trader, especially as a means to gauge commitment to the various spheres of activity in which he might be concerned. An attachment to certain associations could reflect personal convictions, most obviously in the case of religious office-holding, but these networks also served as key agencies in bringing the commercial world together, even though nominally outside the competitive realms of the world of business. It is impossible to separate London society from the structure of its commerce, and it is important to realize that it was to this City focus, rather than the dream of the country estate, that the young merchant was immediately drawn. Inevitably, the best-documented cases of office connection lay with the most successful merchants, who fully realized the potential of their contacts to gain public office, but we must recognize the importance of networks which were subsidiary to the great boardrooms and the aldermanic bench. Not all men reached the top of the socio-political ladder, or even strove to get there; but all realized the importance of cultivating contacts, even if they were reluctant to accept the onerous public duties which their general prominence placed upon them. As the previous chapter demonstrated, the late seventeenth-century merchant was very much a part of the City's hierarchy, a position of comfort, but one which was more likely to bring public commitments with it. Thus, each overseas trader was faced with the competing demands of public and private, and would have to make a trade-off to decide how much of his time and effort he could expend to pursue such mutually fulfilling objectives.

For the newly established merchant in his early thirties, his public advancement would be principally conditioned by his family, location, and religious beliefs. In terms of daily routine, his immediate commitment of time would be to his household, the pivot of his commercial operation and his familial responsibilities. Beyond that obvious focus, the parish figured as the most immediate 'communal' sphere, an importance sanctioned by its overriding influence as the basic unit of English local government. For conforming Anglicans, the official requirement for weekly attendance at the local church helped to cement its place at the centre of neighbourly life, as did the fact that many City precincts were coterminous with parish boundaries. The compactness of the ninety-seven intramural parishes ensured that parochial leaders

[34] See in particular A. Olson, *Making the Empire Work: London and American Interest Groups, 1690–1790* (Cambridge, Mass., 1992). Much fuller discussion of their role comes in the next chapter.

could be on familiar terms with their mercantile neighbours.[35] Some of the parishes in the central City area were very modest in size, with only 100–200 houses, and under 1,000 parishioners. On the other hand, the City's fluid residential patterns worked against such commensality, as did the centrifugal influences of non-parochial organizations, such as the foreign and non-conformist churches. In addition to these competing loyalties, there remained the demands of the greater jurisdictions of the wards and the City. Moreover, given the topographical concentration of merchants in the eastern City, personal loyalties built on commercial connections could even overcome the neighbourhood's prior claims on the time and commitment of the overseas trader. However, analysis of mercantile office-holding demonstrates the enduring importance of this more humble focus for even the greatest of merchants.[36]

While mayoral and aldermanic contests would always make the headlines, the immediate urban loyalties of the merchant can be demonstrated by the less glamorous positions which large numbers of traders were prepared to fill, especially in connection with the parishes and ethnic congregations. A civic elite of 120 traders (14 per cent of the sample) served in the major positions of common councillor, sheriff, alderman, or mayor, but a further 152 (18 per cent) of the sample can be identified as holding parochial or congregational office. Given certain lacunae in the surviving sources, this latter figure is clearly an underestimate, but it still stands as testimony to the commitment of merchants to their definable local communities.[37] It is also clear that parochial life had its attractions even for the richest of London citizens. Many traders were willing to pay fines of up to £20 to duck the burdens of constable, scavenger, or churchwarden, regarding these duties as too troublesome, but it is significant that they chose to sit on their vestries after paying their fines, evidently perceiving them to be an important forum for communal life. When vestry business was so intimately tied to such important business as the administration of local poor rates, the appointment of lecturers, and the status-sensitive arrangement of pew seats, it is predictable that merchants would want to have some say in the running of their parochial neighbourhoods. The regulation of the vestries indeed came to the attention of Parliament in the heightened party tensions of Queen Anne's reign, such was their perceived influence on London life. Thus, even though merchants might

[35] Valerie Pearl has made the strongest argument for the continuing importance of parochial communities—'Change and Stability in Seventeenth-Century London', *London Journal*, 5 (1979), 3–34. Peter Earle has noted the existence of street-clubs as a more immediate orbit, but still sees the parish church as a focus for 'neighbourhood life and pride'—*Making of the English Middle Class*, 240–50.

[36] For analysis of the variety of parochial structures, see Glass in *London Record Society*, 2 (1966), esp. pp. xxxii–xxxv.

[37] Sources for parish office would be too voluminous to list here, but can be exclusively found in the collections at the Guildhall Library. Their coverage of the mercantile eastern City is almost complete for the post-Fire period.

be keen to avoid the strains of local office, and probably paid replacements to undertake some of the more nauseous tasks, they were willing to participate in local affairs, in order to maintain status and contacts with their fellow merchants and tradesmen.[38]

Perhaps the most telling sign of the significance of parochial organization is the apparent willingness of nonconformists and immigrants to undertake vestry duties and offices. At least thirty-three known dissenters officiated at this level, as did thirty-two merchants of Huguenot or Dutch background. Most interestingly, these foreign-born traders all served as either deacons or elders in their respective ethnic churches as well, highlighting the general openness of London society to Christian settlers. In a less harmonious vein, the Jewish community found it much harder to come to terms with parochial duties, and in this period several parishes commenced legal proceedings to enforce fines for their refusal to serve. Their recalcitrance to participate fully in parochial life was exacerbated by their concentration within a handful of parishes, and undoubtedly fuelled traditional resentment towards them.[39] However, other European immigrants were quickly assimilated, and even ethnic cliques could be tolerated if settlers contributed to the administrative stability of their neighbourhood. Adrian Beyer of St Lawrence Pountney is a good case in point, a native of Holland who resided for at least thirty-nine years in the same parish. Naturalized in 1664, he first gained public office in London as deacon in the Dutch church at Austin Friars, but by 1673 had established himself on the parish vestry, and served as churchwarden in 1686–7, shortly before becoming a Dutch elder. He later proceeded up the civic ladder too, serving as a common councilman and deputy of his ward. These offices prove that he was a committed and well-known member of his parish, and his £500 stock assessment under the four-shilling aid of 1693–4 suggests that such responsibilities had done his business no great harm either. Few immigrants were as successful at integration, but many saw the advisability of performing the paternalistic tasks of local government at their most basic City level.[40]

Therefore, on the basis of the sample, it would be hard to make a case for widespread 'elite withdrawal' among the mercantile classes from their traditional responsibilities of urban government, as has been argued for the landed

[38] Metropolitan Whigs and Tories clashed in February 1710 over a Whig-backed bill to regulate vestries within the bills of mortality—*CJ*, xvi. 305, 315. Vestry influence was particularly important in Southwark parishes, where the overseers of the poor could determine voters on the borough's scot and lot franchise.

[39] For Dutch and Huguenot office-holders, see W. J. C. Moens (ed.), *The Marriage, Baptismal, and Burial Registers, 1571–1874 . . . of the Dutch Reformed Church, Austin Friars, London* (London, 1884); R. Gwynn, 'Minutes of the Consistory of the French Church of London, Threadneedle Street, 1679–92', *Huguenot Society*, 58 (1994). For discussion of how the 'passive assimilation' of the Dutch republic was tested by Ashkenazi migration from the 1690s, see S. Schama, *The Embarrassment of Riches* (London, 1987), 587–95.

[40] Significantly, Beyer did not choose to become a freeman until 1691.

elite in their respective rural sphere.[41] The London parish does indeed appear to have continued to thrive as a communal focus for even the most substantial of its citizens, with merchants very much to the fore in the eastern City. Historians have rightly seen a decline in the elaborate local rituals associated with religious festivals in the post-Reformation period, but there remained many opportunities for merchants to partake in parochial life. The evidence of the St Mary at Hill nosegay festival, which took place annually on the Sunday after midsummer, suggests that neighbourly events could both confirm their local status, as well as remind them of their communal responsibilities as parochial leaders. On the Saturday the fellowship of ticket-porters would visit the homes of the merchants of Billingsgate, and present them with posies and nosegays; the following day the porters would process the church, where they and the merchants in turn would donate offerings to the poor. Not all parishes would have such elaborate customs, but there is little doubt that the annual perambulation dinners fulfilled the same communal function, with the merchants presiding over such affairs throughout the eastern half of the City. The enduring popularity of these urban rituals can be inferred by the steps taken by parish elders at St Edmund the King, who in 1707 excluded inattentive vestry members from parochial entertainments. These festivities may have lacked the grandeur of the mayoral show, but they continued as an important focus for the confirmation of City loyalties and personal status.[42]

Elevation to a station above that of parochial level was certainly within the capability of businessmen with wealth and influence. However, office at a ward or City level would require further commitments from the individual, most importantly in the shape of the City freedom. Analysis of the freedom has tended to be overshadowed by historiographic interest in the livery, a sequential stage in the civic cursus honorum which gave its holder the right to vote in parliamentary elections, among other privileges. This elite perspective has again meant that little recognition has been given to the variety of motivation propelling Londoners into public responsibilities. Historians recognize that the City freeman body (of perhaps 20,000 residents) was some three times greater than the liverymen, and had an important electoral role to play in City life. Nevertheless, focus remains on the livery, and individuals who did not vote in parliamentary elections are all too quickly dismissed for being uninterested in civic life, without examination of the reasons why influential Londoners took up the minimum civic qualification and did not proceed to the 'obvious' next step in the corporate ladder. Henry Horwitz has shown that

[41] J. M. Rosenheim, 'County Governance and Elite Withdrawal in Norfolk, 1660–1720', in A. L. Beier et al. (eds.), *The First Modern Society* (Cambridge, 1989), 95–125.

[42] W. Leybourn, *Panarithmologia* (London, 1693), 137; Guildhall MSS 4266/1, vestry order 14 Apr. 1707; Earle, *Making of the English Middle Class*, 243–4. A more authoritarian character has been attributed to London rituals—M. Berlin, 'Civic Ceremony in Early Modern London', *Urban History Yearbook* (1986), 15–27.

the lack of the freedom was no bar to prominence in public life, and has also alerted researchers to the varying degrees of civic commitment discernible among London leaders in the late Stuart period. Clearly, the City was sufficiently flexible in its institutional framework to accommodate the civic patriot and the recalcitrant bigwig, but the broad patterns of such diversity have yet to be identified.[43]

In fact, of the sample 434 (51 per cent) can be identified as freemen, of whom only 321 (38 per cent) have been discovered among the liveries. These overall figures should caution against too hasty a dismissal of the City's ability to attract the mercantile elite in a period when it was clearly failing to maintain its traditional authority over domestic and artisan trade. The lacunae of the City's records mean that both figures are probably a serious underestimate, but the fact that at least half of the resident merchants took up the freedom highlights the continuing influence of civic life within the world of overseas trade.[44] Most significantly, closer analysis suggests that nearly three-quarters of merchants of known native origin were free of the City. Whether London born (74.8 per cent) or provincial (72.8 per cent), traders were still prepared to take out their freedoms, and it is only the impact of foreign immigrants (19.9 per cent) which brings down the overall figure. Their presence also had a deflationary effect on the rate of freedom-taking across the seventeenth century, with a significant decline observable between traders born before 1642 and those born after that date. Nevertheless, even within the identifiable post-Restoration generation, a healthy 60 per cent of traders became freemen.[45] The City would clearly have liked more overseas traders to take up the freedom, judging by the pressure it exerted to impose freedom requirements on the overseas trading companies, but these statistics suggest that there were still sufficient attractions to tempt the greatest of traders to make some commitment to civic life.[46]

While the general reticence of immigrant merchants to take up the freedom

---

[43] De Krey, *Fractured Society*, 40–1; Horwitz, *Change and Continuity*, 2 (1987), 281–2. For a clear outline of the electoral powers of the freemen, see De Krey, 'The London Whigs and the Exclusion Crisis Reconsidered', in Beier et al., *The First Modern Society*, esp. 468. For much higher estimates of freeman totals (of up to 50,000), see V. Pearl, *London Journal*, 5 (1979), 12–14.

[44] For records of freedom admissions, see CLRO, CF1 (although this archive is only reliable from 1681). Particularly valuable has been the almost complete returns for the 1690 poll tax, which required non-freemen to pay surtaxes—CLRO, assessment boxes. For livery sources, company records at the Guildhall Library are essential, combined with the London poll books of 1710 and 1713. The parliamentary inquiry into the City purges (of 1,795 liverymen in 50 companies) of 1687–8 has also proved very useful—House of Lords RO, main paper series 154–9.

[45] The overall figures for the generations represented in the sample are as follows: born pre-1642 (130 traders)—74.6%; born 1642–59 (316 traders)—61.7%; born post-1660 (125 traders)—60%. Archival difficulties have inevitably inflated the number of English-born traders in these subgroups.

[46] Contemporary accounts suggest that freemen numbers were much higher. In 1696 Gregory King only envisaged about sixty unfree merchants living within a 10-mile radius of the capital— J. Thirsk and J. P. Cooper (eds.), *Seventeenth-Century Economic Documents* (Oxford, 1972), 768. The incomplete 1690 poll tax returns identify only 114 individuals as unfree merchants.

is understandable, as settlers in an unfamiliar environment, the motivations of the native trader are more difficult to discern.[47] There simply is no pattern to the identity of merchants who decided to take up the freedom, just as there is none to those who declined to become free. Most importantly for discussion of 'the flight from the freedom', there is no particular correlation between freedom-holding and success in trade, and although the magnate Sir William Scawen might be held forth as the archetypal plutocrat who defied City conventions, his brother Sir Thomas conformed to a more traditional civic stereotype. If brothers could differ in their commitment, then there is little chance that statistical analysis could ignore the overwhelming, but largely immeasurable influence of personal preference on the rate of freedom-taking. However, the discrepancy between the numbers of liverymen and freemen betrays a more basic common feature, in that it demonstrates that merchants did not undertake civic commitments without seriously weighing up their pros and cons. The decision to take up the freedom cannot be indubitably read as evidence of a burning civic patriotism, but it can be regarded as recognition of the importance of City institutions for the operation of overseas trade. At a most basic level, there were the incentives of commercial advantage in terms of reduced tolls in London and in other towns. Just as importantly, the free-man gained the electoral privileges of the wardmote, and could thus influence the key City institutions of the common council and the aldermanic bench. More intangibly, freeman status may have bolstered the individual's repute within the trading community, and perhaps improved his credit-worthiness. There was also the prospect of securing useful contacts in the City livery companies, and the next chapter will demonstrate that the late Stuart merchant was fully alive to the utility of civic connection. All these advantages would be carefully measured against the prospect of the civic duties and obligations which would probably fall to the socially prominent merchant, and the individual would decide in accordance with his personal priorities and ambitions. Given the complex matrix of influences working on freedom-taking, it is predictable that there is no clear pattern, but this confusion cannot obscure the continuing importance of that decision for mercantile self-advancement.[48]

Once initiated into civic life as a freeman, subsequent promotion within the City would proceed on two fronts. First, there was every possibility that the merchant would become a liveryman, and probably a senior officer of his

---

[47] Certain naturalized merchants were overtly hostile to the City regulations which favoured freemen—H. Roseveare, *Markets and Merchants of the Late Seventeenth Century* (Oxford, 1987), 42–4.

[48] For a contemporary account of freemen privileges, see *The Freemen of London's Necessary and Useful Companion, or the Citizen's Birthright with the Foreigners' and Aliens' Best Instructor* (London, 1707). Henry Horwitz has found that one of the supposed disincentives to freedom-taking (the restriction on bequests in accordance with the custom of London) was commonly evaded by freemen in this period—'Testamentary Practice, Family Strategies, and the Last Phases of the Custom of London, 1660–1725', *Law and History Review*, 2 (1984), 223–39.

livery company, a route of advancement which will be analysed more fully in the next chapter. More unpredictably, he could also pursue the treacherous path towards ward and corporate office, which would render him vulnerable to the whims of the City's active electorates. Indeed, such were the obvious political ramifications of the latter route, that previous interest in City office-holding has tended to concentrate on the civic positions of common councillor, sheriff, aldermen, and mayor, reflecting their direct political influence. Of our sample, about one in seven served in these civic offices, with a mere twenty-eight gaining aldermanic status and a further ninety-two acting as common councillors. This is not an overwhelming number of civic activists, especially given the brief tenure of many of these incumbents, and the demands of these high-profile posts can easily explain mercantile reticence towards them. In particular, the fearsome burden of aldermanic office was a major deterrent to great merchants, and it is significant that a quarter of the sample's aldermen were political appointees who quickly resigned their offices.[49] The attraction of serving as sheriff appeared even less welcome, and many merchants were ready to pay fines of up to £500 to avoid a year of heady expenditure and much precious time spent in magisterial chores. This reticence should not, however, be taken as an obvious sign of political indifference, or of a lack of civic patriotism. The geographical density of merchants within certain wards obviously limited the opportunities for political advancement, and the number of common councillors indicates that merchants played a disproportionate part in corporation politics. The role of common councillor was perhaps best suited to the mercantile career, bestowing prestige and influence, but without a concomitant burden of weekly meetings and strength-sapping magisterial duties. Wine importer Abraham Chitty exemplified its importance, since he was prepared to pay the parish of St Helen's a £10 fine in 1697 to avoid the offices of scavenger and constable and ensure his confirmation as common councillor the following year.[50]

Closer scrutiny of the civic merchant highlights how successful candidates for election to the common council fulfilled criteria which went beyond the bare recommendation of personal wealth. Most importantly, in general they could boast longevity of tenure within the precinct or ward, a requirement even apparent in the politicized circumstances of the Augustan period. Moreover, half of them came from a London background, and more than half

[49] For discussion of the aldermanic fear of personal financial exactions by a cash-strapped City and Crown, see R. M. Wunderli, 'Evasion of the Office of Alderman in London, 1523–1672', *London Journal*, 15 (1990), 3–18.

[50] Guildhall Lib. MSS 6846/1, p. 176. Woodhead noted that a quarter of the common councillors in the 1660–88 period were merchants, the dominant source of recruitment among the 140 trades represented among the common councillors—MA thesis, 77–9. He also noted that not one common councillor fined to avoid office, although fifty-one common councillors paid fines to avoid becoming aldermen—pp. 36–42.

had married a London bride, thereby illustrating the importance of local ties for their candidacy. However, the common council should not be represented as a rigid oligarchy, for there remained plenty of opportunity for newcomers. This is best represented by the thirteen councillors of recent foreign descent, three of whom were first-generation immigrants. Civic distinction was thus attainable by such families as the Houblons, Papillons, and Lethieullers, whom Defoe lauded as passing for 'true-born English knights and squires', but their business success did not mean automatic civic advancement. Only after establishing themselves within the City's foreign communities and within the parochial and commercial institutions of the City could they achieve long-lasting prominence within the corporate elite, and true eminence was usually achieved only by the second generation. From their experience, it is clear that the stable combination of business success and civic commitment was still prized within the City's fluid environment.[51]

Significantly, more than half of the civic office-holders also held posts within the City's trading and livery companies. Such a correlation represents the overlap between business and social success, and it is clear that these leaders were the brokers of City business and political life. Even this elite tier should not be regarded as an oligarchy, because the inherent uncertainties of City politics, business, and mortality would continue to undermine the cleverest of personal strategies for self-advancement.[52] Nevertheless, while it is impossible to identify a tightening of political opportunity at the apex of the civic elite, there can be no doubt over the perceived value of maintaining an interest in corporate politics. Amid the party warfare of the late Stuart period there were regular purges of the City corporation, and ferocious contests for common councillor posts, which revealed both local and governmental recognition of the importance of civic office. These disputes also spilled over into appointments to militia offices and hospital governorships, which positions were similarly regarded as symbols of personal esteem and influence. The battle for control of the City corporation and its satellite organizations retained an immense importance even for non-combatants, for at both a personal and institutional level their fate was intimately connected with that of City commerce.[53]

As proof of the enduring importance of civic service, a general survey indicates that even the leading 'brokers' of the mercantile world saw the advisability of holding modest parochial and civic posts. For instance, Sir Benjamin Ayloffe, baronet and governor of the Russia Company from 1700 until his death in 1722, was a true servant to his ward of Aldgate, serving as its common councillor for thirty-one years, and regularly attending his parish

[51] F. H. Ellis (ed.), *Poems on Affairs of State* (New Haven, 1970), vi. 278–9.

[52] Many, but not all of these brokers figure among De Krey's 'City leaders', since his sample did not include all common councillors—De Krey, Ph.D. thesis, 457–73.

[53] De Krey, *Fractured Society*, chs. 5 and 6.

vestry of St Katherine Coleman. The adjoining parish of St Olave Hart Street was also able to entice onto its vestry merchants of the stature of Sir Charles Peers, a leading Mediterranean trader and future MP. However, sensitive to the great demands on the time of the City leader, in 1709 the parish excused him from serving as churchwarden 'upon the account of the dignity of his station'. Conversely, the premature disappearance of a major merchant from the vestry minutes might signal a sudden reversal of personal fortune, as was evident in the case of Sir Bartholomew Gracedieu, a prominent Jamaica trader, who ceased to attend the parish committee of St Magnus the Martyr in 1708, shortly before bankruptcy proceedings were commenced against him. Such dramatic misfortune was not uncommon even among the trading elite, and Gracedieu's fate is a salutary reminder of the importance of the stability sought by both individual, parish, and City.[54]

More generally, nearly all of the thirty-five merchants ranked in the 1695 marriage duty above the status of gentlemen served in some civic or parochial capacity. Furthermore, amongst those recorded as gentlemen in 1695, freedom-taking was well above the average for the mercantile sample as a whole, with over two-thirds becoming City freemen. These impressive rates suggest that the City remained a magnet for its most dynamic commercial element, in spite of an understandable reluctance among busy traders to shoulder corporate burdens. A contemporary expectation of public activity in order to gain respectability was pressed upon the merchant leader, and in the urban context his personal stability was even more valued, given the uncertainties of life in the capital. The complex web of influential authorities within the City defy any attempt to construct a 'typical' cursus honorum of political advancement. However, it is clear that prominent merchants had to establish certain foundations to get ahead: success in business was the immediate and essential objective; such a goal could be facilitated by the close, supportive networks founded on kinship, religious, and business ties, all of which would promote residential stability and a commitment to a particular locality; which in turn would present him as a strong candidate for local office. All these are elements of the ideal interdependent circle of status which promoted the merchant to the forefront of urban society. In fact, Defoe believed that there was no need for the fortunate trader to brag of his abilities, since 'the very station of life he fills up in the place where he lives declares it'.[55]

This endorsement of the continuing importance of parish and civic institutions by a large cross-section of the city's mercantile elite must qualify the impact of those great merchant princes of the Augustan era who gained

[54] Guildhall Lib. MSS 1123/1,2; 858/1, vestry minute 2 May 1709; 2791/1; London Gazette, 31 Jan.–2 Feb. 1710.
[55] D. Defoe, The Complete English Tradesman in Familiar Letters (London, 1726–7), ii. 227. Judging by the 1695 marriage duty returns, there appears a greater inclination among higher-status groups to take up the freedom: gentlemen and above (138 traders)—70.3%; £600 surtax (252 traders)—60%.

national office. Their eminence cannot be ignored, but it must be put into the general context of a merchant body which did not appear to aspire to a higher calling. Of the sample, thirty-seven (4.4 per cent) won election to the House of Commons, but it cannot be said that the success-rate was a radical change from past practice. Beyond the relative popularity of a parliamentary seat, only a handful gained government posts, with Sir John Houblon's Admiralty Lordship, and Paul Docminique's place at the Board of Trade proving very much the exceptions. A handful of merchants did serve the government in positions relating to the customs and excise, but both ministers and traders preferred a less structured partnership. Merchants were willing to act as advisers on commercial and financial matters, were very keen to win government contracts, and were ready to advance impressive sums to bolster national credit, but they did not solicit opportunities to formalize their connection with Whitehall. In a party-riven age, this circumspection was well-advised for the longer-term interests of their trade, but it also reflected the fact that a substantial commitment to national office threatened to take them away from their all-important City connections. Their prominence within the urban business world remained the key to their success at a national level, and even though the common council was increasingly bypassed as a proving-ground of that status, no trader could ignore their broader City 'constituencies'. As we shall see, Augustan merchants could not neglect the national arena, but they continued to influence it through City institutions and associations with which they possessed a reassuring familiarity. The landed hegemony of central power was not a welcoming prospect for the overseas trader, but it is important to see that commercial priorities and City commitments, as much as social obloquy, held the merchant back from strutting the national stage.[56]

iii. Status as an urban phenomenon

Beyond the evidence of office-holding, the centripetal attraction of the City for overseas traders can be further traced in the other forms of activity which represented their essential outlook and interests. Again, a lack of personal papers does not readily permit an insight into the mercantile mind, but much can be learnt from institutional records which reflect their role within urban society. In particular, these records help to define the importance which individual traders placed on their associational ties, and how these

---

[56] These issues will be further discussed in Chs. 4–6. See Ch. 5 for patterns of mercantile representation at Westminster. Until further work is completed on the mid-Hanoverian City, it will be unclear how merchants compensated for the decline of the corporation by involvement in other associations. Peter Clark has recently suggested that voluntary associations may have filled this vacuum—*British Clubs and Societies, 1580–1800: The Origins of an Associational World* (Oxford, 2000).

connections worked to fashion perceptions of social status. Too often, the aspirations of mercantile society have been interpreted from the perspective of a landed society, without recognition of more immediate foci for City loyalty and emulation. The esteem with which a merchant was regarded by his colleagues, clients, and neighbours evidently had a great impact on his effectiveness as a businessman, and his 'credit' would be jealously guarded.[57] Beyond this commercial mandate, however, we still need to know more about the ways in which merchants regarded themselves and their profession within the broader context of metropolitan and national society. The City was far from immune from traditional notions of genteel honour, and historians have recorded at length how the middling orders fed avidly on the entertainment and display of the nearby West End. However, contemporaries commented upon the continuing differences between the gaiety of Westminster and the equally hectic lifestyles of London's business district. In the course of a career, a merchant might seek prominence at both ends of town, but only if he first 'made it' in the City. Thus, while paying tribute to mercantile consciousness of their role within national society, attention must be primarily directed to their status within their immediate urban environment.[58]

For a most direct testimony of mercantile self-regard, we have to look no further than one of the most important foci of extra-commercial life, the parish and congregational churches of the square mile. Adorning the walls of these key communal meeting-points, monumental inscriptions record the aspirations, achievements, and expectations of the urban classes. Their purple prose cannot be accepted uncritically, but it can serve as a guide to common perceptions of the requirements for status within the City context.[59] Significantly, office-holding is the most constant reference-point for proof of the deceased's virtues, and contemporaries paid far more attention than historians to offices below the aldermanic bench, with great care taken to delineate his commitment to parish, ward, and City. It appears that even the chores of minor office-holding could have an important bearing on the general standing of wealthy and successful merchants. Beyond the issue of office, certain qualities were accorded to overseas traders which were praised for their value both in the business world and within the broader associations of London society. Personal integrity was everywhere proclaimed as a virtue which facilitated the workings of trade and society in general, and was even used as a justification for the unashamed amassing of great wealth. For instance, Sir Andrew Riccard's tablet of 1672 at St Olave Hart Street

[57] On the workings of credit, see C. Muldrew, 'Credit and the Courts: Debt Litigation in a Seventeenth-Century Urban Community', *EcHR*, 46 (1993), 23–38.

[58] The influence of the West End on the creation of a metropolitan society is summarized in J. M. Rosenheim, *The Emergence of a Ruling Order: English Landed Society, 1650–1750* (Harlow, 1998), 215–52.

[59] Significantly, David Cressy has recently observed that contemporaries were more concerned with the hyperbole of church memorials, rather than their cost—*Birth, Marriage, and Death: Ritual Religion and the Life-Cycle in Tudor and Stuart England* (Oxford, 1997), 469–73.

applauded him as 'a citizen and opulent merchant of London, whose active piety, inflexible integrity, and extensive abilities alike distinguished and exalted him in the opinion of the wise and the good'. Other qualities commonly claimed also related to mercantile interaction with colleagues, such as an aversion to litigiousness, the Levant merchant Richard Spencer being described in 1667 as 'to many helpful, to most acceptable, to none injurious, to himself and his friends constant'. The bathos of the tomb of Sir Gilbert Heathcote (d. 1733) is particularly telling, for after a career studded with the achievements of the mayoralty, governorship of the Bank, a parliamentary seat for the City, and the bestowal of a baronetcy, the only commercial note struck was the observation that he remained 'in his extensive trade without a lawsuit'. Laid to rest at Normanton in Rutland, Heathcote may have deserted his City power base in his final years, but his urban roots had not been forgotten.[60]

These epitaphs did not merely interpret status in terms of metropolitan life, and it is particularly interesting to note the importance accorded by merchants to their profession as a patriotic endeavour. For instance, the monumental inscription of the great merchant-financier Sir Henry Furnese (d. 1712) highlighted his 'public services to his country', and celebrated his achievement in becoming 'without envy the great and good character of a charitable Christian, a noble benefactor, and a firm patriot'. The tomb of alderman Sir William Gore was equally conclusive on this score, declaring him to have been 'a wise and impartial magistrate, faithful to his prince, and useful to his country'. This emphasis on the service of the nation is far from being a complete departure from the traditional paternalism claimed by rural gentlemen through the exercise of county office, but the readiness of elite merchants to aspire to such leadership suggests that urban culture was spawning its own self-justifications at a time when the hierarchy of wealth was being challenged by the monied and commercial interests. This should not be represented as a revolutionary process, especially since some of the most effective arguments for the patriot merchant can be traced to the 1630s.[61] However, we are perhaps too blinded by contemporary propaganda on behalf of the gentry or the merchants, mostly penned by the radical fringe, to realize that urban society could assuage its leaders with sufficient prestige to stop them hurtling off into a countryside estate. If we recognize the importance of the networks which kept merchants rooted in their urban base, then it is much

---

[60] For transcripts of City epitaphs, many now lost in the blitz, see the Jewer transcripts in Guildhall Lib. MSS 2480, esp. pp. 605, 923; E. D. Heathcote, *Account of Some of the Family Bearing the Name of Heathcote* (Winchester, 1899), 82.

[61] Significantly, Laura Stevenson found that Elizabethan praise for the merchant was not accompanied by the development of a separate system of values to distinguish his contribution, and authors instead relied on gentle notions of honour and service. She argued that their mercantile contribution would only be properly recognized in the Augustan period—*Praise and Paradox* (Cambridge, 1984), esp. 127–9.

more plausible that their perception of status would be primarily determined by their own urban environment.[62]

While stressing the essential urban focus of the Augustan merchant, it is no contradiction to say that the national code of gentility did impinge on their self-perception. The London visitations of 1633–5, 1664, and 1687 were the last of any systematic attempts to define respectability by the rules set down by the College of Arms, and many City merchants were keen to be formally recognized as gentlemen. Predictably, the records of the abortive final visitation of 1687 suggest that merchants were the occupational group deemed to be most worthy of armigerous status. However, the numbers of overseas traders who actually took out coats of arms after 1687 was extremely small, and most of these grantees had retired from City life completely to pursue a more leisured suburban or rural existence.[63] Contemporary complaints of arriviste traders dressing their servants in fine liveries, and covering their possessions in coats of arms, were thus exaggerated. In fact, only a small proportion of the merchants of our sample owned a coach.[64] Analysis of a more subtle index of mercantile self-regard, the title which they adopted in their will, does not suggest any general desire for self-aggrandisement either. The vast majority of our London sample simply described themselves as merchants, while only some 15 per cent adopted the style of esquire or gentleman. Furthermore, for many of the most prominent merchants, the mere appellation of alderman was a sufficient additional dignity, and several even bracketed it with their knighthood.[65]

In the absence of armorial bearings, the most clear-cut distinction within mercantile society remained the knighthood, the achievement of which appears to have been well within the capacity of merchant leaders. No less than thirty-four of the sample gained this honour, many of them in recognition of service in highly unpopular public positions, such as City sheriff. Several traders were honoured in other contexts which suggest that trade was

---

[62] J. Le Neve, *Monumenta Anglicana* (London, 1719), 249; R. Clutterbuck, *The History and Antiquities of Hertfordshire* (London, 1815), i. 508. See Ch. 4 for more extensive discussion of contemporary views on merchant patriotism.

[63] College of Arms MSS K.9, visitation book 1687; W. H. Reynolds, 'Grantees of Arms 1687–1898', *Harleian Society*, 67–8 (1916–17). The visitation book yields good coverage of thirteen wards, broad outlines for another five, and nothing for the other ten. Merchants account for 18.6% (268 ex 1443) of the possible grantees listed, and many of the knights, esquires, and gentlemen recorded made their fortune in overseas trade. Of the sample only twenty took out arms after 1687, and a handful of their offspring did so too. For discussion of the causes of the decline of the visitation, see A. Wagner, *Heralds of England* (London, 1967), esp. 308–18.

[64] Ninety-five (11%) of the sample paid the surtax levied for ownership of a coach in 1692. Not one of these merchants was assessed at less than £300 for stocks under the 1693–4 aid. Further doubts concerning the 'emulative' consumption of the Augustan middling classes have been raised by L. Weatherill, *Consumer Behaviour and Material Culture in Britain, 1660–1760* (London, 1988), esp. 191–200. For an illuminating discussion of the London coach in this period, see S. Whyman, *Sociability and Power in Late-Stuart England* (Oxford, 1999), ch. 4.

[65] Of 276 wills which cited an occupation or title, 174 (63%) described themselves as merchants, and only 41 (14.9%) as esquires or gentlemen.

gaining the respect of the state, if only for the fiscal benefits which commerce begot. Significantly, the elevation of certain mercantile knights demonstrated the variety of political services which the merchant could provide for his country in the changing polity of late Stuart England, such as the presentation of a loyal address from the City, or even the speedy communication of important news or secret intelligence.[66] Their success is all the more impressive in consideration of the noticeable decline in the number of knighthoods awarded in our period, particularly after 1689. Their number would have been even greater, but some merchants went out of the way to avoid public recognition. Most revealingly, the great wine merchant Samuel Shepheard was reportedly 'several times in danger of being knighted', but 'always made his escape'. His aversion to the honour remains in some contrast to his willingness to serve as a common councilman for seventeen years, and demonstrates a desire for direct involvement in City life which went beyond the mere need for hollow titles.[67] He realized, as many of his mercantile colleagues did, that real influence was not exclusively linked to social degree, even if late Stuart governments were keen to fête helpful businessmen. For the most signal services, eight of the sample were accorded the honour of baronet, and two succeeded to that rank, but not one made it into the ranks of the peerage, a failure which illustrates the ultimate limits to the openness of English society. However, as much as merchants valued the esteem of others, there is no evidence to suggest that the formal code of ranks and honours caused them undue concern, or fuelled social resentment. Some traders obviously enjoyed flaunting their heightened status, but all recognized that their credit had to be built on surer foundations than mere acceptance at court.[68]

Mercantile funerals reflected the contrasting attitudes of merchants towards worldly status. Some had magnificent send-offs, the hearse of Sir Charles Thorold in 1709 being adorned with escutcheons and pencels, while officers carried trophies before it. However, this heraldic display was secondary

---

[66] For instance, Sir Henry Furnese was knighted for bringing news of the fall of Limerick to the King at the Hague—W. A. Shaw, *The Knights of England* (London, 1906), ii. 266. More interestingly, Sir William Lewin was commended in 1698 for having undertaking clandestine commerce with the French during the recent war 'with a design to gain as much intelligence as possible in matters relating to the French fleet, and other things of importance'—*CSPD* 1698, p. 7. Thus, although businessmen were not knighted for their success in trade per se, their value to the state was integrally tied to their mercantile operations—Grassby, *Business Community*, 229.

[67] *Whitehall Evening Post*, 30 Dec. 1718. Under Charles II and James II, it was not uncommon for over twenty or sometimes thirty individuals to receive knighthoods each year; in only four years in 1689–1727 did the number exceed twenty—see G. W. Marshall (ed.), 'Le Neve's Pedigrees of the Knights', *Harleian Society*, 8 (1873); Shaw, *Knights of England*. The aforementioned Lewin was one of three City leaders who left a civic feast in October 1702 'to avoid the honour' of being knighted by the visiting Queen—Strathmore MSS at Glamis Castle, box 70, folder 2, bundle 3, newsletter 31 Oct. 1702.

[68] Defoe even claimed that 'trading gentlemen' were refusing to be ennobled, although such claims have to be treated with suspicion—*Complete English Tradesman*, 374. For mercantile baronets, see the notes of Thomas Wotton, Add. MSS 24120, fos. 238, 241, 275, 423; 24121, fo. 9.

in effect to the attendance of 400 boys from Christ's Hospital and the City workhouse, who sang as the cortège embarked on a deliberately circuitous procession through the City's busiest thoroughfares to cover the short distance between his livery hall and his family's parish church. Probate evidence suggests that most merchants envisaged a more modest send-off.[69] Levant trader John Beare exemplified this hatred of pomp, confessing that 'I never loved popularity in my lifetime'. Significantly, Beare hailed from a gentle Devon background and appears to have maintained close links with his relations in the West Country, but after a career in the City he now espoused a common mercantile dislike of excessive show. Moreover, while his monument celebrated his Devon ancestry, it also declared his forty-two-year residency of St Olave Hart Street, as if that was cause for pride by itself. Other merchants with gentle backgrounds could be much more elegiac about their forefathers, such as Hamburg trader Jeremy Elwes, whose self-professed aim was 'as much as in me lies to keep up my name with reputation in some measure suitable to the family I came of'. The social pressures of having a baronet and knight for brothers might partly explain this self-regard, but it does not appear that ancestor worship was a great preoccupation with most merchants. Indeed, some of the greatest merchants were keen to expose the humbleness of their roots, the aforementioned Sir Henry Furnese making provision in his will that his monument acknowledge 'God's great goodness . . . in advancing me to a considerable estate from a very small beginning'.[70]

Perhaps the most obvious indication of the limited social aspirations of the merchant body as a whole was their indifference to investment in land and the establishment of great country estates. Several historians have recently questioned mercantile ambition on this account, stressing the variety of factors which affected all potential landowners.[71] Of course, examples of the super-wealthy's immersion into country society attracted great contemporary comment, as Sir Gilbert Heathcote's Normanton or Sir William Scawen's Carshalton rivalled the architectural pretensions of the most fashionable local gentry. However, testamentary records suggests that such profligacies were relatively rare among our sample, and that if merchants bought a country

---

[69] Thorold's cortège passed from Throgmorton street to St Andrew Undershaft via Lothbury, King street, Cheapside, Cornhill, and Leadenhall street—College of Arms MSS I. 30, esp. pp. 139–41. Despite widespread criticism of ostentatious funerals, social pressures ensured that the wealthy could not ignore the necessity of a decent burial—Cressy, *Birth, Marriage, and Death*, 421–55.

[70] PCC 1696, fo. 86; 1697, fo. 116; 1712, fo. 234. In general, the genealogical interests of the newly rich were not markedly different from those of more established merchant households.

[71] Note, in particular, the magisterial work by J. Habakkuk, *Marriage, Debt, and the Estates System: English Landownership, 1650–1950* (Oxford, 1994), esp. chs. 6 and 7; also L. Stone and J. C. F. Stone, *An Open Elite? England 1540–1880* (Oxford, 1984), 212–25. Habakkuk observed that government financiers were the most likely land-purchasers within the ranks of new wealth, and that in general mercantile profits were not solely responsible for the creation of large estates in the seventeenth and eighteenth centuries—420–5, 438–43. For an impressive list of property investment by City men (although not exclusively merchants), which was concentrated overwhelmingly in the Home Counties, see Jones, *War and Economy*, 330–1.

retreat, it would most likely to be a modest 'retiring house' with immediate access to the City. More generally, although evidence concerning landed investment is patchy, the bulk of mercantile property was to be found in the City itself and its surrounding region, and the alacrity with which merchants were prepared to sell off these purchases at their demise suggests that there was no inherent social strategy behind such ownership.[72] Business priorities may have again predominated, as in the case of Sir Francis Brewster, who ventured into property investment at the age of 31 'being importuned by friends to fix something on the land and not have all on the sea'. Very few merchants can be identified as the possessors of higher-status manors, and properties beyond the London region can usually be attributed to some familial link. Given the depression in the land market in the South-East, which, with only a brief respite, lasted into the 1730s, it is of little surprise that merchants looking for investment opportunities were attracted to government securities and shares, or to the more assured London property market. Poll books for the Home Counties which distinguish between the freehold and residence of voters also suggest that mercantile landowners were apt to remain City based, and few traders cited any other address than London in their wills.[73]

Retirement into the Home Counties was sought by a small group of the sample, but this did not mean full integration into county society, which in general would take generations for a mercantile family to accomplish. Furthermore, only a handful served as sheriff of their adopted county, and one of them, Sir Samuel Moyer, still kept his 'winter house' in St Stephen's Walbrook, where his monument proudly declared him a parish resident for forty years. Analysts of the office of justice of the peace have also detected little mercantile impact on the county benches of the late Stuart period.[74] A further question mark against merchant aspiration may be highlighted by one final category of office-holding, the commissioners for tax assessment in the

---

[72] Of 389 wills traced, 87 (22.4%) mention properties in London, 131 (33.7%) record properties in the South-East, and only 67 (17.2%) list estates elsewhere in England. Rogers suggests, on the basis of Woodhead's evidence, that a high proportion of aldermen owned properties at a distance from London, but does not discuss the miscellany of reasons which could have influenced such investment (beyond social aspiration)—*Social History*, 4 (1979), 448. For an architectural appreciation of the limited pretensions of London migrants to the Home Counties, see P. Hunneyball, 'Status, Display, and Dissemination: Social Expression and Stylistic Change in the Architecture of Seventeenth-Century Hertfordshire', D.Phil. thesis (Oxford, 1994), esp. ch. 4.

[73] Brewster, *Essays on Trade and Navigation*, 116; Habakkuk, *Marriage, Debt and the Estates System*, 503–13. G. S. Holmes notes how land prices and taxation inhibited the landed investment of the great trader Heathcote until late in life—*The Making of a Great Power* (London, 1993), 289. Only 18 (4.6%) mercantile wills mentioned manors. In this period, printed poll books which distinguish the residence and the electoral freehold of our sample include Surrey (1705), Middlesex (1705) and Essex (1715).

[74] Guildhall Lib. MSS 2480, pp. 1027, 1030. Moyer was one of only four non-metropolitan sheriffs in the whole sample. Norma Landau has noted that the Blackheath division of the Kent commission of the peace was changing in character by 1700, but notes no significant alteration to its predominant landed leadership until the 1740s—*The Justices of the Peace, 1679–1760* (Berkeley, Calif., 1984), 136–45, 316–18.

Home Counties. Taking four sample years between 1692 and 1713, it appears that while Middlesex, Surrey, and Essex saw a significant influx of merchants into the ranks of the assessors, there was no revolution in the numbers holding county office. Surrey saw the steepest rise, and this influx of traders may help to explain why there was such an animus against City-based candidates at the county elections of 1710 and 1713. However, it is hard to detect similar concerns in either Middlesex or Essex, and with merchants making a minimal impact in Hertfordshire and Kent, there was no obvious challenge to the pre-eminence of the existing landowning class.[75]

All these indices of social aspiration and advancement demonstrate that the Augustan period did not mark a dramatic watershed in the centuries-old osmotic process between land and money, most famously detailed by Defoe, and increasingly recognized by modern commentators. A tiny fraction of the new rich would seek to escape the perils of their profession and take refuge in a nearby estate, but few could have shared the illusion that land was an automatic passport to social mobility.[76] Even for the most successful merchant, social climbing was a very slow process, and in practical terms entrance into gentry society would take generations rather than a single lifetime. Doubtless many a merchant on the Exchange dreamed of a life free from the toil and worry of running his business, but the sage pragmatism of the mercantile career path informed their general social outlook. After a life spent in the City it would have been an immense wrench for many traders to leave the scene of their professional success, where their name was both known and probably respected. Colonial trader Thomas Tryon highlighted this essential attachment when he observed that 'the citizen can rarely be long easy in the country, but complains he's melancholy for want of company and knows not how to spend his time'. Accustomed to the rhythms and associations of City life, merchants predictably judged themselves and others by their own standards, and did not hopelessly pursue an amorphous 'gentility'. Without the claims of descent or connection, the self-made merchant could still achieve a comforting prominence within the context of his immediate urban environment. The more elevated standards of a crest and broad acres were not beyond the City prince, but doubts must remain whether many traders actively sought to meet them.[77]

---

[75] For lists of tax assessors, see *Statutes of the Realm*, vi. 257–7, 268, 285–6, 271 (1689); vi. 528–9, 519, 539 (1694); viii. 101–2, 106–7, 113–14, 126–7 (1702); ix. 822–3, 828–9, 837–8, 851–2 (1713). W. D. Rubinstein drew similar conclusions from a study of county JPs and lieutenants in the late nineteenth century—'Businessmen into Landowners', in N. Harte and R. Quinault (eds.), *Land and Society in Britain, 1700–1914* (Manchester, 1996), 110–11.

[76] Defoe, *Complete English Tradesman*, 366–80.

[77] *Memoirs of the Life of Thomas Tryon*, 47.

iv. Provincial parallels

Although the prospect of forging a mercantile career in a provincial town might have been a less daunting prospect than advancement in the capital, there were still considerable challenges involved. In purely financial terms, the young provincial apprentice would need fewer resources to set himself up in trade, but he would be just as careful to cultivate contacts both at home and abroad in order to make his way in the business world. Moreover, when established, the provincial overseas trader would be under much greater pressure to undertake public offices and responsibilities, such was his prominence within the more limited social orbit of the outports. Thus, even though the provinces provide more modest examples of the commercial and social success enjoyed by the late Stuart merchant, their most favoured sons were all too aware of the difficulties in building a career in overseas trade, and recognized that advancement would be linked to urban associations. Although the commercial and corporate structures of York and Liverpool were very different, the career paths taken by our two prosopographic samples provide ample evidence of a close relationship between business success and civic activity, which, in turn, had a marked impact on their perception of personal status.[78]

York will again be studied first, since it poses particularly pertinent questions concerning the relationship of commercial opportunity and the traditional structure of a regulated economy. Unlike London, where overseas traders managed to elude the civic obligation of the freedom, York merchants and all other traders were forced to become free of the city, or face a legal challenge from the corporation or the established trading companies. Throughout our period these authorities stood firm, and thus the whole of our sample shared a minimum commitment to the ancient corporate structure of the city. Having become free, the merchant might have to make a series of choices of affiliation, which would necessitate a personal assessment of the benefits and burdens of accepting additional responsibilities. In a town which continually complained of the decay of its trade and a declining number of overseas traders, successful merchants were in higher demand for service in both commercial and civic office, which pressure may even have deterred many potential recruits from setting up in business in the city. However, the sample demonstrates that the suffocating regulations of York's society and economy did not deter all newcomers, and that in general its merchants

---

[78] In recent years there have been an increasing number of prosopographical studies of provincial urban elites, but their focus has almost exclusively remained on councillors rather than merchants per se. For notable exceptions, see P. McGrath, *The Merchant Venturers of Bristol* (Bristol, 1975); G. Jackson, *Hull in the Eighteenth Century* (Oxford, 1972). Richard Grassby supplies a useful survey of available provincial data, although his figures are not specific to merchant recruitment, and (as he acknowledges) mainly relate to those apprentices who successfully became freemen—*Business Community*, 155–8.

showed considerable commitment to the wider responsibilities of their urban environment.[79]

Given the general tie of the freedom, the most obvious difference within mercantile ranks related to the backgrounds of traders, and, more specifically, whether they were York natives or not. Of the 288 merchant freemen of the 1640–1740 period, 110 (38 per cent) can be identified as York-born, and all but twelve of these natives were sons of freemen. As the previous chapter demonstrated, the proportion of native traders rose after the Restoration, and this increasing reliance on home-grown talent is highlighted by the fact that two-thirds of York-born traders were the sons of local merchants. Seventeen other occupations were represented among the fathers of native traders, but the advantage of having an existing familial interest in overseas commerce is clear to see. The greatest of the merchant houses could boast several generations of York-based trade, and in the case of the Dawsons they ran to no less than five.[80] Such continuity may suggest that the contraction of town trade made the city increasingly inhospitable to non-native merchants, but the fact remains that nearly two-thirds of the sample were not the sons of freemen. Undoubtedly the shortcomings of local genealogical sources have inflated the number of 'outsiders', but it remains clear that York, as with other early modern towns, had always relied on non-townsmen to maintain its trade. Fortunately, the apprenticeship records of York's merchant companies have survived in some abundance for the later seventeenth century, and provide evidence of both the successes and failures of the port in attracting new recruits. Table 2.3 examines the background of apprentices registered to merchants from 1680, when the town's economic decline was all too evident.

Predictably, the most important source of apprentices was the county of Yorkshire, with all three of the Ridings providing a steady stream of recruits. Several came from further afield, but York's merchants increasingly had to rely on townsmen and nearby gentlemen to provide their apprentices.[81] The town's commercial difficulties saw a steady fall in the number of mercantile trainees after 1700, and in the 1720s there were only ten indentures taken out. The prospect of commercial success, especially in comparison to the more prosperous centres of Leeds and Hull, was the principal cause of this decline in applications. Even more gloomily for the town's future, it is clear that many of these recruits never served out their time. In fact, only fourteen of the

[79] The York corporation was active in its support for guild-led campaigns against non-citizen traders until the late eighteenth century—*VCH Yorkshire: The City of York* (London, 1961), 215–18. The development of formal structures to oversee international trade are discussed in D. Palliser, *The Company of Merchant Adventurers of the City of York* (York, 1985), 1–9.

[80] For the Dawsons, see J. W. Walker, *Harleian Society*, 94 (1942), 143–4; York City Library, Skaife notes, i. 203–12, 266ᵛ.

[81] Jenny Kermode concluded that Yorkshire and northern Lincolnshire had been York's principal mercantile recruiting-ground in the late medieval period—*Medieval Merchants: York, Beverley, and Hull in the Later Middle Ages* (Cambridge, 1998), 73–7.

TABLE 2.3 *Origins of apprentices to York merchants, 1680–1720*

Town/region	Total number	Father				
		Esquire	Gentleman	Merchant	Tradesman	Other
York	39	0	11	8	13	7
Yorkshire Town	18	0	7	2	7	2
Yorkshire County	52	4	32	1	2	13
Rest of England	9	3	3	1	1	1
TOTALS	118	7	53	12	23	23

Sources: Apprenticeship records survive in the minute books of the mercantile companies at Merchant Adventurers' Hall, York—The Company of Merchant Adventurers of York, 1677–1736, fo. 225 and ff.; The York Residence of the Merchant Adventurers, 1693–1815, fo. 88 and ff.; The York Residence of the Eastland Company, 1645–97, fo. 213 and ff.

apprentices in the table became freemen of York, which remains a damning indictment on the port's ability to nurture the personal resources at its disposal.[82] There can be little doubt that opportunities were missed, for several ambitious local apprentices actually went on to become successful businessmen in the capital, most notably the Hamburg trader Francis Boynton and the Baltic merchant Philip Nesbit. Hull also appears to have benefited to some extent from recruits within Yorkshire.[83] National commentators bemoaned the wastefulness of aborted apprenticeships as a general commercial problem, and with so little new blood even venturing to take out indentures at York, these failures spelt great future difficulties for the city. By the turn of the century, York alderman Andrew Perrot was prepared to spend £300 to bind his son to a London Barbary merchant rather than seek to train him locally, thus revealing an informed concern at the future of the town's overseas trade.[84]

While these basic problems must be highlighted, it would be premature to suggest that York was not prepared to accommodate new mercantile arrivals. In fact, if the civic careers of native York traders are compared with those of merchants from outside the town, it is clear that newcomers could be rapidly

[82] *A Brief History of Trade in England* (London, 1702), argued that only one in fifteen or twenty apprentices became masters in the domestic trades. Grassby, *Business Community*, 139–40, suggests a failure rate of 50% for the major provincial towns. With regard to York's fourteen successful apprentices, there is no positive correlation between trading background and freedom-taking. However, the high proportion of recruits from gentle backgrounds may account for York's poor completion rate.

[83] Jackson, *Hull*, 99–106. Boynton was one of the many London dealers who shipped goods directly via Hull—E190/331/15.

[84] Borthwick Institute, prerogative will, Nov. 1702. Little evidence has been found concerning the cost of a mercantile apprenticeship at York, although a legal dispute from the 1660s records that the merchant Robert Hilary had been paid £100 for binding Timothy Hawksworth. The dispute suggests that York's failure to train new recruits can in part be linked to the familiar problems of indiscipline among the young—York City archives F8, p. 161.

assimilated into town society. For instance, while some 48 per cent of York-born merchants served in corporate office at or above the level of chamberlain, the corresponding figure for 'outsiders' stands at 42 per cent, and a very similar proportion from each group were prepared to take on the most burdensome commitment of becoming aldermen.[85] These rates are significantly higher than those found in the capital, and can be largely attributed to the stronger centripetal focus of York society, and the greater pressure on wealthier inhabitants to serve in local government. Several leading merchants paid substantial fines to avoid the most senior corporate offices, but their recalcitrance cannot be interpreted as a rejection of their communal responsibilities. Nathaniel Wilson, who was fined £200 to be relieved of aldermanic office in March 1705, remained a key figure in sustaining the commercial institutions of the city, and was very much prepared to fight York's corner in disputes with regional and national authorities. Although refusing to follow the mayoral example of his father and grandfather, Samuel Dawson (d. 1731) was another influential advocate for the town, and his epitaph still saw fit to record that he 'modestly declined' the civic honour. The careers of Wilson and Dawson thus reveal that they recognized that their businesses could only flourish if York's general commercial interests were preserved, even if they were unwilling to undertake all the rigours of local government. For its own part, the corporation could on occasion be sympathetic to the business concerns of its officers, granting an annual pension of £30 to alderman William Ramsden in August 1695 after he had suffered losses at sea and other misfortunes.[86]

The mutuality of interest between merchant and city is further illuminated by the activities of our sample in their private capacities. In particular, despite the town's evolution as the centre for the entertainment of the Yorkshire gentry, York merchants were not keen to ape the lifestyles of their social 'betters'. Of eighty-five identified first marriages, 60 per cent were matches with York brides, and it is significant that even the most 'gentrified' of the merchants, such as the influential Thompson family, saw the attraction of securing alliances within their traditional power base.[87] Greater traders did acquire modest country estates, but only while maintaining their York

---

[85] These must remain minimum figures, since the corporation records yield only erratic coverage of membership of the 72-strong common council—York City archives, B34-44; P. Withington, 'Urban Political Culture in Late Seventeenth-Century England: York 1649-88', Ph.D. thesis (Cambridge, 1998), ch. 3. The researches of Robert Skaife, preserved at the York City library remain invaluable for tracing corporation service.

[86] York City archives, B40, fo. 201; Royal Commission on Historical Monuments, *City of York* (London, 1972), iii. 25; Skaife notes, ii. fo. 593. For discussion of the victory of the merchants over the 'rentier patricians' within the late fourteenth-century corporation, see Kermode, *Medieval Merchants*, ch. 2.

[87] For York marriage licences, see *York Archaeological Society*, 40, 43, 46; Skaife notes, iii, fo. 739-47. For the gentrification of York, see J. J. Looney, 'Cultural Life in the Provinces: Leeds and York, 1720-1820', in Beier et al., *The First Modern Society*, 483-510.

residences at the heart of the mercantile community, and their colleagues were even less eager for a country retreat. Probate evidence once again suggests that traders were not enamoured of gentle titles, with about half of the sample's wills resting content with the soubriquet of 'merchant'. Most interestingly, in comparison with the capital there appears a greater readiness to give notice of civic honours, and corporate dignities are mentioned in more wills than the esquires and gentlemen combined. Monumental inscriptions also accord with this civic attachment, and while some epitaphs echoed the commercial values of their metropolitan counterparts, the overt appeal to mercantile patriotism was largely absent. Their more buoyant brethren at Hull were clearly more alert to national trends, with the tomb of the merchant MP William Maister (d. 1716) proclaiming him as 'so great and good a patriot'. In a more pretentious vein, several York traders bequeathed personal items emblazoned with coats of arms, but others used their merchant marks, or simply issued token rings to pass on their memory.[88]

Although it would be foolish to ignore the numerous associations which tied York to its county hinterland, to London, and abroad, the essential world of its merchants appears much more immediate in scope than that of either the capital or other outports, Liverpool in particular. As the next chapter will show, York was not without connection to the highest authorities in the land, but its diminishing commercial importance ensured that York traders were rarely prominent at a national level, leaving others to represent their interests. Three of the sample gained a knighthood, but only one even advanced to the status of city MP, and his family later rued the cost of such prominence, as election expenses conspired to undermine their fortunes. Without the wealth, and, as vitally, the contacts of the London elite, York merchants predictably became political players within a more limited orbit, and could only make a public impact with the full weight of the corporation behind them. Individuals could still prosper at York by undertaking a career in overseas trade in 1720, but the numbers endeavouring to do so had severely declined, and the rewards of success remained largely defined in terms of urban, rather than county or national status. Significantly, the close alliance of mercantile and civic communities had yet to break down, and remained a fundamental influence on the perspective of the York merchant.[89]

This impression dovetails with the frustrated commentary of local historian Francis Drake, who complained in 1736 that magistrates had guarded their

[88] T. Gent, *Annales Regioduni Hullini* (1735), 36. Most of the mercantile wills can be found at the Borthwick Institute in the records of the Prerogative Court of York. For monumental inscriptions, see the aforementioned RCHM reports, vols. iii–v, and the Skaife collections at York City library. The limited gentrification of the York merchant largely accords with Kermode's late medieval findings— Kermode, *Medieval Merchants*, ch. 9.

[89] For the electioneering of the Thompson family, which may have cost them £13,000 at the 1741 York election, see J. F. Quinn, 'York Elections in the Age of Walpole', *Northern History*, 22 (1986), 175–97.

privileges too jealously and had 'locked themselves up from the world'. His impatience was fuelled by the progress which he espied across the Pennines, and he lamented how the town had passed up on the chance to accommodate 'the late famous Mr. (William) Clayton of Liverpool, who raised the tobacco trade in that town to the greatest height it was ever at'. To Drake, Liverpool presented a significant contrast as a centre which nurtured entrepreneurial talent, and had enjoyed spectacular success as a reward for its far-sighted openness. Clayton's mercantile colleagues also appeared to recognize the importance of courting individuals, with Thomas Johnson observing in 1702 that if trade declined 'the people go too, and then you have done with the new improvements'. However, while lionizing the importance of active merchants to the urban economy, Johnson was only too aware that newcomers to Liverpool did face obstacles, even if the town lacked the constitutional baggage of chartered companies to limit participation in overseas trade. Most importantly, the Liverpool corporation was just as keen to defend the economic privileges of its freemen, and to capitalize on the wealth and influence of its leading traders. Thus, Liverpool's rise cannot be simply attributed to commercial democratization, and analysis of the local mercantile life-cycle demonstrates many parallels with the more traditional centres of York and London.[90]

The previous chapter highlighted how the number of merchants taking up the freedom of Liverpool increased significantly after 1690, with the vast majority gaining their admission by purchase or apprenticeship. By the reign of George I, the town appeared less reliant on redemptions as a means of maintaining a complement of active traders, and was consequently able to reproduce successive generations of merchants by means of apprenticeship and patrimony. Even so, the town still appeared to welcome newcomers who were able to pay substantial fines for admission to the freedom.[91] However, the mere purchase of the freedom did not commit the trader to longer-term residence, and town records suggest that many newcomers made little impact on local society. Scottish and Irish migrants may simply have been acting as temporary factors for businesses at home, and thus saw the freedom as a commercial convenience rather than as the first step towards a greater investment of time and money in the port's future. The same may be said for mercantile purchasers from towns closer to home, such as Manchester and Warrington, who could conduct their business operations at a convenient distance, perhaps

---

[90] F. Drake, *Eboracum: Or the History and Antiquities of the City of York* (London, 1736), 240; Heywood (ed.), *Chetham Society*, 9 (1846), 82. The absence of mercantile MPs remains a significant contrast to late medieval York—Kermode, *Medieval Merchants*, 47–8, 52–3.

[91] For discussion of the commercial advantages of the freedom, and the corporation's battles to preserve them, see J. Picton, *Selections from the Municipal Archives and Records* (Liverpool, 1883), esp. 79–85, 264–5, 296–305. Liverpool freemen did enjoy reciprocal trading rights with several ports on the Irish Sea, although this did not ensure cordial relations—ibid. 76–7. Defoe thought these links to be of 'some advantage'—*A Tour throughout the Whole Island of Great Britain*, ed. G. D. H. Cole (London, 1927), 666.

in partnership with a Liverpool merchant. Their role in linking the port with its industrial and commercial hinterland was undoubtedly vital to the port's growth, but these individuals did not seek to become a force within Liverpool itself.[92] Therefore, for proof of Liverpool's real openness to outsiders, it is necessary to examine the apprenticed merchants in greater detail, since this form of entry would necessitate a substantial period of local residence. Table 2.4 analyses the origins of apprentices during its second phase of expansion, when the port's reputation as a mercantile centre was well established.

TABLE 2.4 *Origins of mercantile apprentices at Liverpool, 1707–27*

Place	Total	Father status/occupation		
		Tradesman	Esquire/ gentleman	Yeoman/ husbandman
Liverpool	6	5	0	0
Lancashire	32	7	5	8
Cheshire	22	4	3	3
Yorkshire	7	3	4	0
Rest of England	14	1	6	3
Wales	2	0	1	0
Scotland	2	0	0	0
Ireland	4	1	2	0
Colonies	2	1	0	0
Unknown	9			
TOTAL	100	22	21	14

Sources: The table is compiled from Liverpool RO, 352/CLE/REG/4/1. The table does not include apprentices taken on by merchants to be trained merely as 'mariners'.

Liverpool's recruiting ground falls between the extreme cosmopolitanism of the capital and the more limited horizons of York. Its colonial and Irish Sea trade encouraged newcomers from far afield, but the most important source of apprentices remained the adjoining counties of Lancashire and Cheshire. Although imperfect in its recording of the status of the apprentice's father, the indentures suggest that in these two counties it was possible for rural families of more humble means to set their offspring up in business at Liverpool, in some contrast to York's relationship with its immediate hinterland. Significantly, despite the eye-catching connections abroad, Lancashire and Cheshire remained the source of some of Liverpool's earliest great merchants, and such

[92] For intra-urban commercial links within Lancashire, see D. M. Forshaw, 'An Economic and Social History of Liverpool, 1540–1680', BA thesis (Nottingham, 1953), 117. Once the port had grown, Liverpool merchants also took advantage of local ties to gain the freedom of other towns such as Chester and Lancaster—T. C. Hughes (ed.), 'Rolls of the Freemen of Lancaster', *Record Society of Lancashire and Cheshire*, 87 (1835), 90 (1938); J. Bennet (ed.), 'The Rolls of the Freemen of the City of Chester', ibid. 51 (1906), 55 (1908).

local recruitment highlights the enduring importance of regional ties. Apprentices of more distant origin appear to have come from more elevated social backgrounds, a trend which reflects Liverpool's growing reputation as a prosperous centre, in which gentle sons might make their own fortune. The town in fact boasted of its success in attracting these recruits, claiming in 1699 that 'many gentleman's sons of the counties of Lancaster, Yorkshire, Derbyshire, Staffordshire, Cheshire, and North Wales are put apprentices in the town'. However, once again a caveat must be entered to this seemingly limitless opportunity, since only thirteen of these 100 apprentices ever became freemen of the town, a success rate very much akin to declining York. Uncertainties surrounding the future of the freedom may have helped to limit the number of applications in the early eighteenth century, but such a high degree of failure highlights the difficulties of building a career in a new urban environment, even with the help of an established local master.[93]

The challenges facing the Liverpool newcomer are thus plain to see, and they add a more significant lustre to the achievements of the merchants who dominated the town's trade and society. However, in common with the aspirant apprentice, their success could not have been maintained without the establishment of strong local associations which could promote the endeavours of these enterprising individuals. At the Restoration, it does not appear that Liverpool could boast organizations capable of fostering sustained economic growth, and there was little prospect that it would emerge as a major international port. In particular, the ruling corporation had a distinctively genteel flavour as a result of the interference of the Crown and the local gentry. Many civic historians have chartered the corporation's subsequent emergence as an independent force, but it is only the recent work of Michael Power which has highlighted the commercial significance of having the town hall controlled by a dynamic group of traders bent on personal and communal self-aggrandisement. A vital stage in advancing this mercantile interest was taken in the early 1680s, when the corporation managed to bring to heel several recalcitrant traders who had refused to take out the freedom, a test of strength as important as any won against great local landowners such as the Molyneuxs. This battle secured the supremacy of the freedom for a crucial generation of growth, but the corporation still had to work hard to ensure that newcomers would fulfil its offices and play an active part in overseeing the town's expansion.[94]

Of the 177 merchants who took up their freedom between 1660 and 1719, about half were prepared to serve in corporation office. This figure compares

[93] Picton, *Selections*, 325–6. Nevertheless, the enrolment of apprentices from far afield highlights Liverpool's dynamism, even when compared to prosperous Hull and Bristol—Jackson, *Hull*, 99–106; P. McGrath, 'Merchants and Merchandise in Seventeenth-Century Bristol', *Bristol Record Society*, 29 (1955), 275–6.

[94] M. Power, 'Councillors and Commerce in Liverpool, 1650–1750', *Urban History* 24 (1997), 310–23. The 1680s struggle can be followed in the corporation books—Liverpool RO: MF2/3, pp. 236–43.

favourably with the success of York in attracting its wealthier inhabitants to undertake unpaid responsibilities. It is all the more impressive considering the fact that nonconformity was stronger in Liverpool, and many merchants might have been deterred from office by the penal laws. Predictably, there is a wide discrepancy in the commitment of individuals, but it is significant that the town was able to rely on freedom purchasers (presumably with little prior connection to Liverpool) to undertake the most onerous posts. Overall, freemen by patrimony or apprenticeship do appear more active than merchants who simply bought their freedoms, but prominent traders such as Thomas Clayton, John Cleveland, Thomas Coore, and Owen Prichard demonstrated that newcomers were willing, and able, to climb to the top of the corporate ladder. Increasingly, the town could rely on locally born or trained merchants to take on these responsibilities, but it was important for the town's general growth that newcomers were not excluded from town government. This observation does not suggest that Liverpool merchants lived in an idyll of unity and fraternal love, but the port's commercial interests dictated that influential traders be given a voice in their councils, whatever their origin. The presence of great numbers of merchants within the corporation might lead observers to conclude that it was a commercial oligarchy, but this would be to ignore the new blood which sustained the corporation in its earliest phases of expansion.[95]

On a more personal basis, it appears that merchants were rapidly assimilated into this evolving urban environment. Of fifty-two known first marriages, some two-thirds were to Liverpool women, an impressive rate given that the size and attractiveness of the local marriage market was dependent on the growth of the town. This endogamy helped to strengthen their ties with boom-time Liverpool, and although only 13 per cent of mercantile freemen admitted after 1660 were freeborn, over 60 per cent of them can be identified as Liverpool residents when they died.[96] As analysts of the early modern town have rightly pointed out, migration was a key socio-economic process, which helped to sustain urban populations. However, in the particular case of Liverpool, its success in retaining a potentially mobile mercantile elite was fundamental in ensuring its longer-term growth. A few traders retired to a country estate after a successful career in trade, but the most significant feature of their non-mercantile investment was the ownership

[95] P. G. E. Clemens noted the commercial importance of new capital to the sustained rise of Liverpool—'The Rise of Liverpool 1665–1750', *EcHR* 29 (1976), 219–20. As elsewhere, I am hugely indebted to Michael Power for providing biographical information on Liverpool councillors. For unpublished mercantile biographies, see Liverpool Record Office, Wakefield notes, vols. 45–47; E. Glasgow, 'Liverpool People' (transcript).

[96] For Liverpool marriage licences and bonds, see *Record Society of Lancashire and Cheshire*, 65 (1912), 69 (1914), 73 (1918), 77 (1924), 82 (1933), 85 (1935), 97 (1942). The vast majority of mercantile wills can be found within the records of the Diocese of Chester at the Lancashire Record Office. For emphasis on the transitory character of Liverpool society, see D. Ascott, 'Wealth and Community: Liverpool, 1660–1760', Ph.D. thesis (Liverpool, 1996), ch. 4.

of properties within the town and its immediate neighbourhood, where profits beckoned as Liverpool rapidly expanded. Moreover, only a handful of traders adopted gentle titles in their wills, and even one of the few self-proclaimed esquires, Richard Norris of Speke, could hardly be said to have deserted Liverpool. He may have retired to his gentle roots shortly before his death, and requested to be buried with his Lancastrian ancestors at nearby Childwall, but only did so after over thirty years of corporate service had given ample testimony of his commitment to the prosperity of the port.[97]

Norris's surviving correspondence with other Liverpool leaders reveals that signs of increasing 'concentration' within the mercantile elite did not undermine the basic associational ties between lesser and greater merchants. Undoubtedly families such as the Claytons, Johnsons, and Clevelands dwarfed their mercantile colleagues in wealth, but this did not cause them to spurn their broad responsibilities to the port. The success of these supertraders directly benefited the town, since it facilitated their role as town representatives both within the region and in the capital. As the next chapter will show, the likes of William Clayton had to work hard to earn the respect and trust of their fellow Liverpudlians, who closely scrutinized the activities of all those who acted on their behalf. The acute embarrassment (whether feigned or real) of Thomas Johnson testifies to their vigilance, for he thought that he might incur 'a great many censures' after receiving a knighthood in March 1708. This was not merely a question of petty jealousies among status-conscious townsmen, since Johnson recognized that he faced particular opprobrium for having secured personal advancement while going about the town's business. Putting his own interest before that of the town would have been a most serious crime in the eyes of his commercial colleagues, entailing a loss of local prestige for which no title could compensate. Although sensitive to local censure in the course of town affairs, Liverpool merchants also recognized that they could gain great credit for their efforts. As a sign of this, town MP William Clayton's epitaph of 1715 simply declared him to have been 'a great encourager of trade, and having good judgement in it, represented the borough in six Parliaments'. Within a generation, mercantile tombs in Liverpool claimed patriotic status for their contribution to both town and nation, Foster Cunliffe being hailed in 1758 as 'a merchant whose sagacity, honesty, and diligence procured wealth and credit to himself and his country'. The monument also paid due tribute to his magisterial prowess, thus ensuring that Cunliffe's success stood as lasting testament to the fruitful relationship between corporation and port interests in early modern Liverpool.[98]

[97] For the Norris family, see *Chetham Society*, 9 (1846), introduction. For the importance of Liverpool as a commercial and social centre for local gentry, see the diaries of Nicholas Blundell for 1702–28 in the *Record Society of Lancashire and Cheshire*, 110, 112, 114 (1968–72).

[98] *Chetham Society*, 9 (1846), 170–1; *Transactions of the Historical Society of Lancashire and Cheshire*, 59 (1908), 57, 139. Outsiders were clearly struck by the power of the mercantile elite, Thomas Patten of Warrington rebuking Richard Norris thus in 1702: 'everybody you deal with must be obliged to you for

Liverpool might not be the open society which its apologists averred, but inequalities of wealth within the town could not obscure common mercantile interests which local magnates had to respect. As merchants battled their way through the particular perils of their profession in Liverpool's expanding arena, the fortunes of both individual and town were peculiarly intertwined in a dynamic partnership which worked to ensure general benefits. Thus, although oligarchic in appearance, Liverpool's mercantile society remained essentially pluralistic in character, thereby fostering the competitive edge which drove it into the front rank of English provincial towns. Harnessing the ambitions of potentially volatile mercantile interests was a demanding challenge for town leaders, but individual traders realized that their future was bound up with that of the port, and were prepared to sacrifice time and money to achieve mutually sustaining commercial and civic objectives. Thus, even though lacking the formal mercantile structures of London and York, Liverpool provided a supportive environment in which all overseas traders could hope to prosper.[99]

This account has endeavoured to show that in order to understand the public merchant, you have to understand the private man, and appreciate how his activity was inseparably linked to business and personal associations. Brewster's portrayal of the bewildering round of engagements facing the prominently placed citizen would certainly have been endorsed by the vast majority of the merchants examined here, and can be illuminated further by the personal archives of important traders such as Sir Thomas Rawlinson (1647–1708). Alderman, East India Company director, and wine trader, he benefited greatly as the heir to a successful City business, but he had to establish his personal credentials for the impressive succession of posts he undertook in City life. It was a remarkable feat to balance those competing demands on his time, which ranged from securing the advancement of his sons, to assuring company officials in India of his support, and to attendance on the weekly chores of aldermanic office. The reward for such industriousness came with elevation to the mayoralty in 1705, when he had the honour of acting as intermediary between the Crown and the greatest city in the realm. At the end of his year in office, he confessed that 'the trouble that attends the post I am in hath been exceeded by the pleasure of doing good', and, although trite and suspect, this observation might be taken as a summary of the personal and communal benefits which public life could bring to the active

buying your goods; perhaps it['s] so in Liverpool, but it's otherwise elsewhere'—Liverpool RO, 920 NOR 2/254.

[99] A striking example of the collectivism of mid-Hanoverian Liverpool merchants remains in the form of the Ugly Club, all of whom were 'remarkable for their ugly grotesque phizzes as for their several great abilities and extensive knowledge'—E. Howell (ed.), *Ye Ugly Face Clubb, Leverpoole, 1743–53* (Liverpool, 1912).

merchant. Not all chose to follow his civic route, but none could ignore that 'something of his own trade and employment' was invested in relationships that had little overt relevance to his balance sheets.[100]

Significantly, analysis of the varying stages of the mercantile career suggests that there was no radical change in the urban associations which influenced business endeavour. Clearly, the financial and commercial 'revolutions' created new foci of business interest and power, but this did not mean that the traditional career path taken by the merchant was changing, or that customary forms of interpersonal contact had diminished in importance. Many merchants did call for fundamental change in the organization of trade, particularly with regard to government regulation, but, as ever, contemporaries met problems with tested methods as well as novel solutions. There are indeed many continuities to this era of commercial 'revolution', especially if focus is brought to bear on the men who were at the heart of economic development—the merchants themselves, who performed a variety of roles to ensure the commercial success of their urban power base. The merchant was a middleman by profession, as well as in the course of his public life, and to understand his impact, we must recognize those broader responsibilities. His objectives may have been very individualistic, but his strategy for self-advancement could never have succeeded without informal and formal connections. The next chapter will analyse how these socio-political intermediaries influenced the development of mercantile associations in the Augustan period, and how in turn these organizations sought to capitalize upon the obvious 'political' skills of the overseas trader.

[100] Bodl. Rawlinson Letters 63; D862(4), esp. fo. 89. His offices included alderman (1686–7, 1696–1708); committeeman of the East India Company (1685–9, 1690–2, 1693–8, 1700–7); master of the Vintners' Company (1687 and 1696); colonel of militia (1690 and 1705–7); and president of Bridewell and Bethlehem Hospitals (1705–8). His career as a moderate, although much-reviled, Tory is also a good example of how party passions affected office-holding and threatened to curtail urban networks.

CHAPTER THREE

Mercantile Association and Commercial Politics

'Some men's business lies abroad, and cannot be so well managed at home, and . . . these meetings of societies are advantageous to them. As first, merchants, by these clubs and meetings, have intelligence of ships going out and coming in, and also of the rates and prices of commodities, and meet with customers by accident, which possibly might never make inquiry at their homes or warehouses. The like excuses all men of business and trade pretend.'[1]

THIS lively portrait of the merchant as a sociable, ever-alert man of business was not meant to be flattering, but it serves to highlight the essential importance of association for the overseas trader. The author in fact castigated the trader for haunting taverns and coffee-houses, and exhorted him to stick to a more regular orbit, arguing that 'the Exchange is appointed for the merchant's intelligence, and his warehouse is his shop'. However, as the first two chapters have argued, the advancement of the overseas trader was determined by connections of varying degrees of formality. Even if we acknowledge the importance of the family as the primary focus of a trader's economic and social perspective, international commerce could not have functioned as a completely atomized set of mercantile units. The challenges of overseas trade, particularly to far-distant lands, would simply have overwhelmed many familial businesses, unless they could rely on the support of trading associations and government-backed organizations. The early modern town could provide the physical environment for business, in the form of the aforementioned exchanges for dealing, and warehousing for storage, but the increasing competitiveness of international commerce demanded ever more of the resourcefulness of the individual, and ineluctably forced him to rely on greater associations, and ultimately the state itself.[2]

Recognizing the importance of commercial networks, historians have been quick to study formal merchant organizations, prompted not least by con-

---

[1] R. T., *The Art of Good Husbandry, or The Improvement of Time* (1675), reproduced in J. Thirsk and J. P. Cooper (eds.), *Seventeenth-Century Economic Documents* (Oxford, 1972), 97–9.

[2] Peter Clark has recently provided a tantalizing glimpse of the huge range of commercial clubs in the late seventeenth century, and notes that a contemporary defined 'club' as a group designed 'to promote trade and friendship'—*British Clubs and Societies, 1580–1800: The Origins of an Associational World* (Oxford, 2000), 9–12, 53–4.

temporary concern about their impact on the development of English trade, and even on Augustan party politics.[3] This exciting research has highlighted the potential sophistication of the political machinery available to merchants, even though concentration on party affiliation has largely precluded a more searching examination of mercantile associations during the age of commercial 'revolution'. These studies have also been largely compartmentalized into studies of individual companies, or limited geographical areas, which approach minimizes the significance of more general developments.[4] Each trade certainly had unique demands to make on the individual and the state, but this chapter will demonstrate that mercantile associations cannot be considered in isolation, and that a rigid subdivision of trade does not take into account important coordinating agencies which gave commercial 'politics' much of its force. Beyond the companies, analysis of informal merchant organization is only beginning, and we are still unaware of the wider significance of routine collective action in the commercial world, which can be perceived in the arbitrational process used to resolve trade disputes. There remains a pressing need for studies of both the formal and unregulated sectors, and we have yet to discover how individual traders interacted with these commercial associations in order to secure influence on a wider political stage.[5]

Current economic research would suggest that patterns of commercial activity in the late seventeenth century could promote the creation of powerful associations. The most authoritative study of the organization of trade in London has demonstrated a high degree of specialization among merchants, even to the extent of a viable distinction between importers and exporters within the same geographical sphere of commerce. When combined with signs of an increasingly oligarchic trend in the control of some trades by small

[3] Although concentrating on the joint-stocks, the best general account of corporate activity remains W. R. Scott, *The Constitution and Finance of English, Scottish, and Irish Joint-Stock Companies to 1720* (Cambridge, 1919). For a brief, although illuminating, account of the development of the companies in the post-Restoration period, see C. Wilson, *England's Apprenticeship, 1603–1763*, 2nd edn. (London, 1984), 172–6.

[4] For published company histories covering the Augustan period, see A. C. Wood, *A History of the Levant Company* (Oxford, 1935); R. Davis, *Aleppo and Devonshire Square* (London, 1967); K. N. Chaudhuri, *The Trading World of Asia and the English East India Company* (Cambridge, 1978); L. S. Sutherland, *The East India Company in Eighteenth-Century Politics* (Oxford, 1952); K. G. Davies, *The Royal African Company* (London, 1957); R. W. K. Hinton; *The Eastland Trade and the Commonweal* (Cambridge, 1959); W. E. Lingelbach, 'The Internal Organization of the Merchant Adventurers of England', *TRHS* NS, 16 (1902), 19–67; E. E. Rich, *The History of the Hudson's Bay Company, 1670–1870* (London, 1958–9); J. Carswell, *The South Sea Bubble* (London, 1960). For the unregulated trades, see the path-breaking A. G. Olson, *Making the Empire Work: London and American Interest Groups, 1690–1790* (Cambridge, Mass., 1992); L. M. Penson, *The Colonial Agents of the British West Indies* (London, 1924).

[5] For an excellent example of the impact of commercial combinations on overseas trade, see H. Roseveare, 'The Damned Combination: The Port of London and the Wharfingers' Cartel of 1695', *London Journal*, 21 (1996), 97–111. The potential importance of commercial arbitration is highlighted by C. Rawcliffe, '"That Kindliness should be Cherished More and Discord Drawn Out": The Settlement of Commercial Disputes in Later Medieval England', in J. Kermode (ed.), *Enterprise and Individuals in Fifteenth-Century England* (Stroud, 1991), 99–117.

groups of greater merchants, economic preconditions would appear ripe for a similar stratification in the structures of mercantile political life. Indeed, Gary De Krey's key study of Augustan merchants politics, while remaining flexible on the subject of mercantile organization, divided the London traders into various geographical spheres of predominant commercial interest for the purpose of his analyses. This chapter will show that such associations are indeed valid at a general level, reflecting the views of contemporaries such as Nicholas Barbon, who observed in 1690 that 'the merchant is distinguished by the name of the country he deals to, and is called Dutch, French, Spanish, or Turkey merchant'.[6] However, this specialization could not preclude division within these trades, and the competitive climate of international trade hampered the cause of mutual understanding, as Jacob Price's study of 'gang' warfare within the tobacco trade has most ably demonstrated.[7] Furthermore, the organization of trade was inevitably more complex than a simple geographical model, and traders could specialize by commodities as much as by countries, becoming 'wine' or 'cloth' merchants in the process. General traders were also a significant exception to this picture, and we must recognize the wider trading circles in which the greater traders could move. Therefore, in line with the arguments of the two preceding chapters, analysis will not be confined to purely commercial associations, but will also cover institutions which acted as informal foci of commercial-political activity, the City livery companies in particular. This approach will highlight the adaptability of the merchant, and demonstrate that commercial political activity was far from restricted to the occasional appearance at the parliamentary poll.[8]

At root, this methodology seeks to establish how merchant politics really worked in an era of profound challenge for traditional commercial associations. Historians have recognized the importance of these upheavals, and have even suggested that ideological influences could intrude into the commercial sphere, as ministers avidly sought to tap the wealth and influence of the City. However, even though party interest in metropolitan affairs has been acknowledged, the impact of Whig and Tory on international commerce is much less clear. At present, we know far more about the needs of the state and its rarefied political networks than about the priorities of merchants and their collective organization.[9] From a trader's perspective, the essential *raison d'être*

---

[6] D. W. Jones, *War and Economy in the Age of William III* (Oxford, 1988), 249–73; *idem*, 'London Overseas Merchant Groups at the End of the Seventeenth Century and the Moves against the East India Company', D.Phil. thesis (Oxford, 1970), esp. 193–216; J. M. Price and P. G. E. Clemens, 'A Revolution in Overseas Trade: British Firms in the Chesapeake Trade 1675–1775', *Journal of Economic History*, 47 (1987), 1–43; G. S. De Krey, *A Fractured Society: The Politics of London* (Oxford, 1985) 121–76; N. Barbon, *A Discourse of Trade* (London, 1690), 2.

[7] J. M. Price, 'The Tobacco Adventure to Russia', *Transactions of the American Philosophical Society*, NS, 51 (1961), esp. 29–37, 62–8.

[8] For a striking portrayal of the breadth of the portfolio of Charles Maresco and associates, see H. Roseveare, *Markets and Merchants of the Late Seventeenth Century* (Oxford, 1987), esp. 17–120.

[9] For the interaction of politics and the great financial companies, see P. G. M. Dickson, *The*

for mercantile political associations remained the prosaic search for profit, for which end merchants would engage in collective activity to secure commercial benefits from the wide range of national authorities with jurisdiction over international trade. Their political activity was thus geared to access those levers of power, a stratagem of increasing difficulty during the Augustan period as constitutional change threatened the existing status quo. With the balance of power shifting uncomfortably from Whitehall to Westminster, particularly after 1689, merchants had to adapt accordingly, and the period predictably saw a major reassessment of the role of the merchant in public life. The second half of this book will be largely preoccupied with the ways in which this shift of power affected the status and influence of the merchant, but as a preliminary to these discussions it is important to see how commercial associations functioned in general. Successive governments still permitted mercantile groups to retain the initiative in formulating commercial policy, and thus trading associations were put on their mettle to secure advantage from the post-Revolutionary regimes. As sectional interests, merchant groups recognized that they faced potential indifference or hostility, and had to work hard to garner support for their particular causes. This basic challenge put great pressure on these associations, and, by extension, on the members who were burdened with the tasks of lobbying. The relationship of the individual trader with the larger mercantile association is thus crucial to our understanding of the realistic impact of mercantile politics in this age of uncertainty and change. As we shall see, merchants increasingly frequented the lobbies of Whitehall and Westminster, and thus we have to understand the organizational forces which put them there.[10]

It should it be stressed that re-establishing merchant networks on a general scale is not easy, given the paucity of individual business records, and the aforementioned fluidity of merchant life. Ascertaining the numbers of merchants active in each trade is especially difficult, particularly given the opportunities for new investment over the course of a merchant's career. Historians have made excellent use of surviving port books for the period to determine commercial affiliation, but there are serious reservations concerning their reliability as a guide to any individual's business portfolio, or especially his market share over any particular length of time. Even the

Financial Revolution in England, 2nd edn. (Oxford, 1993). For a more commercial emphasis, see H. Horwitz, 'The East India Trade, the Politicians, and the Constitution, 1689–1702', *JBS* 17 (1978), 1–18; De Krey, *Fractured Society*, 23–9.

[10] Jacob Price once characterized the Augustan period as a 'transition from court mercantilism to parliamentary mercantilism'—*Transactions of the American Philosophical Society*, NS, 51 (1961), 82. For analysis of the state's reliance on commercial wealth, see J. Brewer, *The Sinews of Power: War, Money, and the English State, 1688–1783* (Oxford, 1989); P. O'Brien, 'Inseparable Connections: Trade, Economy, Fiscal State, and the Expansion of Empire, 1688–1815', in P. J. Marshall (ed.), *The Oxford History of the British Empire: The Eighteenth Century* (Oxford, 1998), 53–77. For a more general discussion on the functional relationship of the state and trade, see M. N. Pearson, 'Merchants and States', in J. D. Tracey (ed.), *The Political Economy of Merchant Empires* (Cambridge, 1991), 41–116.

archives of the great companies have to be treated with circumspection. Membership of a regulated overseas trading company can certainly be taken as a sign of an active interest in that particular trade, but investment in a joint-stock cannot be taken as proof of close involvement. In fact, it is becoming clear that the name on the stock cannot even be taken as conclusive proof of proprietorship. These interpretative difficulties must be acknowledged in any reconstruction of the political world of the Augustan overseas trader, but the very complexity of urban society, and its essential associational culture, ensures that we can still obtain a multidimensional picture of the collective activities of a large number of individuals. Most importantly, the records for studying the *political* associations of merchants are in general more plentiful than sources for their commercial interests, thus permitting a more confident general survey of the relationship of the trader with the state.[11]

Although focusing on group activity, the ensuing sections will stress that these mercantile associations could have a variable impact on the individual merchant. Within any organization there could be huge disparities in the commitment of the traders involved, just as there could be enormous differences in the benefits accruing to its membership. Moreover, although the chapter is structured to analyse in turn the trading companies and the unregulated trades, there will be no attempt to suggest that merchants rigidly adhered to this division. When it came to making money, a sage pragmatism could quickly overturn any attachment to theories of economic regulation.[12] Ensuing analysis of mercantile networks does not assume any sense of class solidarity among merchants either, since it is clear that they were a highly competitive breed, who would not let ideals of common interest interrupt their search for profit. According to commercial commentator John Houghton, ''tis a maxim in our merchants that there is no friendship in buying or selling'. Alarmist fears were periodically expressed at the onslaught of new wealth, but such conspiracy theories conveniently ignored the difficulties of ensuring common purpose within a fast-moving and uncertain commercial world.[13]

On the other hand, the nature of the mercantile profession required multiple forms of association for traders to succeed, and encouraged regular contact between merchants which could become of more permanent political force. Early modern dealing by necessity involved a great deal of face-to-face contact, and from our limited knowledge of proceedings at the Exchange, it is clear that there could be a high degree of recognition between merchants. For instance, the merchant author Charles King claimed in 1721 that he could

[11] For discussion of the accuracy of port books, see E. B. Schumpeter, *English Overseas Statistics 1697–1808* (Oxford, 1960). For discussion of the problems of identifying share ownership, see Dickson, *Financial Revolution*, 251–3. Concern for the elusiveness of the early modern association was recently echoed by Peter Clark's major study of voluntary clubs and societies—*British Clubs and Societies*, 9–10.

[12] C. Wilson notes that the free-trade doctrine only came after the successful campaigns against the monopolists—*England's Apprenticeship*, 270–1.

[13] J. Houghton, *A Collection of Letters for the Improvement of Husbandry and Trade*, 9 Nov. 1682.

vouch for the mercantile credentials of over 400 of the traders who appeared in Samuel Lee's path-breaking *London Directory* of 1677, not to mention 'their families left behind them'. Furthermore, we must not forget that the merchant was also at the centre of a spider's web of connections involving a myriad of other trades and professions, which were vital to the success of his business.[14] Awareness of these multifarious contacts does not diminish the immediate importance of merchant organizations to the overseas trader. The simple fact remains that above and beyond the overwhelming priority of their own businesses, merchants were prepared to join together on a regular basis to pursue common objectives. Given the propensity of these mercantile interests to fragment with variable commercial circumstances, it would be very hard to ascribe to them common sociological perceptions, but in a political sense they could have a durable and effective influence. The changing political and economic landscape of Augustan England was a very real challenge to existing forms of mercantile organization, and thus provides an excellent opportunity to study their development.

i. *The formal organization of overseas trade*

Commercial commentators of all shades of opinion were united in thinking that the formal organization of overseas trade was highly idiosyncratic, a jumble of regulated and joint-stock companies existing side-by-side with areas of completely open access. Apologists for the companies might stress in mitigation the variable demands of far-flung spheres of commerce, but there remained little rationality behind the regulatory system of the Restoration period. This state of affairs reflected the turbulent history of internecine warfare within English commerce, particularly since the Elizabethan period, and this conflict remained a significant feature of the post-Restoration commercial 'revolution'.[15] Not surprisingly, historians have concentrated heavily on the tensions between proponents of a free and regulated economy, which was a dominant theme of debate concerning commercial organization throughout the Augustan period. Jacob Price's work on the battle for the Russia trade has provided a most stimulating model of mercantile association at this time, identifying three broad categories of trader in this City struggle: an 'old gang' based in the oligarchic trading companies; a 'new gang' who

---

[14] C. King, *The British Merchant* (London, 1721), i. p. xxxv. Analysis of court depositions suggests that traders could be familiar with a very wide circle of associates. For instance, in 1689 George Jackson confessed to knowing Daniel Allen 'by sight and hath but a small acquaintance with him'. Nevertheless, he knew where Allen lived—HCA13/79, 2 Nov. 1689.

[15] For the early Stuart and Interregnum battles, see R. Brenner, *Merchants and Revolution* (Princeton, 1993), esp. chs. 2 and 3; R. Ashton, *The City and the Court, 1603–43* (Cambridge, 1979), esp. 106–20; B. Supple, *Commercial Crisis and Change in England, 1600–42* (Cambridge, 1959); M. Ashley, *Financial and Commercial Policy under the Cromwellian Protectorate* (Oxford, 1934), 111–31.

thrived in the more open institutions of the 1690s; and the unregulated transatlantic traders. Gary De Krey has since argued that these affiliations were a basis for London's Whig–Tory divisions, but both scholars remain wary of rigid categorization, Price viewing these distinctions as neither 'precise nor exclusive'. This caution is well merited because ideology (whether political or economic) always had to compete against profit for the allegiance of the individual trader.[16] Nevertheless, their work has highlighted the importance of the free-trade debates for the development of mercantile association, and we need to know more about the merchant response to the challenges of the age. Mercantile attitudes towards trading organizations were inevitably complex, reflecting the variety of motivations which coaxed their membership to join. Under pressure, even free-marketeers were apt to act in a coordinated fashion, and ultimately accept the need for a regulatory body above them, as D. W. Jones has demonstrated in his analysis of the attack of the wine merchants on the East India Company in the 1690s. The inherent flexibility of the merchant politician is clear from this scholarship, but so is his dependence on broader associations, and there can be no doubt that his loyalties were tested to the full by the upheavals of the Augustan era. This section will thus undertake further analysis of the 1692 sample to probe the relationship between the companies and their members, and to ascertain why merchants could be committed to their cause.[17]

In general, the post-Restoration period is held as the nadir of the overseas chartered company, with major defeats for the cause of the monopolists across a very broad front. Of the leading companies, only the Levant managed to reach the Hanoverian age with its constitution and privileges largely intact. Economic viability had brought about the demise of the corporate activity on certain trade routes, most notably in the case of the Greenland Company, but the abrogation of others was the direct result of external assault. The Canary Company was the first major casualty, losing its chartered existence altogether in 1667, and in succeeding years the champions of freer trade scored several successes, prizing open the trade routes of the Eastland Company in 1673, the Merchant Adventurers in 1693, the East India Company and the Royal African Company in 1698, and the Russia Company the following year. The subsequent creation of the United East India (1709) and South Sea (1711) companies by governments eager for financial backing could hardly be said to have compensated for such corporate reverses, and simply demonstrated that only ministerial priorities could overcome the prevailing free-trade wind.[18]

---

[16] J. Appleby, *Economic Thought and Ideology in Seventeenth-Century England* (Princeton, 1978); 158–98; Scott, *Joint-Stock Companies*, esp. ch. 8; Price, *Transactions of the American Philosophical Society*, NS, 51 (1961), 26–37; De Krey, *Fractured Society*, esp. ch. 4; ; Horwitz, *JBS* 17 (1978), 1–17. In his forthcoming work on ideological developments in the late seventeenth century, Steve Pincus argues for a hardening distinction between Whig and Tory views on the origins of national wealth.

[17] Jones, *War and Economy*, 288–301.

[18] Scott, *Joint-Stock Companies*, i. chs. 14–21; G. L. Cherry, 'The Development of the English Free

The significance of the period for the development of associations is thus obvious, but caution should be heeded before heralding the dawning of a new era of freer trade. In particular, it is important to see that several of the reformed companies had an important role to play in eighteenth-century commerce, even though their independence had been severely compromised. In uncertain times of crippling wartime hardship, the political advantages of collective organization were evident, and even the looser associations of the colonial trades may have become more regularized in this period. Thus, closer inspection of merchant networks will show important themes of continuity within merchant politics which have been sometimes ignored by advocates of a revolution in the organization of City life.[19]

These continuities reflected enduring commercial necessities and the essential reluctance of ministers to take more direct responsibility for the advancement of English trade. Historians have argued that the decline of the companies after 1660 was linked to increasing governmental concern to take over the representation of trade at home and abroad, but it would be hard to identify any such consistent policy before 1720.[20] In fact, Hanoverian ministers continued to rely on the companies as conduits of information, and even former enemies of the incorporated system were happy to take advantage of these connections. Whatever the mercantile merits of corporate organization, the political attractiveness of the companies for minister and merchant alike was well established, reflecting the fact that the Crown had long granted privileges to incorporated groups of merchants in the belief that they would act as stewards of that trade in the general interest of the nation. Of course, these monopolies were attacked for their jealously guarded control of lucrative business, but the very success of the East Indian and Levant trades reflected the fact that the companies did perform services which were at a premium for all merchants.[21] In particular, the close relationship of the companies with the Crown highlighted the importance of executive power for the promotion of overseas trade. Whether it was a need for diplomatic representation abroad, or for a protective convoy, the companies could act as

Trade Movement in Parliament, 1689–1702', *JMH* 25 (1953), 103–19; G. Anderson and R. D. Tollison, 'Apologiae for Chartered Monopolies in Foreign Trade', *History of Political Economy*, 15 (1983), 549–66. The Hudson's Bay Company (created 1670) stands as a modest success within this era of free-trade onslaught.

[19] Olson, *Making the Empire Work*, esp. ch. 5.

[20] B. Dietz, 'Overseas Trade and Metropolitan Growth', in A. L. Beier and R. Finlay (eds.), *London, 1500–1700* (London, 1986), 130. Hinton's analysis of the declining Eastland Company suggested that the demise of the companies was a result of the government's readiness to take over many of their functions—*Eastland Trade*, 121. However, it is significant that the government was still keen to contact officers of the reformed Eastland Company under George I, over forty years after the trade had been thrown open. In 1719, the government was informed that the Eastlanders had 'now united in interest with the Muscovy Company', and would be represented by them—CO389/27, pp. 110–11, 134.

[21] For a classic analysis of the self-interest served by the companies in maintaining the market price of their goods, see Brenner, *Merchants and Revolution*, 83–9.

effective spokesmen, particularly after decades of experience in the vagaries of the English political system. Merchants recognized this, and, even when successfully challenging the justice of the company system, they strove to maintain a smooth line of communication with the powers of Westminster and Whitehall. Thus, while the privileged status of the companies might have been under fire, the advantages of a politically active commercial association were widely recognized within the capital and the provinces.[22]

Several studies have revealed how close a relationship was maintained between the state and the major companies, and their archives remain an enduring testament to the formal and informal channels which connected Westminster and the City. After 1660 the Royal African and Hudson's Bay companies actually boasted royalty among their shareholders, a presence which encouraged many peers to invest as well.[23] The East India Company lacked such direct patronage, but its fearsome reputation ensured it a generally cosy relationship with Whitehall even during one of its stormiest eras. Payments to William Chiffinch, Charles II's groom of the stole, highlighted the backstairs politicking in which the company indulged, but the prominence of some its leading officers was sufficient to merit close ministerial attention. The 'casual discourse' on East India business which took place between Sir Richard Ford and Lord Chancellor Clarendon in October 1661 was the kind of contact to which all companies aspired, and it is particularly frustrating that the archives remain so coy about these private audiences. More publicly, loans to the state would maintain cordial relations, and the companies could also be tapped for a wide range of government business abroad.[24] For their own part, City institutions would endeavour to remind the Crown of their distinctive contribution to the nation by gifts of special merchandises. The Russia Company were accustomed to giving hawks, the Eastland Company sturgeon, the Levant Company carpets, while the East India Company actually presented an elephant in 1676. Even though the rising influence of Parliament represented a major challenge to these traditional forms of political access, the executive powers of the Crown remained of vital importance for the regula-

---

[22] Significantly, John Houghton sought to rise above the free-trade debates of his day by proposing that company regulation be adapted to suit the *political* character of the trading area. Well-ordered states (France, Spain) could be left unregulated, but arbitrary states (Turkey, Russia) needed regulated companies, and vulnerable, ungoverned states (India, Africa) needed a joint-stock venture—*A Collection for Improvement of Husbandry and Trade*, 10 Jan. 1696.

[23] E. E. Rich, 'Minutes of the Hudson's Bay Company, 1671–4', *The Hudson's Bay Company Series*, 5 (1942), pp. xx–xxvii. Royal and aristocratic investors in the Royal Adventurers into Africa, founded in 1660, made up more than half its membership. However, its subsequent incarnations became increasingly mercantile in character—Davies, *Royal African Company*, 63–5. Several companies appointed royalty as governors—Davies, ibid., 156; Rich, ibid., pp. xvi–xvii; Carswell, *South Sea Bubble*, 58–61. The Levant Company turned to aristocratic governors from 1673 onwards—G. P. Ambrose, 'The Levant Company, mainly from 1640–1753', B.Litt. thesis (Oxford, 1933), 414–17.

[24] *Calendar of the Court Minutes of the East India Company, 1660–3* (Oxford, 1922), 114, 134. The best study of the politics of the East India Company after 1660 remains P. Loughead, 'The East India Company in English Domestic Politics, 1657–88', D.Phil. thesis (Oxford, 1981).

tion of overseas trade, and thus Whitehall retained an especial appeal for the incorporated City sector. After the Revolution their royal charters appeared vulnerable, and companies increasingly had to learn the difficult arts of parliamentary management, but the Crown remained a vital ally, whose influence was assiduously courted by all mercantile interests.[25]

Although these continuities must be recognized, it is still true to say that the merchants of our sample were on the threshold of one of the key periods of change in the structure of London commercial life. The financial revolution of the stock market in the 1690s provided businessmen with a giddying selection of avenues for investment, several within the sphere of overseas trade, and the decade also saw perhaps the deepest examination yet of the advisability of organizing overseas trade by monopolistic companies. Thus the commercial allegiance of merchants would be tested to the full, as they sought to make a profit amidst the difficulties of a war-weary economy. For the historian, the profusion of such investment choices provides an excellent opportunity to espy the priorities of the merchants, and, more importantly, to assess the actual function of City institutions. A recent sociological analysis of investment in City joint-stocks under William and Anne highlighted the possibilities of the period, espying party motivations among some investors in times of political crises. Due to the study's overwhelming fiscal interest, the fundamental mercantile objectives of these trading organizations were somewhat underplayed, and we have yet to achieve a full appreciation of the motivations of company supporters. Using the 1692 sample, analysis will start with the individual, in an effort to detect the essential attraction of companies for their membership.[26]

In terms of overseas trade, the merchants of our sample had the choice of entering four major regulated companies (the Levant, Russia, Merchant Adventurers', and Eastland companies), or investing in four joint-stock companies (the East India, Royal African, Hudson's Bay, and Greenland companies).[27] Together, these institutions controlled a vast sphere of world

[25] Guildhall Lib. MSS 11471/2, pp. 169, 182, 191; Hinton, *Eastland Trade*, 152; SP105/153, fo. 186; *Calendar of the Court Minutes of the East India Company, 1674–6* (Oxford, 1935), p. xxxvii.

[26] Horwitz, *Continuity and Change*, 2 (1987), 267–9; B. G. Carruthers, *City of Capital: Politics and Markets in the English Financial Revolution* (Princeton, 1996). Unlike Carruthers, De Krey saw the essence of 'Whig' investment in a commercial context, thereby acknowledging the frustration felt among merchants at the lack of opportunities for reinvesting surplus wealth in the 1690s—*Fractured Society*, 134–5. For recent emphasis on the importance of the development of the joint-stocks before 1689, see A. M. Carlos, J. Key, and J. C. Dupree, ' Learning and the Creation of Stock-Market Institutions: Evidence from the Royal African and Hudson's Bay Companies, 1670–1700', *Journal of Economic History*, 58 (1998), 318–44.

[27] This survey has not included the short-lived Company of Merchant Adventurers to North-West America, whose founding charter of 1691 included ten of the sample—*CSPD* 1690–1, p. 527. For the overwhelming significance of mercantile investment in the public funds (including the East India and South Sea companies) from the 1690s onwards, see Dickson, *Financial Revolution*, 253–84. For examples of the sample's investment in non-mercantile ventures in the 1690s, most notably the Copper Mines Company, the Irish Royal Fishery, and the Company of Glass-makers, see *CSPD* 1690–1, pp. 459,

trade, even while leaving the way clear for their countrymen to trade to the Americas, the Caribbean, North Africa, and a host of European countries. The decision to enter a company would reflect a multiplicity of factors, relating to the personal circumstances of the individual, and the character of the institution. As the previous chapter pointed out, for a young trader just out of his apprenticeship, his initial choice of trade would be predominantly determined by familial background or the identity of his master, but with experience and capital came greater opportunity for the merchant. Foremost in the mind of all traders was the likely profitability of joining such a company, and in general the timing of company admission by our sample suggests that the economic health of the organization was the crucial factor in determining recruitment. The secrecy with which the companies went about their business revealed an acute sensitivity over their commercial repute, but indices of economic vitality, such as stock values or commodity prices, were widely available to City merchants, who could thus make an informed assessment of company prospects.[28]

While these general observations can be made, an important distinction must be drawn between the commitment of membership to a regulated company and that demanded by a joint-stock. Regulated companies, which were in essence loose associations of merchants trading on their own capital, would only appeal to merchants planning to engage directly in the company's sphere of commerce. Admission fees could be most prohibitive, and in order to protect markets for their members these companies had traditionally accepted only 'mere merchants', i.e. overseas traders.[29] Joint-stocks, on the other hand, did not impose high entrance fines, and investment in the stock was the principal requirement for joining the company. Set limitations on the company's total stock was the most immediate bar to admission, and ensured great resentment among outsiders should the stock prices and dividends prove lucrative. However, the joint-stocks proved far more open to new investment, and could boast a very catholic membership, ranging from great merchants to the more leisured classes of the peerage and gentry. Given these essential constitutional differences, it is clear that the commitment of individuals to commercial organizations could vary enormously, particularly over time. The

540–1; 1691–2, p. 3. More generally, see C. T. Carr, 'Select Charters of Trading Companies, 1530–1707', *Selden Society*, 28 (1913).

[28] Davies, *Royal African Company*, 160–1, has shown that the weakness of the company could be obscured by the eminence of its stockholders. In the case of the African Company, its decline (from the late 1670s) was only mirrored by the diminishing quality of its stockholders in the early 1690s.

[29] For instance, in March 1670 the Levant Company ruled that a mere merchant was defined as an individual who had only practised merchandising for at least the preceding year—SP105/3, fo. 18ᵛ. The Hamburg Company ruled that retailers had to give a year's notice of quitting their profession before joining as a merchant, and then could not return to retail for five years—W. E. Lingelbach, *The Merchant Adventurers of England: Their Laws and Ordinances with Other Documents* (New York, 1971), 115–16. The Eastland Company expected members to have 'traded at home and abroad . . . merchantlike' for 'some good continuance not less than three years'—Hinton, *Eastland Trade*, 56.

diarist John Evelyn is a good example of the passive company member, who held East India stock for over twenty years with little attention paid to the company's affairs. At the other end of the scale were the likes of Sir Josiah Child, Sir Thomas Vernon, or Sir John Ward, all of whom played a very public role as champions of their particular corporate causes. The impact of the latter is more familiar to historians as the recognizable 'face' of City interest, but the diversity of commitment within these institutions must be recognized. Adversaries perceptively observed that in practice the companies tended to degenerate into closed oligarchies, but it would be unwise to discount the influence of the wider membership.[30]

Fortunately, surviving company records can provide a more informed picture of mercantile commitment to the regulated and joint-stock trades. Thus, Table 3.1 examines the relative commercial 'allegiances' of three of the four major regulated companies, whose records provide a realistic picture of their membership. Comparison is made here on the basis of the first company which the merchant joined and those of which he became a member in the subsequent course of his career.

TABLE 3.1 *Membership of overseas trading companies within the City sample*

Company (of 1st membership)	Only 1 company	+1 regulated company	+1 joint-stock	+2 other companies
Eastland	16	16	8	7
Levant	47	14	17	4
Russia	14	14	8	1
TOTAL	77	44	33	12

Sources: Hinton, *Eastland Trade*, 221–5; PRO, SP105/152–6; A40/1–2, A43/1–2; T70/186–8; Guildhall Lib. MSS 11741/1–4; BL, Oriental and India Office MSS B36–50; Harleian MSS 7497–8; *Statutes of the Realm*, vi. 405–10; *A List of the Names of the Subscribers to a Loan of Two Millions* (1698).

Although lacking any data from the Merchant Adventurers' Company, the table immediately reveals the proliferation of commercial allegiance possible within the City. From this evidence, it would appear impossible to talk meaningfully of durable, independent company 'interests', since it is clear that in the course of a career a trader could have several, perhaps competing, mercantile loyalties. Potential conflict of interest may have caused a reduction in cross-company commitments in sensitive areas of trade, for instance in the case of the Levant and the East India companies. Prominent individuals such

[30] *The Diary of John Evelyn*, ed. E. S. De Beer (Oxford, 1955), iii. 201–3, 365, iv. 297. Members of regulated companies could also vary in their commitment, Levant trader Henry Ashurst being 'ashamed' to admit in 1687 of 'never much appearing in the company'—Bodl. MSS Don.c.169, fo. 56.

as Lord Berkeley acted as an informed intermediary between the two City giants, but periodic clashes, most notably that of the early 1680s, could only have led to a stricter segregation between them.[31] However, the diversification of merchant investment in general served to encourage smoother relationships between the companies, rather than engender antagonism. When the bottom line of any merchant's commitment to his commercial institution was profit, there is no reason to doubt his readiness to defend each and all of his investments when threatened. The point was succinctly put by a provincial branch of the Merchant Adventurers that although the trader 'cannot serve two masters, yet he may be free of two companies, and use a good conscience to them both'. Company development in the later seventeenth century would bear out this testimony, since attacks on corporate privileges in general came from outside the company sector, and were not the result of inter-company disputes. The ties of mutual interest between the companies were in general far stronger than their differences. Moreover, as the table makes clear, beyond the issue of privilege there were evidently strong personal connections helping to smooth relations between these organizations.[32]

A significant proportion of the overlapping personnel in Table 3.1 were the predictable consequence of regional commercial interests. Most notably, the opening up of the Russia Company in 1699, when admission fees were lowered from over £50 to just £2, saw an influx of Eastland Company members keen to exploit new markets to the Baltic. More occasionally, specialists in certain exports might join a company in a bold effort to gain new markets. In this regard it is particularly unfortunate to have so few records survive for the Merchant Adventurers' Company, which almost certainly would have revealed even greater proliferation of allegiance among traders seeking outlets for English cloth.[33] In the course of a career a merchant had to be extremely flexible if he was to avoid ruin during the depressions which

[31] Loughead, D.Phil thesis, 134–46, 158–9. Berkeley, when governor of the Levant Company in March 1686, informed his fellow East India officers of the Turkey merchants' forthcoming attack on imported Indian textiles—Oriental Library, B38, fo. 204. Inter-company investment in a joint-stock has been analysed by K. G. Davies, who discovered that in 1675 a quarter of Africa stock was held by Levant members, while Northern European and colonial merchants were also prominent— *Royal African Company*, 66–7.

[32] M. Sellers, *Surtees Society*, 129 (1917), p. lxvii. The minute books of the overseas trade companies betray little formal contact with each other, and common interests only rarely promoted coordinated action, such as the export of cloth in 1686, or customs house abuses in 1700—Oriental library, B38, p. 216; SP105/156, p. 22. Significantly, companies endeavoured to avoid overt hostilities by pretending to be unincorporated merchants. For example, the petition of London merchants against the Russia Company in December 1697 was immediately recognized as the work of the Eastland Company by the beleaguered Muscovites—Guildhall Lib. MSS 11471/2, p. 202.

[33] The Merchant Adventurers represent a very important omission since it claimed 'about 400' members in England in 1691—PC2/74, 219. For a survey of the company's post-1660 development, see E. K. Newman, 'Anglo-Hamburg Trade in the Late Seventeenth and Early Eighteenth Centuries', Ph.D. thesis (London School of Economics, 1979). She notes that the Hamburg residence itself fell from 40 to 13 in the course of 1691–1728; p. 289. An impressive list of their honorary members survives—Add. MSS 28079, fos. 59–60.

periodically hit all trades, and several found it necessary to join a series of companies. The small group of merchants who can be identified as members of more than two regulated companies include some of the leading names in Baltic and Mediterranean trade such as Sir Benjamin Ayloffe, Sir Thomas Vernon, and Sir Joseph Woolfe. These prominent traders are the closest to earning the soubriquet of 'general merchant', even though they only became a dominant force in one sphere of commerce. Their number was necessarily limited by the forbidding economic challenges of conducting multi-regional trade, but their connections with several companies were of undoubted significance within the world of London commercial politics. Jacob Price has shown how 'informal' groupings of traders could develop around a few notable individuals, who could engineer associations 'bound together by kinship, partnership, and previous business experience'. In fact, their prominence within the City was directly related to their ability to act as go-betweens between the compartmentalized units of England's regulated economy. Influential outsiders could also learn to respect these metropolitan grandees. In particular, the preference of Whitehall governors to work through personal contacts enabled them to become political brokers, ready to act as a conduit for City opinion across a wide spectrum.[34]

The major free-trade victories of the Augustan age worked to promote such commercial brokers, allowing merchants to enter other companies with a minimum outlay of money or other commitment. The reality of such change is demonstrated by analysis of company recruitment during the free-trade assault. Table 3.2 records the admissions of our sample to three regulated companies, marking the Glorious Revolution as a convenient dividing-point from which to chart Augustan trends.

TABLE 3.2 *Admission to regulated companies by the City sample*

Company	Patrimony	Service	Purchase	Gift	Uncertain	Total
Eastland						
pre-Revolution	9	6	43	0	0	58
post-Revolution	2	2	24	0	0	28
Levant						
pre-Revolution	13	31	20	1	9	74
post-Revolution	2	9	15	0	10	36
Russia						
pre-Revolution	1	6	0	0	1	8
post-Revolution	1	1	78	0	2	82

Source: Guildhall Lib. MSS 11892; 11741/1–4; PRO/SP105/152–6.

[34] Price, *Transactions of the American Philosophical Society*, NS, 51 (1961), 26–37.

The high proportion of merchants who simply bought their way into these companies is the surest sign of their increasing accessibility. The failure of the Eastland and Russia companies to retain high admissions fees in 1673 and 1699 respectively opened the floodgates to a much greater number of merchants, who could easily afford the 40 or 50 shilling fees, and saw this outlay as a reasonable exchange for the benefits of membership. The general demise of patrimony and apprenticeship as a method of entry was an inevitable accompaniment to the increase in purchased admissions, and signalled the decline of an oligarchic trend within the companies. The Levant Company was the last real bastion of a strictly regulated admissions policy, insisting on the requirement of 'mere' merchanthood, and on the production of the City freedom before contemplating the acceptance of any applicant. Several studies have commented upon the special character of the company, in which the passage of a family business through several generations was not unrare, and tight control over admission procedures evidently facilitated this continuity. However, the company was not inhospitable to newcomers who were willing to pay up to £50 for admission, and company leaders knew that the most effective bar to a host of new entrants was the forbidding expense of setting up as a trader to the Near East. Only in 1754 would they suffer the fate of the other regulated companies and bow to the call for lower fees, and until that time they maintained a special distinction within the City as an institution of limited access.[35]

Predictably, the relationship of the sample with the joint-stock companies reveals no patterns of comparative clarity. In general, the decision to invest in a joint-stock would involve little more than the initial purchase, and their commitment to company affairs could be limited to the perusal of prices listed in the press, attendance at the occasional meeting of shareholders, and the odd conversation with their broker. More encouragingly for the active merchant, the East India and Africa companies did license some private trade by their members, but the numbers involved were not great, and such commerce was limited to a few commodities. In the special case of the East India Company, Whig and Tory ideology may have had a limited impact on the investments of some of our sample in the highly charged political atmosphere of the City in the latter 1690s, and perhaps in 1710–13, but it would be unwise to place too much emphasis on the longer-term influence of party allegiance. In general, the relationship of most merchants with the stocks was largely pragmatic, ruled by the likelihood of a dividend pay-out, rather than the more pressing need to establish the right to trade in a specific geographic area. This is not discount the passions which the joint-stocks could engender, such as were raised after 1689 by discussions over the future of the East India and

---

[35] Davis, *Aleppo and Devonshire Square*, 60–74; De Krey, *Fractured Society*, 141–4; Brenner, *Merchants and Revolution*, 72–4. For a good example of the costs of avoiding membership of a major company, see Roseveare, *Markets and Merchants*, 41–4.

Royal African companies, but the advantages to be drawn from the stock were by nature different from those expected of a regulated company, and merchant investment reflected this distinction.[36]

Despite the essential differences between the general membership of the regulated and joint-stock companies, it is possible to make meaningful parallels about the commitment of individual traders at the level of the boardroom. Although admission policies might differ, the essential governance of all the City companies was remarkably similar, with the daily running of corporate business left in the care of a small board of annually elected directors and senior officials. These officers were directly responsible to the company membership for their actions, but general meetings of freemen or stockholders were infrequent, and in their absence these boards would take full responsibility for the advancement of the company's affairs. Thus, these officers were burdened with very important duties, a fact recognized by the companies themselves when setting minimum stockholding requirements for their committeemen or directors. The commitment of the traders who staffed the boards of directors could not be left to chance, and these posts were far from sinecures or political appointments.[37] Attendance on the business of equipping the great ships which sailed to distant continents was a most challenging task, and ensured that all the companies evolved sophisticated organizational systems to prepare for these voyages. It was common to have committees for finance, correspondence, shipping, sales, purchases, and overseas administration; all of which required smooth integration for the longer-term success of the enterprise. Moreover, all companies found it necessary to appoint ad hoc committees to attend to urgent business, particularly when political assistance was required. On top of this committee work, routine board sessions were frequent and attendance strictly enjoined. Leaders of the East India Company met over 100 times a year, and attendance records published at the time of the annual spring elections bespoke the significance of diligence in office. Even the more humble Hudson's Bay Company required its handful of assistants to meet c. 60–80 times a year, concentrating their efforts into a few months of voyage preparation. Thus, to be a member of the board revealed a real commitment to the trade in question, and predictably it was the more dynamic of the directors who came to personify the companies in the eyes of the City.[38]

When joint-stock and regulated companies are taken together, at least 148

[36] Davies, *Royal African Company*, 109–12. Significantly, Carruthers concludes that mercantile investment in the stocks was more profit-oriented than in the case of the gentry—*City of Capital*, 191.

[37] Recognition of the responsibility of office resonates from a pamphleteer of 1691, who delineated a tripartite division of the East India Company membership according to commitment to the stock: managers of the trade, ex-managers, and basic adventurers—Loughead, D.Phil. thesis, 308.

[38] For analysis of the domestic organization of the companies, see in particular, Davies, *Royal African Company*, 153–65; Wood, *Levant Company*, 205–11; Chaudhuri, *East India Company*, 22–39; Carswell, *South Sea Bubble*, 48–53; E. E. Rich (ed.), 'The Minutes of the Hudson's Bay Company, 1679–82', *The Hudson's Bay Company Series*, 8 (1945), pp. xi–xvi.

TABLE 3.3 *Company officers and the 1693–4 assessment (City sample)*

Assessment	Number	% of total company officers	Number in tax bracket	% of tax bracket
Under £200	2	1.4	96	2.1
£200–99	24	16.2	179	13.4
£300–99	28	18.9	146	19.2
£400–99	23	15.5	96	24.0
£500–99	39	26.4	94	41.5
£600+	17	11.5	43	39.5
Unrecorded	15	10.1		
TOTALS	148	100	654	22.6

Sources: The table has been compiled mainly from surviving company minute books, which are listed among the sources to Table 3.1. The only serious omission here is once again the Merchant Adventurers' Company.

merchants of our sample (17 per cent) can be identified as officers in the major overseas trading companies.[39] Within this group there are wide disparities of tenure, some remaining in office for merely one year, while several spent decades at the helm of their firms. Given the demands of these officers, and the inherent uncertainties of a commercial career, this variation in personal commitment is to be expected. Although these duties would ultimately work to their professional advantage, it cannot be assumed that merchants would commit so much of their time to these posts. The companies themselves were not unmindful of the burdens which they placed on their principal officers, providing allowances to encourage attendance at meetings. Even the powerful East India and Levant companies struggled to maintain loyalty to the corporate cause, and had to bully prominent merchants into accepting office. For instance, in April 1664 Sir William Thompson had to take on the governorship of the East India Company despite 'his public occasions, which take up much of his time', while the Levant Company showed even less consideration in February 1687 when re-electing a recalcitrant Sir John Buckworth as deputy-governor for the seventeenth time. More positively, the opportunity for influencing the councils of such major City concerns, and the personal status accorded to presence at the board, were much more efficacious in persuading the greater merchants to devote their time to company affairs.[40]

In fact, the companies were fairly successful in attracting the support of the City's leading merchants, and Table 3.3 suggests that even in an age of freer

[39] These figures must again be regarded as minimum totals due to the limitations of certain company archives, most notably those of the Merchant Adventurers and the Eastland Companies.

[40] *Calendar of the Court Minutes of the East India Company, 1664–7* (Oxford, 1925), p. 31; SP105/155, fo. 16ᵛ. Economic interest did not guarantee diligence to office in the eyes of City journalist James Whiston, who, when discussing the organization of a mercantile council of trade, envisaged an attendance rate of only 40–60%—*A Discourse on the Decay of Trade* (London, 1693), 5–6.

trade a substantial number of London merchants were prepared to play a leading role in the overseas companies.

The broad correlation between wealth and active commercial leadership is striking, and further supports the idea that the late Stuart period saw 'concentration' in its organization. However, even allowing for the fluctuations in the wealth of individuals, the table reveals that the boardrooms of the City were not the exclusive domain of the super-rich traders, a finding which suggests that the company electorates had other criteria in mind than mere wealth when choosing their leaders. Commercial experience and diligence to duty were equally important as recommendations for office as a fortune made in trade, even though personal success would evidently impress mercantile colleagues.[41] Company charters paid indirect tribute to these fundamental requirements, insisting on a limited rotation of officers in order to relieve the burdens on individuals while maintaining continuity in the direction of the trade. Adversaries were quick to condemn such practices as proof of increasing oligarchy, but there was a sound commercial imperative underpinning this regulation. In fact, the company constitutions were most concerned to counteract the influence of potentially overmighty members, although they recognized that a great magnate could prove of direct benefit to their membership. For instance, the East India Company may have appeared ill-served by its controversial leaders Sir Josiah Child and Sir Thomas Cooke in the 1690s, but there can be little doubt that the personal influence of these supertraders had performed singular service for the company in the recent past. Economic muscle and commercial privilege were the basic strengths of the companies, but they needed leaders who could fight their corner in various arenas of political power, and thus the calibre and connections of officers retained a great appeal for the incorporated electorates.[42]

Potentially of greater concern for the proponents of commercial freedom, it appears that several corporate leaders were directors of more than one City institution. Within the office-holding cadre of our sample was an elite of forty-six merchants who achieved high office in more than one company. They are almost exclusively to be found in the £500-plus bracket for stocks, and the apparent necessity for such wealth highlights the difficulty of achieving pre-eminence in more than one trade. Unless blessed with considerable reserves of capital and spare time, the leaders of the regulated companies would find it nigh on impossible to devote their energies to the stewardship of two trades. In the case of the joint-stocks, the requirement for officers to possess sizeable company investments ensured that only the very wealthy

[41] In order to defend the commercial competence of the Royal African Company in 1709, Charles Davenant actually provided pen-portraits of all twenty-four directors—*The Political and Commercial Works*, ed. C. Whitworth (London, 1771), v. 264–8.

[42] On Child's political skills, note the argument of Loughead, D.Phil. thesis, 184–5. The attachment of the companies to certain national figures doubtless reflects their desire to maintain continuity in political access.

would be able to gain such advancement. In 1711 legislation was passed to debar City magnates from simultaneously holding directorships in the East India Company and the Bank of England, but these moves reflected political and financial priorities, rather than any real concern for a tightening oligarchy within English commerce. None of the companies saw fit to pass by-laws against multiple directorships, recognizing that they were only within the grasp of the very few, and there were many practical obstacles to the establishment of merchant empires within the City.[43]

Although the government had its own agenda in moving to legislate against dual directorships, their concern reflected an acute assessment of the general importance of such officers in late Stuart England. The elite forty-six merchants of our sample included many of the nation's leading traders, whose commercial prosperity had helped to earn them prominence in civic and national circles. Despite the onerousness of the tasks of running a company, sixteen of this group found time to serve in Parliament, and several more attained national office. This activity ensured them a high public profile, and over half gained the recognition of a knighthood or a baronetcy. Although nationally prominent, they did not neglect their London base, since some three-quarters of these company officers were City freemen, and most of them were prepared to act in some civic capacity. Indeed, their prominence was essentially founded on their ability to act as brokers between commercial, civic, and national authorities. Thus, even if committed to the service of their commercial organizations, which remained a key element of their elevated status, they had to serve non-commercial 'constituencies' if they were gain maximum political impact. These brokers were nothing new in the politics of English commerce, and their survival bespeaks the vitality of traditional forms of trading association amid a period of great upheaval in City organization. Despite the startling shock which the free-trade assault had delivered to the company system, and wider constitutional change within the state, personalities retained an importance as coordinating agencies within the fractured world of overseas trade, and from this perspective there was no revolution in commercial politics. With the exception of the Canary Company, the combined offensive on the monopolists had failed to remove the essential structures of corporate life, and there was little attempt by the members of the reformed companies to temper their oligarchic constitutions. All companies maintained strong democratic features in the form of annual officer elections, but the administration of their affairs was left in the hands of a powerful few, who would come to represent the public face of the company in its dealings with other authorities.[44]

Crucial to the maintenance of this status quo was the attitude of successive governments, who showed little inclination to become more involved in the

[43] Holmes, *British Politics*, 178; De Krey, *Fractured Society*, 239–41.
[44] For discussion of early Stuart 'brokers', see Brenner, *Merchants and Revolution*, 89–91.

daily affairs of trade, and preferred to deal with small groups of merchants to secure the support of the City at large. Government attitudes to trade regulation will be examined at greater length in the second half of this book, although here it may be noted that in spite of many experiments the daily interaction between the commercial world and the executive did not change fundamentally. The relationship between merchants and the legislature was far more unpredictable and problematic, but Chapter 5 will show that the trading companies were able to adapt to a more permanent and powerful Westminster assembly. Increased parliamentary activity did not mean that corporate groups were less dependent on individuals or small committees to fight their cause, and thus external change did not necessarily advance the case for internal corporate reform. For their own part, merchants found that the reformed companies were well adapted to the cultivation of state support, and that the sanction of a parliamentary statute was an even more effective means to secure special consideration than their former royal charters. This perspective does not ignore the serious misgivings which corporate leaders retained about some of the reforms enforced upon them, but they were undoubtedly glad to see that the success of their interloping rivals had seen little change in the way in which the companies went about their business. The experience of our sample certainly suggests that it would be unwise to have too structured an impression of company and non-company men, or even of 'old gang' against 'new gang', for it is clear that all merchants could see the advantage of preserving a special corporate tie to the state.[45]

Of course, while the company records provide us with an insight into the often sophisticated mechanisms of large-scale mercantile organizations, due proportion must be given to their impact on the merchant population as a whole. Despite frustrating lacunae in corporate archives, it is clear that the majority of overseas traders were predominantly active in the unregulated trades, especially to continental Europe and the Americas. Table 3.1, although lacking any returns from the Merchant Adventurers of England, suggests that only one in five merchants joined regulated companies. The numbers investing in the joint-stocks were predictably much greater, but the variable nature of their investments makes it difficult to credit them as active members of those trades on a longer-term basis. However, records of the political activity of the unregulated trades survive in adequate numbers to permit a general survey of an undoubtedly powerful force within City life.

[45] Government attitudes towards the representation of merchant views are discussed in Ch. 4, section iii. For Price's own caveat concerning the old/new gang distinction, see *Transactions of the American Philosophical Society*, NS, 51 (1961), 31–2.

ii. The unregulated trades

The hundreds of merchants who commanded the trade routes to the North American colonies, the Caribbean plantations, the Mediterranean, and much of continental Europe, rank amongst the most dynamic element of the period of 'commercial revolution', their successes seemingly defying the need for an organizational framework to oversee their activities. Several attempts had been made to enforce company governance in these areas, particularly in the early Stuart period, but the Restoration saw their continued demise, most notably in the case of the Greenland, Bermuda, and Canary companies.[46] Instead, as the work of Alison Olson has suggested, the initiative for supplying political services for these trades appears to have come from the merchants themselves, working in tandem with the planters, traders, and governors of the countries with which they dealt. However, while the Olson thesis brings much important method to the apparent madness of the unregulated trades, there has as yet been no attempt to test her ideas with respect to trades outside the Americas. Moreover, the welcome breadth of her work has raised many issues concerning Augustan mercantile activity which she could not hope to cover in any detail. This section will thus seek to test out her ideas, and consolidate our understanding of the workings of these loose associations within a fluid City environment. Further research may in fact give more credit to the government's initiative in promoting organizational discipline among traders, as ministers sought to benefit from their expertise and connections. In this light, the distinction between the regulated and unregulated trades becomes even less apparent on closer inspection, and it is clear that significant interaction occurred between the two sectors, especially on a personal basis.[47]

Before attempting to bring order to the unregulated sector, its less disciplined characteristics should be acknowledged first of all. For all the encouraging signs of merchant association which Olson lists, such as the signing of petitions, the emergence of coffee-house foci for social and political integration, and subscription societies, it is reasonably clear that the unregulated trader thrived on his independence, and that any attempt at a stricter organizational framework might be resisted. Particularly in wartime, both merchant and administrator often lamented the indiscipline of the unregulated traders, who spurned the potential benefits of coordinated commercial operations in order to secure markets ahead of their rivals. This

---

[46] Scott, *Joint-Stock Companies*, ii. 69–75, 288–97, 379; C. A. J. Skeel, 'The Canary Company', *EHR* 31 (1916), 529–44. For the early Stuart period, see in particular P. Croft, 'Free Trade and the Commons, 1605–6', *EcHR* 2nd ser., 28 (1975), 17–27; Brenner, *Merchants and Revolution*, esp. chs. 3 and 4.

[47] Olson, *Making the Empire Work*, esp. chs. 2–6; also *idem*, 'The Virginia Merchants of London: A Study in Eighteenth-Century Interest-Group Politics', *William and Mary Quarterly*, 3rd ser., 40 (1983), 363–88; J. M. Price, *Perry of London: A Family and a Firm on the Seaborne Frontier, 1615–1753* (Cambridge, Mass., 1992), 52–9, 72–90. Penson, *Colonial Agents of the British West Indies*, retains particular value as a study of the development of mercantile politics in 1660–89.

competitiveness has to be acknowledged alongside their common interests. Moreover, although the leaders within each trade can be identified with relative ease, since they often became the official agents for merchants and colonists abroad, the apparent order which they instilled into merchant politics may well have been compensating for the half-heartedness of their colleagues, who might even agitate against them if their own interests were directly threatened. In this regard, the possible conflicting allegiance of other associations must be considered, whether of a mercantile or non-commercial character. As Olson and Price suggest, when religious, social, and economic ties coalesced, such as in the case of the Quaker merchants trading to Pennsylvania, then a durable political force might be identified. However, indicators of social and political interaction suggest that merchants could be at the centre of a very wide network of contacts, which could counteract the impact of loosely constructed trading associations.[48]

More encouragingly, it is clear that common trading interests worked to ensure that informal associations could become of more permanent force. Especially in wartime, when the pressures working on merchants escalated, there was much greater need for mercantile coordination to ensure that strained resources were applied to best effect for the defence of trade. However, even in this context, political coordination could not be taken for granted, and in this process the government could be instrumental in galvanizing the overseas trader into collective action. Although mercantile petitioning impresses as a sign of business concern to influence policy-making, the government itself usually sought to gauge commercial opinion by engaging certain well-placed overseas traders on an individual basis. Furthermore, collective merchant action must be placed within the context of the hundreds of petitions addressed to government departments from individual traders or small cartels seeking personal redress. These appeals rarely raised the general issues championed by the companies or semi-formal commercial associations, but they nevertheless made traders very conversant with the political machinery of Whitehall. This broader perspective in fact enhances the potential dynamism of the merchant politician, and such activity also highlights the challenges confronting the commercial lobbyist wishing to discipline his unregulated colleagues towards a common goal.[49]

In order to ascertain the effectiveness of the unregulated trades in the

---

[48] J. M. Price, 'The Great Quaker Business Families of Eighteenth-Century London: The Rise and Fall of a Sectarian Patriciate', in R. S. Dunn and M. M. Dunn (eds.), *The World of William Penn* (Philadelphia, 1986), 363–99. Olson does suggest that mercantile associations were not as strong as ethnic or religious links, and that they could be riven by internal divisions—*Making the Empire Work*, esp. 55, 72, 92. For discussion of the fragility of mercantile communities overseas, see G. B. Nash, 'The Early Merchants of Philadelphia: The Formation and Disintegration of a Founding Elite', in Dunn and Dunn, *World of William Penn*, 337–62.

[49] P. Crowhurst, *The Defence of British Trade* (Folkestone, 1977). In 1692 alone, 29 of the sample transacted private business with the Treasury—*CTB*, ix.

political sphere, analysis has been undertaken of 279 London petitions from the 1660–1720 period, all of which addressed a general commercial issue rather than an individual cause. No attempt can be made to suggest that they are uniquely representative of merchant activity, but they do cover a wide range of sectional interests, as well as huge range of mercantile affairs. Moreover, these addresses were directed to an assortment of executive and legislative authorities, most notably the monarch, Houses of Parliament, and the Board of Trade. Unlike the representations of the trading companies, which in this period were usually signed by a leading company official on behalf of its membership, the numbers of signatories of 'unregulated' petitions could number over 300, and thus can provide a great deal of information concerning the mechanics and passions of these trades over key commercial issues. Frustratingly for historians, little hard evidence has emerged of the ways in which these petitions were organized and collected, but the scale of the sample will allow certain insights into this important political process.[50]

Before examining the patterns which emerge from the thousands of signatures within these petitions, some prefatory remarks should be made about their reliability as a guide to the activities of the unregulated traders. Most importantly, caution must be employed when considering their claims to representativeness. Particularly over divisive issues, merchants were apt to make exaggerated boasts of their universal support as a means to deceive unsuspecting authorities. On a more practical basis, the widely acknowledged problems of gaining signatures ensured that lobbyists struggled to gain a full complement of traders affected by their campaign. There were certain venues where signatories could be found fairly easily, most notably the walks of the Exchange or the taverns and coffee-houses nearby, but the collection of names could involve a bothersome trip around the City, and perhaps into the suburbs and certain rural retreats too. When the Board of Trade made periodic demands for information and opinion from London merchants, they were often greeted by requests for extra time to permit consultations with mercantile colleagues, especially during the summer when the seasonal pre-occupations of business and leisure tempted merchants away from the City's stifling atmosphere. In 1691 the authorities were actually requested not to summon traders on Fridays, with 'most of the considerable traders being out of town at the end of the week'. Thus, although Olson is right to see certain foci of business as facilitators of merchant interaction, it would be unwise to assume that the unregulated trades enjoyed a well-oiled political machinery, finely tuned to suit the conflicting demands of independence and common interest. In fact, their organizational engines often had to be kick-started by government before they sprang into life. For instance, when postponing a

---

[50] About two-thirds of the petitions can be found among the Board of Trade papers at the PRO, esp. class CO389. Other important collections include the House of Lords main paper series and the State Papers, Foreign.

decision on the fate of the Cadiz consul in mid-1675, the Council of Trade encouraged Spanish merchants to 'in the meantime . . . meet among themselves in order to come the better prepared in this matter'. In contrast, the trading companies appear much more sophisticated in political organization, and it was entirely predictable that the unregulated trades were forced to produce their most effective lobbying to overcome the trading privileges of their chartered rivals.[51]

A general survey of the identity of the petitioning groups suggests that geographic specialization was the guiding principle in the organization of the unregulated commercial world, just as it was in the regulated sector. Some three-quarters of the petitions were issued in the name of a regional interest group, while the rest came from a miscellany of specific commodity traders, none of whom have left more that the occasional record of a coordinated foray into public activity. The most well-represented geographic areas in this sample are predictably the important trades to North America and the Caribbean, with especial prominence given to those merchants handling Virginian and Maryland tobacco, Newfoundland fish, and Jamaican and Barbadian sugar. These findings endorse Olson's and Price's account of the vibrant activism of the colonial trader, but it is important to note that the merchants trading to Italy, Spain, and Portugal appear equally adept at co-ordinating their activities. Elsewhere in Europe, the unregulated trades appear rather mute, although the dominant influence of the chartered companies in certain areas was an important inhibiting factor. The records of central government and Parliament indicate that many petitions have not survived, but these sources also suggest that these surviving addresses do not present a radically inaccurate impression of the relative political activism of specific trades. Thus, even though the sample cannot give a precise picture of the mercantile lobby of Augustan London, they can illuminate its workings.[52]

The most striking feature of the sample is the proliferation of petitions after the Revolution, with nearly three-quarters submitted after 1688, but this pattern on its own cannot be interpreted as proof of increasing organization among independent traders. While Chapter 5 will show that unregulated traders became a significant lobby in the late Stuart Parliament, the sample cannot provide a comprehensive account of the incidence of mercantile petitioning, and its representativeness is necessarily conditioned by the chance survival of records. More importantly, the clustering of addresses in the 1689–1713 period was evidently a direct consequence of war-induced

---

[51] CO388/1, p. 271; CO388/2, fo. 350; CO388/18, no. 90; CO388/17, nos. 38, 82, 86; CO389/3, p. 12. For reservations concerning the reliability of petitions, see J. M. Price, 'Who Cared about the Colonies? The Impact of the Thirteen Colonies on British Society and Politics, c.1714–75', in B. Bailyn and P. D. Morgan (eds.), *Strangers within the Realm* (Chapel Hill, NC, 1991), 405–6.

[52] Virginia and Maryland supplied 30 petitions in this sample, averaging 19 signatures; Jamaica, Barbados, and the Leeward Islands 61 (mean 19 signatures); Newfoundland 16 (mean 29 signatures). When combined, Spanish, Italian, and Portuguese traders yielded 84 petitions (mean 25 signatures).

hardship, and did not necessarily signal a long-term change in the political sophistication of the unregulated trades.[53] These considerations must also inform more specific issues, such as the relative political activity of the trades. In general, it appears that the prosperity of each trade was crucial to the timing of these petitions, since they were designed to address particular common grievances, and collective merchant action would vary in accordance with perceived commercial difficulties. Without a clear mandate for coordinated activity mercantile associations proved noticeably sluggish. Most significantly, in an age when political groups of all kinds increasingly published their opinions on great occasions, merchants were not apt to congregate to sign addresses commemorating events such as battles or the royal accessions. Traders did sign such addresses, but only as officers in urban government, and not as a commercial entity. This distinction is important, since it highlights the fact that the purpose of association was crucial in defining the identity of the lobby, and commercial interests found it difficult to maintain unity if the common goal was not clearly defined.[54]

As importantly, such organization would almost certainly be linked to the expectation of success, and the task of coordinating unregulated traders often hinged on the perceived likelihood of overcoming the suspicions or ennui of government officials and MPs. As the experienced lobbyist Sir William Hodges lamented to the secretary of the Board of Trade in May 1714, he had yet to contact several important Spanish traders since some were 'in the country' and others were 'apprehending such discouragements in their trade that they desire to be excused'. His observation hints at the possible unpopularity which merchant leaders could earn if the government was unresponsive to their demands, or should the lobby espouse controversial views. A constant intercourse with Whitehall did not necessarily guarantee a fruitful relationship for either merchants or ministers, and both groups could express frustration with each other's motives and priorities. Nevertheless, even groups who made few addresses, such as the Geneva or Norway merchants, could not fail to recognize the importance of maintaining access to powerful authorities. Their inactivity could simply be attributed to the lethargy of the traders themselves, but it more plausibly reflected the government's lack of urgency in supporting those trades, especially when its attention might be distracted by the hundreds of thousands of pounds of customs revenue rolling in from American tobacco

[53] Number of petitions: 1660–89: 33; 1690–9: 85; 1700–9: 87; 1710–20: 57; undated: 17. The sample cannot provide an adequate number of subscribed parliamentary petitions to substantiate Olson's claim that Parliament provided a more dependable focus for mercantile petitioning than executive bodies. Access to the requisite power, rather than personal connections, appears to have ruled the strategy of the mercantile lobby—*Making the Empire Work*, 6.

[54] The companies, with their closer ties to the Crown, did present commemorative addresses. However, the mass petition appears a feature of Hanoverian mercantile politics and not that of late Stuart London. Note, in particular, the petitions of 1744 (542 signatories) and 1760 (810 signatories)—Chapman, *Merchant Enterprise*, 30.

or West Indian sugar. Refined by constant communication with the authorities, the arguments of the lobbyists from these lucrative trades are as striking in their consistent claim to national fiscal importance as for the monotony with which the same names appear as signatories.[55]

While this collective action is impressive, it appears that the unregulated trades failed to produce any lasting organizational structures before the mid-eighteenth century. In their absence, the success with which merchants coordinated their political activities must be related to the initiative of the traders themselves, especially the leaders of their respective trading groups. Olson identified a 'core group' of merchants within each interest, and credited it with a key role in harnessing the political potential of their mercantile associates. Jacob Price has provided an excellent account of the brokership of the Perry family within the tobacco trades, but historians would still like to learn more about their organizational methods. It may safely be assumed that in general these leaders had natural claims to pre-eminence within their trade by dint of their personal fortune, market share, and connections both at home and abroad. With these recommendations, a merchant could effectively play the role of representative of his trade, and such recognition clearly informed the choices made by the colonial assemblies for their London agents.[56] The colonial petitions were usually headed by the official agents, many of whom served in that capacity for a number of years, such as Bastian Beyer for Antigua, or Sir Bartholomew Gracedieu for Jamaica. Their outstanding leadership could also be espied within the unregulated European trades, with Sir William Hodges and Sir James Doliffe frequently acting as the contact for the Iberian traders, while former consul Sir Samuel Stanier and Sir Charles Peers publicly endorsed the grievances of the Italian merchants. There are tantalizing signs that metropolitan traders were encouraged by authorities to elect some of their colleagues to oversee the enforcement of mercantile policy, such as the allocation of seamen to ships under convoy. This democratization, if widely practised, would have worked to curtail the growing influence of the greater merchants in certain trades. The sources are largely silent on such matters, but in general it appears that the 'core group' could not afford to ignore the wishes of their colleagues. When dealing with government officials, leading traders often confessed their fear of misrepresenting fellow merchants, and it is clear that the petitioning process was as important for establishing a common front as for communicating it to others.[57]

---

[55] CO388/17, no. 5. Jacob Price has shown that even the powerful colonial lobbies could only expect to influence specific reforms, rather than general government policy—Bailyn and Morgan, *Strangers within the Realm*, 395–436.

[56] Olson, *Making the Empire Work*, 55–6, 103; Price, *Perry of London*, 52–9; Penson, *Colonial Agents*, 114–36.

[57] In October 1691, the allocation of seamen for the transatlantic marine was managed by four traders, who had been 'nominated' by the commissioners for customs and 'unanimously chosen by the Virginia and Maryland traders'—CO1/68, fo. 201. After long-term residence in London, merchants

The maintenance of a close personal connection with Whitehall appears a most important priority for the unregulated trades. Although many petitions impress with their long lists of signatures, their organizers were as concerned with the quality of their supporters as their simple number. In particular, the reassuring inclusion of leading traders would aid any application to Whitehall. In the course of routine Treasury and Customs business, the leading figures in the unregulated trades could become very familiar to civil servants and even ministers, who were accustomed to meeting with small deputations of mercantile leaders to resolve disputes. The configuration of the signatures within the petitions reflect the manner in which such commercial business was handled. It was common practice for the most prestigious of the traders to sign immediately below the petition, generally to the right hand side of the page. The lead of a well-known trader would encourage others to join the lobby, and would also warn government officials of the importance of the issue raised by the address. This pre-eminent position was often taken by government contractors or colonial agents, clearly in the hope that personal recognition would influence the relevant authorities. The significance of such positioning was not lost on the merchants themselves, many of whom were quite prepared to ignore the symmetry of the roster of names to insert themselves at the head of one of the columns. On the other hand, some petitions remain curiously unbalanced in appearance, possibly as a result of the failure of the organizers to attain the signature of an important trader for whom they had courteously left a space of some prestige. Most significantly, when copying petitions to circulate their contents, government officials were usually careful to copy out the spacing of signatures exactly as they appeared in the original.[58]

While it was important for petitioners to impress the authorities with the eminence of their supporters, they also saw the benefits of gaining as many signatures as possible to strength their case. Solomon Merret, a tireless supporter of the Newfoundland fishery in the early eighteenth century, actually felt constrained to apologize for being the only merchant of note to champion its revival, admitting that 'it may seem strange that none of London besides myself rarely appear in this matter, unless it be considered that few merchants here besides myself are concerned thither this year'. Further illustration of the need for numbers comes with the embattled defence of the Russia Company in the latter 1690s, whose leaders, stung by the charges of exclusivity levelled by their interloping rivals, managed to gather together every surviving member to muster a half-respectable thirty-two traders. This remains a rare example of a trading company mustering its support on paper in this period, but it highlights the onus on a petitioning party to appear the voice of a

could be very reticent when asked to venture opinion concerning trading conditions overseas—CO388/18, no. 89; CO388/19, no. 114; CO389/23, pp. 145–7.

[58] Price is thus right to see the upper-right corner as the accustomed position of honour, but the larger petitions posed particular problems for assuring traders of a respectable spot—*Perry of London*, 53.

particular merchant community. In general, most of the petitions from specific regional trades numbered less than thirty, and very often below twenty, but when a divisive issue came to the boil, numbers could rise well above this, and extra support would be sought from the provinces or from the English factories abroad. However, it is significant that overseas traders chose to act as distinct commercial interests, especially when they could have sought subscriptions from concerned individuals in the manufacturing, retailing, or primary industries. The only real exception to this rule was the colonial traders, who were apt to join with planters to advance common grievances. Most merchants stood aloof from other economic interests, often conniving at the submission of other petitions, but appearing eager to represent their views independently. The advanced specialization of metropolitan trade may partly explain such distinctive petitioning, and City merchants were always keen to stress their particular expertise as justification for their stance on the matter at hand. National authorities, although suspicious of mercantile motives, also appear to have supported this politics of specific interest, reluctantly accepting that overseas traders possessed a uniquely informed view of their respective spheres of commerce. In this case, City practice presents a definite contrast with provincial petitions, in which the overseas traders were often submerged by mass subscriptions of all the local inhabitants affected by the fortunes of a certain trade.[59]

Although the general organization of trades by geographic specialism must be acknowledged, attention must also be given to petitions which crossed these well-established lines of demarcation. Their existence does not invalidate the overwhelming importance of specific interest groups, but demonstrates the fluidity of commercial political allegiance, and highlights the fact that there were forces working for coordinated mercantile activity within the City. Most importantly, these petitions reveal that there were issues of common resonance for overseas traders, which could promote collective activity on a very wide basis. The apparent efficiency with which the geographic trades could organize their lobbying was undoubtedly tied to basic mutual interest, and the fact that most merchants at this time were still tied to a single trade deterred collective commercial activity on a wide scale. Nevertheless, on occasion the City could rise above its divided interests and give an uncompromising expression of its unified discontent.[60]

The protection of trade fell naturally into this category of widespread concern, even though, under government direction, the issue was generally handled on a trade-by-trade basis. However, the intense pressure of the wars

---

[59] *CSP Col.* 1702, p. 599; Lords main paper series 1275, fo. 85; 1366, fo. 64. For examples of provincial petitioning, see section iv of this chapter, and Ch. 5.

[60] Olson's description of associational interest groups as 'competitive, co-operative, overlapping' accurately represents the complex dynamics of mercantile politics, but further research is needed on the nature of these integrative forces—*Making the Empire Work*, 6.

of William and Anne saw mercantile anger over the inefficiency and under-funding of convoys manifest itself in mass petitions. For instance, in November 1692 a general petition of London merchants, shipowners, and ship captains represented their anguish over recent losses to the House of Commons, which was forced to appoint a committee of inquiry to assuage City fears. Unfortunately, the original petition does not survive to analyse the leaders of this campaign, but other important addresses reveal that the independent trades were capable of significant interaction when roused. On occasion, there is even evidence of active cooperation between the unregulated and regulated trades, such as a petition of 1690 which praised William III for maintaining higher duties on aliens who exported English goods. Dominating the eighty-nine signatories were Levant, Hamburg, and Eastland company members, evidently drawn together by their mutual interest in securing the country's vital export of woollen manufacturers. However, there were also key figures from the American trades such as Micajah Perry, and the important West Indian merchant William Wrayford, both of whom shared a common interest with the company men. Similar influences lay behind another major petition of 1693, which was signed by sixty-four leading merchants in the name of 'the cloth exporters'. Although only eleven signatories of the 1690 petition appended their name, there was once again a strong representation of Levant and Hamburg merchants, and this time they managed to secure the support of a significant core of Mediterranean merchants to strengthen their cause.[61]

These examples highlight the importance of a common cause for achieving coordinated action within the City, but they also pinpoint the key role played by those individuals who could overcome the accustomed parochialism of London's trading groups. The value of their leadership is most apparent in addresses such as that of November 1707, when 153 City merchants from the Mediterranean, American, and Caribbean trades joined to protest at the inadequate convoy protection provided during the War of the Spanish Succession. This lobby helped to stir up a major political furore, in the course of which ministers found great difficulty in disciplining their accustomed mercantile supporters. Most interestingly, further evidence of significant political coordination between these unregulated trades was demonstrated by the subsequent emergence of a novel 'Newfoundland interest', which put immense pressure on the government to secure an advantage against the French in the closing years of the war. This change of heart was a welcome tonic for the lone voice of Solomon Merret, who had the satisfaction of heading petitions of up to fifty traders, boosted in particular by the presence of some of the City's leading Mediterranean merchants, eager to seize the lucrative fishing grounds from the French. In this campaign, great merchants

---

[61] H. Horwitz, *Parliament, Policy, and Politics in the Reign of William III* (Manchester, 1977), 105–6, 116; SP8/8, no. 27; Lords main paper series 692, fo. 33. Henry Roseveare notes that 294 traders signed a petition against the dominance of a cartel of wharf-owners in 1705—*London Journal*, 21 (1996), 98.

such as Samuel Shepheard, Sir William Hodges, and Sir James Doliffe emerged as effective brokers for a wide spectrum of overseas traders, articulating their concerns to ministers and civil servants, who in turn used them to gain information about the commercial matters at issue. For all the merchants concerned, these relationships were a workable substitute for the establishment of a regulated company, and could reap valuable political dividends in return for relatively little commitment of time or money.[62]

Given sufficient motivation, it is clear that the loosely associated trades were capable of very sophisticated organization and discipline. Perhaps the most significant illustration of their potential are the early records of the New East India Company. D. W. Jones has demonstrated that in origin this cartel was a group of wine merchants who wished to take on one of the City giants in order to invest surplus trading capital in wartime. Although only a band of some twenty traders, their political skills more than made up for their lack of numbers. Over the course of a seven-year campaign, they proved most adept at finding influential friends in Westminster and Whitehall, coordinated extensive petitioning and pamphleteering, and secured first-rate legal counsel to argue their case. However, the generic independence of their steering committee caused many problems, most notably a repeated failure to secure attendance. Moreover, the group had to acquire various corporate characteristics to sustain their campaign, finding it necessary to hire rooms to provide a convenient base, to make financial demands on their membership, and to enjoin committeemen to keep their debates secret. In all these ways they were imitating the company whose monopoly they were seeking to overthrow, and the pressures evidently told on a membership unaccustomed to such strictures. That they were ultimately successful in their aim pays ample testament to the discipline of their cause, but it would be dangerous to infer from their example that the unregulated trades were as efficient in their general organization. An element of coordination was welcomed as a means to gain favour from government and to protect common interests, but private business and other competing personal loyalties would inhibit the establishment of firm associations.[63]

This section has stressed the extraneous factors which could promote collective merchant activity, beyond the more straightforward bonds of a common commercial interest. When merchants in the same trade could rightly look upon their fellow traders as rivals as much as brethren, it is not surprising that external pressures were a precondition of coordinated effort.

---

[62] Lords main paper series 2401, fo. 1; W. Cobbett (ed.), *Parliamentary History of England* (London, 1806–20), vi. 603; CO194/24, no. 7. For discussion of the contentiousness of the Newfoundland Trade, although with little discussion of the London lobby, see R. G. Lounsbury, *The British Fishery at Newfoundland* (New Haven, 1934), esp. chs. 6–8. D. W. Jones notes that wine merchants had often invested in the Newfoundland trade in the 1690s, but their political support for the trade can only be traced to the reign of Anne—*War and Economy*, 269.

[63] Jones, *War and Economy*, 295–301; Horwitz, *JBS* 17 (1978), 1–17; Bodl. Rawlinson MSS C449.

Whether inspired by the prestige of leading traders, or encouraged by government intervention, these associations remained extremely fluid in both form and membership. As Olson has rightly suggested, the City's social and commercial environment was geared to serve these distinct interests, whether formally via the walks of the Exchange, or informally through the establishment of coffee-houses dedicated to the indulgence of specific trading groups. In this respect there may well be many forms of association whose commercial importance has yet to be uncovered, for instance the City's county feasts or its pot clubs.[64] Although these assemblies were overtly apolitical, contemporaries remarked on their widespread importance, and apologists argued that such conviviality was essential for advancing their businesses. Given the fluid bonds within the unregulated trades, these organizational foci could have played a significant role in advancing general commercial interests, although it is notoriously difficult to pinpoint their precise influence. The next section will briefly analyse one such type of City structure, the livery companies, each of which acted as a City forum providing the 'institutional' informality attractive to both regulated and unregulated traders. The electoral privileges of the liverymen have alerted historians to their parliamentary significance, but their socio-political character must also be recognized, particularly as their brand of corporatism was rightly attuned to respect mercantile independence.[65]

iii. The livery companies

The study of political relationships through company records and petitioning remains an important corrective against too atomized an impression of commercial organization, but these associational influences did not exist in a social or institutional vacuum. In particular, due credit must be given to the unique spider's web of formal and informal contacts which each merchant enjoyed. Historians have been rightly suspicious of their ability to reconstruct the effective 'world' of the overseas trader from fragmentary personal records, principally because of their inability to ascertain the precise significance of a range of contacts in any general context. The records of a few prominent individuals do survive to give an insight into the general circle in which a City

[64] For insights into the political significance of the county feasts, see N. E. Key, 'The Localism of the County Feast in Late Stuart Political Culture', *Huntington Library Quarterly*, 58 (1996), 211–27; *idem*, 'The Political Culture and Political Rhetoric of County Feasts and Feast Sermons, 1654–1714', *JBS* 33 (1994), 223–56.

[65] For contemporary accounts of London clubs, see Thirsk and Cooper, *Seventeenth-Century Economic Documents*, 97–9; J. Macky, *A Journey through England in Familiar Letters* (1714), i. 189–90. For analysis of more formal organizations, see N. Rogers, 'Clubs and Politics in Eighteenth-Century London: The Centenary Club of Cheapside', *London Journal*, 11 (1985), 51–8; H. Horwitz, 'Minutes of a Whig Club', *London Record Society*, 17 (1981); D. Allen, 'Political Clubs in Restoration London', *HJ* 19 (1976), 561–80. For a recent reappraisal of the role of the coffee-house, see S. Pincus, 'Coffee Politicians Does Create: Coffee-Houses and Restoration Political Culture', *JMH* 67 (1995), 807–34.

leader could move, and their wide orbit impresses as an indication of their potential influence in contemporary society. However, less thought has been given to the ways in which institutions might have shaped, or were influenced by, the existing bonds between City merchants. In this context, the livery companies are of especial interest, since they retained an overtly political role, and were popular with merchants well into the eighteenth century. Furthermore, as a crucial stepping-stone for a career in City politics, they can highlight the social and political influences abetting or inhibiting the organization of trading interests in Augustan London.[66]

Although hierarchical, the structures of the livery companies mirrored the fluid organization of mercantile society, and historians have encountered understandable difficulty in charting their influence through formal and informal channels. These associations faced fundamental problems in the later seventeenth century, with growing opposition to their regulation of trades, and widespread financial difficulties, particularly after the Great Fire. Such challenges have led some historians to belittle their importance as foci of London life, and it has been recently suggested that new forms of voluntary association attracted the City elite of the late Stuart and Hanoverian era.[67] However, as Chapter 2 demonstrated, the livery companies remained central to the organization of City public life, and still managed to recruit the greatest of merchants after 1660. Membership of a livery company was clearly not a prerequisite for prominence within the trading world, but large numbers still enlisted, most evidently as a boost to business and reputation. The fiscal and legal advantages of the freedom of the City were an obvious incentive, but the civic sphere also provided access to informal influence and favour, conveniently situated as the livery halls were for after-hours socializing. Historians have rightly concentrated on the importance of the livery as a means to gain the parliamentary vote, but the broader socio-political role of the companies needs to be highlighted. The experience of the sample suggests that attitudes towards the companies were far from tied to the simple issue of the franchise, and merchants were ready to incur heavy fines to avoid the livery. For instance, in 1678 French trader Abraham Caris offered to pay the Leathersellers' Company £25 for the privilege of remaining a simple freeman. It was not absolutely necessary for an overseas trader to ascend the corporate ladder after gaining the freedom of the City, and this element of choice must

---

[66] Brewer, *Sinews of Power*, 237–42. For a brief survey of the constitutional development of the livery companies in this period, see I. Doolittle, *The City of London and its Livery Companies* (Dorchester, 1982), 1–20. For a stimulating discussion of the continuing importance of the companies, see J. P. Ward, *Metropolitan Communities* (Stanford, Calif., 1997). Carruthers also noted their 'considerable organizational vigour'—*City of Capital*, 185.

[67] T. Reddaway, *The Rebuilding of London after the Great Fire* (London, 1940), esp. ch. 9; J. R. Kellet, 'The Breakdown of Guild and Corporation Control over the Handicraft and Retail Trade in London', *EcHR* 2nd ser., 10 (1957–8), 381–94; Clark, *British Clubs and Societies*, 23–4, 35, 154. For their political travails, see M. Knights, 'A City Revolution: The Remodelling of the London Livery Companies in the 1680s', *EHR* 112 (1997), 1141–78.

TABLE 3.4 *Merchant admission into the City livery companies (City sample)*

Company	Total	Method of admission			
		Patrimony	Service	Redemption	Unknown/ Uncertain
Mercers	57	7	33	12	5
Haberdashers	30	3	20	5	2
Drapers	28	6	12	8	2
Merchant Taylors	26	3	17	5	1
Grocers	25	1	9	2	13
Fishmongers	22	0	12	8	2
Clothworkers	18	4	11	1	2
Vintners	15	2	5	3	5
Skinners	12	3	4	3	2
Ironmongers	10	1	8	1	0
Dyers	10	0	7	1	2
Shipwrights	10	0	0	7	3
Salters	8	1	2	0	5
Embroiderers	8	1	2	1	4
Leathersellers	6	2	3	1	0
Weavers	5	0	2	0	3
Others					
(11 companies)	31	1	2	11	17
TOTAL	321	35	149	69	68
%		11	46	21	21

Sources: Most livery company records used in the compilation of this table can be found in the Guildhall Library, although several prominent companies still retain their archives, including the Mercers. The London poll books for 1710 and 1713 were also very useful for identifying mercantile liverymen.

be recognized, since it reflects the appealing flexibility of these traditional City institutions.[68]

Surviving records do not always permit a complete picture of the liveried merchant, but the continuing significance of the livery hall can be inferred from general patterns of recruitment. At least 321 (38 per cent) of our mercantile sample can be identified as liverymen, and their distribution is analysed in Table 3.4, which also distinguishes their mode of admission by patrimony, apprenticeship, and redemption.[69]

The general favouritism of merchants for the most prestigious of the City livery companies conforms to traditional recruitment patterns. In particular, the premier livery company, the Mercers, had long been associated with

[68] Leathersellers' Company MSS, court minutes 27 May 1678.

[69] The only other major survey of Augustan merchants identified 42% of a sample of 1,339 traders as liverymen—De Krey, *Fractured Society*, 128–9. A further 113 (13%) of our merchant sample can be identified as City freemen, but have not been linked to a City company.

London's commercial elite, and its membership reflected its pre-eminent status. However, while it has been argued here that City repute was keenly sought by the overseas trader, the heavy concentration of merchants in the traditionally regarded great twelve companies cannot be attributed to status considerations alone. When deciding whether to enter a City company, there were evidently several factors playing on each merchant's mind. As already stressed, for certain trades, most notably those governed by the Levant, Eastland, Russia, and Merchant Adventurers' companies, the freedom was an absolute prerequisite, and there would be pressure on the wealthy trader to assume a prominent role within a livery company commensurate with his general City standing. However, each individual had to balance against this confirmation of status the costs of admission and livery fees, as well as the likelihood of civic responsibilities. Therefore, livery companies had to provide some attraction for wealthy merchants, who, although having no livery company of their own, could choose to spend their time and energies as members of other City associations.[70]

Most interestingly, there is much evidence to suggest that certain livery companies were successful in attracting recruits from particular spheres of trade, according to geographic or commodity specialisms. For instance, when Anthony Cornwall sued for his freedom in June 1689, he chose not to enter the Clothworkers' Company, the livery of his master, 'but dealing in tobacco desires his freedom in the Company of Grocers', the current home of the Bristows, and at least three other leading Virginia traders. For their own part, it is clear that the Grocers' Company were keen to enlist the leading specialists in their sphere of commerce, going out of their way to poach a well-connected future MP from the Haberdashers in the early 1690s.[71] Other companies reveal similarly suggestive clusters of merchants. A third of the Merchant Taylors of our sample can be linked to the Iberian and Madeiran wine trade, while at least a third of the Fishmongers were cloth merchants. Most significantly, nearly half of the mercantile Mercers were also members of the Levant Company, thereby reinforcing both the superiority of the premier livery company, as well as the distinctiveness of the Turkey traders. Merchants such as Caleb Hooke were willing to pay fines of £50 to switch from his company of apprenticeship (the Haberdashers) to the Mercers. The fact that at least a fifth of the merchants in Table 3.4 were prepared to pay higher redemption fees to enter companies illustrates the careful deliberation which accompanied the merchant's choice of livery, as well as the flexibility of the system in general. Many factors would be involved in his selection, but membership patterns do suggest that civic ties could bolster trading associa-

---

[70] For excellent studies of the prominence of the Mercers' Company, see I. Doolittle, *The Mercers' Company, 1579–1959* (London, 1994); J. Imray, *The Mercers' Hall* (London, 1991).
[71] Freeman petitions can be found at the CLRO, esp. CF1/23, no. 166; History of Parliament, 1690–1715 section, draft biography of Edmund Boulter.

tions, helping to bring together smaller groups of merchants united by commercial or familial interests. Thus, while it is impossible to segregate all the mercantile livery into such neat geographical or commodity areas, they do appear as an important source of political connection in the mercantile sphere.[72]

Although the aforementioned movement between companies is highly significant, admission patterns indicate that the choice of company was still heavily influenced by the young merchant's master. Nearly half of the liveried merchants were made free by service, simply following in the civic footsteps of their mercantile tutor. Very often there existed a familial tie between master and apprentice to render the company even more attractive, and the livery hall could indeed become a home-from-home for certain merchants. While familial connection is a predictable feature of choice of company, a more interesting pattern emerges concerning the importance of ethnic ties, with several lesser companies appearing popular with immigrant merchants, most notably the Shipwrights and Embroiderers. The concentration of several trading dynasties in the companies is highly illustrative of the potential sociability of merchants within City institutions, which bolstered the more assured bonds of marital ties within their circle. An excellent example concerns the extended Huguenot network of the Houblons, Lethieulliers, Denews, and Carbonnels, all of whom could boast members of the Dyers' Company. Livery membership undoubtedly reinforced ties between four of the leading lights of the Threadneedle Street congregation, even though the French church took priority over the company as the topographical hub of Huguenot life. Nevertheless, the proximity of Dyers' Hall, off Thames Street, like all the leading mercantile companies, was sufficiently accessible for overseas traders to involve themselves in its activities. The extensive use of the company halls for private and group celebrations could only have helped to cement professional and personal ties within trading circles still further.[73]

While membership patterns suggest that the livery halls did provide a semi-formal associational focus for merchant groups, it is important to stress that the companies did not play an overt role in the politics of overseas commerce. John Brewer and others have recently highlighted the importance of the livery companies for promoting the parliamentary campaigns of artisan and retail-

---

[72] I. Doolittle noted a rise in freedom redemptions after the 1690s, and linked it to the desire of 'outsiders' to participate in City politics—'The Government of the City of London, 1694–1767', D.Phil. thesis (Oxford, 1979), 31–2. Olson sees political significance in the fact that active colonial traders accounted for 22% of the liveried merchants in the 1690s (according to De Krey's figures)—*Making the Empire Work*, 33.

[73] The Merchant Taylors' Hall appears to have been in great demand for musical events and feasting—Guildhall Lib. MSS M F331, *passim*. Of published works, note in particular Imray, *The Mercers' Hall*, which describes the multifaceted uses of the livery halls, including the three-day celebrations at Drapers' Hall for the nuptials of Sir John Frederick's eldest son in 1676—pp. 261–2. In general, the histories of the overseas trading companies do not suggest that they fostered a clubbable attitude on the basis of their essential business unity—Davies, *Royal African Company*, 162.

ing groups, but their significance for the interests of overseas traders is far harder to discern. On the one hand, it is clear that merchants could share common commercial interests with the domestic traders in their livery companies, but surviving records do not indicate that merchants used the companies as a platform from which to champion their mutual causes. Their reticence reflects the perceived institutional responsibilities of the livery companies, since ministers and parliamentarians would expect them to comment on their restricted sectors, and turn to the overseas companies or unregulated traders for specialized comment. However, given the clustering of merchants in certain companies, it would be naive to suggest that leading liverymen were not enjoined by their brethren to act on behalf of mercantile interests, and on behalf of artisanal and retailing members too. Predictably, the less prestigious companies appeared keen to curry the favour of leading mercantile members. For instance, when Sir John Fleet moved from the Coopers to the Grocers in 1692 in order to qualify himself for the mayoralty, the former commissioned his portrait 'in perpetual memory of so honourable and worthy a member'. Indeed, the maintenance of such informal personal influence was probably the most potent form of liveried political activity. Voting preferences have been readily studied by psephologists, but the socio-political role of the livery companies has yet to be explored for the later seventeenth century, and they may well have acted as informal meeting-places for merchants to discuss matters away from the Exchange, trading company headquarters, local tavern, or coffee-house. It would have been particularly odd for the livery hall not to have evolved as such a forum when they were essential elements in the formal structure of City politics.[74]

Less doubt surrounds the general appeal of the livery companies to the status of the businessman. The hierarchical distinction between liverymen and the lesser freemen, journeymen, or yeomanry was suited to flatter the pretensions of any wealthy trader to elevated City status, and overseas merchants were in general rich enough to gain promotion to the upper strata of the companies with little effort. Alert to their needs, companies were also careful not to overburden merchants with yet more offices, and many traders rested content with the political and fiscal rights of the freedom and livery. It was clearly in the interest of the Merchant Taylors' Company to show sympathy to busy MP Sir Henry Ashurst, who was allowed to postpone his tenure of the mastership on four occasions when 'concerned in public business', and thus

---

[74] Brewer, *Sinews of Power*, 237–42; W. Foster, *A Short History of the Worshipful Company of Coopers of London* (Cambridge, 1944), 129. A suggestive example of the subtle influence of livery ties on business relates to the Company for Winding Fine Silk. The company started in 1692, and three of its first investors were John Barkstead (its governor), John Franks, and Humphrey Simpson, all of whom had become Mercers in 1690—*CSPD* 1691–2, pp. 302–3. Livery links can also be espied in the lists of witnesses to brokers' bonds, although common interests in overseas trade appear a more obvious focus for collective activity—CLRO, BR/P.

'could not in person attend the affairs of this company'.[75] Given the potential burdens involved, it is all the more significant that at least seventy-four (23 per cent of the identified livery merchants) of the sample were prepared to undertake high office within the companies, and thirty-six of these liverymen served as head of their company. Several wardens and masters were also the leaders of several other City institutions, and their willingness to accept livery office speaks volumes for the continuing prestige of the companies. The example of colonial trader Robert Bristow is particularly interesting in this regard, for in July 1692 he agreed to serve as warden of the Grocers, even though professing himself to be 'wholly a stranger to the company's affairs'. The high profile of the companies within the civic calendar, especially at the time of elections and inaugurations, was an understandable attraction, giving livery officials the opportunity to preside over an influential group of fellow citizens. However, it is more likely that at root the real attractions of the livery hall centred on the contacts to be made there, rather than the pomp of its ritual ceremonies.[76]

The kaleidoscope of connections which might be mediated through the livery company did not accord the civic hall a greater significance than the merchant's counting-house or the floor of the Royal Exchange. Nevertheless, when personal association was so important for the advancement of business, there is no doubt that a large cross-section of City merchants found to their advantage that membership did have its privileges. To this day the commercial hub of national life has been criticized for having too 'clubbable' a feel in certain quarters, and that the golf course or old school tie can bar advancement to all but the favoured few. These inequalities clearly existed in early modern London, and were preserved in institutionalized forms. Not every liveryman gave slavish devotion to his company, and as with any association various degrees of commitment could be espied among the membership. Yet, beyond the pomposity of civic ceremony, there remained an informality in which businessmen could indulge their passion for networking in a convivial, but controlled atmosphere. Undoubtedly there were individuals who found livery life stuffy and uncongenial, but many more thrived in its surroundings, and secured advancement on many personal fronts thanks to this fluid form of political association.[77]

---

[75] Ward, *Metropolitan Communities*, 83–5; Guildhall Lib. MSS MF331, court minutes 19 July 1689, 27 July 1691, 29 June 1692, 17 July 1696. In July 1698 Ashurst fined for £80 to avoid the office 'by reason of his living at distance in the country' (i.e. Oxfordshire). In November 1681 the company ruled that no new motions could be moved in the court of assistants after noon so that members could 'go to the Exchange about their several and respective concerns'.

[76] Guildhall MSS 11588/6, p. 6. At the same time as Bristow's election, two other merchants each paid £25 to escape office as wardens. Surviving portraits of liveried benefactors highlight the essential link between the companies and the City hierarchy.

[77] On the variety of commitment evident in the livery companies, see Ward, *Metropolitan Communities*, 145–6. Significantly, few merchants left bequests to the companies, even those who had served company offices with some distinction.

iv. Provincial parallels

Once again, when turning from the complex structures of London life to the more modest scale of the provincial town, patterns of mercantile interaction appear much clearer at first sight. In comparison with the metropolis, the confined commercial orbit of the provincial ports and their limited mercantile numbers would seem undoubted forces for encouraging collective action, especially since a narrower spectrum of economic function would promote immediate awareness of common interests. However, while these factors undoubtedly aided local commercial association, the diminutive size of the mercantile sector also posed fundamental problems for provincial leaders. In the absence of magnates of the stature of the great City tycoons, there was an obvious concern that a provincial cause would make little impact at national level. Formal provincial associations indeed recognized this weakness, and although principally designed for the regulation of local commercial life, one of their key priorities was to establish connections with governmental authorities in London. As we shall see, a variety of local organizations could provide such brokerage, and provincial merchants knew that they had to be flexible in their political strategies if they were to achieve their aims. During a period of constitutional upheaval there was an even greater premium on their adaptability, and the examples of Liverpool and York will demonstrate that local commercial structures of very differing character could respond positively to the political and economic challenges of the period.[78]

The commercial structure of York was one of the most complex of all provincial ports, and underwent profound changes during the difficult trading times of the post-1660 period. Indeed, the city's commercial decline has been traditionally mirrored by, or partly blamed on, the withering vitality of York's company system. At the Restoration, there were three corporate mercantile bodies: the Company of Merchant Adventurers, whose membership included grocers, apothecaries, and ironmongers as well as overseas traders; the residency of the Merchant Adventurers of England, or Hamburg Company; and the residency of the Eastland Company. Although there was a certain overlap in membership between all three groups, their respective constitutional roles gave each very different commercial priorities, and ensured them varying fortunes during a period of general decay in the town's trade. By 1702 the York Eastland Company had ceased to function, a running feud with its ailing London headquarters having put the final nail in a commercially moribund coffin. The Hamburg Company proved more resilient, but struggled for numbers, and shared in the travails of its German-based and London masters. The more relaxed admissions policy of the Company of

---

[78] For important studies of mercantile political association, see P. McGrath, *The Merchant Venturers of Bristol* (Bristol, 1975), 124–49; G. Jackson, *Hull in the Eighteenth Century* (Oxford, 1972), esp. 234–61, 300–16.

Merchant Adventurers ensured it a respectable complement of traders in 1720, but a declining number were directly involved in overseas trade. Only in the face of determined external assault had any liberality been extended by these institutions to a wider mercantile constituency, and to outsiders the York companies appeared to exhibit the classic obduracy of their London and provincial counterparts. However, closer analysis suggests that the companies were not ignorant of the common concerns of York traders, and that they continued to function as active political associations, dedicated to increasing local trade. In particular, by exploiting their direct influence with the civic corporation and the city's MPs, they maintained a successful campaign for local improvement, even if unable to mount a real challenge to the superior commercial centres of Leeds and Hull.[79]

It is easy to see the reasons why historians have given little credit to the York companies for their leadership in local trade, since in appearance their oligarchic constitutions precluded any service to the general interest of the town. The strictness with which all three companies supervised local trade ensured that no rival mercantile association ever manifested itself within the city. The role of the Company of Merchant Adventurers was crucial here, since it enforced wide-ranging regulations over weights and measures, apprenticeships, and unfree trading. Although a few local men dared to raise a challenge to their monopoly of trading privileges, each was rebuffed with force, and the companies could rely on full civic cooperation to maintain their position. Their success can be measured by the case of the recalcitrant William Garforth, who was forced to take up his freedom in 1701 after a two-year struggle, and later became both governor of the company and a deputy of the Hamburg residency. More generally, even in an era of decline the companies appear to have suffered little internal division, in significant contrast to the often stormy relationship of the residencies with their London and regional counterparts.[80]

Although forced to respect the rule of the companies, local merchants exhibited varying degrees of commitment to corporate life. Probably the most significant feature of York's shrinking mercantile sector was the prominence of a small elite of traders who were members of more than just one company. In

---

[79] For detailed analysis of the constitutional development of the York companies, see M. Sellers, 'Acts and Ordinances of the Eastland Company', *Camden Society*, 3rd ser., 11 (1906); *idem*, 'The York Mercers and Merchant Adventurers, 1356–1917', *Surtees Society*, 129 (1917); W. E. Lingelbach, in *TRHS* NS, 16 (1902), 19–67; B. Johnson, *The Last of the Old Hanse* (York, 1949). For an instructive regional comparison, see J. R. Boyle and F. W. Dendy (eds.), 'Extracts from the Records of the Merchant Adventurers of Newcastle-upon-Tyne', *Surtees Society*, 93 (1895) and 101 (1899). For a positive view of the role of the York companies in the late eighteenth and nineteenth centuries, see D. Palliser, *The Company of Merchant Adventurers of the City of York* (York, 1985), 11–12.

[80] Merchant Adventurers' Hall, York, Company of MA MSS, minute book 1677–1730, fos. 95ᵛ–99ᵛ. Jenny Kermode has recently argued that the priority which guided guild development in York had been an elite desire for local control—*Medieval Merchants: York, Beverley, and Hull in the Later Middle Ages* (Cambridge, 1998), 55–6.

1660 many traders could have boasted these multiple loyalties, but their number had dropped significantly by the time of the Revolution. York leaders reacted to this development with concern, for the corporate constitutions required that certain officers had to be associated with another local company. In 1707 the Company of Merchant Adventurers made a major break with tradition when it ruled that its governors no longer had to be free of 'the Old Hanse', i.e. members of the Hamburg residency who had become free by patrimony or apprenticeship. The shortage of eligible candidates represented a direct threat to the very existence of the companies, and inevitably put even greater pressure on local traders to undertake company office. Predictably, those who were ready to serve in two or more companies included some of the wealthier of the town traders, whose multiple affiliation was doubtless a boon to their prominence within York society in general, as well as within its commercial sector. Francis Drake acknowledged their commercial status in 1736, reporting that merchants who had become free of the Old Hanse were 'esteemed a degree before any of the rest'. In fact, this small group, which by 1715 numbered only about ten regular members, represented the rump of the town's active overseas traders, a dying breed but sufficiently influential to maintain a rigid enforcement of a regulated economy. More than any other feature of York's mercantile decline, they appear to personify the commercial ossification which condemned the city to its economic fate.[81]

However, while the appearance of decline is compelling, the vitality of the corporate system should not be underestimated. In particular, although oligarchic in structure, York's companies adapted to the wave of free-trade reform, and were able to capitalize on their traditional strengths to act as spokesmen for local commercial concerns. Of course, the York residencies of the Eastland and Merchant Adventurers' companies fought hard to prevent the reduction of admissions fees, but it is important to note that once the national battle was lost, the influx of new members, including merchants from Leeds, boosted their position as representatives of regional mercantile interests. Furthermore, these commercial organizations did not permit these newcomers to become influential members, and the common corporate concern remained the promotion of York trade. As a sign of its limited tolerance, in 1702 the Company of Merchant Adventurers made it very clear that its own members had precedence over any Hamburg trader who had bought his freedom since the residency reduced its fees. After centuries of strict regulation, the commitment of these new members could only be regarded with suspicion, but traditional rivalries cannot obscure the advantages won by these freedom purchasers. For an admission price of 40 shillings, the York companies had a great deal to offer in terms of political connection, particularly in terms of local contacts and access to influential figures in the

---

[81] Company of MA MSS, minute book, fo. 118; F. Drake, *Eboracum* (London, 1736), 228. Concern for the declining number of Old Hanse merchants was first aired within the Company in 1698—fo. 91.

London. Outsiders never achieved corporate office, but they could benefit from the formal and informal influence of institutions well versed in the art of commercial lobbying.[82]

Political effectiveness was not achieved by internal corporate discipline and a gesture of openness alone. Within York, the companies had always been able to rely on close links with the corporation, and as the preceding chapter demonstrated, even in a period of declining numbers there remained a significant overlap in the leaderships of local government and commerce. The close relationship between merchants and major retailers in the Company of Merchant Adventurers also ensured the town's commercial sector extensive influence in corporate affairs, which was put to the service of overseas trade on frequent occasions during the post-Restoration period. For instance, when York merchants complained of the duties levied by the port of Hull in 1682–3, it was the corporation which brokered a compromise. At the turn of the century civic rulers were instrumental in leading opposition to the Aire and Calder navigation scheme, which threatened to advance the commercial viability of Leeds at their expense. More positively, it was the corporation which finally achieved improvement in the navigability of the Ouse after a two-year parliamentary struggle in 1725–7. For this success York's citizens had to thank their MP Edward Thompson, a local gentleman closely related to one of the City's most important merchant dynasties. Although his recent election had confirmed a trend for the city to choose gentry rather than townsmen as their spokesmen, his service demonstrated a strong continuity with that of his York predecessors. Of course, he could not guarantee the town a future in overseas commerce, but his actions demonstrated that its political machinery was still attuned to economic interests. At this time provincial corporations throughout the country were making a more forceful contribution in the sphere of overseas commerce, and in York's case this can be viewed as a response to the perceived decline in its mercantile companies.[83]

Despite their close relationship with the York corporation, the companies could not rely on the town hall to do its bidding, particularly when time and money would have to be spent to serve their interests. The Company of Merchant Adventurers, able to muster attendances of over fifty leading traders in the reign of Charles II, could lay the best claim to representing the broad commercial interest of the town, and, despite declining numbers, could

---

[82] Company of MA MSS, minute book, fo. 104ᵛ. The MA of England were thrown open in 1693, and thirty-nine individuals had taken out 40–shilling freedoms by 1700, including seven applicants from other towns. In the same period only thirteen became free via paternity or apprenticeship—Hamburg court book 1693–1797, fos. 88–98. Admission rates in the York Eastland residence did not noticeably dip until the 1690s—Merchant Adventurers Hall, York, Eastland residence MSS 2/1, fo. 243 and ff.

[83] York City archives E85, Letters concerning City affairs 1663–1718, pp. 35–42, 51, 126–8; B38, fo. 197v; B39, fos. 112–13, 117, 119, 121; B42, fo. 61, 71ᵛ, 78ᵛ, 87, 92ᵛ. The 1727 Act did meet resistance within the town, with opposition to the imposition of new local taxes—Drake, *Eboracum*, 232–3.

still play an important political role. In 1695, it unashamedly revealed its true priorities by appointing a committee to liaise with the town's MPs 'to consider of trade in the city and what may be advantageous to the company'. Two years later, another committee was ordered to procure a parliamentary ban on the import of Irish yarn. In subsequent years, the Company also sought to promote the navigation of the Ouse, and a petition to the House of Lords in 1698 actually boasted 118 signatures. Only about a quarter of the signatories can be identified as active merchants, and thus we can see that overseas traders could find ready support from retailers and domestic wholesalers to present an impressive united front to national authorities. The eighteenth-century trader increasingly saw the wisdom of challenging such common initiatives through the corporation, but the ancient Merchant Venturers' Hall remained an important forum for commercial initiatives.[84]

Although suffering acute uncertainties during this period, the two residencies at York also found that their political functions commanded the respect of local merchants. York's overseas traders had clearly enjoyed significant advantages from their direct links to the commercial institutions of London, and even though these connections were often under great strain in the post-Restoration period, these local-central disputes did not represent any fundamental dissatisfaction with the residency system per se. There were undoubtedly tensions arising from arguments over company duties or the appointment of officials, but these differences could be overcome on occasions when the company actually served the general interest of London and the provinces. The York residency of the Eastland Company is a particularly good example of this schizophrenic tendency, even in its most difficult years following the opening up of the trade in 1673. In the wake of that calamity the residency was at continual loggerheads with its London colleagues, but in September 1689 it sent warm thanks to the governor for having gained an exemption for the company from the provision of an act to allow the freer export of woollen cloth. Moreover, as late as 1698 a petition in the name of the residency was presented to the Commons in support of the London company's campaign to open up the Russia trade. This activity reflected the residency's commitment to join with the Londoners 'in anything that may conduce to the good of the fellowship in general'. Within a few years the York Eastland Company had ceased to appoint any officers, its demise as a political force anticipating that of the London company by over a decade. The unpopularity of its London headquarters appears the most obvious cause of its dissolution, and York merchants evidently felt that they could expect little favour from City traders who were over-authoritarian in their dealings with

[84] Company of MA minute book, fo. 81, 88ᵛ; House of Lords RO, main paper series 1274, fos. 60–1. Both the corporation and the Company of Merchant Adventurers actively sought improvements in the navigation of the Ouse in 1699–1700. For the politicking of York's commercial elite in the fourteenth and fifteenth centuries, see Kermode, *Medieval Merchants*, 32–7.

the provinces. The residency was already weakened by the success of their commercial rivals in Hull and Leeds, and there appeared little point in continuing if their London brethren refused to respect the federal spirit which had served the provinces well in the past.[85]

Outlasting the Eastland men in both duration and importance, the residency of the Hamburg Company proved that corporate organization could still be used to good effect even in an age of freer trade. The enforced relaxation of its entry requirements posed an even more significant rupture with traditional practice than in the case of the Eastlanders, but both the London and York branches of the company appear to have quickly accepted the need to adapt to changing times. For instance, in December 1694 the London residency sought to mobilize its brethren of York to secure parliamentary recognition of exclusive trading privileges on three German rivers, and even sent a specimen petition for them to study. Significantly, in spite of its historic insistence on 'mere merchant' members, it urged the York residency to 'procure unto it as numerous a subscription as you can of all sorts of people, especially such as are any way concerned in the trade of the woollen commodities of our nation and the manufacturing the same, for the Members in Parliament have generally a good regard unto such subscriptions'. Even more illuminatingly, the petition was made in the name of York's inhabitants, with the local company deputy forbidden to add his office, 'but in case your lord mayor should favour us with his hand to it, we desire he will add also that his title'. By adopting this strategy the York residency was able to muster 120 supporters on paper to aid the corporate cause. These orders reveal the defensiveness of the companies at this time, but they continued to play a forceful role in the political arena, even if they had to tread warily and respect public opinion. Over thirty years later, the Hamburg Company could still inspire a more general campaign, gaining the support of the mayor, several aldermen, and about 100 'principal inhabitants' for a petition to the newly enthroned George II to intercede in a dispute between the Danes and the city of Hamburg. Encouragingly, the monarch assured the company of royal protection, and thereby endorsed the value of York's traditional political connections. On their own, York's commercial associations could not save the city's overseas trade, and even townsmen would have realized that they were often swimming against a strong commercial tide. Nevertheless, their failures should not condemn these companies to insignificance, for their development reveals an inner vitality fuelled by the enduring need for influence at home and abroad. It would be most erroneous to suggest that by 1720 the mercantile

---

[85] *CJ*, xi. 697, xii. 93. Sellers, in *Camden Society*, 3rd ser., 11 (1906), provides plenty of evidence on the tempestuous relationship between London and its provincial residences, but these published extracts must be supplemented by the original York Eastland minute book for 1645–97. For evidence of the rewards gained by York through this association (in 1665, 1670, and 1689 respectively), see fos. 39, 45–6, 88ᵛ.

community had been reduced to an impotent group of dining clubs, toasting their past glories with their sole remaining import.[86]

In comparison with York, Liverpool entered its first great era of expansion with little formal structure to its mercantile activities. With Irish trade remaining the staple of the port in previous centuries, the town had escaped the attention of the London companies, and, as elsewhere, the only surviving trace of an earlier mercantile guild was the ruling corporation. During its late Stuart boom there was no serious challenge to this status quo either from within or outside the town, since their lucrative American and West Indian trades were unregulated. However, even though Liverpool merchants could pride themselves on their independence, individuals could not conduct such long-distance commerce without significant aid from local and national authorities. As the port expanded, its leaders found it increasingly necessary to learn political as well as commercial skills, particularly in its relationship with the capital. Their overall success in gaining leverage within national circles was vital to their achievement of sustained economic growth, especially in their battles with significant commercial rivals. Local associations were thus fluid in character, but common interests could prove just as effective a stimulus to collective action as the agency of traditional forms of company organization.[87]

Given the absence of any formal mercantile structure, the Liverpool corporation was the most likely focus for the promotion of the port on a regional and national scale. Michael Power's analysis of the mercantile forces behind the building of the docks in 1709–15 accurately identifies a powerful clique of leading aldermen as key figures in securing the long-term future of the port. More generally, his observations on the growth in mercantile representation on the aldermanic bench and common council leave little room to doubt that the corporation served as a forum for the advancement of the port's commercial interests. Mutual business priorities could not pre-empt serious divisions over issues such as the town charter or religion, but once the corporation had secured the services of its leading merchants, it could not afford to alienate them by neglecting their particular concerns. Of course, consensus could be as elusive in the purely commercial sphere, but even in tense moments local merchants were aware of the need to secure general interests, a concerned merchant remarking in 1702 that 'we must not be angry with one another that we differ in judgement; nothing [is] more common'. The town's

---

[86] Hamburg court book 1693–1797, fos. 10–33. Petitions to the Commons were also circulated for subscriptions in November 1693, October 1698, and December 1707. For the vibrancy of the Newcastle residence in this period, which saw periodic cooperation with their York brethren, see *Surtees Society*, 93 (1895), 199–252. The Bristol Merchant Venturers were also resilient, seeking influence via the creation of honorary freemen in the later eighteenth century—McGrath, *Merchant Venturers*, 102–23.

[87] For discussion of the medieval Liverpool guild and the Hanse of local freemen, see J. Picton, *Selections from the Municipal Archives and Records* (Liverpool, 1883), 79–85.

success in maintaining the overall unity of its mercantile sector is all the more impressive in consideration of the potential interference of local gentry, whose interests often ran counter to those of the borough. These challenges were overcome, but not without cost and great sacrifices on the part of the corporation and leading individuals. Most significantly, their efforts demonstrate how local traders were alive to political and commercial changes at both regional and national level.[88]

The Liverpool corporation appeared at its most resourceful in its relationship with Westminster, particularly through its ready adaptation to the annual sessions of Parliament after 1689. Having failed to solicit the Commons once on mercantile matters under Charles II and James II, in the 1690–1715 period the town submitted no less than twelve petitions to the Commons on issues affecting overseas trade, most of them in the name of the corporation. Liverpool was also prepared to join with neighbouring towns to achieve regional commercial objectives, and in 1697–8 sought alliance with West Country interests to promote the local salt trade. The all-important dock campaign of 1709 thus benefited from the experience of several recent legislative initiatives, the town having learnt how to impress the gentry-dominated Lower House with their plea for special consideration.[89] Several petitions made a particular point of Liverpool's value as a centre for training young gentlemen in trade, but their more general propaganda focused on the town's role as a breeding-ground for mariners, and its substantial contribution to Treasury coffers. Few opportunities were spurned to remind outsiders of Liverpool's commercial merit, a gentle visitor to the town in October 1701 being informed that the port had yielded some £60,000 in customs in the past year. The town's reputation was certainly closely guarded, and traders were most concerned to ensure that Liverpudlians were seen as 'an honest, industrious people, and that we deserve encouragement'. Presiding over an expanding centre, town traders had good cause to crow over local achievements, but they needed to tailor their demands to a specific audience, which might be indifferent or even hostile to the benefits of the port. Liverpool was not always successful in its aim, but its readiness to turn to Parliament revealed

[88] M. Power, 'Councillors and Commerce in Liverpool 1650–1750', *Urban History*, 24 (1997), 301–23; Heywood (ed.), *Chetham Society*, 9 (1846), 89. For the tempestuous party divisions in Liverpool over the town's charter, see M. Mullet, 'The Politics of Liverpool, 1660–88', *Transactions of the Historical Society of Lancashire and Cheshire*, 124 (1972), 31–56. I am indebted to Richard Harrison for permission to read the excellent unpublished articles on Liverpool which will appear in the History of Parliament's forthcoming volumes for the 1690–1715 period.

[89] J. Longmore, 'The Liverpool Corporation as Landowners and Dock-Builders, 1709–1835', in C. W. Chalklin and J. R. Wordie (eds.), *Town and Countryside* (London, 1989), 116–46. The Liverpool corporation reportedly fought against bills affecting the navigation of the Mersey, and the erection of a new lighthouse in 1663–4—see Picton, *Selections*, 241–2. For Liverpool's interaction with other regional political interests, see S. Handley, 'Provincial Influence on General Legislation: The Case of Lancashire, 1689–1731', *Parliamentary History*, 16 (1997), 171–84; T. S. Willan, 'The Navigation of the River Weaver in the Eighteenth Century', *Chetham Society*, 3rd ser., 3 (1951), esp. 142–59.

a sensitive appreciation of the changing political landscape, and of its need for external help to sustain its recent development.[90]

Liverpool's chief political operators were the town's two MPs. During this period the port made a noticeable break with recent practice by choosing two merchants to represent their views at Westminster, rejecting the influence of local landlords. This development has been represented as a symbol of urban independence, but it also had the practical value of ensuring that the town had an informed and supportive voice in the capital. The excellent Norris papers reveal the full extent of the heavy workload which a demanding borough could place on its representatives, not only while dealing with Parliament but also with a whole range of government departments which handled mercantile matters. Most interestingly, they reveal that even local magnates such as William Clayton and Sir Thomas Johnson could not expect to hold sway over their mercantile colleagues, and that on sensitive commercial issues they had to tread very carefully for fear of accusations of self-interest. Labouring under such pressure, they often bemoaned their lot, and expressed a wish never to stand for the borough again. Even former MPs were not spared if there were pressing matters at hand, and Jasper Maudit actually complained in 1700 that he had been 'forty weeks absent from my concerns in the service of the town'. That these representatives persevered in such tiresome duties for many years suggests that the personal compensations of status and contacts largely made up for attendance on a multiplicity of town and private business.[91]

Norris's correspondence also illuminates the manner in which Liverpool mobilized its mercantile forces to impress external authorities. Most interestingly, although Liverpool might appear a homogeneous mercantile society, ever ready to jump to the defence of town interests, MP Johnson complained that it was 'an endless work to get persons together to sign letters or petitions . . . you can never expect much from pressed men'. This frustration echoed the difficulties of merchant leaders in the capital, and again credits the drive of town leaders who were prepared to undertake such a thankless task for the general interest. For a borough such as Liverpool, which lacked a major political patron, the importance of effective petitioning was even greater, and their determination to marshal their mercantile forces must be linked to the self-dependence of the borough. Despite Johnson's complaint, surviving petitions prove that Liverpool traders could be dragooned into an effective lobby, with no less than ninety-three 'merchants and traders' signing an

---

[90] Picton, *Selections*, 325–6; *CJ*, xvi. 102; M. R. Wenger (ed.), *The English Travels of Sir John Percival and William Byrd II* (Columbia, NY, 1989), 140–1; Liverpool RO, 920 NRO, 1/189.

[91] Heywood, *Chetham Society*, 9 (1846), esp. 46–7, 114; R. Sedgwick (ed.), *The History of Parliament: The House of Commons, 1715–54* (London, 1970), i. 559; ii. 63, 180–1. The growth of the town also put increasing pressures on corporate leaders, especially the mayor, whose burdens were noted in 1707—Liverpool RO, MF2/4, p. 175. For an example of how this parliamentary aid encouraged civic pride, see W. Enfield, *An Essay towards the History of Leverpool* (Warrington, 1773), 15–18.

address of March 1718 in support of the establishment of a marine insurance society. In its feverish attempts to convert authorities to its cause, the town courted ministers and other influential figures, but did not develop any close relationship with a local peer to secure longer-term advantage. Thus, it sought to impress authorities by dignifying their causes with corporation approval, or by enlisting the support of other commercial interests. Politic awareness certainly resonated from the verdict of Liverpool rock-salt traders that a 'multiplicity of petitions will favour our case' against rival brine-pit owners in December 1697. By the end of Anne's reign town merchants had even influenced nationwide campaigns, joining their interest to attacks on the Royal African Company and the French commerce treaty of 1713. In all these efforts, internal unity was deemed essential. This fact of political life was viewed most clearly by London-based representatives such as MP Johnson, who stressed in 1702 that their cause would 'not do well' under national scrutiny unless the port could secure 'a general consent of the merchants and dealers'.[92]

Although vital, the formal process of petitioning was only one facet of a commercial campaign, and both before and after the presentation of their case Liverpool's agents faced an immense task in managing the cause in London. Significantly, the completion of town business in the capital was facilitated by close commercial links between Liverpool and London merchants, even though the two ports were competitors in transatlantic trade. During the period two City merchants with Lancashire connections, John Dubois and Robert Heysham, proved valuable servants of the town, the latter without even serving for Liverpool. These ties should not obscure the evident hostility which many Liverpudlians bore towards London traders, but it was clearly in the town's interest to maintain contacts with the nation's leading merchants. Norris himself, as a contact of important City merchants such as Samuel Shepheard and Alexander Cairnes, was in an excellent position to act as broker between local and central interests, a role shared by other leading Liverpool traders. When dealing with the London elite, the town's interests were served by having merchants of true stature, and in this manner 'concentration' within the trading community probably aided its political cause. The greatest of Liverpool traders were also more likely to have diversified their mercantile investments, and could thus more readily represent the port's various economic interests. Interestingly, stories of the fabled wealth of certain Liverpool leaders circulated within the City during Anne's reign, spread by commercial rivals in an effort to discredit the town. These rumours reflected the growing reputation of the port throughout the country, which sparked

[92] Heywood, *Chetham Society*, 9 (1846), esp. 81, 151–2; CO389/19, no. 296; Liverpool RO, 920 NOR 2/115. At least one economic analyst gave credit to Liverpool's effective politicking as a cause of its growth—P. G. E. Clemens, 'The Rise of Liverpool, 1665–1750', *EcHR* 29 (1976), esp. 216–17. For discussion of the national campaigns for and against the French Commerce Treaty of 1713, see Ch. 6.

both admiration and jealousy. In response the town kept a close watch on the activities of their mercantile representatives, and ensured that personal ambitions or ideological extremism did not bring the town into disrepute.[93]

Liverpool thus presents a very different case-study from either York or London. As a growing port, it lacked the traditional institutions or connections which might have helped it secure the political favours required for the advance of its trade. However, having undergone significant internal reforms, and taken every opportunity to exploit national constitutional change, the town had proved itself a formidable adversary in the political arena by 1720. Its heightened national profile was the key to its success in gaining governmental favour, but much credit must be given to its greater traders who worked hard to secure its commercial objectives both within Liverpool and in the capital. Political advancement was not always easily achieved, as one would expect from a system of political access so heavily reliant on individuals, but the corporation played a crucial role in overseeing the port's development. It was fortunate that its case for special pleading was far stronger than that of the York corporation, but even in its expansionist phase Liverpool could never take the outcome of its commercial campaigns for granted. Indeed, even in an age of corporate decline the fate of these two provincial towns suggests that the politics of trade became much more organized, whether contested on a local, regional, or national stage. In this new era we can observe traditional forms of political activity at work, with corporate and individual agencies used to achieve economic ends. However, changing commercial circumstances, such as those experienced at Liverpool, meant that new political interests could become well established. The respective influences of commercial and political change were seen most clearly at Westminster and Whitehall, but it is important to trace their impact within the towns themselves, where mercantile associations energetically adapted their strategies to secure advantage at a national level.

This chapter has demonstrated how merchant organizations were fashioned by the need for political services to obtain commercial ends. If merchants were independent economic units in the late Stuart period, they could not afford to be so isolated within a political sphere undergoing profound change. The great trading companies took the principal buffeting during a period of radical reassessment of the structure of English trade, but their value as political agencies ensured that the reformed companies were still very much at the forefront of national commerce under the Hanoverians. Prominent individuals could perform very important roles in coordinating and articulating a common

---

[93] B. D. Henning (ed.), *The History of Parliament: The House of Commons, 1660–90* (London, 1983), ii. 237–8; Sedgwick, *House of Commons*, ii. 136; *Chetham Society*, 9 (1846), esp. 114. Heysham's west-coast commercial links were noted by Defoe—*A Tour throughout the Whole Island of Great Britain* ed. G. D. H. Cole (London, 1927), 667.

voice across the fragmented world of English trade, both within the regulated and unregulated sectors. They personified the mutually supporting structures of commerce and the state, which needed well-placed leaders to broker agreement between a potentially vast array of interests. One cannot assume that common commercial causes were readily identified, or that little effort was needed to maintain unity among traders. Furthermore, the complexity of international trade ensured that there were plenty of issues which could divide the most steadfast of allies, and we should not underestimate the difficulties of sustaining a commercial interest. Moments of particular crisis could cause a trading group to establish a formidable united front, but there were no guarantees of longer-term consensus. The fluid format of mercantile association was well attuned to the essential independence of the overseas trader, and it was entirely appropriate that trading alliances were often maintained by agencies without a specific mercantile brief, such as the City livery halls or the provincial corporations. There are certainly signs that changes within the superstructure of the state entailed innovations in mercantile organization, but it would be hard to ignore the traditional continuities at work within mercantile politics. Merchants had always sought to exploit existing constitutional realities, and the Augustan trader still presented no overt challenge to the authorities of his day.

Awareness of the competing forces for continuity and change within English commercial politics argues for more thorough analysis of merchant activity in the public domain. In the first half of this book, the overriding concern has been to outline the background and outlook of the merchant, but these perspectives have to be related to his impact in the national sphere. So far the overseas trader has been rooted in his urban base in order to appreciate the real nerve-centre of his operations, and the most immediate source of his personal prestige. Moving to the national theatre, he was on less certain ground, where claims to prominence and special consideration were largely judged by unfamiliar aristocratic and gentry codes. However, the next three chapters will stress that the adaptability of the merchant classes ensured that they did make their mark within that potentially inhospitable world, although such flexibility did not entail the desertion of their urban roots. In this process, the mutability of the state itself was crucial in assuaging the general interests of businessmen, with national leaders much readier to embrace the merchant as a valued member of the realm, even while the country remained conservative in its social and political instincts. As the English nation entered its British and imperial destiny, the domestic relationship of commerce and land remained a vital test of its ability to embrace rapid change at a non-revolutionary pace.

CHAPTER FOUR

The Merchant, Politics, and the Press

'There are not more useful members in a Commonwealth than merchants. They knit mankind together in a mutual intercourse of good offices, distribute the gifts of nature, find work for the poor, add wealth to the rich, and magnificence to the great'.

(Joseph Addison in *The Spectator*, May 1711)

'I do not pretend to love my country so much better than myself as to encourage a trade which would be to my prejudice . . . I must speak as a merchant who judges his trade only by the measure of profit'.

(Naval contractor John Taylor to the Board of Trade, 1694)[1]

WHEN transferring one's attention from the world of the merchant to a more public sphere, it is hardly surprising that there should be contradictory views of the relationship between overseas traders and the state. Addison's oft-quoted views on the benefits of commerce reflect a perceived trend in Augustan literature to laud the merchant as a patriotic adventurer, a model which proved the focus for social commentary throughout the eighteenth century. However, Taylor's more sanguine assessment of his relationship with the state poses questions concerning the reality behind the nation-loving portrait found in the works of such luminaries as Defoe, Steele, Prior, and Gay.[2] As the preceding chapters have suggested, although in need of state support, the merchant can be distinguished for his essential independence and readiness to take advantage of any opportunity to advance personal interest. Many literary sources continued to recycle a less public-spirited image of the trader, and there remained an onus on the mercantile apologist to explain away such unpatriotic tendencies. Thanks to John McVeagh and James Raven, we know a great deal about this public debate, but as yet it is far from clear how the activities of the traders themselves contributed to the lionization of their profession. It is tempting to link this positive image to the commercial 'revolution' of the post-1660 period, but we still know little of the trader's views towards such celebrated images as Sir Andrew Freeport, the mouthpiece for

---

[1] J. Addison and R. Steele, *The Spectator*, ed. D. F. Bond (London, 1965), i. 296; *CSP Col* . 1693–6, pp. 263–4. Taylor was offering advice on the importation of naval stores from New England.

[2] J. McVeagh, *Tradefull Merchants: The Portrayal of the Capitalist in Literature* (London, 1981), esp. 53–82; J. Loftis, *Comedy and Society from Congreve to Fielding* (Stamford, 1959), 77–100. For a review of the merchant in the literature of Elizabethan England, see L. C. Stevenson, *Praise and Paradox* (Cambridge, 1984), 75–158.

Addison's mercantophile sentiments. The riches of Augustan literature have been skilfully mined to demonstrate a significant change in attitudes towards the merchant, but this apparent shift in opinion needs to be tested against other forms of media, and against social and political realities. In the second half of the book we will explore the impact of both the real and the imagined merchant on the national stage. In particular, the next three chapters will ask if these much-trumpeted patriotic credentials actually made any difference to their position within the state.[3]

The contrasting tone of Addison and Taylor highlights the fact that there was *continuing* debate concerning the value of the merchant to the state in the Augustan period. Furthermore, Taylor's comments reveal that discussion of the patriot trader resounded far beyond the confines of the theatre and social commentary, and it is important to recognize that it was not an idle debate on the personal merits of the men of new wealth. Steve Pincus has shown how controversy over the value of trade animated political thinkers in the 1640s and 1650s, which discussion (in his view) accelerated the creation of 'a truly self-conscious commercial society'.[4] After 1660, commerce came to be debated in the same breath as the European balance of power and even the nature of political representation, and thus had serious repercussions for domestic and international development. Merchants had thus much more than personal pride at stake when partaking in these debates, and few could ignore their significance, even the straight-talking Taylor. Indeed, the apparent contradiction of Addison and Taylor is less evident on closer inspection, for both were prepared to employ the vocabulary of the patriot trader, thereby highlighting its impact as a contemporary idiom in public discourse. In the gentry-dominated political world addressed by Taylor there was an added onus on merchants to convince their social betters that they were worthy of special consideration, and Taylor used the appeal to patriotism in a subtle way, hoping that the commissioners of trade would actually trust him *more* if he demonstrated the self-interest which traditional accounts had accorded to the early modern businessman. As with so many other elements of mercantile life, this business strategy involved risks, but Taylor gambled in the knowledge that his supplies of timber were of great importance for the national war effort,

[3] J. Raven, *Judging New Wealth* (Oxford, 1992); M. Hunt, *The Middling Sort: Commerce, Gender, and Family in England, 1680–1780* (Berkeley, Calif., 1996), 172–92. For a stimulating debate concerning the patriotic credentials of the eighteenth-century merchant, see L. Colley, *Britons: Forging the Nation, 1707–1837* (New Haven, 1992), esp. 59–107; K. Wilson, 'Empire, Trade, and Popular Politics in Mid-Hanoverian Britain: The Case of Admiral Vernon', *Past and Present*, 121 (1988), 74–109; R. Harris, 'American Idols: Empire, War, and the Middling Ranks in Mid-Eighteenth Century Britain', ibid. 150 (1996), 111–41.

[4] S. Pincus, 'Neither Machiavellian Moment nor Possessive Individualism: Commercial Society and the Defenders of the English Commonwealth', *American Historical Review*, 103 (1998), 705–36. Note, in particular, his emphasis on economic questions as issues of political resonance, which to a certain extent represents a departure from the important work of Joyce Appleby, *Economic Thought and Ideology in Seventeenth-Century England* (Princeton, 1978).

and hoped that his profits would be protected by his very real value to the state.[5] This exchange highlights the knife-edge of interdependence between merchant and state, and reflects an element of the real-life theatre which was played out on a number of public stages not far from the more imaginative arenas of the fashionable West End. The skill of Addison might have left more memorable images, but it is important that we consider how merchants attempted to manipulate their public image in an era of political and commercial transition. We still only have a very limited view of the impact of the merchant on the public stage, and we must appreciate the wider currency of the patriotic trader if we are to understand its real significance.[6]

When moving from a comfortable prominence within urban society to the more unpredictable environment of a gentry-dominated state, the Augustan merchant in public life betrayed understandable trepidation rather than confidence. Centuries of ingrained social prejudice represented a formidable challenge for the merchant, and many spheres of public life remained off limits to the business elite. Most notably, despite the greater welcome accorded to the patriot trader in certain literary circles in the later seventeenth century, there appears little sign that traders were rewarded with heightened social status or political power. Even those historians who regard the late Stuart merchant to be on the ascendant would hesitate to suggest that he had been wholeheartedly embraced by the nation's natural rulers by the Hanoverian age.[7] As the preceding chapters have suggested, on an individual basis it does not appear that overseas traders were in the vanguard of significant social change, and gave little cause for the gentry to reconsider their attitudes towards the business world. In common with previous generations, mercantile fortunes were attractive to genteel suitors, and a career in trade remained a useful stand-by for the troublesome younger son, but financial benefits did not necessarily ensure enhanced status for overseas traders, or increasing concern for their interests among the traditional governors of the land. Nevertheless, the findings of literary historians have clearly demonstrated that a reappraisal of the role of the overseas trader was under way as British trade expanded in the long eighteenth century, and that the Augustan period remains a significant era of reassessment for such social commentary.[8]

[5] Taylor is a good example of the perceived rise of the 'great' merchant, dominating smaller contractors, and acting as their intermediary with government officials. For excellent analysis of the reciprocation of state and contractor, see J. Ehrman, *The Navy under William III* (Cambridge, 1953), esp. 59–65.

[6] For parallel developments in the worlds of market and theatre, see J.-C. Agnew, *Worlds Apart* (Cambridge, 1986), esp. 152–77.

[7] Note the mistrust of Sir George Downing towards merchants, despite his active support for a most constructive series of commercial measures—H. Roseveare, 'Prejudice and Policy: Sir George Downing as Parliamentary Entrepreneur', in D. C. Coleman and P. Mathias (eds.), *Enterprise and History* (Cambridge, 1984), esp. 147–8.

[8] In this regard, James Raven's work represents a significant advance on that of McVeagh, since it reveals that a positive image of the overseas trader was maintained after 1750—*Judging New Wealth*, 256–8.

Beyond the realms of fiction, the professional needs of business ensured that there were perennial issues which could test the receptiveness of the patriot trader in governing circles. Significantly, several political studies have indicated that changing attitudes towards the merchant may have led to more concrete rewards than the mere approbation of commentators such as Addison. For instance, historians have noted some improvement in the navy's protection of trading convoys, advances in the diplomatic representation of trade abroad, and, most tellingly of all, a shift in fiscal legislation from revenue priorities to commercial sponsorship. More generally, the innovatory debates of the political arithmeticians after 1660 helped to promote commercial issues as central to the discussion of state policy.[9] These are encouraging signs of a state supportive of trade, and seemingly bespeak an increasing regard for the patriot trader in the corridors of power. On the other hand, occasional alarm was expressed at the political pretensions of well-placed businessmen, whose financial clout threatened the accepted hegemony of the nobility and gentry. Moreover, the work of J. G. A. Pocock has shown that the moral character of commerce could be attacked in heated discussions concerning the future of state and society. Even though the overseas trader offered little direct threat to the gentry's stranglehold on positions of political or social pre-eminence, in certain governing circles the jury on the merchant was clearly still out. However, although there were undoubted limits to the effectiveness of mercantile claims to patriotic status, they cannot obscure the significance of the Augustan debates reflecting on the relationship between the trader and the state, which peaked during the great wars of 1689–1713. Ossified social attitudes and the continuing hegemony of land remained as facts of English life, but that did not preclude a most significant exchange of views on the role of the merchant within the state.[10]

The following sections examine debates which both highlight and define the importance of the Augustan period for the merchant in public life. Most importantly, they will illuminate contemporary discussion on the overseas traders from a mercantile point of view. As literary historians concede, the most influential authors were largely non-commercial in origin, and were

[9] P. Crowhurst, *The Defence of British Trade* (Folkestone, 1977); R. Hinton, *The Eastland Trade and the Commonweal* (Cambridge, 1959), 121; C. D. Chandaman, *The English Public Revenue, 1660–88* (Oxford, 1975), 11–21; R. Davis, 'The Rise of Protection in England, 1689–1786', *EcHR* 2nd ser., 19 (1986), 307–17; J. Hoppit, 'Political Arithmetic in Eighteenth-Century England', *EcHR* 49 (1996), 516–40. Diplomatic activity is largely beyond the remit of this study, but by the reign of Anne there appears a more systematic approach to commercial affairs in the work of the consuls—D. B. Horn, *The British Diplomatic Service, 1689–1789* (Oxford, 1961), 237–58.

[10] J. G. A. Pocock, *The Machiavellian Moment* (Princeton, 1975), 423–61. For a general critique of Pocock's views, see Pincus, *American Historical Review*, 103 (1998), 705–36. For further exploration of the contemporary debate concerning the relation of trade and politics, see I. Hont, 'Free Trade and the Economic Limits to National Politics: Neo-Machiavellian Political Economy Reconsidered', in J. Dunn (ed.), *The Economic Limits to Modern Politics* (Cambridge, 1990), 41–120. The variety of mercantile imagery in this period is discussed in N. A. F. Glaisyer, 'The Culture of Commerce in England, 1660–1720', Ph.D. thesis (Cambridge, 1999).

thus at best unacquainted with the business world. Defoe was very much the exception as a former trader with literary genius, and it was thus predictable that portrayals of the merchant ranged from the hopelessly idealistic to the positively hostile.[11] Inevitably, most social commentators approached the question of the merchant in society from the perspective of the gentleman, in order to see how the trader fitted into the predominant culture of the governing classes. Even among historians, there has been less concern to discover mercantile self-perception, especially to see how the trader regarded his contribution to state and society. In this chapter these perspectives will be examined by analysing understudied forms of mercantile expression, in particular the voluminous literature which survives from commercial tracts. Recent bibliographic studies have revealed that the late Stuart period saw significant change in the economic press in England, and it is thus doubly important to study the message emanating from this vibrant source.[12] Analysis of the ways in which merchants and others characterized the role of overseas trade within the state will demonstrate the real and imagined obstacles which traders perceived to be in their path towards political and social acceptance. As with literary evidence, there must be reservations about some of the more extreme claims made for the values and virtues of the trader, especially from publishers and authors wishing to boost sales, but the press can illuminate the evolving relationship of the merchant and the state. In fact, the Augustan discourse of commercial patriotism was severely tested after 1660 by an intermittent campaign for a greater mercantile presence in governing circles, which debate will form the last section of this chapter. However, as a necessary preliminary to these important exchanges, we must first delineate the circulation of literature about trade, and to identify the forces which promoted it.

i. The mercantile press

Few historians would quibble that there were far more publications about commerce produced in the second half of the seventeenth century than in the first half, but in itself this does not prove that trade had captured a greater share of the national consciousness. In the course of the century the press underwent profound change, and trade was but one of the many areas to benefit from an expansion in the market for the printed word. The commercialization of print found a ready audience among merchants, who possessed

---

[11] McVeagh stressed the essential vagueness of the literary ideal of the merchant in the early eighteenth century—*Tradefull Merchants*, 65–7.

[12] J. Hoock and P. Jeannin, *Ars Mercatoria* (Paderborn, 1991), esp. vol. ii. For an imaginative use of commercial tracts to investigate general attitudes towards trade, see T. Keirn, 'Monopoly, Economic Thought, and the Royal African Company', in J. Brewer and S. Staves (eds.), *Early Modern Conceptions of Property* (London, 1995), 427–66.

the wealth, literacy, and the professional need to promote the growing media for information and opinion. In particular, analysts of the early stock market have demonstrated the increasing circulation of printed data in City circles from the late 1660s onwards, and merchants clearly patronized the capital's first advertising gazettes.[13] However, even at the end of the century trade was still a very poor cousin in terms of both readership and publication rates when compared to the serious standard fare of politics, religion, and foreign developments. There is also little reason to suppose that it posed a real threat to travel tales or imaginative literature in the market for works of instruction and entertainment. As late as 1680 William Petyt's influential *Britannia Languens* could lament a lack of published commercial authorities, observing how the subject of trade was 'so copious and so little laboured by other writers that I have no common places or beaten tracts to follow as in other studies', a view endorsed by Nicholas Barbon a decade later. Nevertheless, these reservations should not obscure the ways in which trade had benefited from a revolution in the press, and several initiatives demonstrated that a wider audience had been generated for commercial issues.[14]

Until 1660 public debates concerning trade had been largely advanced by polemical treatise, the most influential of which were penned by former merchants. They could vary enormously in length, depending on the precise reasons for their publication, and could be broadly classed into two: the longer general discourse about trade, and the shorter tract aimed at a specific commercial controversy. Neither format kept rigidly either to a specific or general brief, and, as we shall see, they could range far beyond their ostensible commercial remit. As contributions to particular controversies, their incidence in the first half of the century was largely determined by the occurrence of acute economic hardship, most notably in the 1620s. Emboldened by a parliamentary forum for the discussion of commercial grievance, a wide range of groups and individuals sought to impress their views at a national level. Relatively few took the trouble to publish their opinions for a wider audience, but these disputes helped to establish a public forum for economic issues. Not uncoincidentally, it appears that from the 1620s onwards it became increasingly common for interest groups to distil their arguments into a single page

[13] L. Neal, *The Rise of Financial Capitalism* (Cambridge, 1990), 20–34; J. Price, 'Notes on some London Price Currents', *EcHR* 2nd ser., 7 (1954–5), 240–50; J. J. McCusker and C. Gravesteijn (eds.), *The Beginnings of Commercial and Financial Journalism* (Amsterdam, 1991), 291–352. For general discussion of the mercantile contribution to the growth of the press, see J. Sutherland, *The Restoration Newspaper* (Cambridge, 1986); R. Harris, *Politics and the Rise of the Press: Britain and France, 1620–1800* (London, 1996), 24–6.
[14] *Britannia Languens* (1680), 153–4; N. Barbon, *A Discourse of Trade* (London, 1690), preface. In the most comprehensive study of seventeenth-century economic literature, J. Appleby found that only a dozen economic titles appeared in the 1620s, while hundreds were being produced by the 1670s—*Economic Thought*, 5. She based this assessment on the great repositories at the British Library, the Goldsmiths Library of Economic Literature, and the Kress Library at Harvard.

for the purposes of influencing Crown and Parliament.[15] As in so many other fields, the 1650s proved particularly fertile for the printed economic controversy, prompting some of the more radical reassessments of the role of foreign trade within the state. The upheavals of these two decades thus ensured that post-Restoration commentators could invoke a wide range of native authorities to support their arguments, especially on the perennial issues of freer trade and monetary policy. It is thus unsurprising that the format of much of the commercial debate under the later Stuarts was maintained largely through these two kinds of publication.[16]

However, while commercial disputes gave encouragement to authors and publishers to promote trade literature, their polemical origins did not serve to inculcate respect for this genre of writing, and the authors themselves acknowledged that the common format of trade controversy was not geared to win over a wider audience. As Charles Davenant later observed, 'set a white dog and a black dog together by the ears in a dirty kennel, it is odds but that they will come out both alike, black'. A most sympathetic gentle observer of the 1690s could still describe self-interest as 'a fault common to all the rest that have written upon that subject, being merchants'. Even traders showed a similar weariness with the pitch of commercial debate, Sir Francis Brewster observing in 1695 that he knew 'no subject that has been more writ on and worse handled than that of trade'. He attributed such unproductive in-fighting to the fact that commerce was not 'in the hands of philosophers or men bred to the liberal sciences, but such whose education has been more in the Cantore than schools'. The West Indian trader Thomas Tryon also lamented the opportunities spurned by the commercial press, calling for merchants, domestic traders, and manufacturers to concentrate on 'the universal notions and methods of trade' for 'then our country gentlemen must be convinced and made sensible that it would be their principal interest to propagate and advance trade'.[17] Factionalism was merely one cause of gentry indifference, and other writers agreed that the presentation of economic debate had failed to capture public attention. Several commercial writers even felt obliged to apologize for the limitations of their style, and the only commercial polemicist to be widely acknowledged for literary ability was Defoe. The aforementioned

[15] R. Ashton, *The City and the Court, 1603–42* (Cambridge, 1979), 106–35; B. Supple, *Commercial Crisis and Change in England, 1600–42* (Cambridge, 1959), 58–64. Appleby, *Economic Thought*, 51, stresses the novelty of the 1620s in moving debate to a new public forum of print, thus removing economic discussion from the politicized court and Parliament to a more scientific arena. I am indebted to Chris Kyle for this observation on the emergence of the single-page résumé in the 1620s.

[16] M. Ashley, *Financial and Commercial Policy under the Cromwellian Protectorate* (Oxford, 1934); Pincus, *American Historical Review*, 103 (1998), 705–36.

[17] *The Political and Commercial Works of Charles Davenant*, ed. C. Whitworth (London, 1771), v. 305–6; Add. MSS 5540, fo. 56; F. Brewster, *Essays on Trade and Navigation* (London, 1695), preface; T. Tryon, *England's Grandeur and Way to Get Wealth* (London, 1699), 21. For discussion of mercantile self-interest in the press, see W. Letwin, *The Origins of Scientific Economics: English Economic Thought, 1660–1776* (London, 1963), 87–96.

Petyt highlighted the diffident response for works on commerce, fearing that the public would condemn his treatise merely 'upon the sight of the title page . . . (because it is of trade)', and would thus dismiss it 'as fit only to be read by milliners and exchangemen'. The disparagement of the mercantile press was a serious hurdle for the commercial world to overcome if it really was to make an impact on other sectors of society, and thus rise above the petty parochialism which had alienated potentially sympathetic observers. Given this reputation for narrow-mindedness and inelegance, it is predictable that both contemporaries and historians have turned to respected penmen such as Addison and Steele to gauge the advance of trade in the Augustan press.[18]

Mercantile authors recognized that the potential readership for the commercial treatise was limited, and that they faced an uphill task in broadening the appeal of the subject beyond particular vested interests. Many works made an overt attempt to win a different audience, but the success of their efforts in attracting new readers is very difficult to ascertain. Historians of the press have demonstrated the difficulties in discovering circulation figures for all types of publication, and although subscription lists, stamp duties, and personal libraries all indicate a wide circulation of commercial ideas, the survival of such illuminating sources remains erratic. A literary expert indeed concluded that 'we have to accept that ignorance will remain about many aspects of the historical sociology of popular literature'.[19] Only in the most bastardized format of the single-page summary can editions of trade literature be determined with any certainty, with perhaps between some 500 and 1,000 copies printed. These limited editions reflected their authors' primary interest in influencing Parliament and Whitehall, although they could easily find their way into the provinces from Westminster. With longer treatises, the circulation figures are even more uncertain, although the increasing volume of economic literature on offer suggests that the market for these publications was growing. On the other hand, the experience of merchant writer John Cary should sound a note of caution in the apparently effortless rise in the trade press, for in 1696 he was explicitly warned by a correspondent at Ipswich that even the Suffolk seaport would be a poor market for his important treatises. More positively, the ensuing sections will indicate that certain types of commercial tract could sell in their thousands, which suggests a readership far beyond the confines of the merchants themselves.[20]

[18] *Britannia Languens*, preface. The difficulties of applying literary styles to economic debate, especially for commercial audiences, are noted by J. Viner, 'Satire and Economics in the Augustan Age of Satire', in H. K. Miller, E. Rothstein, and G. S. Rousseau (eds.), *The Augustan Milieu* (Oxford, 1970), 77–101.　　　　　　　　　　　　　　　[19] Raven, *Judging New Wealth*, 252.

[20] Add. MSS 5540, fo. 64. Appleby, *Economic Thought*, 5, suggests that the normal print-run for economic tracts was in the range of 500–2,000 copies. An estimate for printing 1,000 'half-sheets' remains among the jottings of Levant trader Charles Cooke, who calculated that it would set him back a relatively modest 66 shillings and 8 pence—Bodl. folio theta 665, fo. 106ᵛ.

The key to the advancement of the mercantile press was diversification in the format of commercial debate, and the most important sign of growing interest in trade was the appearance of several periodicals dedicated to commerce, a clear innovation on pre-Restoration discourse. John Houghton's *A Collection for Improvement of Husbandry and Trade* was the most significant new publication, running weekly in its second series of 1692–1703, during which time he covered a huge range of economic issues in the hope that 'trade may be better understood, and the whole kingdom made as one trading city'. In this vein, he provided the uninitiated with several extensive accounts of overseas trade and the workings of the City, and was willing to commentate on commercial issues of moment, such as the new Board of Trade in 1696, and the calico riot of 1697.[21] More generally, as a member of the nascent Royal Society, the apothecary Houghton symbolized the importance of changing scholarly attitudes for the advancement of debate about commerce, as greater credit was given in some quarters to its contribution to national strength. Samuel Fortrey, an influential pamphleteer, captured this spirit of patriotic inquiry, insisting that 'the genius and disposition of the times [is] to study more the interest and improvement of the nation than usually heretofore'. Historians have shown that there was considerable support among the early members of the Society for disseminating information about trade, and they were willing to turn to merchants to discuss commercial matters. However, their record of publication never matched such enthusiasm.[22] The justly famous work of the political arithmeticians such as Petty, Graunt, and King significantly advanced ideas on demographic and fiscal issues, but the Royal Society contributed little to the advancement of trade. Houghton, however, continued to highlight the significance of overseas commerce for national strength, and was not averse to directing Parliament to attend to matters of pressing concern. As such, he was much more obviously the forerunner of Charles Davenant, who by the turn of the century had established himself as the leading commentator on the relationship between commerce and the vitality of the state.[23]

---

[21] *A Collection*, 27 Apr. 1692. Houghton's first series, *A Collection of Letters for the Improvement of Husbandry and Trade*, ran for 21 issues in 1681–5. Margaret Hunt has recently stressed Houghton's educational role—*The Middling Sort*, 183–5. For discussion of Houghton's wide-ranging importance, see Glaisyer, Ph.D. thesis, ch. 5.

[22] S. Fortrey, *England's Interest and Improvement, Consisting in the Increase and the Store and Trade of this Kingdom* (Cambridge, 1663), preface. For discussion of the link between economic thinking and the Royal Society see W. E. Houghton, 'The History of Trades: Its Relation to Seventeenth-Century Thought', *Journal of the History of Ideas*, 2 (1941), 33–60; Letwin, *Origins of Scientific Economics*, esp. chs. 4 and 5. In the late seventeenth century only 7% of Royal Society fellows were merchants or tradesmen, and Houghton was exceptional as a very active member—M. Hunter, *The Royal Society and its Fellows* (Chalfont St Giles, 1982), 24–8.

[23] For discussion of the general role of political arithmetic in state policy, see J. Hoppit in *EcHR* 49 (1996), 516–40. For evidence of King's close interest in foreign trade, see *Two Tracts by Gregory King*, ed. J. H. Hollander (Baltimore, 1936), 59–76. As Hollander notes, Davenant did have access to King's unpublished work.

Davenant published in a traditional treatise format, leaving Houghton's mantle as trade journalist to be taken up by Charles Povey and Daniel Defoe. Although the lesser-known of this pair, Povey probably represented a truer metropolitan perspective than Defoe, albeit to promote his various commercial schemes via his main publishing venture, the twice-weekly *General Remark on Trade*, which ran from 1705 for at least three years. Most ambitiously, Povey wanted his paper to be 'universally approved of, not only by those who are concerned in trade and business, but likewise [to] become acceptable to all persons whatsoever rank and degree'. Like Houghton, he evidently thought that his audience required an education in the mysteries of trade, and thus inserted a series of articles detailing the operation of both domestic and international commerce. With circulation figures of some 3,500, Povey claimed a readership even beyond that of the *London Gazette*, and its distribution to 'taverns, booksellers, stationers, strong-water shops, inns, coffee-houses, victualling-houses, and other places of popular resort' doubtless ensured his desired cosmopolitan audience.[24] At the same time, Defoe's *Review* of 1704–13 was achieving even more publicity for commercial issues, keen as he was to mix his informed views on trade with staple commentary on domestic and foreign politics. Not only was he accustomed to pronounce his views on specific issues such as the commercial consequences of the Act of Union, or parliamentary efforts to regulate credit, but he also was keen to lecture his audience on the general benefits of trade for society as a whole.[25] His success was an encouragement to other publishers to combine standard political fare with commercial items, as with the *Weekly Packet* of 1712, which boasted its credentials as 'a methodical collection of the most material occurrences in matters of state, trade, arts, and sciences'. Whatever the success of these innovations, their impact pales in comparison with the journalistic bout of 1713–14, when two papers exclusively dedicated to trade, the *Mercator* and the *British Merchant*, ran for over a year. Such was their importance for the development of commercial debate that chapter 6 will examine this controversy in great detail, for it serves to show how the printed word was circulating new ideas about both trade and its practitioners across a very wide social spectrum. At its peak, over 10,000 copies of trade-related journals were being produced each week, a figure which gave ample testimony to the power of the printed commercial word.[26]

Thus, even though it is difficult to gauge the audience for commercial

---

[24] *The General Remark on Trade*, 16–20 Nov. 1705, 4–7 July 1707. Povey actually planned to enlarge his circulation to 8,000–10,000 copies. For the development of the more factual *Price Courants*, see J. M. Price in *EcHR* 2nd ser., 7 (1954–5), 240–50.

[25] *Defoe's Review*, ed. A. W. Seard (New York, 1938).

[26] J. M. Price, 'A Note on the Circulation of the London Press, 1704–14', *BIHR* 31 (1958), 215–24. T. Keirn has shown that some 200 titles were published in the course of the controversy over the Africa trade between 1689 and 1714, 80% of which contained only one or two pages—Brewer and Staves, *Early Modern Conceptions of Property*, 437.

issues, these journalistic innovations suggest that the merchant and his concerns were increasingly in the public eye, and that there had been significant changes in the presentation of commercial issues. The development of the economic press could not be ascribed to merchants alone, but the successful integration of commerce with more traditional public debate in the *Review* and the *Spectator* speaks greatly for contemporary reaction to perceived changes within state and society. Most commercial commentary was still focused on particular issues, but the resonance of these public exchanges could be very broad. Most interestingly, several general themes of commercial debate suggest that the role of the merchant within the state had come to the fore, as a matter of interest for all classes. In particular, discussion focused on the development of the merchant as a recognizable profession, the perceived importance of tracing the history of English trade, and the representation of commercial interests within the national polity. Analysis of these debates will illuminate the forces which influenced changing attitudes towards the merchant within the period.

ii. The press and the profession

One of the most interesting developments for analysts of Augustan society has been the rise of the professions within English society, a phenomenon which reflected important changes within the upper tier of the urban middling orders. A number of occupations gained increasing influence and respect, from traditional careers in medicine and the law to the burgeoning sectors of the civil service and armed forces. Although lacking the acres to become members of the gentry, these professionals came to be regarded as gentlemen due to their expertise and perceived value to the state. Regularization of standards of training and practice considerably enhanced their status, and the jealous protection of 'secret knowledge' ensured them a lucrative monopoly of certain social services.[27] There has been little discussion of the merchant from such perspectives, even though there are signs that his occupational status may have undergone similar transition. In particular, historians have yet to discover whether the development of a more 'concentrated' elite of overseas traders significantly altered attitudes towards the merchant, especially in the course of debates on the patriot trader in the late Stuart period. There were no professional examinations or supervisory institutions to dignify career structures within commerce, but in common with the accepted professions the particular functions of the trader were lionized in many quarters for fulfilling a specialized and important service for the country. There were in fact calls for the establishment of colleges for merchants, in response to the perceived

[27] G. S. Holmes, *Augustan Society* (London, 1982); P. Corfield, *Power and the Professions in Britain, 1700–1850* (London, 1995); W. Prest (ed.), *The Professions in Early Modern England* (Beckenham, 1987).

failure of conventional curricula to prepare youngsters for a career in trade, and to the threat of foreign competition. These appeals went unheeded, and the merchant was never ranked among the true professionals, but the didactic mercantile literature of the 1660–1720 period suggests that the overseas trader claimed important professional attributes. Many of these works were written by merchants and thus provide a sensitive guide to their broader occupational concerns, so often subsumed by more particular priorities. Thus, it is all the more significant that these sources lauded the qualities of the overseas trader for their potential benefit to society as a whole, and as arguments for according heightened respect for the merchant within the state.[28]

The magisterial survey of Hoock and Jeannin has established that the late Stuart period saw a fundamental shift in the publication of English commercial instruction, with a huge increase in such literature. Since the fifteenth century England had lagged behind the commercial powers of Italy and the Netherlands, but after 1660 there appeared an unquenchable demand for works on trading skills.[29] Many of these publications were specifically targeted at the merchant, reflecting a common perception that he held a distinct position of authority within the business world. However, while this boom is one of undeniable significance, post-Restoration development cannot be understood without reference to early Stuart innovations. More precisely, the post-1620 period was a most fertile era, producing several works whose ideas on the professional attributes of the merchant became standard for the rest of the century. Elizabethan precedents could be found for their arguments, for instance John Browne's successful *Marchant's Aviso* of 1591, but Augustan commercial debate looked principally to early Stuart authorities for their inspiration, thereby ensuring them an enduring popularity.[30] Their unequivocal endorsement of the overseas trader as a valuable citizen predictably pre-dates trends in the literary world, and can explain in part the positive response of the post-Restoration public to the mercantile ideal. Although purely practical in purpose, these guides helped to define the claims of the merchant to special consideration, and in the process developed the parameters of a sophisticated discourse of commercial patriotism.[31]

---

[28] For discussion of the need for mercantile colleges, see *Britannia Languens*, 100–2, 198; Add. MSS 5540, fo. 75; Brewster, *Essays on Trade and Navigation*, p. vi.

[29] Hoock and Jeannin, *Ars Mercatoria*, esp. ii. 668–72. Significantly, Natasha Glaisyer has recently argued that the growth in didactic mercantile literature after 1660 was steady in character, and cannot be simply linked to specific bursts of interest—Ph.D. thesis, ch. 6.

[30] For discussion of Browne's writings, see D. H. Sacks, *The Widening Gate* (Berkeley, Calif., 1991), 332–8. Laura Stevenson notes that Elizabethan praise for the merchant was not linked to their trade per se, but to their service for the Crown—*Praise and Paradox*, esp. 127–9. Although noting support for traders in the writings of the late sixteenth century, McVeagh sees equivocation in the portrayal of the merchant until the late seventeenth century—*Tradefull Merchants*, chs. 1 and 2.

[31] Significantly, Steve Pincus's important argument concerning the increasing respect accorded to the value of trade/traders during the 1640s and 1650s does not seek to link such views to pre-1640 authors—*American Historical Review*, 103 (1998), esp. 717–22.

As an apologist for the merchant classes, none was so enduringly authoritative as Gerard de Malynes, an adviser on trade and exchanges to the governments of Elizabeth and James I. Malynes's principal fame rests with *Consuetudo: vel Lex Mercatoria* of 1622, an ambitious work aimed at an audience of 'statesmen, judges, magistrates, temporal and civil lawyers, mint-men, merchants, mariners, and all others negotiating in all places of the world'. To this diverse group he not only sought to propound the laws of the seas, but imparted informed opinion on a wide range of mercantile activities in the course of his discussion of commodities, money, and exchanges. He hoped that this knowledge would help 'to maintain equity and justice by the law of nations', and underlined the value of merchants to the nation as 'the means and instruments' to enrich the kingdom. Therefore, it seemed 'questionless' to him that 'the state of a merchant is of great dignity and to be cherished; for by them countries are discovered, familiarity between nations is procured, and politic experience is attained'. There was no claim that the merchant should direct commercial policy, but he clearly had a role to play in society which elevated him above charges of self-profit, and even gave him patriotic status. Malynes's other works, which were issued in a more conventional polemical format, revealed that he could be most critical of the potential harm inflicted on the realm by merchant self-interest, and indeed insisted that 'princes and governors are to sit at the stern of the course of trade and commerce'. However, the respect with which the *Lex Mercatoria* was regarded in the mercantile press highlighted its importance in cementing an image of the merchant as the servant of the state.[32]

Malynes's most obvious successor was Lewes Roberts, a director of both the Levant and East India Companies. His *Merchant's Map of Commerce* of 1638 developed Malynes's arguments, and earned enduring repute among commercial writers for classifying the merchant as a distinctive and valued member of society. For Roberts, it was the professional expertise of the merchant which set him apart from both the landed gentry and other members of the trading classes, and the sheer size of the tome still impresses with its coverage of the specialisms of the mercantile sector. As the title suggests, its principal aim was to instruct in matters of global economy, informing the reader of the customs, produce, and trade of the known world. The result is nothing less than a staggering account of global trade, with data supplied on a myriad of social, economic, and political practices, from Brazil to Mozambique to China. In fact, as both contemporaries and modern analysts have stressed, the seventeenth-century merchant was generally a regional or commodity specialist, but Roberts highlighted the necessary cosmopolitanism of the successful merchant. Indeed, Roberts laid great stress on skills beyond

---

[32] G. de Malynes, *Consuetudo: vel Lex Mercatoria* (1622), preface; Appleby, *Economic Thought*, 42–5, 108. Letwin regarded Malynes as the author of the most popular mercantile handbook of its time – *Origins of Scientific Economics*, 101.

the usual remit of the overseas trader, insisting that 'a merchant's judgement must not be limited within the compass of any one particular trade or vocation: for herein must his mystery, skill, and art exceed all other, as requiring by necessity a more general knowledge than any other tradesman'.[33] Further lionizing his subject, Roberts also stressed the technical expertise required by the overseas merchant, insisting that 'merchandising may well be said to be an Art or Science invented by ingenious mankind for the public good, commodity, and welfare of all commonwealths'. In this light, he considered mercantile ability to be superior to that of a poet 'whose excellency must consist in a cursory judgement in all sciences . . . the difference being that the merchant's skill must be real, solid, and substantial, and the poet's may be feigned and poetical'. Therefore, for the young merchant's enlightenment he supplied separate articles on customs duties, coins, weights and measures, accounting, arithmetic, and exchanges, to the last-named of which he devoted over 100 pages in order to explain the mysteries of transmitting credit overseas. The perceived need for such accomplishments ensured a steady stream of publications devoted to inculcating one or more of these particular skills for the rest of the century. There can be little doubt that such talents were not shared by every merchant, especially across a wide range of languages and customs, but Roberts had successfully represented the intricacies of his calling, and displayed appropriate pride in having mastered its many challenges.[34]

Roberts was not content with mere professional attributes, and extrapolated from these merchant abilities a wider virtue based on their collective and individual value to the state. He easily dealt with the problem of mercantile self-profit, by insisting that the benefits of the exchanges in which he was involved brought much-needed provisions and wealth into the country. More significantly, he argued that the merchant's work, and especially his experience of foreign countries, rendered the merchant an especially worthy citizen. Roberts asserted that 'neither is it a rare or extraordinary thing to find those that have had their education thus to have proved not only good commonwealthsmen, but also excellent statesmen: our own country hath afforded some examples in all ages, but in other countries many more are daily found'. Significantly, he did not invoke any specific mercantile heroes, but the Venetians, the Dutch, the Tuscans, and the Hanse towns were all held forth as examples of successful states for whom 'merchandizing is found to be the school from whence they gather their first principles, and indeed the chief foundation upon which their fabric of political government is raised, the scale by which their counsels are framed and the pillars by which the same is seen to

---

[33] L. Roberts, *The Merchant's Map of Commerce* (London, 1638), esp. 36. For an account of his life, see *DNB*. In the dedication, Roberts stressed twelve years of overseas travel as his credentials for relating the merchandising of four continents, although it appears that his main spheres of experience had been the Mediterranean and the Levant.

[34] Roberts, *Merchant's Map*, 36, 38. The swipe at poetical skills reflects ongoing debate concerning the relative merits of differing forms of knowledge for the benefit of mankind.

be supported and maintained'. On a more individual basis, the merchant was seen as a prime candidate for magistracy, 'his wisdom, travel, and experience abroad' suiting him for the role of governor and 'good patriot'. In Roberts's eyes, there was little that the merchant could not do, and such evident utility demanded the respect and thanks of the rest of society.[35]

Of course, these personal views cannot be accepted uncritically as a sign of the confidence of a rising bourgeoisie, or as a general measure of merchant aspiration in the late 1630s. However, it appears that his work was well received, since it underwent three further editions by the close of the century. More pertinently, it had an undoubted influence on mercantile writings throughout the century and beyond, for other authors directly echoed his views on the skills and social contribution of the merchant. The impressive growth of English trade under the early Stuarts also appears to have stimulated the market for professional guides, and several of Roberts's contemporaries saw fit to publish works to give instruction in mercantile skills. Most notably, only three years before Roberts had appeared Richard Dafforne's *Merchant's Mirror*, a guide to the intricacies of accounting, whose preface lamented the lack of English authorities in this field. James Peele had published two works on accounting in the mid-sixteenth century, but now there appeared a new impetus to the trade, with Ralph Handson, Richard Hodges, John Marius, John Collins, and others ensuring a stream of works on the calculation of interest, exchange, and accounting over the ensuing twenty years. The broadening range of this literature was highlighted in 1660 by Abraham Liset, who felt compelled to encourage sales of his accounting manual with a handbook of instructions to would-be gentleman merchants, outlining the main points of Malynes into the bargain. Most interestingly, the mathematics teacher endorsed Malynes's views on the utility of the overseas trader, stressing that 'right merchants are taken to be wise in their profession for their own good and benefit of the commonwealth; for . . . they are the principal instruments to increase or decrease the wealth thereof'.[36]

The demand for instructive manuals on trade if anything increased in the early Restoration, doubtless encouraged by the appearance in 1664 of Thomas Mun's posthumous *England's Treasure by Foreign Trade*. This work had probably been composed by this experienced trader in the 1620s, but was published by his son 'for the common good', reasoning that the 'serious discourses' of major merchants were 'commonly not unprofitable'. Mun's

---

[35] Roberts, ibid. 1, 11, 198.

[36] Accounting works were mostly penned by teachers and pubic notaries—R. Dafforne, *The Merchant's Mirror* (London, 1635), dedication; R. Handson, *Analysis or Resolution of Merchant's Accounts*, 4th edn. (1669); R. Hodges, *Enchiridion Arithmetica*, 2nd edn. (London, 1653); J. Collins, *An Introduction to Merchant's Accounts* (1653); J. Marius, *Advice Concerning Bills of Exchange*, 2nd edn. (1670); A. Liset, *Amphithalami* (1660), 14–18. For discussion of the contribution of several English authorities in the field of accountancy, see M. F. Bywater and B. S. Yamey, *Historic Accounting Literature: A Companion Guide* (London, 1982).

essential aim was to remind his readers of the importance of trade for national wealth, but he opened his work by stressing in even more cogent terms the all-round abilities of the merchant. He also stressed additional accomplishments to be gained, such as a knowledge of insurance and navigation, concluding that 'I find no other profession which leadeth into more worldly knowledge'. Like Roberts, he drew attention to the positions of civil authority gained by merchants in Italy and the Netherlands, and made a powerful critique on the lack of respect shown to 'the nobleness of the profession' in early Stuart society. He even claimed that social disparagement ensured that merchants did not 'labour to attain unto the excellence of their profession', and lamented how 'the memory of our richest merchants is suddenly extinguished; the son being left rich, scorneth the profession of his father, conceiving more honour to be a gentleman (although but in name) to consume his estate in dark ignorance and excess, than to follow the steps of his father as an industrious merchant to maintain and advance his fortunes'. He also could not resist a swipe at the legal profession, contrasting 'the plainness of our dealing' with 'the workers of lying wonders'. Mun thus showed an explicit impatience with the social mores of his day which was less obvious in Roberts's work, but his answer to such prejudice was to put forward exactly the sort of arguments which the latter had championed for the merchant in *The Map of Commerce*. It is therefore of no surprise that an enterprising publisher printed both treatises together in 1700.[37]

Thus, by the reign of Charles II, merchants had ventured into print to put forward a positive portrait of the ideal merchant, which both integrated their profession into society (by stressing their value to the national revenue) and set the merchant apart (by outlining the special skills necessary for a successful career in trade). Over the next sixty years the economic press would continue to highlight the distinctive characteristics of the role of the merchant within society, which ideas were widely discussed in other forms of publication, and ultimately find their place in the fashionable works of Addison and Steele. However, the most sensitive debate on the role of the mercantile profession was maintained in commercial handbooks, an innovative and increasingly popular genre after 1660. Although most of these works were not penned by active merchants, in content and tone they mirror the works of Malynes and Roberts, and were indeed prepared to acknowledge their debts to these commercial authorities. Providing instruction in a far more accessible format, often pocket-size, they achieved great sales, exploiting a demand fuelled by the expansion of the nation's trade. Several only dealt with certain aspects of the merchant's work, most notably accounting, their publishers hoping thereby to

[37] T. Mun, *England's Treasure by Foreign Trade* (London, 1664), esp. dedication, 2–10, 116–17. For Mun's economic ideas, and his importance in differentiating economic factors from social and political influences, see Appleby, *Economic Thought*, 37–41. His emphasis on the professional value of the merchant was invoked in the late eighteenth century—Thomas Mortimer, *The Elements of Commerce, Politics, and Finance* (1772), 208.

gain as wide an audience as possible. For instance, the *Debtor and Creditor Made Easy*, written by London merchant Stephen Monteage, aimed to reveal the mysteries of Italian bookkeeping to farmers, gentlemen, artisans, and shopkeepers, as well as to young merchants. The second edition of 1682 even included an appendix which encouraged women to learn, reasoning from Dutch example that it was in the family's interest that the wife be thoroughly conversant with her husband's business affairs. Historians have rightly questioned their success in instilling good practice in business accounts, but they retain much value for their illumination of the continuing debate on the status of the overseas trader.[38]

The first in importance for the post-Restoration period was John Vernon's *The Complete Comptinghouse* of 1678, whose success is attested by the five editions it had gone through by 1722. In his epistle to his readers, Vernon stressed that he wished to ensure that apprentice merchants were respected by their masters, and not treated as a drudge and errand-boy while there were so many skills to be learnt. In accordance with this aim, the 248-page book was structured as a conservation between an apprentice and a kindly master, who guided him through his first steps at the customs house, dockside, Royal Exchange, and counting-house. Most interestingly, Vernon was keen to delineate the exact function of the merchant, and took evident pride in the pre-eminent position which the merchant enjoyed within commercial life. As the master opined: 'I hate to think a man should pretend to pass for a merchant and yet the shopkeeper stand and laugh in his sleeve to see his ignorance and folly; and not only cheat him of his money, but jeer [at] him when he is gone.' Modern research has often lamented the blurring of distinctions within the early modern economy, as merchants flitted between various wholesaling, retailing, and rentier investments, but Vernon had little doubt that the function of the merchant was supreme. He even attacked the daily publication by the customs house of the bills of entry, which was seen as 'a thing exceeding prejudicial to merchants and which makes the trade and mystery of a merchant as free and open to a cobbler as to a merchant that hath been bred 40 years to the trade'. His extensive coverage of the many skills necessary for the merchant somewhat undermined this bizarre claim, but he had demonstrated that the pride of the merchant still burned as bright as in the days of Mun and Roberts.[39]

More diffuse in aim, William Leybourn's *Panarithmologia* of 1693 set its sights firmly on the trading community, but sought to serve as both a general

[38] Stephen Monteage, *Debtor and Creditor Made Easy*, 2nd edn. (1682); Grassby, *Business Community*, 184–9. Monteage worked as a fiscal agent for several notable clients, including the Duke of Buckingham for 14 years—Bywater and Yamey, *Historic Accounting Literature*, 127–30; C24/1135, case 18.

[39] J. Vernon, *The Complete Comptinghouse* (London, 1678), esp. 135, 197–8. Further editions appeared in 1683, 1698, 1708, and 1722. Little is known about Vernon, although his published work suggests that he may have taught accounts in the capital. His wife ran a coffee-house near Vintners' Hall in Thames Street.

almanac for inland and overseas dealers. Nonetheless, there was no mistaking the principal thrust of the work, since it lauded the value of foreign trade to the nation in the highest terms. The structure of this work clearly owed a great deal of inspiration to Lewes Roberts, and Leybourn was keen to update his Caroline hymn of mercantile praise. Stressing the need for action above theory, this mathematician-cum-surveyor cited commerce as 'the main sheet anchor of us islanders, without which the genius of all our useful studies, which renders men famous and renowned, would make them useless and insignificant to the public'. Moreover, summarizing the merchant's claim to true patriotism, he asserted that 'it's foreign trade that renders us rich, honourable, and great, that gives us a name and esteem in the world'. He reserved particular pride for the contribution of London to national prosperity, boasting that it produced two-thirds of the annual customs revenue of £600,000. Accordingly, it was entirely appropriate that the London customs house had been rebuilt after the Great Fire 'in a much more magnificent, uniform, and commodious manner', and could thus accommodate the transaction of the country's vital overseas trade. Leybourn's handbook enjoyed phenomenal success, going through twenty-three editions stretching into the nineteenth century.[40]

Leybourn had thus great claims to merchant patriotism, but even he could not match the service which Edward Hatton performed for the trading classes from 1695 onwards. In that year appeared *The Merchant's Magazine*, a conventional guide to accounting and exchanges, which went through seven editions by 1721, selling (so the publishers claimed) some 8,000 copies. When reviewed by *The Works of the Learned* in 1695 it was evident that Hatton had gauged his subject-matter well, since it was hailed for 'being calculated for the improvement of trade and commerce, to which our English nation is so much indebted for their fame and grandeur, and that great figure which they make in the world'. The reviewer even went on to commend it to the gentry, 'not a few' of whom now 'run towards trade and merchandise'. Hatton was not slow to tap such potential custom, and the third edition of 1699 even included an extract from Sir Josiah Child's *Discourse of Trade*, in which the great merchant had appealed to the gentry to respect foreign trade, insisting 'the employment of a merchant is as valuable as that of a lawyer, physician, or any other profession whatsoever; for if the necessary perfections and qualities of a truly accomplished merchant be considered with respect to his natural, moral, and acquired parts, it will place him (in the opinion of the judicious) far above contempt'. At about this time Hatton published his pocket-sized *Comes Commercii*, which combined interest tables with a general guide to the shipping of goods in the capital. Another great success, it went through four editions by 1722, by which time it had sold over 5,000 copies. Hatton was still keen to emphasize

[40] W. Leybourn, *Panarithmologia* (London, 1693), esp. 41, 47. His debt to Roberts is exemplified by his account of the five sites necessary for a commercial centre—p. 4.

the value of trade to the nation, enthusing in the third edition of 1716, that 'the subject itself is in no way despicable, but of general use in this nation, where the current of most men's geniuses tend toward trade'. This final claim was somewhat undermined by Hatton's critique of those gentlemen who thought their offspring 'to be above the sphere of commerce', but the buoyancy of the market for mercantile handbooks suggested a genuine interest in overseas trade. For certain, these works demonstrate that Mun's and Roberts's arguments had been far from lost on their successors, who promulgated patriotic themes to flatter a growing trading constituency.[41]

These arguments for the merchant patriot were the forerunners of the famous justifications put forward by Defoe, Addison, and Steele, to which historians have usually turned to judge attitudes towards the mercantile classes. Of course, despite the obvious utility of the merchant, it did not mean that he was suddenly invulnerable to attacks concerning self-interest, covetousness, and ungentlemanly behaviour. Nor was he accorded the status of a 'true' professional, since his role lacked the cerebral, educated character of the lawyer, doctor, and don. Yet, the trade periodicals and handbooks suggest widespread recognition that the role of the overseas trader was regarded as distinct from the rest of the trading world, and that this special position at the very least deserved some respect. Furthermore, recognition of the important functions of merchants begged wider questions concerning the social and political role of the overseas trader, as many mercantile authors had pointed out. Thus, increasing professionalism prompted a more searching debate about the state's response to the expansion of trade, which went far beyond the realms of the didactic economic press. Particular credit can be given to the outlook of the political arithmeticians in this regard, whose quest for useful knowledge in the service of the state encouraged more commercial authors to consider 'national' perspectives after 1660. Although the principal interest of most trade journalism remained the advancement a specific cause, whether it be the naturalization of foreign artisans or the spoils of the East India trade, these works frequently illuminated more general themes concerning the merchant classes. In particular two prominent issues deserve especial attention with regard to the public role of the merchant: the historic debt owed by the nation (and other European powers) to the increase of trade; and the demand for an effective council of trade. The former highlighted the real sense of achievement felt by the trading classes, which manifested itself most directly by a claim to patriot status; while the latter betrayed the undisguised desire of merchants for a greater say in matters affecting their business interests. The assertiveness with which such claims were put forward undoubtedly bespoke a vulnerability to counter-charges of self-interest and even

---

[41] E. Hatton, *The Merchant's Magazine*, 7th edn. (London, 1721), esp. the preface; *idem, Comes Commercii*, 3rd edn. (London, 1716), esp. the epistle. Hatton's evident civic patriotism is shown by his best-known work, *The New View of London* (London, 1708).

unpatriotic behaviour, but in the next two sections these debates will serve as key sources for ascertaining the changing status of the merchant.

iii. The histories of trade

Although a leading authority dismissed the importance of historical analysis of the economy before the mid-eighteenth century, the Augustan period saw increasing interest in England's commercial past. This oversight is under-standable, since commercial histories were motivated by contemporary ambitions, and their published researches would never match up to the standards of modern historiography. On the other hand, their overt con-cern for current affairs ensured that they were sensitive towards changing attitudes concerning trade and its practitioners. In argument they were over-whelmingly sympathetic towards commerce, and shared a concern to educate an English audience about its fundamental importance to the future of the state. A correspondent of John Cary's underscored this didactic need by observing in the 1690s that 'a good history of the rise and progress of trade' would 'instruct men in a multitude of particulars that are not known or not well considered'. Always the innovator in matters of commerce, in 1713 Defoe embarked on a short-lived monthly periodical *The General History of Trade* to cure 'the ignorance of our people in matters of trade'. In this proselytizing vein, authors were prepared to go back to the Phoenicians to examine the fiscal and other benefits of trade, although it is significant that they generally concentrated on the economic upheavals of the seventeenth century to bring home their message. They may have fallen well short of the all-embracing vision of a 'History of Trades' espoused by luminaries such as Robert Boyle and Sir William Petty, but they reflected a perceived need to take stock of English commercial development. Most were dedicated to the rise of native trade, but it is significant that authors were eager to trace its growth within the context of general European developments. This awareness did not derive solely from recognition of the interdependence of world commerce, but reflected the essential motivation for discussion, which increasingly focused on the protection, consolidation, and extension of the current limits of English trade. In particular, the Dutch and the French were heralded as the exemplars of commercial prudence, whose lessons England had to learn for fear of tumbling down the European league of nations.[42]

Although great play was often made as to the antiquity of England's revered cloth trade, most economic writers saw England's emergence as an overseas

---

[42] D. C. Coleman, *History and the Economic Past* (Oxford, 1987), 6–8; Add. MSS 5540, fos. 59–60; *The General History of Trade*, issue 1, p. 12; Houghton in *Journal of the History of Ideas*, 2 (1941), 33–60. For a good example of the educational tone directed specifically at the gentry and nobility, see *A Brief History of Trade in England* (London, 1702), esp. 109–14.

trading power as a Tudor phenomenon, with Sir Josiah Child referring to the fifteenth century as the time 'before trade was understood in England'.[43] Some eulogized Henry VII for his patronage of the Cabot brothers, and Defoe credited the first Tudor King with breaking the monopoly which Northern Europeans held over English commerce. In fact, Defoe, alongside most authors, saw the Elizabethan age as the launching pad for England's true maritime greatness. Indeed, one author of 1691 went as far as to describe the adventurers of the late sixteenth century as 'heroes equal to Alexander and Caesar', forging into the unknown 'in the early days of trade when navigation was judged a mystery next to that of the black art'. John Evelyn, in his *History of Commerce and Navigation* of 1674, described Drake as a 'demi-god', and Raleigh would be continually extolled as an active and contemplative supporter of English trade expansion. Elizabeth herself was given due respect for her role, Defoe thinking her 'particularly espousing' to merchants, sending 'formal embassies with splendid retinues and in the most honourable manner, for opening the sluices of trade to her subjects'. However, while these paeans of praise for Elizabethan initiative were meant to remind Englishmen of their basic commercial interests, it is significant that these heroes were not celebrated primarily as patriotic merchants, but more as anti-Spanish colonizers. In particular, no overseas trader was elevated to the status of national hero. Even the most celebrated figure of the Elizabethan mercantile community, Sir Thomas Gresham, whose renown was enshrined by a statute at the Royal Exchange, was in the press heralded more for his charitable works than his commercial activity. Lingering suspicions of the greed inherent in commercial gain evidently held back the apotheosis of the merchant, and even sympathetic gentle commentators such as Evelyn felt constrained to recall Greek and Roman distaste for the rapaciousness of traders.[44]

This prejudice would never be completely overcome, but in the intense interstate rivalry of late seventeenth-century Europe, it was clear that historians of trade found it much easier to champion commerce as a vital prop of national power. Charles Davenant frequently plundered the past to warn statesmen and traders of the progress of England's commercial competitors, finding the European upheavals of the seventeenth century particularly fertile sources for his arguments. He thus monitored the history of international commercial relations with some care, and, reasoning that 'no profession of men sooner feel the effects of national increase or decrease in reputation than merchants', warned in 1711 that 'if your country is thought weak, declining,

[43] Child, *New Discourse of Trade*, 4. Edward III was occasionally given credit for his commercial foresight.

[44] Defoe, *A Plan of the English Commerce* (London, 1731), 15–38; *The Linen and Woollen Manufactory Discoursed, with the Nature of Companies and Trade in General* (London, 1691), 3; J. Evelyn, *Navigation and Commerce: Their Original and Progress* (London, 1674), esp. 11–13, 57–8. For a more realistic picture of the contribution of the state to the advance of Tudor and early Stuart trade, see K. R. Andrews, *Trade, Plunder, and Settlement: Maritime Enterprise and the Genesis of the British Empire, 1485–1630* (Cambridge, 1984).

and afraid to resent injuries, you are oppressed and overborne by all that have dealings with you'. He did not neglect to relate international developments to the history of domestic change, and in the process produced a most ingenious thesis to explain why the nation had come to recognize the importance of trade for state development. Henry VII and VIII were credited with a key role, since their breaking of the power of the Church and nobility had caused a great deal of landed wealth to be released for investment in trade. He still dated the first flourishing of overseas commerce to the latter end of Elizabeth's reign, and only under her successor did he see 'an extended trade' accelerate the process of landed subdivision. Ultimately, this redistribution of land had encouraged the participation of the new propertied classes in the governmental process to advise on wars, treaties, and alliances. This is a very idiosyncratic angle on the 'gentry debate' which has galvanized modern historians on the causes of the civil wars, but Davenant's attempt to explore the connections between economic and socio-political change marked out the importance of the late Stuart period for commercial commentary. Many other writers shared his perception that England, in common with other European states, had accorded greater recognition to commerce from the mid-seventeenth century onwards.[45]

Of all passages in commercial history, the wonderful success of the Dutch Republic in the seventeenth century attracted most attention, especially from advocates arguing for increased state support for trade. Dissection of the causes of Dutch greatness would almost become a science in the hands of Josiah Child, and many followed his lead in tracing the roots of Dutch supremacy to its carrying trade, sound economic infrastructure, and fishing industry.[46] Three wars and the Navigation Laws demonstrated that the government shared at least some of their concern over Dutch superiority, and accounts of commercial incidents fuelled popular prejudices against the Dutch for many decades. Indeed, an alarum against the Dutch was seen within mercantile circles as the most direct way to provoke government action on trading matters.[47] Beyond its value as a demagogic slogan, however, anti-Dutch sentiment was seen in some mercantile quarters as proof of a more fundamental change in attitudes towards trade. For instance, proponents of the Navigation Act regarded the re-enactment of 1660 as an important watershed, Sir Francis Brewster musing in 1695 that 'the disposition of those

---

[45] Davenant, *Political and Commercial Works*, v. 457. Davenant's stress on the socio-political consequences of economic change echoed many of the contributors to the gentry debate of the 1950s—see R. C. Richardson, *The Debate on the English Revolution* (London, 1977), 90–4, 116–19.

[46] For general discussion on the impact of the Dutch on domestic economic thinking, see Appleby, *Economic Thought*, 73–98. For Child's influences, see Letwin, *Origins of Scientific Economics*, 14–15. The root causes of Dutch economic supremacy are analysed with masterly precision in J. I. Israel, *Dutch Primacy in World Trade, 1585–1740* (Oxford, 1989).

[47] For new insights into stormy relationship between the English and Dutch, see S. Pincus, *Protestantism and Patriotism* (Cambridge, 1996). For illustrations of anti-Dutch prejudice in the seventeenth and eighteenth centuries, see M. Duffy, *The Englishman and the Foreigner* (Cambridge, 1986).

times seemed to tend another way, for pleasure more than trade: but this act stood as a sentinel for the traffic of the nation, and put them in mind of other things'. He also observed that in 1660 'there was a set of people in trade that had been bred up in it in the time of the Parliament, and these men having the money, as well as the trade of the kingdom in their hands, were at that time easier heard than they have been since'. Even as he wrote, concerns were being voiced that the government's fiscal needs had directly increased the political power of the businessman, thus endorsing this correlation between the weakness of governments and the enhancement of their commercial priorities. No minister liked to go cap in hand to their business elite, but commentators remarked that all European nations were acting as if the struggle for international supremacy was linked to the strength of their overseas commerce. As we shall see in the next section, Dutch success led to calls for a reorganization of the relationship between the state and the trader, in recognition of the heightened importance of commerce in the course of the seventeenth century.[48]

Suspicion of the Dutch would die hard, and long outlast the official cessation of open warfare between the two maritime powers. However, following the end of the Dutch wars France became the *bête noire* of the commercial classes, and from the 1670s onwards the rise of French trade was conscientiously mapped out by a succession of writers, who looked to Richelieu and Colbert as the master exponents of mercantilism.[49] Distrust of the Stuart rapprochement with Louis XIV helped to fuel debate on the imbalance of England's trade with France, which was seen as the precursor to the complete maritime dominance of the Bourbon monarchy. Richelieu, in particular, was heralded as the architect of French sea-power, usually as a device to expose the failings of the current ministry. In a censorious vein, several authors recalled Elizabeth's upbraiding of the French for building a single warship of only fourteen guns, and wished for a return to such aggressive maritime superiority. More constructively, Richelieu's innovations, such as colleges for merchants, were endorsed by writers such as Evelyn as solutions for more fundamental problems within English trade. These concerns would be increased by the adoption of French innovations in other countries, especially in Sweden, Germany, and Portugal. Charles King drew attention to these European developments in 1721, and, having reflected on the rise of France as the latest of the great trading nations, concluded that the correlation of state and trading power was 'a truth that ought to be written in letters of gold in

[48] Brewster, *Essays on Trade and Navigation*, 92–109; *Britannia Languens*, esp. 199–200. Note how Child emotively described the Navigation Act as the nation's 'Charta Maritima'—*New Discourse of Trade*, preface.

[49] For the reality of French economic advance in the seventeenth century, see C. W. Cole, *Colbert and a Century of French Mercantilism* (New York, 1939). For the role of government agents in spreading alarm at French economic growth, see Roseveare, 'Prejudice and Policy', in Coleman and Mathias, *Enterprise and History*, 135–50.

all the cabinets of princes and ministers, to admonish them to consider the husbandmen and traders as they deserve'.[50]

Thus, even though no individual merchant was immortalized in print, histories of national trade had been used to promote the general benefit of the trading sector. By the early eighteenth century authors were prepared to give both monarchs and royal councillors increasing credit for their commercial acumen, a development which suggests that the political interest of trade had been advanced. Many economic writers sought ministers as patrons, lauding them in their dedications for their commercial knowledge. Self-interest must be acknowledged here, but it is significant that ministers could be flattered for recognizing the importance of trade as an issue of state. Most notably, Paul Methuen, negotiator of the 1703 Anglo-Portugal commercial treaty, was lionized in certain quarters, and there were calls in the press for his statue to be erected throughout the country as a continual reminder of his service to the nation.[51] A generation later, *The Golden Fleece* of 1736 demonstrated that history could still be ransacked for ministerial heroes of native origin, with Lord Burleigh celebrated as a commercial visionary for his protection of the cloth trade. Of more general significance, this pamphlet observed that it was 'not possible for any minister to give sound advice to his prince, either in peace or war, who is not thoroughly acquainted with the trade, riches, and power of his country, nor can any matter of state be more worthy the eloquence of a great man in either House of Parliament than a true knowledge of our foreign manufactures and foreign commerce, on which the grandeur and prosperity of his country so much depends'. With a burgeoning empire to manage, Hanoverian Britain looked to the past for instruction in charting an uncertain future, and thus commercial history continued to be fashioned to suit present needs. However, Augustan debate on the history of trade had far from produced a complacent consensus on the record of past or present governments as guardians of commerce. Seemingly imbued with the findings of the modern scholarship, several authors reviewed the contribution of the state to the advance of English trade with a very critical eye, and used the past as a pretext for making significant demands for reform in the management of trade. These debates further illuminate the development of merchant pro-

---

[50] Evelyn, *Navigation and Commerce*, 47; Davenant, *Political and Commercial Works*, i. 386–8, 419–20, ii. 260 (which includes citations from Richelieu's *Testament Politique*); C. King, *The British Merchant* (London, 1721), i. pp. xxix–xxx. For discussion of the influence of anti-French feeling on commercial debate under Charles II, see M. Priestly, 'London Merchants and Opposition Politics in Charles II's Reign', *BIHR* 29 (1956), 205–19; *idem*, 'Anglo-French Trade and the Unfavourable Balance Controversy', *EcHR* 2nd ser., 4 (1951), 37–52. For a more sanguine, contemporary view of French shortcomings as overseas traders in the 1630s, see Roberts, *Merchant's Map of Commerce*, 188.

[51] *The British Merchant*, 16–19 Feb. 1714. For the delay in recognition of the importance of the Methuen treaty, see A. D. Francis, *The Methuens and Portugal, 1691–1708* (Cambridge, 1966), ch. 8. Adam Smith's famed attack in 1776 highlighted widespread admiration for that 'so much commended' treaty—*An Inquiry into the Nature and Causes of the Wealth of Nations*, ed. E. Cannon (London, 1904), ii. 47.

fessionalism, as well as the apparent value which the state placed upon overseas commerce.[52]

iv. The representation of commerce

It is easy to see why seventeenth-century merchants might call for a fundamental review of their relationship with the state. As outlined in the previous chapter, the government of English trade was maintained in a fairly ad hoc fashion, both by the executive and the legislature. The Crown's continuing pre-eminence in matters of overseas commerce saw it jealously guard its privileges against external interference, and as late as 1685 royal proclamations could declare that it was 'the undoubted prerogative of the Crown to license, limit, and regulate foreign trade'. The legislature provided another avenue for mercantile advantage, but Parliament was subject to royal summons, or to the vagaries of national events. In the absence of regular parliamentary sessions, Whitehall remained the daily forum for commercial political activity until the Revolution, and even after that upheaval historians have concluded that *raison d'état* usually prevailed over the needs of trade. Studies of the succession of trade councils and Privy Council committees which appeared after 1620 have found little to enthuse about, and have identified their powerlessness as the root of their ineffectuality. However, while historians are right to see little change in the executive's handling of commercial affairs, the Augustan period did see generalized debate on the state's management of trade, reflecting widespread concern for its importance to the nation's future. Of particular interest for this study, many schemes were proposed which argued for a more prominent role for the merchant in public life, and one campaign saw the approbation of a very wide mercantile constituency, the need for an experienced board of trade. Several governmental experiments, such as those of 1660 and 1669, actually acknowledged the utility of mercantile leaders working in partnership with traditional landed governors. Thus, even though political priorities ultimately prevailed throughout the Augustan period, it is clear that this era saw important debate concerning the credentials of the merchant as a public figure. Most significantly, many merchants were eager to contribute to these discussions, and this issue managed to cut through the divided world of commercial interests because it was perceived as a fundamental precondition of England's growth as an economic power, and reflected a widespread urgency to provide direction for national growth. Although focused on a lost cause, deliberation of the board of

---

[52] S. Smith, *The Golden Fleece, or the Trade, Interest, and Well-Being of Great Britain Considered* (London, 1736), pp. vii–viii. For discussion of the influence of historiography in framing public opinion, see J. Black, 'Ideology, History, Xenophobia, and the World of Print in Eighteenth-Century England', in *idem* and J. Gregory (eds.), *Culture, Politics, and Society in Britain, 1660–1800* (Manchester, 1991), 184–216.

trade is all the more significant when it is considered how little serious debate centred on the general representativeness of the English constitution in this period.[53]

Demands for commercial familiarity within the highest circles of government were aired well before the Restoration, with economic analyst John Keymer (writing in the guise of Sir Walter Raleigh) calling for a 'state-merchant' at the outset of James I's reign. Under the early Stuarts several investigative commissions were appointed to investigate specific commercial matters, but none had pretensions to permanence or extensive mercantile expertise.[54] More promisingly, the experimental councils and committees of trade of the Interregnum period revealed a radical departure from past practice, and saw leading merchants such as Maurice Thompson, Martin Noell, and Thomas Povey acting as official advisers to the republican regimes in commercial affairs.[55] Although now characterized by some historians as the era of a triumphant gentry, the Restoration actually saw a continuation of such policy, with Charles II establishing a separate Council of Trade of sixty-two members, at least twenty of whom were selected from the nominations of London merchant groups. Charles announced that he had seen the 'wonderful benefit' of such an institution during his exile, and trading groups registered their approval by eagerly petitioning the new body for the redress of grievances. Sitting at Mercers' Hall in the heart of the City, and with an extensive agenda for the care of domestic and foreign trade, it took on the appearance of a commercial senate.[56] However, its role was strictly limited to a mere advisory role, and the experiment does not appear to have survived the crises of 1664–7. Thereafter, the early promise of the Restoration was not fulfilled, and the government of trade was subsequently entrusted to a succession of assemblies and Privy Council committees, only one of which, the ineffectual council of 1668–72, contained a significant mercantile presence. Stuart governors viewed the prospect of a large assembly of trading representatives as an inefficient and potentially disorderly body, and thus relegated merchants and traders to a subsidiary role, as informants and petitioners.

[53] R. Steele, *A Bibliography of Royal Proclamations of the Tudor and Stuart Sovereigns, 1485–1714* (Oxford, 1910), i. 459. The best works on governmental attitudes to trade remain C. M. Andrews, *British Committees, Commissions, and Councils of Trade and Plantations, 1622–75* (Baltimore, 1908); I. K. Steele, *Politics of Colonial Policy* (Oxford, 1968). For a recent challenge to the notion that the new boards of trade were proof of a more vigorous, coordinated policy towards the colonies, see M. J. Braddick, 'Government, War, Trade, and Settlement', in N. Canny (ed.), *The Oxford History of the British Empire: The Origins of Empire* (Oxford, 1998), 286–308.

[54] On Keymer, see A. R. Beer, *Sir Walter Raleigh and His Readers in the Seventeenth Century* (Basingstoke, 1997), 157–9. Significantly, four editions of the *Observations* appeared between 1653 and 1720, including one in 1696, at the height of the council of trade debates. Supple, *Commercial Crisis*, 233, sees the 1622 commission to examine trade as a most significant turning-point in the government's handling of trade.

[55] For a brief history of the councils of trade of 1650 and 1655, see Andrews, *Committees*, 24–60.

[56] The surviving papers of the 1660 Council of Trade can be found at the PRO, CO389/1–2. See C. M. Andrews for innovations in the administration of the colonies and their trade—*Committees*, 61–95.

Ministers had evidently seen little advantage in formalizing the public role of the merchant, and trade reverted to aristocratic and gentry control as before.[57]

In spite of this failure, mercantile participation in these Restoration assemblies promoted a more generalized debate concerning the government of trade, and it is clear that this discussion encompassed both the legislative and executive sphere. In the late 1660s Josiah Child, a current member of the Council of Trade, commented hopefully of trade's increasing attraction to gentry households, and wondered whether commerce might become 'so familiar amongst us that our gentlemen who are in our greatest councils will come to understand it, and accordingly contrive laws in favour of it'. He noted that 'even as the world now goes' Parliament was in the habit of passing useful commercial legislation each session, and prayed for further enlightenment in the corridors of power. He, like the rest of the trading nation, was keeping an envious glance on the activities of the Dutch, whose rise to power status was seen as a triumph of trade. Significantly, the very first of the fifteen Dutch advantages listed by Child was the presence in the councils of state of 'trading merchants that have lived abroad in most parts of the world, who have not only the theoretical knowledge, but the practical experience of trade'.[58] This view was heartily endorsed by Roger Coke, who in 1670 called upon Parliament to establish 'a constant council of trade' of commercial experts, reasoning that an experienced merchant was bound to know more about trade than a privy councillor. He was prepared to acknowledge the intense factionalism of the commercial world, observing that 'the trade of England is managed confusedly, distractedly, and sharkingly by the traders', but this lament only added fuel to his argument that the state take the initiative in the regulation of commerce. The reform of the Council of Trade in 1675, which saw supervision of trade returned to a Privy Council committee, reflected pressure for a more effective forum for commercial matters, but it is clear that this was not a sufficient sop to mercantile opinion. Even though several of the new 'Lords of Trade' could claim commercial interests, the committee never boasted a significant trading presence, and thus fell short of direct mercantile representation.[59]

[57] Charles Wilson saw the emergence of a 'third force' of junior ministers in the 1670s and 1680s (such as Sir George Downing and Sir William Coventry) who were sufficiently experienced not to be steam-rollered by trading interests—*England's Apprenticeship, 1603–1763*, 2nd edn. (London, 1984), 165–9.

[58] Child, *New Discourse of Trade*, esp. 42–4. Child had composed this piece as a contribution to the current controversy over interest rates, but shelved it when Parliament failed to take up the matter. For the debt owed by Child to the views of Henry Robinson on the Dutch, see Letwin, *Origins of Scientific Economics*, 14–15. Colbert's new Council of Trade of 1664, complete with real power, doubtless encouraged debate too—Cole, *Colbert and A Century of French Mercantilism*, 357–63.

[59] R. Coke, *A Discourse of Trade* (1670), esp. 65–7; Andrews, *Committees*, 111–13. Roger Coke was of solid gentry stock, but clearly had some direct experience of trade—*DNB*. For evidence of distrust towards merchant self-interest within ministerial circles in 1670, see P. Laslett, 'John Locke, The Great Recoinage, and the Origins of the Board of Trade, 1695–8', *William and Mary Quarterly*, 3rd ser., 14 (1957), 377.

The problems inherent in establishing an efficient and effective board of trade were well understood by contemporaries, who foresaw great difficulties in reconciling so many competing trading interests. Even when writing in support of the much-criticized East India Company in 1681, a pamphleteer was willing to concede that self-interested merchants 'are not always the best judges of trade, as it relates to the profit or power of a kingdom'. Overall, the regulation of commerce was best left in parliamentary hands, he reasoned, having found by experience that 'a mixed assembly of noblemen, gentlemen, and merchants are the best constitution that can be established for the making rules, orders, and by-laws for the carrying on any trade for the public utility of the kingdom'. This system of checks and balances would ensure that traders would find it difficult to overawe inexperienced gentlemen in commercial disputes, and thus preserve government in the interest of all subjects rather than for a particular economic constituency. Child's arguments from the successful Dutch model of government were also met by reference to Sir William Temple, whose famed *Observations* recorded that few active merchants featured on Dutch councils.[60] Mercantile apologists thus still had to convince doubters that traders could put the interest of the nation before their own, and thus when William Petyt proposed in 1680 that the balance of trade be referred to experienced traders, he stressed that these experts be 'curious, intelligent, and impartial and have minded the public interest as well as their own'. These qualities clearly dovetailed with conventional ideas on the independent wisdom of Members of Parliament, but Petyt's scheme offered no assurances that traders would remain stoically patriotic. Beyond this difficulty, Petyt also recognized that Westminster alone had the authority to introduce the far-reaching measures needed to remedy the nation's economic plight. However, for most of the 1680s the country lacked a parliamentary forum in which trade debates could be regulated in the interests of all, and even the Lords of Trade were in decline as an effective supporter of commerce.[61]

The Glorious Revolution, with its profound repercussions for the government of the realm, saw no immediate change in the sphere of executive control of trade. However, the unmistakable accretion of parliamentary authority after 1688 ensured that mercantile opinion increasingly focused on the legislature's regulation of commerce, and it soon transpired that many traders believed that Westminster was not up to the job of serving the nation's economic interests. Despite the advent of annual parliamentary sessions after 1689, which enabled MPs to consider more economic business than ever

---

[60] *A Treatise [Concerning the East India Company]* (London, 1681), 1–3. The authorship of this tract is discussed by Letwin, *Origins of Scientific Economics*, 234–6, and tentatively attributed to Thomas Papillon or one of his allies.

[61] *Britannia Languens*, 152–3, 303. Note how Andrews's verdict of 'eminent success' for the Lords of Trade after 1675 has been qualified by subsequent research—Steele, *Colonial Policy*, 11. William III was clearly concerned at their performance in 1690, observing that their business was 'much behind at present'—PC2/74, p. 447.

before, several critiques of parliamentary inefficiency appeared in the 1690s, reflecting the turbulence in commercial activity caused by the ravages of war, the recoinage crisis, and the battle for freer trade. As early as 1690 the colonial trader Dalby Thomas was ready to widen the scope of his attack on heavy sugar duties to consider the general government of trade. He perceived the current problem in its bluntest terms: 'how indeed can the divines, lawyers, nobility, and great gentry of this kingdom be nice judges and right distinguishers between the clashing and tangling interests of so great a mystery as universal trade, when few or none of them ever had the least occasion to inspect or experiment any part of it?' He viewed the current lordly council of trade as hamstrung by such inexperience, 'whereby at last the secretary or clerk to such a board becomes the only oracle to it' and could thus manage debate as he felt fit. Thomas called for 'an able, diligent, impartial, and constant-sitting council of trade', which would be accountable to the Privy Council and Parliament for their decisions. Its members would receive supportive salaries, and were to be 'elected and deputed by every plantation, maritime city, company, constitution, and trade which would desire to send members to it'.[62] The following year a pamphleteer echoed his frustration, broadcasting 'the complaint I have heard from the generality of merchants' that commercial regulation had been left to 'the ravages of strangers and the worst confusions of an ungoverned multitude in trade'. A council of trade 'composed of merchants from all parts of the kingdom' was the author's answer to the perceived decay in English commerce, reasoning that trade could not be reformed without 'men of practical heads in trade appropriated to the work'. Most significantly, this council was deemed all the more necessary because of the current failure of Parliament to attend to these matters, its Members having ceased to act as the efficient representatives of old, who appeared 'no less than a county or borough, and spake not [for] himself, but [for] them'. The appearance of Child's *New Discourse of Trade* in 1693 added further fuel to arguments for a reformed council of trade, and its timing was geared to appeal to a mercantile world reeling from very heavy shipping losses. He was prepared to admit that the interest of the merchant and that of the state were 'so far from being always parallels', but he was clearly impatient with the regulation of trade being governed by the principles of 'soldiers, huntsmen, and herdsmen'.[63]

The most energetic and ambitious proposals for a commercial council came from James Whiston, who, as the publisher of a tri-weekly bulletin of commodity and share prices, could claim great familiarity with the mysteries of trade. He ventured into print on at least three occasions to promote the

---

[62] D. Thomas, *An Historical Account of the Rise and Growth of the West India Colonies* (London, 1690), 6–8, 45–7. Steele, *Colonial Policy*, 22–3, argued that William Blathwayt enjoyed great informal powers as Secretary of Trade (until replaced by William Popple in 1696).

[63] *Linen and Woollen Manufactory Discoursed*, 13–14; Child, *New Discourse of Trade*, preface.

establishment of 'a standing council for the regulation of trade', most notably in 1693 when he outlined plans for an advisory body of some 100 experts to speak on behalf of the nation's merchants and manufacturers. Reasoning that it was 'impossible for noblemen and gentlemen not educated in trade ever to arrive at a perfect understanding of the matters in question', he called for the annual election of representatives of all the leading overseas and domestic trades, who would act as a source of commercial expertise for the benefit of Crown and Parliament. The council would meet three times a week, and all matters would be heard on three separate days before any decision, which would be recorded in a register of members' voting. At a projected annual cost of £4,000, this system would easily pay for itself, and at a stroke reform the negligent and haphazard supervision of trade. Although prepared to acknowledge the problems Parliament faced due to 'the multiplicity of their other affairs and fatigues', Whiston could not ignore the need to educate the nation's governors in trading matters, 'for want of which their judgements are abused by clamour, importunity, prejudice, partiality, or some other prevailing bias . . . to the manifest abuse of the people, damage of the nation, and disparagement of such unexperienced and unqualified judges'. He believed that 'there are thousands who would offer considerable matters of vast improvements did they know once whom to apply to', and argued that the council be empowered to reward those who could advance the cause of national commerce. Once again the spectre of Dutch and French commercial domination was invoked to highlight the real urgency for change, but he was confident that an effective regulation of the government of trade would maintain the national war effort and ensure England's general standing within Europe. Such was the clamour for reform that orders were given for the appointment of an advisory body to discuss the promotion and security of trade, and newsmongers reported that a committee of trade 'composed of merchants' would liaise with the Admiralty to ensure the protection of the nation's merchant marine.[64]

Predictably, this campaign reached a crescendo in 1695–6, the hardest years for the commercial sector as the coinage crisis compounded the difficulties of imperilled sea-lanes. Sir Francis Brewster's *Essays on Trade and Navigation* highlighted the depth of feeling over the council of trade in the early months of 1695, the author observing that 'this has been the common theme of men of all understandings, on which so much is said and writ that it looks like remonstrating against the government to print more, since there seemed not a tendency towards it'. Most interestingly, Brewster confessed that there were differences of commercial opinion concerning the composition of the new

---

[64] J. Whiston, *A Discourse of the Decay of Trade* (London, 1693); H. Horwitz, *Parliament, Policy, and Politics in the Reign of William III* (Manchester, 1977), 161, 201; *CSPD* 1693, pp. 408, 426. Another of Whiston's pamphlets, *To the King's Most Excellent Majesty*, has been tentatively dated to 1693, although with no internal evidence to suggest that date. Its proposal for a council of 40–50 merchants and tradesmen is much less systematic, and the title may even suggest a pre-1689 publication date.

council. One group wanted an assembly consisting of 'men of all qualities in trade and manufactories', which would in fact appear 'more like a Parliament'. Others wanted merely wanted a council of 'a great number of merchants, as believing them the best judges of trade'. A veteran of thirty years in 'universal trade', Brewster sympathized with the latter, but also betrayed a weary awareness of commercial self-interest, stressing that they be retired merchants, and thus less susceptible to charges of partiality. As a further precaution, he ruled that only three of his council of nine were to be former merchants, the rest being made up of ministers and officials from the Customs and Admiralty Offices.[65] Pressure for an experienced board was also maintained by Roger Coke, who castigated Parliament for its poor record of regulating trade over the previous eighty years, especially for having rarely met for considerable periods, whereby 'grievances have been so multiplied and fixed and so many interested in them, that the body of the Parliament has been distempered thereby, not only in electing Members, but in their sessions'. Holland was again upheld as the exemplar of mercantile prudence, its officers being 'generally merchants . . . and sit all the year round and so no grievances arise in trade but they take notice of them and redress them'. He was optimistic for future improvement, no doubt encouraged by the recent passage of the Triennial Act which guaranteed successive Parliaments, but he evidently perceived Westminster as an inefficient headquarters for English trade. Another pamphlet of that year took up a similar theme, perceiving Parliament to be 'too numerous a body to have particulars examined, debated, and resolved; the generality of her Members unacquainted with trade, the Houses taken up with multiplicity of business'. This author also thought the lack of resident borough Members in the Lower House an impediment to trade, and called for a council of merchants in London to make up for Westminster's shortcomings, arguing that 'right reason dictates that merchants should direct in affairs of traffick'. Even the provinces became animated by the debate, Bristol merchant John Cary urging the new Parliament of November 1695 to establish a standing committee of trade, consisting of experienced businessmen. Significantly, he thought that there were signs in the last Parliament that 'a great many Members . . . began to be much in love with trade', and hoped the 'dark notions' of trade apparent among MPs would soon be a thing of the past.[66]

This public debate must be credited as an important influence behind the

[65] Brewster, *Essays on Trade and Navigation*, 37–40. Interestingly, he noted that the government had the issue 'under consideration'. Perhaps this a reference to a proposal for a council of fourteen merchants and seven nobles/gentlemen which can be found in an unsigned paper in the Shrewsbury papers—*HMC Buccleuch*, ii. 738.

[66] R. Coke, *Reflections on the East India and Africa Companies* (London, 1695), 23–4; J. Cary, *An Essay on the State of England* (Bristol, 1695), dedication, 139–40. Significantly, this flurry of tracts pre-dates parliamentary discussion of a reformed council of trade, and thus can be seen as a genuine expression of mercantile opinion.

creation of a new Board of Trade in May 1696. Historians have in general regarded the controversy surrounding its establishment as a political contest, or as an 'incidental' result of the coinage crisis, thereby belittling the contribution of the commercial sector to discussion of the issue. In fact, in the summer and autumn of 1695 ministers were in contact with leading merchants in an effort to resolve the country's pressing economic problems, and the resultant proposals owed much to post-Restoration debates concerning a reformed board of trade.[67] Even as the government received these advices John Houghton's weekly *A Collection for Improvement of Husbandry and Trade* highlighted widespread interest in the issue with its call for 'a set of men to enquire what arts or policies of getting wealth are used the world over' for the benefit of 'some higher powers'. These potentates would not be stampeded into radical reforms, but advisers such as Charles Davenant were ready to recommend significant innovations in the regulation of trade. His scheme of November 1695 aimed to relieve hard-pressed officials from 'the troublesome, perplexed, and tedious concerns of trade', and centred on the creation of a small council of peers, MPs, and 'some wealthy merchants not engaged in trade'. Most controversially, it would have extensive supervision of commerce, and even have powers to declare embargoes.[68] His plans caused friction within court circles, and were predictably watered down in the new commission of December 1695, which only betrayed 'vague' instructions concerning foreign trade. When the Commons debated the matter in the parliamentary session of 1695–6 the government's scheme was countered by a rival plan promoted by their opponents, who proposed a parliamentary-controlled board of trade for their own factious purposes. A major controversy ensued in which commercial advantages were sacrificed to political advantage, and the resultant, court-backed board was clearly designed to outmanoeuvre a promising opposition attack on prerogative powers, rather than answer mercantile grievances. 'An awkward compromise' was thus reached, in which royal control of trade policy was nominally upheld, and reassurance given to the commercial classes that their concerns were shared by ministers. Preserving a limited independence from the Privy Council, the new body was given marginally greater authority than its predecessor, but remained an advisory council, great alarm having been aired that Davenant's scheme might usurp some of the Crown's executive powers. Only one of its seven members had direct mercantile experience, and the government put its faith in administrative, rather than commercial expertise. Therefore, the composition of the board had gained a

[67] Note in particular, M.-H. Li, *The Great Recoinage of 1696–9* (London, 1963), 63–82.

[68] Houghton, *Collection*, 15 Nov. 1695. He concentrated on overseas trade 'for the benefit of my country' until March 1696, when the council matter had been settled. For the controversy, see Steele, *Colonial Policy*, 10–18; Horwitz, *Parliament, Policy, and Politics*, 164–5; R. M. Lees, 'Parliament and the Proposal for a Council of Trade, 1695–6', *EHR* 54 (1939), 38–66; Laslett, in *William and Mary Quarterly*, 3rd ser., 14 (1957), 370–402.

full hearing before ministers and Parliament, but the supervision of commerce remained firmly in gentry hands.[69]

This inertia cannot be interpreted simply as a rebuff to commercial opinion. In fact, rival politicians were keen to claim credit for reforming the administration of trade, recognizing the real hardship which the war had inflicted on the economic sector. Analysis of a possible forecast of a Commons division on the issue has indeed concluded that trade interests may have affected the political loyalties of some MPs.[70] More significantly, surviving evidence suggests that the government was alive to mercantile demands for fundamental reform, for among the Duke of Shrewsbury's papers is a list of sixteen leading merchants with their respective commercial expertise identified.[71] Furthermore, although political priorities overtook commercial concerns with respect to the new board, it is clear that ministers accepted criticisms of the handling of trade. Most notably, the creation of the post of inspector-general of imports and exports in 1696 was tantamount to official recognition of the need to record and study overseas commerce for the purposes of policy-making. The appointment of the experienced William Culliford to the office suggested that it was no sinecure, and the subsequent elevation of Davenant himself to the post would be welcomed by critics of national commercial policy. Another chance had been missed to produce an effective council of trade, but the 1696 reform was not the end of the matter, and ambitious plans for the government of commerce continued to surface. Even as ministers returned to their more familiar constitutional and religious fare, it is clear that the new Board of Trade could not curtail criticism of the regulation of commerce.[72]

The most eloquent exponent of such dissatisfaction remained James Whiston. In the course of 1695–6 controversy there appeared his *Causes of our Present Calamities*, a treatise which was presented to the MPs in the midst of the

---

[69] For a contemporary discussion of the constitutional issues involved, see Burnet, *History*, iv. 294–5. The parliamentary proposal did not specify the character of the membership of its projected board, even though endorsing many of Davenant's proposals. However, among the ministry's advisers, Christopher Wren shared Davenant's reservations concerning active mercantile participation on any advisory committee, although he could only offer the lame alternative of appointing 'persons of good understanding, public spirited, vers'd in trade, but not traders themselves . . . if such can be found'— Steele, *Colonial Policy*, 11.

[70] I. F. Burton, P. W. J. Riley, and E. Rowlands, 'Political Parties in the Reigns of William III and Anne', *BIHR* special supplement 7 (1968), 6–12. When the matter was brought to parliamentary debate in December 1695, the Whigs were quick to claim that they had thought of the reform before their Tory opponents—*EHR* 54 (1939), 48–9.

[71] *HMC Buccleuch*, ii. 738. Although the author of the list is unknown, its contents suggest a most informed familiarity with London's mercantile elite. Laslett notes that this scheme must have pre-dated 25 July 1695—*William and Mary Quarterly*, 3rd ser., 14 (1957), 383–4. Shrewsbury was Secretary of State for the Southern department, and Steele notes that he received other proposals concerning a reformed council of trade at this time, although all frustratingly unsigned—*Colonial Policy*, 12–14, 17–18.

[72] Brewer, *Sinews of Power*, 223–4; G. N. Clark, *Guide to English Commercial Statistics, 1696–1782* (London, 1938), 1–42. Steele, *Colonial Policy*, 38–41, notes that the Board largely concentrated on colonial affairs, since their advice on trade matters was usually overruled by higher powers.

parliamentary battle over the council. True to his earlier stance, Whiston again stressed the value of commerce to the kingdom, and lamented the lack of informed opinion in Whitehall and Westminster to guide it. The call for a board of experienced traders was duly made, but he modified his scheme, clearly responding to criticisms of his commercial senate. This time he envisaged a committee of only thirty-six members, whose background was almost exclusively mercantile and metropolitan. All but eight were to represent overseas trading groups, and there would also be members chosen by the silk manufacturers, shipmasters, and shipwrights. Predictably, the new Board of Trade of May 1696 did not meet with Whiston's approval, since in 1704 he issued *The Mismanagements in Trade Discovered*, in which he urged the continuing necessity of his scheme, observing that the current Board had 'men of natural ingenuity and acquired learning' but who lacked understanding of trade's 'different policies and various methods'. He claimed that his scheme had originally met with general approval, but the Board was not the fulfilment of his dream, and he cited reports that its members were attracted there by its 'very extravagant salaries'.[73] Other authors echoed Whiston's frustration much earlier. Within months of the Board's first session, John Cary used the continuing coin controversy to renew his call for an effective council, perceiving the nation's trade to lie still neglected. Significantly, he stressed the need to end the government's ad hoc management of trade, insisting that 'trade requires as much policy as matters of state, and can never be kept in a regular motion by accident'. Also animated by recent debates, Simon Clement, a London merchant, called for Davenant's original scheme to be put into effect, specifying a complement of two peers, three or four MPs, and four or five retired merchants. In the same year he also penned an imaginary dialogue between an overseas trader and a gentleman, in which the former patiently lectured the latter on the mysteries of foreign exchange, being 'sorry' to see how misunderstandings had taken hold of 'many honest gentlemen, who are not acquainted with foreign affairs'.[74]

During the difficult 1690s debate over the representation of commercial views was also fuelled by a continuing campaign to enforce landed property qualifications for MPs. There was clearly a political agenda behind this campaign, as opponents of the court sought to limit the influence which the 'monied' supporters of the government could exert on the Lower House.

---

[73] J. Whiston, *The Causes of our Present Calamities* (1696); idem, *The Mismanagements in Trade Discovered* (1704). The *Causes* were presented to MPs on 20 Jan. 1696—*EHR* 54 (1939), 50–1. Whiston's anger at sinecurists reflects a personal campaign against venality.

[74] J. Cary, *An Essay on the Coin and Credit of England* (Bristol, 1696), 29–30; Simon Clement, *A Letter to a Member of Parliament Concerning a Committee of Trade* (a manuscript copy of which can be found in the Cary papers—Add. MSS 5540 fos. 104ᵛ–106); S. C., *A Dialogue between a Country Gentleman and a Merchant Concerning the Falling of Guineas* (London, 1696). Clement's frustration resembles that of an East India Company petition to the House of Lords in December 1695, which tried to explain the correlation between prices and commodity volumes by reference to chicken-eating—House of Lords RO, main paper series 955, fo. 18.

These moves were not specifically targeted against the merchant per se, but had obvious ramifications for the future of the trader on the national stage.[75] With the nominal objective of ensuring the independence of Members, proposals were first introduced in the sessions of 1695–6, requiring all knights of the shire to prove real-estate holdings to the annual value of £500, while borough MPs were to have a minimum rental of £200. The corporation of the City of London led resistance to the bill, which was only defeated after a rare exercise of the royal veto. In the very next session another attempt was made to set landed qualifications, and on this occasion met with widespread opposition. Ten boroughs petitioned against the bill in the Commons, while another fourteen addressed the Lords against it, all of them arguing that it was against the rights of electors to limit their choice of Member. They also agreed that it was folly to exclude merchants and greater traders from the House, reasoning, as the Plymouth corporation did, that such men 'may be the best able and fittest to represent this trading town'. Significantly, in the Commons this concerted pressure succeeded in the addition of a proviso to the measure in favour of resident merchants worth over £5,000 in real or personal wealth, but the bill was rejected before its second reading in the Upper House.[76] However, as mercantile opinion had found to its cost in the case of the new Board of Trade, the case for effective trading representatives could not ultimately prevail against gentry-dominated assemblies, or those animated by factional objectives. Similar bills managed to pass the Commons in the 1702–3 and 1704–5 sessions, and the passage of the Qualification Act in 1711 demonstrated the tenacity with which 'Country' opponents sought to combat the influence of moveable wealth. As the next chapter will demonstrate, the significance of this statute for the representation of mercantile issues was far from disastrous, and the debate on landed qualification actually helped to keep the issue of commercial representation alive. Indeed, the controversy of 1696–7 had highlighted considerable support both within and outside Parliament for the presence of mercantile voices at Westminster. Recent debate over the need for commercial experience among the nation's rulers had rallied support for the business politician, and would resonate in continuing discussion of the future regulation of English trade.[77]

While Country polemicists fumed at the monied interest, mercantile groups continued to attack the state's attitude towards commerce, and

---

[75] For an outline of the qualification bill debate, see H. E. Witmer, *The Property Qualifications of Members of Parliament* (New York, 1943); Horwitz, *Parliament, Policy, and Politics*, 168, 177, 187, 189.

[76] *CJ*, xi. 460, 556, 591–9, 607, 612, 614, 630–2; *LJ*, xv. 699; xvi. 80–1; House of Lords RO, main paper series 1093 (A1–18). G. S. Holmes argues that mercantile pressure did provoke the royal veto in 1695–6—*British Politics in the Age of Anne*, 2nd edn. (London, 1987), 178–82. Petitioning boroughs were Bridgwater, Fowey, Callington, Tregony, Penryn, New Sarum, Rye, Winchelsea, Tiverton, Weymouth and Melcombe Regis, Dorchester, Exeter, Winchelsea, Plymouth, Ashburton, Lyme Regis, Barnstaple, Norwich, Taunton, London, Southwark, Nottingham, Poole, and Honiton (thus covering eleven counties).

[77] *HMC Lords*, NS ii. 199–201, 216–17.

several authors still identified fundamental problems with the regulation of trade. For instance, Simon Clement was moved to write a treatise concerning Irish trade after viewing committee proceedings in the Upper House, which 'brought me to consider that how clear soever it may seem to men that have been conversant in the practice of trade, yet it must be a matter of great difficulty for your lordships to determine in such things, where the judgement is directed from information only, since those informations are generally given with the greatest partiality'. In 1699 appeared James Puckle's *England's Way to Wealth and Honour*, in which a Dutchman gloated over his country's commercial advantages, which were promoted by 'the great care and prudent conduct of our magistrates, who court trade as a rich mistress, and spare neither charge nor pains to attain her'. Significantly, international interest in the issue was signalled by the reorganization of the French Council of Trade in 1700, which permitted twelve major cities to send deputies to Paris to represent their views. The following year calls were made in Scotland for a board of trade consisting of noble and commercial interests.[78] Expressing a more traditional respect for the commercial acuity of the United Provinces, in July 1707 Charles Povey lamented how Dutch merchants ensured that their state always secured key concessions in the negotiation of treaties, and simply attributed this trend to prudent foresight, 'the concerns of traffic being accounted among them a matter of state (a maxim which ought to be observed in other countries)'. The English executive continued to suffer by such comparisons, with Sir Francis Brewster lambasting the reformed Board of Trade as a mere sinecure and another lost opportunity to prepare commercial matters for Parliament. As he wryly observed, 'when government is made a trade, trade will have no government'. Probably goaded by the recent debates on the qualifications of Members, he also asked why there were not more tradesmen at Westminster, reasoning that 'no man would envy the advance of a true patriot as he would be that employed his talent for the advance of manufactures, fishing, and navigation'. He hoped to see more 'corporation men' returned soon, and concluded by calling on electors to choose 'men among ourselves, of known integrity and fortune in the place they are chose for'.[79]

The most significant of the chorus of dissatisfied observers was Charles Davenant, the inspector-general in 1705–14, who approached the subject of English trade with an almost messianic zeal. Although possessing a far from mercantile pedigree, he recognized the value of overseas trade to the nation, and one of the underlying themes of all his writings is a mission to convert the

[78] S. Clement, *The Interest of England as it Stands with Relation to the Trade of Ireland* (London, 1698), 1–2; J. Puckle, *England's Way to Wealth and Honour* (London, 1699), 18; W. C. Scoville, 'The French Economy in 1700–1: An Appraisal by the Deputies of Trade', *Journal of Economic History*, 22 (1962), 231–52; *Proposals and Reasons for Constituting a Council of Trade* (Edinburgh, 1701).

[79] *The General Remark on Trade*, 7–9 July 1707. F. Brewster, *New Essays on Trade* (London, 1702), esp. 4–5, 14–15, 63, 126–7.

gentry to the cause of commerce, since 'in our great assemblies it has never been sufficiently thought a matter of state, but managed rather as a conveniency or an accidental ornament than the chief strength and support of the kingdom'. However, these views did not blind him to the possible self-interest of any commercial group, and he advocated the mercantile education of the gentry in order to protect the landed from manipulation at the hands of the trader. He thus spoke as an informed and committed commercial observer, who could still laud the merchant as 'the best and most profitable member of the commonwealth' while suspecting him of the self-interest so vilified by critics. Given this qualified regard, it is particularly significant that he appeared unimpressed by the record of the Board of Trade, and he argued in 1697 that the great East India question be referred to a commercial council 'composed of the ablest men in the kingdom'. The following year he stressed the general need for the regulators of trade policy to be 'experienced and knowing therein', and, endorsing Child's observation on Dutch wisdom in this regard, he observed how 'the concerns of commerce being among them a matter of state (as it should be in other nations) they commit the care of it to the ablest hands they have'. He showed great exasperation with the economic analysis behind current policy decisions, and enthused that an able council would produce accurate statistics which could advance the cause of constructive trade debate. Closely involved in the daily regulation of trade, Davenant was well aware of governmental shortcomings, and his proposals for national commercial growth reflected a desire to tap the experience of the merchant in the interest of the nation. His assessment of the potential value of the merchant in public life merely echoed the views of Roberts and Mun, but as a government officer ready to turn such praise into actual reform, his stance highlighted the cumulative significance of debate on the 'patriot' trader among the post-Restoration generation.[80]

Despite this chorus of disapproval, the fact remains that the Board of Trade never became the commercial meritocracy desired by so many writers on trade. However, this failure should not be interpreted as the consequence of landed indifference or hostility. Even amid the politicking of 1695–6, governing circles had acknowledged that commerce was too important a matter to be left to chance, and although gentry dominated, the new Board of Trade showed a commendable determination to take advantage of expert opinion. The Board may also have remained a talking-shop without effective power, but it did become more integrated into the workings of government, especially through interaction with Parliament. The prescient Davenant indeed remarked in 1698 that the promotion of trade would need 'the concurrent

---

[80] Davenant, *Political and Commercial Works*, esp. i. 89, 120, 146, 422, 449–50; ii. 1–2. Davenant was even prepared to commend his protagonist Henry Pollexfen as a 'good patriot' for attempting to improve the nation's trade—ibid. ii. 162. For Davenant's more general contribution to political economy, see I. Hont in Dunn, *Economic Limits to Modern Politics*, 57–101.

assistance of the whole legislative authority', and both Houses of Parliament used the Board to address commercial problems. This development suggested that the landed elite had at least given formal notice of their responsibility for commercial advancement, even if constitutional conservatism acted as a break on far-reaching reform of the management of trade. Even with retired merchants at its helm, the Board could not have played a more forceful role without a fundamental transference of executive powers from the ministry, an unlikely occurrence in a post-Revolutionary age. Thus, political uncertainties, rather than landed attitudes towards the trader, remained the most effective block to more efficient commercial regulation.[81] An experienced council of trade was still desired by some merchant patriots, but commercial leaders did not seek to challenge the system, and continued their attempts to make an unyielding state structure work more productively in their interests. Concentrating their efforts on Parliament and the ministry, where the real power to influence policy was perceived to lie, they skilfully adapted their patriotic rhetoric to achieve less revolutionary ends. The next two chapters will examine this concurrent debate to gauge the reaction of ministers and parliamentarians to the increasing volubility of the merchant in public life. Discussion surrounding a reformed council of trade had demonstrated that the country's rulers could not ignore the claims of the patriotic merchant, but it remains to be seen if these far-reaching proposals provoked any practical benefits for trade and its supporters.

Examination of the merchant and the Augustan press faithfully reflects the turbulence within English commerce, with schemes advanced for funda- mental reform in the ways in which trade was managed, represented, and promoted. Aside from the storming of certain monopolies, none of these campaigns achieved its specific aims, and such failure may be interpreted as a crushing defeat for the trading classes. Undoubtedly, supporters of these reforms were disappointed, but, as John Taylor found to his general advan- tage, the state was prepared to acknowledge its debt to commerce in less radical ways. Crucial to the success of the merchant classes was the celebration of their economic role as a patriotic endeavour, which claim gained increasing force in a militarized Europe, and as the English state slowly evolved into the British Empire. Commerce still had an image problem under the early Georgians, with accusations of greed and factiousness remaining the most serious obstacles to ready acceptance in either social or political circles. However, the innovations in the form and content of the commercial press

---

[81] Davenant, *Political and Commercial Works*, i. 422; Steele, *Colonial Policy*, 38–41. See Brewer, *Sinews of Power*, 221–32, for discussion of the increasing use of commercial information by the state. For a positive view of the Board's role as an intermediary between commercial interest groups, see A. Olson, 'The Board of Trade and London Interest Groups in the Eighteenth Century', *Journal of Imperial and Commonwealth History*, 8 (1980), 33–50. For its relationship with Parliament, see below, Chs. 5 (section iii) and 6.

reflected a genuine movement of interest in trade, and the periodicals, histories, and handbooks devoted to the subject were not a faddish frenzy stirred up by publishers eager for sales. The vitality, modernity, and resilience of the Augustan commercial apologist is most striking, but these were necessary attributes when faced with the innate conservatism of state and society. Even though snobbery and social tensions persisted, the cause of trade and its practitioners had been more stridently advanced since 1660, and eventually gained the key conversions of Addison and Steele. Ultimately, however, the real testing-ground for acceptance remained the most public stage of all, Parliament, whose establishment as the effective sovereign power in the Augustan period appeared as both a challenge and an opportunity for traditional forms of mercantile activity. An immense surviving literature testifies to the importance of Westminster for the merchant at this time, and can further illuminate the perspectives of both polite and commercial society. The next chapter will therefore analyse this key relationship as a sensitive guide to both the social and political impact of the overseas trader.

CHAPTER FIVE

The Merchant and Parliament

'It is said, some have travelled as the tartars do, in hordes with their whole family, their sons, packers, brokers, book-keepers, and other officers that make-up the equipage of a wealthy merchant; all in hopes to be elected through the powerful recommendation of money.'[1]

THUS wrote Charles Davenant in 1701, employing his commercial expertise to provide a powerful image of the merchant and his professional entourage, albeit in a negative light. Reacting in part to a major scandal surrounding the electioneering of several leading City merchants associated with the New East India Company, the author was one of several critics to express alarm at the political impact of the great changes in City finance and commerce, but few succeeded as he did in capturing a prevailing distaste for the potential challenge of new money. The following year he created Double as the nemesis of the country gentlemen, who 'wallowing in wealth' would easily usurp their social and political ascendancy within the country.[2] The informed Davenant's principal concern was reserved for the activities of the jobbers and brokers of Exchange Alley, but among the less familiar social prejudice could easily rebound upon the overseas trader. In fact, the leading authority on the politics of Anne's reign has suggested that open conflict between the forces of old and new wealth was only avoided by the end of the War of the Spanish Succession. In the absence of direct collision, measures such as the Members' Qualifications Act of 1711 testify to an obvious disregard for moveable wealth, as the gentry-dominated Parliament set property requirements for MPs which could only be aimed at reducing the number of businessmen in the Commons. As the previous chapter indicated, in other parliamentary contexts Davenant could be very generous to the trading classes, but he remained most sensitive to the role of the merchant at Westminster. In response to this contemporary interest, this chapter will undertake a thorough analysis of the mercantile relationship with Parliament to investigate how commercial aspirations

---

[1] C. Davenant, 'An Essay upon the Balance of Power' (1701), in *The Political and Commercial Works of Charles Davenant*, ed. C. Whitworth (London, 1771), iii. 326.

[2] Davenant, 'True Picture of A Modern Whig' (1701–2), ibid. iv. 215–16. Double is clearly a broker, and thus Davenant can be seen to be swinging back to his more accustomed defence of overseas trade. For similar concern, see *Considerations upon Corrupt Elections of Members to Serve in Parliament* (1701). For the East India controversy, see R. Walcott, "The East India Interest and the General Election of 1700–1', *EHR* 71 (1956), 223–39.

and priorities were accommodated by the landed in an era of economic and political upheaval.[3]

In comparison to the huge outpouring of commercial commentary directed at Parliament in the late seventeenth and early eighteenth centuries, the number of works on the relationship of the merchant classes with Westminster is surprisingly limited.[4] In particular, modern commentators have paid little attention towards Parliament's role as a forum for the resolution of social tensions. Historians have shown that latent animosities between landed gentlemen and businessmen could surface in the course of the discussion of public policy at Westminster, but our understanding of their impact remains largely impressionistic. With the honourable exception of the historians of the great free-trade debates of the period, and certain case-studies of the economic lobbyist, there have been few attempts to discern whether the commercial and financial 'revolutions' did in fact cause a major reorientation of the relationship between the trading classes and Parliament.[5] The most recent research, most notably that of Julian Hoppit and Joanna Innes, suggests that Parliament underwent a very significant transformation in terms of legislative performance after 1689, and the economy appears to be one of the principal motive forces behind such change. These important findings argue for further research into the shift of power from the executive to the legislature, and this chapter will offer a fully rounded account of the reaction of the overseas trader, by examining both the extra-parliamentary and the Westminster politicking behind commercial legislation.[6]

Previous work has rarely aimed to discover the specific role of the overseas trader in the political process. Conflating them with bankers, manufacturers, and retailers in a 'business interest', analysts have yet to isolate the particular political advantages enjoyed by the merchants, nor have they chartered their relationship with other commercial groups. As the previous chapters have suggested, business competition did not aid coordinated activity even within

[3] G. S. Holmes, *British Politics under Anne*, 2nd edn. (London, 1987), ch. 5; *idem*, *The Making of a Great Power* (London, 1993), 287–91. For the emergence of trade as part of the vocabulary of political thought in the later seventeenth century, see J. G. A. Pocock, *The Machiavellian Moment* (Princeton, 1975), esp. 423–61.

[4] A point reiterated recently by T. Keirn—'Monopoly, Economic Thought, and the Royal African Company', in J. Brewer and S. Staves (eds.), *Early Modern Conceptions of Property* (London, 1995), 427–66.

[5] G. L. Cherry, 'The Development of the English Free Trade Movement in Parliament, 1689–1702', *JMH*, 25 (1953), 103–19; H. Horwitz, 'The East India Trade, the Politicians, and the Constitution, 1689–1702', *JBS* 17 (1978), 1–18; K. G. Davies, *Royal African Company* (London, 1957), 123–52. For excellent studies of parliamentary lobbying by commercial groups in the Augustan period, see L. Davison, T. Hitchcock, T. Keirn, and R. B. Shoemaker (eds.), *Stilling the Grumbling Hive: The Response to Social and Economic Problems in England, 1689–1750* (Stroud, 1992); S. Handley, 'Local Legislative Initiatives for Economic and Social Development in Lancashire, 1689–1731', *Parliamentary History*, 9 (1990), 231–49; J. Brewer, *The Sinews of Power: War, Money, and the English State, 1688–1783* (Oxford, 1989), 221–49. For the parliamentary response, see H. Roseveare, 'Prejudice and Policy: Sir George Downing as Parliamentary Entrepreneur', in D. Coleman and P. Mathias (eds.), *Enterprise and History* (Cambridge, 1984), 135–50.

[6] J. Hoppit (ed.), *Failed Legislation, 1660–1800* (London, 1997).

specific trades, and this chapter will demonstrate that there was little common purpose across the commercial sector as a whole. In general, trade lobbies were formulated with very specific objectives in mind, and during our period there was no profound change in the essential particularism of commercial politics. However, analysis of the mercantile lobby will suggest that all trading interests were galvanized by the political changes of the Augustan age, and that there was widespread recognition of the growing importance of a voice at Westminster. In turn, the challenge of securing parliamentary favour would stretch the political abilities of overseas traders to the full, and prove the acid test of their heightened public profile after 1660. The records of semi-formal organizations do not always illuminate the associations and tactics behind parliamentary endeavour, but sufficient evidence survives of how commercial groups attempted to influence members of both Houses. More importantly, we can identify their key arguments for change, which remain a much under-studied aspect of merchant politics when compared to the solicitation, and even bribery of MPs. It would be naive to suggest that personal influence played no significant part in the success or failure of certain issues, but Davenant's colourful images should not lead us to assume that Westminster could be swayed by a cause which lacked coherent and plausible justification.[7]

In order to outline the broad parameters of these momentous changes in the politics of trade, this chapter will study in turn four key themes. The most obvious manifestation of mercantile influence at Westminster will be analysed first by charting the election of overseas traders to the House of Commons between 1660 and 1754. These trends on their own do not provide a comprehensive picture of the influence of overseas trade at Westminster, and more significant patterns emerge from subsequent study of extra-parliamentary agitation concerning commercial issues. Thanks to significant changes in parliamentary practice, the post-1689 period was highly important for the development of commercial politics, both in terms of the intensity of debate and the presentation of economic grievance. Parliament's response to these key developments will then be examined in order to see if an evident increase in commercial lobbying had any impact on Westminster's approach to economic problems. A final section will then examine the contribution of the Members themselves, both in terms of legislative activity and in the course of parliamentary debate. All these sections will suggest that the 1690–1715 period saw an important readjustment of the interaction between a gentry-

---

[7] The most comprehensive surveys of 'business interests' remain the introductory volumes in the History of Parliament series—P. W. Hasler (ed.), *The History of Parliament: The House of Commons, 1558–1603* (London, 1981); B. D. Henning (ed.), *The History of Parliament: The House of Commons, 1660–90* (London, 1983); R. Sedgwick (ed.), *The History of Parliament: The House of Commons, 1715–54* (London, 1970); L. Namier and J. Brooke (eds.), *The History of Parliament: The House of Commons, 1754–90* (London, 1985). Also note the broad commercial grouping of M. D. McHattie, 'Mercantile Interests in the House of Commons, 1710–13', MA thesis (Manchester, 1949). A very idiosyncratic category of 'non-elite' MPs has been studied by I. Christie, *British Non-Elite MPs, 1715–1820* (Oxford, 1995).

dominated Parliament and overseas trade, which saw the interests of both advanced without any more than the occasional moment of tension. Westminster can thus reveal a most dynamic relationship between the forces of land and trade, analysis of which will illuminate the reasons why the state experienced no serious upheaval as its rulers emerged as a commercial power in the course of the eighteenth century.

i. Merchant representation at Westminster

The direct participation of the merchant in the parliamentary process has aroused the interest of both contemporaries and historians, with the latter taking it for granted that the number of 'merchant' MPs in the Commons can be read as a guide to the perceived social acceptance of business within the nation at large.[8] This belief reflects Parliament's status as the exemplar of landed hegemony, and the early modern period in general appears untroubled by any noticeable increase on the part of the commercial classes at Westminster. In fact, it appears that the number of businessmen in the Lower House fell between the reigns of Elizabeth and Charles II, and between 1660 and 1690 their complement hovered at a level of 10 per cent of the Commons, a rate which was largely maintained for the majority of the eighteenth century.[9] However, the Augustan period remains a major gap in our understanding of these trends, especially as this apparent stability does not accord with the vituperative attacks against the rising corruption of the City interests, nor does it explain why the gentry should have taken such remedial action against the nouveau riche in the form of landed qualifications. In order to shine light on these issues, Table 5.1 analyses MPs for three distinct periods, distinguishing those Members who were actively engaged in overseas trade for a significant period of their career.

The table immediately highlights a significant rise in the numbers of overseas merchants entering the House after the Glorious Revolution, in the process of which they far outstripped other sectors of the commercial world. Thus, even though remaining an insubstantial minority of the Commons membership, overseas traders were able to assert their prominence within urban society, founded on both their professional connections as well as the simple criterion of superior wealth. This increase in mercantile representatives was more obviously at the expense of domestic traders rather than the gentry, and the overall number of businessmen in the House did not pose a threat

[8] Holmes, *Making of a Great Power*, 289–91.

[9] Hasler, *House of Commons, 1558–1603*, i. 20, 56; Henning, *House of Commons, 1660–90*, i. 7–10; Sedgwick, *House of Commons, 1715–54*, i. 148–50; Namier and Brooke, *House of Commons, 1754–90*, i. 131–4. For a brief overview of other surveys of mercantile representation, see R. Grassby, *The Business Community of Seventeenth-Century England* (Cambridge, 1995), 223–4.

TABLE 5.1 *Mercantile MPs (English and Welsh constituencies), 1660–1754*

Period	1660–90	1690–1715	1715–54
Number of Parliaments	7	10	6
Total number of MPs	2,040	1,874	1,869
Total number of merchant MPs	75 (3.7%)	148 (7.9%)	136 (7.3%)
Other commercial MPs	98 (4.8%)	70 (3.7%)	51 (2.7%)
Number of first-time merchant MPs	62 (3.0%)	118 (6.3%)	93 (5.0%)
Number of first-time merchant MPs per Parliament	8.9	11.8	15.5

Sources: All tables in this section are based on the findings of the History of Parliament volumes for the 1660–90 and 1715–54 period, supplemented by the author's own research and the unpublished biographical articles of the History's 1690–1715 section (due for publication in 2001). The table does not include MPs who only sat for Scottish constituencies after 1707, who numbered 108 in 1707–15 and 172 in 1715–54. The category 'other commercial MPs' encompasses several occupations, most notably banking, brewing, domestic wholesaling, mining, and manufacturing.

of alarming novelty to the landed classes.[10] More significantly, beyond the question of basic numbers, it appears that merchants were able to secure election to a far wider range of constituencies. First-time mercantile MPs in 1660–90 represented only thirty-seven different boroughs and two counties; but under William and Anne they were returned for eighty towns and five counties, and for eighty-five urban constituencies under the first two Georges. From this general overview, this extension of mercantile influence is indeed impressive, and would certainly help to explain the concerns of commentators like Davenant, which on occasion were even echoed on the hustings when merchants made a rare challenge for county seats, such as at the Surrey election of 1710. However, such clashes were rare, and it would be wrong to attribute this proliferation of merchant influence to any broad social agenda. In order to understand its causes, closer analysis is needed of the political motivations of the growing band of mercantile Members.[11]

From the outset it must be acknowledged that it is very difficult to generalize about the causes for this rise in mercantile Members, since their motivation, in common with all MPs, could vary according to the individual, and range from ideological conviction to hopes of future preferment. Moreover, even though they were predominantly urban representatives, their borough constituencies could vary wildly in character, from the twenty-two parish-

[10] The published History of Parliament volumes suggest that the figure for the broader 'business' interest could fluctuate from one Parliament to the next, but the overall figure did not alter significantly. None of the domestic trading groups experienced a significant upsurge in parliamentary representation in this period.

[11] In the wake of the dramatic defeat of Sir Richard Onslow and Sir William Scawen at the Surrey election of 1710, it was reported that local gentlemen would not suffer 'the City of London to choose the representatives for Surrey'—Devonshire MSS at Chatsworth, Finch-Halifax papers, box 5, bundle 13, Henry Weston to Lord Guernsey, 29 July 1710.

pump politicians of Gatton to the 8,000-strong electorate of London. Thus, it would be difficult to talk of the character and responsibilities of the 'typical' merchant Member. Nevertheless, certain general factors clearly advanced the electoral success of overseas traders, most obviously the increasing incidence of parliamentary elections after 1690, which created more opportunities to gain a seat. Furthermore, whatever their personal reasons for standing, there can be little doubt that their burgeoning parliamentary presence bespoke a growing respect for the importance of that institution. Merchants were busy men who would not unthinkingly take on potentially onerous parliamentary commitments, and thus it is significant that so many overseas traders were willing to seek a place at Westminster. However, while the enhanced authority of the post-Revolutionary Parliament was an evident attraction, more specific causation is needed to explain the rise of the merchant Member. Anxious commentators might pinpoint money and ambition as basic motivational forces, but, as with any Member, there were a number of key variables which determined their appearance and impact at Westminster, ranging from age to wealth to constituency interest. Subsequent analysis will concentrate on the patterns of parliamentary service exhibited by merchants entering the House *for the first time*, all of whom served initially for borough constituencies. This general survey cannot account for specific motivations for entering the House, but can demonstrate broader influences promoting the rise of the merchant MP after 1690.[12]

As a priority, we must ascertain whether the parliamentary career of the merchant MP was changing in tandem with their increased numbers at Westminster, an issue addressed by Table 5.2.

In general, the table does not suggest that merchants were keen to relinquish their place after merely one assembly. There was a noticeable rise in the number of merchants only serving for one Parliament after 1690, but approximately a third of these traders met defeat at the hustings on at least one other occasion, and several more died while in the House. Thus, there can be little doubt concerning the general desire among merchant politicians for a sustained parliamentary career, a finding all the more significant when it is clear that the demands of Westminster were increasing in this period. In July 1690 Sir Samuel Dashwood, a two-time Member, lamented the 'many a pound' his parliamentary activity had cost him already, and hoped that it 'may happen but seldom and not long continue'. Lumbered with the (more remunerative) post of excise commissioner too, Dashwood bemoaned his 'often going to the other end of town', and 'the great inconveniences my servants and family receive thereby'. Even merchants who sat for many Parliaments felt the burden of office, a friend of Sir Henry Ashurst com-

---

[12] There is surprisingly little written on the motivations of those entering Parliament. The introductory volumes for the History of Parliament volumes supply the most instructive surveys.

TABLE 5.2 *Parliamentary service by first-time merchant MPs, 1660–1754*

Number of Parliaments	1660–90	1690–1715	1715–54
1	13 (21%)	32 (27%)	35 (38%)
2	16 (26%)	21 (18%)	23 (25%)
3	9 (15%)	15 (13%)	17 (18%)
4–6	16 (26%)	33 (30%)	17 (18%)
7–9	7 (11%)	15 (13%)	1 (1%)
10+	1 (2%)	2 (2%)	0
TOTALS	62	118	93

Sources: See Table 5.1.

miserating with him in 1696 on the loss of his seat as 'a writ of ease to you from a great deal of trouble, which hath heretofore had too much influence upon the impairing your bodily health'. Ashurst himself had complained of being 'forced to serve my dear country and the public to the neglect of my private affairs', but personal sacrifice could bring its rewards. The status and influence of the position offered the most obvious compensations, and a seat could protect the incumbent from other responsibilities, John Ward pleading his parliamentary status to avoid the London shrievalty in 1706.[13] Despite these advantages, the enhanced status of Parliament could not disguise the increased workload of annual sessions, which would not necessarily appeal to the merchant politician. The financial and personal commitment necessary to retain a seat had evidently begun to take its toll on the merchant MP by the early Hanoverian period, which saw an overall contraction in the parliamentary career of merchants. In common with the experience of the gentry, traders found opportunities for securing a seat curtailed by the Septennial Act of 1716, which had an inflationary effect on already forbidding levels of electoral expenditure. Nevertheless, overseas traders still managed to find success across a wide spectrum of constituencies, even if they were less prepared to answer the increasing demands of political management under the Whig ascendancy.[14]

The political ambitions of overseas traders can also be illuminated by analysis of the ages at which merchants first entered the House. Augustan political commentators were most concerned that the Commons be regarded as an experienced senate, and fears were occasionally expressed that too many

[13] Bodl. Dashwood MSS A.1.6, Dashwood to Sir Francis Dashwood, 5 July 1690; Add. MSS 45538, fos. 22–3; Bodl. MSS Don. C. 169, fo. 71ᵛ; N. Luttrell, *A Brief Historical Relation of State Affairs* (Oxford, 1857), vi. 61. Ashurst actually served for two more Parliaments after 1696.

[14] An interesting early Hanoverian case-study has been supplied by Jacob Price's *Perry of London: A Family and a Firm on the Seaborne Frontier, 1615–1753* (Cambridge, Mass. 1992), 72–84, which demonstrates that the anti-ministerialist activity of Micajah Perry III had an impact, but not necessarily a decisive one, on his commercial decline.

TABLE 5.3 *Age of first-time merchant MPs on entering Parliament, 1660–1754*

Age	1660–90		1690–1715		1715–54	
under 30	1	(2%)	9	(7%)	6	(6%)
30–9	8	(13%)	30	(25%)	22	(24%)
40–9	28	(45%)	32	(27%)	19	(20%)
50–9	18	(29%)	19	(16%)	12	(13%)
60–9	3	(5%)	7	(6%)	5	(5%)
70–9	1	(2%)	4	(3%)	1	(1%)
Unknown/uncertain	3	(5%)	17	(14%)	28	(30%)
TOTAL	62		118		93	

Note: Of all data, those concerning age must be regarded with particular caution, and regarded as approximate. Any real doubts have been classed as 'uncertain'.

Sources: See Table 5.1.

youngsters were being introduced into the House. Table 5.3 demonstrates that mercantile Members did not give any undue cause for alarm on this score.[15]

Although the table suggests that most merchants would be comfortably into their middle age before they considered a parliamentary career, there was a notable increase after 1690 in the number of traders who gained election to the House before their fortieth birthday. In the world of business, a merchant's thirties would have been critical years of consolidation for his commercial career, allowing little time for the distractions of parliamentary office. Thus, the willingness of younger merchants to enter Parliament is further confirmation of Westminster's increasing attraction within commercial circles. In the 1690–1715 period these younger Members were in general promoted by familial interests, whose influence could compensate for their inexperience and possible anonymity. Political naivety was certainly an issue for the aforementioned Sir Henry Ashurst when standing as a 25-year-old contender for a by-election at Liverpool in 1670, with opponents reasoning that as 'a very young man, neither does he understand the interest of the town, nor so much as (that) of the county'. Significantly, his Hanoverian counterparts increasingly lacked direct local connections, and a much higher proportion of them were London merchants. These trends suggest a more ruthless political ambition, although as much on the part of their local or governmental patrons as on themselves. In general, however, the forties and fifties remained the more 'natural' age at which merchants took themselves to Westminster, and most of the top traders had proved themselves in the commercial world before undertaking a parliamentary career. Having estab-

[15] In some contrast to the agitation surrounding qualifying measures, there was little concern for the youthfulness of mercantile MPs in electioneering material—*The Six Distinguishing Characters of a Parliament Man* (London, 1700); *Honest Advice to the Electors of Great Britain* (London, ?1708).

lished both fortune and reputation, they stood more chance of success at the polls, and could also contemplate the burdens of public office with greater equanimity.[16]

Choice of constituency is a further test of the motivation of merchant newcomers to Westminster, especially as a measure of their commitment to public life. The widening geographic coverage of mercantile representation has already been highlighted, but it remains to be seen if this change denoted a growing ambition among the mercantile classes to break new political ground. Table 5.4 thus seeks to probe the reality of Davenant's travelling tartar by studying the constituencies held by merchant Members in the course of their career.

TABLE 5.4 *Constituencies represented by first-time merchant MPs, 1660–1754*

Constituencies represented	1660–90		1690–1715		1715–54	
1 borough	50	(81%)	92	(78%)	67	(72%)
2 boroughs	8	(13%)	15	(13%)	21	(23%)
3 boroughs	2	(3%)	5	(7%)	4	(4%)
4 boroughs	0		1		1	
1 borough/1 county	0		1		0	
2 boroughs/1 county	1		2		0	
1 county	1		1		0	
2 counties/1 borough	0		1		0	
TOTAL	62		118		93	

Sources: See Table 5.1.

The picture which emerges here is a pretty emphatic rebuttal to any suggestion that merchants were mere carpet-baggers, buying up the votes of venal constituencies as their whim took them. The table demonstrates that merchants in general were not successful in gaining election to more than one constituency. In common with some two-thirds of all MPs, the vast majority of merchants were content to represent one borough only, and across the whole period only a handful of these loyal members campaigned for election elsewhere. Furthermore, their general failure to gain election to county seats reflects a limited political ambition, which did not constitute a threat to the supremacy of the landed gentleman for the prestigious status of knight of the shire. Mercantile county Members were extremely thin on the ground, and

[16] Henning, *House of Commons, 1660–90*, i. 558. It is difficult to gauge whether the opportunities presented by the financial revolution encouraged overseas traders to withdraw from active commerce at an earlier age, a development which would have facilitated the political career of the merchant MP. It is clear that the greater City magnates became financiers later in their career, but they had continued their mercantile activity during their initial service in Parliament. For further discussion of the merchant life-cycle, see Ch. 2.

their success was only achieved in alliance with local gentle support.[17] It is most interesting to note a slight rise in the proportion of multi-constituency merchants in the Hanoverian period, despite the fact that electoral opportunities had been severely cut by the Septennial Act. However, this increment should not be interpreted as evidence that merchants were willing or indeed able to wield increasing political influence. In fact, this trend more readily reflects governmental willingness to find borough constituencies for their loyal mercantile supporters, doubtless for their credit and contacts. Late Stuart ministers had clearly aided the parliamentary careers of helpful contractors, but the Septennial era saw a closer working partnership between the City and Whitehall, with eleven of the eighteen merchants who served in four or more Parliaments after 1715 boasting government connections. Overall, at least a quarter of the merchants entering the House for the first time in 1715–54 can be linked to the service of the state in a business capacity.[18]

These patterns of parliamentary tenure suggest that traders were still very much in the electoral shadow of the landed gentleman, despite their more frequent appearance in Parliament. The formidable task of establishing an electoral interest was a considerable obstacle for a busy merchant, requiring an extensive investment of time and money.[19] Given this forbidding challenge, the strategies which they evolved to secure their seats obviously bear testimony to their reasons for entering Parliament. Although it is notoriously difficult to identify the decisive factor in any success at the polls, such are the paucity and bias of existing records, Table 5.5 focuses on certain electoral connections which contemporaries and historians have regarded as critical to the establishment of a secure parliamentary interest. In no way does the table pretend to identify the principal cause of electoral victory.

The table suggests that despite the general pattern of mercantile loyalty to a single constituency, a decreasing proportion of overseas traders could boast a direct link with their constituents on the firm recommendations of residence or family. This finding suggests that overseas traders had become increasingly adept at securing seats in unfamiliar constituencies, but it is important to note that even after the intense politicking of the rage of party, half of the merchants entering the House still sought to take advantage of their immediate contacts of kin and neighbourhood. For a merchant to succeed without such recommendations, the aid of an influential patron or the government would be necessary, especially if he wished to secure re-election. After 1715 several leading merchant contractors were prepared to take advantage of their minis-

[17] Beyond the seven successful mercantile knights of the shire in Table 5.4, only one further merchant can be identified as contesting the poll in a county election. I am indebted to David Hayton for the general figure for constituency loyalty.

[18] The number of first-time merchant MPs whose entry to Parliament was facilitated by government contacts rose from 8 to 17 between 1690–1715 and 1715–54. These must be regarded as minimum figures.

[19] Walcott, *EHR* 71 (1956), 223–39.

TABLE 5.5 *Constituency interest of merchant MPs on first entry into Parliament,*
1660–1754

Connection	1660–90	1690–1715	1715–54
Borough resident	29 (47%)	33 (30%)	22 (24%)
County resident	3 (5%)	4 (3%)	5 (5%)
Family link	14 (23%)	28 (24%)	21 (23%)
None of the above	16 (26%)	53 (45%)	45 (48%)
TOTAL	62	118	93

Sources: See Table 5.1.

terial contacts to enter the Commons, but the more modest resident MP had not yet become extinct.

It is at this point that acknowledgement be given to the particular impact of London merchants, and their differences from provincial overseas traders. In some ways it is difficult to isolate the 'London' merchant, since several metropolitan traders kept a residence many miles from the capital, for the convenience of business, family, or even political management. Nevertheless, it is possible to distinguish those members whose public careers largely depended on advancement in the capital, and thus may be broadly defined as 'Londoners'. Across 1660–1754 there was a steady rise in the numbers of City merchants entering the House, with them accounting for 63 per cent of all first-time mercantile MPs in the Restoration period, and 75 per cent under the first two Georges.[20] Furthermore, a handful of overseas traders with London parents provided additional evidence of the extensive influence of the capital on mercantile representation. The inexorable rise of the successful London merchant accords with common perceptions of the superior influence and wealth of the great mercantile princes of the City, and it is clear that the number of provincial merchants dwindled in absolute terms, and that their parliamentary tenure was curtailed. After 1690 a much higher proportion of provincial merchant MPs served for only one Parliament, as they struggled to compete against the electioneering of local county magnates and government agents. The customary recommendations for a provincial merchant were his intimate ties to the borough, and until 1715 the vast majority of provincial trading MPs were borough residents. However, by the dawn of Hanoverian rule several of the larger provincial ports such as Kings Lynn, Great Yarmouth, and Exeter were increasingly turning to the local gentry to

[20] The Hanoverian figure only matches the proportion of national trade channelled through the port of London—C. French, 'Crowded with Traders and a Great Commerce: London's Domination of English Overseas Trade, 1700–75', *London Journal*, 17 (1992), 27–35. The respective figures for our three periods are: Londoners 39, 82, 70, and non-Londoners 22, 34, 21. In addition, merchants with London backgrounds were a corresponding 1, 2, 2.

represent them at Westminster, and thereafter even buoyant Bristol and Liverpool were more willing to choose country gentlemen. The rising cost, and the increasing workload associated with a parliament seat were evidently major deterrents for provincial merchants, and seaport constituencies adapted to Members who were less acquainted with their commercial affairs, but attentive nonetheless.[21]

However, what was the attraction of a provincial seat for the London merchants, who were clearly the key motive force behind the rising numbers of first-time merchants in the House? Evidently, one major reason for their activity in the provinces was a negative factor, in that the chances of serving as one of the four members for the City were slim unless the overseas trader had extensive contacts, great energy, and a high public profile. Historians have noted that a declining number of 'business' MPs were City freemen, but it appears that the representatives of London still had to work extremely hard to prove their worth to the City liverymen. In general, London members were the cream of the mercantile elite, often with long service in the corporation and the major overseas trading companies. Only thirty-one of the 191 London merchant MPs in the 1660–1754 period ever succeeded in gaining the most prestigious of urban seats, and only two others went as far as being listed in the poll. Thus the vast majority had to look elsewhere for access to Westminster, and accordingly ran the risk of being viewed as rapacious carpet-baggers. However, their attachment to their parliamentary seat is attested by the fact that few of these merchants were content with one term of parliamentary office, and sought a more permanent residence at Westminster. In fact, the number of single-Parliament London merchants dropped in the course of the 1690–1715, only to rise again in the Hanoverian period. At one level, it only made good business sense to seek further dividends for the costly investment of time and effort in gaining a seat, but it is still a surprising number who showed a sustained commitment to the maintenance of their position at Westminster.[22]

The choice of constituency of these London traders suggests that there was no great discontinuity with the practices of previous generations of merchants, even if the number of successful merchants was on the rise. A handful of boroughs became especially notorious for the bidding war for votes conducted between rival City magnates at election time, most notably New Shoreham, Stockbridge, and Great Grimsby, but this was not common practice. At least a third of the first-time Londoner MPs of the 1690–1754 period could boast

---

[21] Hull was the most notable provincial port to continue to choose mercantile Members on a regular basis—G. Jackson, *Hull in the Eighteenth Century* (Oxford, 1972), 300–2.

[22] H. Horwitz, 'Party in a Civic Context: London from the Exclusion Crisis to the Fall of Walpole', in C. Jones (ed.), *Britain in the First Age of Party* (London, 1987), 173–94. Analysis of the late 18th-century City suggests that the aldermanic bench was still seen by merchants as a necessary step towards a parliamentary seat—S. Brown, 'Politics, Commerce, and Social Policy in the City of London, 1782–1802', D.Phil. thesis (Oxford, 1992), 36–45.

important familial connections to the borough they served. Another quarter were brought in by borough patrons, and, as already mentioned, an increasing number by government. All these connections suggest that the simple use of money to buy a place at Westminster was not the common cause of London success in the provinces, although it would be naive to suggest that electoral douceurs were not essential to maintaining an interest over any course of time. In fact, mercantile ambitions were more likely to be checked by financial considerations, rather than advanced by them, especially if they envisaged an extended tenure in the Lower House. Given the increased premium on a parliamentary seat, the prospect of being brought in by a patron was particularly appealing to the merchant, for such agency conveyed prestige upon the trader with little commitment of time and resources. The example of Nathaniel Newnham is instructive in this regard, for he was reluctant to accept a government seat at Bramber because it was sufficiently close to his Sussex residence to threaten additional trouble and expense. Too close a personal connection with the constituency may actually have dissuaded traders from standing, and set merchants on their electoral travels in the manner which Davenant depicted. However, the experiences of successful mercantile candidates suggest that it would take more than money to buy their constituency of choice, and in general merchants were keen to represent boroughs with which they could boast several kinds of interest, whether they be linked to family, property, patron, government, or indeed business.[23]

'Professional' connections remain the most elusive and little-studied area of the London merchant interest, but there is little doubt that they were an important determinant of the political ambitions of our sample. At the height of the East India electoral scandals of 1701 John Toland claimed that commercial rivalries had divided London 'and consequently all the boroughs by reason of their dealing there', with supporters of New and Old Companies 'threatening even to turn off their workmen if they will not vote as they would have them'. Davenant painted an even more compelling image of the politicization of commercial connections, with the notorious Double boasting that 'we had persons at Blackwell Hall, who . . . told the clothiers as they came up (that) England, and particularly the woollen manufacture, would be ruined if Mr. Howe was chosen'. Even in less factious times, it is clear that provincial merchants reaped great political capital from their prominent position within the local economy, and historians have given increasing attention to the economic 'constituency' within the Augustan electorate.[24] More specifically, there are several excellent examples of London merchants establishing close

---

[23] Sedgwick, *House of Commons, 1715–54*, ii. 293. Even corrupt boroughs such as Great Grimsby necessitated more careful management than simple bribery, an aspirant MP at the turn of the century offering an array of services, many of which promised the economic regeneration of the town—'Diary of Abraham De La Pryme', *Surtees Society*, 54 (1869), 153–6.

[24] J. Toland, *The Art of Governing by Parties* (1701), 120–1; Davenant, *Political and Commercial Works*, iv. 192–3; R. Sweet, *The English Town, 1680–1840* (Harlow, 1999), 27–73.

links with the outports on this basis, such as the Hernes who represented Dartmouth for over thirty years, having used it as a base for their extensive trade to the Mediterranean. On the other hand, the traditional suspicion of the outports towards monopolistic London cartels was well founded, and the maintenance of a 'business' interest could be very difficult. Certain ports did use London merchants on a regular basis for representing their affairs in executive councils without ever electing them as Members, as has been noted with Liverpool's employment of the Heyshams, but this practice does not appear to have been replicated on an extensive basis in a parliamentary context. The inherent uncertainties of trade probably argued against too heavy a reliance on business connection as a basis for political interest, and even a government contractor in an 'Admiralty' borough could not be confident of longer-term support from his constituents or his patron.[25]

The profound parliamentary changes of the post-1690 period can thus be shown to have had an important, but far from dramatic impact on mercantile representation at Westminster. There was a huge increase in the number of merchants entering the House, and the tenacity with which many of these traders held onto their seats suggests that they shared common perceptions concerning the increasing significance of a voice in the Commons. On the other hand, there was no widespread attempt to use their increasing wealth to storm the gentry-dominated House, and most mercantile MPs opted to serve for constituencies with which they boasted some familiarity. After 1715 an increasing number of merchants had to thank electoral patrons or the government for their place at Westminster, and it is this accommodation of the forces of land and money which most readily represents how the state assuaged commercial demands for political influence. The gentry, as sitting tenants, would not tolerate a vast increase in the number of traders in their midst, and the Qualifications Act of 1711 revealed the limits of their regard for commerce and its practitioners. However, that measure should be read as an exceptional response to the recent excesses of the monied interest, most notably the Bank of England, rather than as a rebuff to the mercantile Member.[26] It is important to see that the hurdles which they placed in the way of merchant ambition did not reflect antipathy to the trading classes in general, and that their principal aim was to uphold the sanctity of representation against the threatening forces of new wealth. This latitude can only be observed by taking a broader view of Parliament's response to commercial developments.

---

[25] Henning, *House of Commons, 1660–90*, i. 195–7. For Liverpool and the Heyshams, see Ch. 3.

[26] Historians now regard the act as an ineffective barrier for the political ambitions of the greater merchants, who could easily afford the £300 p.a. estate requirement. Nevertheless, it continued to be a source of 'Country' interest—P. Langford, *Public Life and the Propertied Englishman, 1689–1798* (Oxford, 1991), 288–95; H. E. Witmer, *The Property Qualifications of Members of Parliament* (New York, 1943). For contemporary reaction to the attempt of a Bank delegation to influence the royal choice of ministers in 1710, see *The Wentworth Papers, 1705–39*, ed. J.J. Cartwright (London, 1883), 120; *HMC Portland*, ii. 222.

ii. Parliament and the representation of overseas trade

While analysis of patterns of merchant representation can suggest general attitudes both within and towards the commercial classes, electoral behaviour supplies merely one perspective on the impact of overseas trade at Westminster. As virtual representative of the whole nation, Parliament was supposed to pay heed to the interests of all subjects, the merchant included, and thus the significance of a direct mercantile presence in the Commons should not be exaggerated. In general, it does appear that trader MPs were under greater pressure than their gentle colleagues to pay heed to the wishes of their urban constituents, but Parliament's response to commercial issues was far from contingent on such direct delegation.[27] In order to gauge the real significance of the period for the politics of trade it is necessary to consider how commercial interests attempted to influence both landed and trading Members. The need for such research has been highlighted by the recent work of Julian Hoppit and Joanna Innes, who have emphasized the importance of the Augustan period for the advancement of economic legislation, and exposed our limited understanding of the reaction of Parliament to a new era of regular sessions and increased responsibility for affairs of state. It appears that Westminster was committing more time and energy to the resolution of economic problems, and thus it is imperative to understand the broader influences working to promote such issues at Westminster.[28]

The Hoppit–Innes examination of longer-term trends is the obvious starting-point for assessing the significance of commerce as an engine of parliamentary change in the Augustan period. Their methodology, of examining failed parliamentary initiatives exclusively on the evidence of the Journals of the House, can certainly be questioned for its potentially uneven coverage of lobbying in the 1660–1800 period, but the scale of their study remains impressive. As they concede, there is a further problem in distilling a mass of parliamentary endeavour into meaningful categorization, even though such a process must be attempted to address the variety of forces behind a major increase in Westminster's daily workload.[29] Fortunately, these obstacles have been largely circumvented by a well-designed and comprehensive survey, and their findings have demonstrated that the number of economy-related initiatives was rising in the Augustan period. More significantly still, the success-rate for such measures was dramatically enhanced after 1690. Across the 1660–1800 period they found that economic measures were a

---

[27] For the views of a conscientious constituency MP on the relationship between the borough and the Commons, note the speech of Sir William Coventry, MP for Great Yarmouth, in March 1671—A. Grey, *Debates of the House of Commons, 1667–94* (London, 1769), i. 401.

[28] Hoppit, *Failed Legislation*, 1–25.

[29] For the Hoppit–Innes classification of the economy, see *Failed Legislation*, 8–10. For discussion of the more specific difficulties inherent in codifying economic activity, see M. R. Julian, 'English Economic Legislation, 1660–1714', M.Phil. thesis (London School of Economics, 1979), ch. 5.

standard fare of parliamentary debate, and in the 1660–88 period they were the leading category of legislative activity with 287 initiatives, although experiencing a dismal 81.1 per cent failure rate. Between 1689 and 1714 they were ranked second after personal legislation, but the proportion of unsuccessful measures had dropped to 68.2 per cent, which improvement was continued under the first two Georges to a figure of 32.1 per cent. This survey also demonstrated that the Commons had become the dominant instigator of economic legislation, with the Lords declining appreciably in this respect in the post-Restoration period. Thus, even at a broad 'economic' level we again see that the late seventeenth and early eighteenth centuries were particularly important for the development of commercial politics.

Of course, such an all-embracing category as the economy, which in the Hoppit–Innes scheme ranged from enclosure to import duties, has only a general relevance to the specific matter of overseas trade, but it does substantiate their general thesis that Parliament was becoming a more efficient legislative machine in the Augustan period. Numerous factors are invoked to explain this wider phenomenon, most notably the regularity of parliamentary sessions and the increasing organization of Westminster lobbies, but further research is needed to attribute specific causation to each field of parliamentary activity. As Hoppit and Innes would be the first to admit, in the case of overseas trade it is particularly difficult to isolate legislative endeavour, as so many of their categories could have a direct impact on mercantile concerns. For instance, revenue bills affecting import and export duties could have an enormous influence on international markets, and the determination of governments to see such legislation through ensured a very high success rate for these measures, despite often considerable opposition from vested interests.[30] Even within the Hoppit–Innes scheme, certain areas such as harbour improvement (bracketed with 'communications') or shipbuilding (located in 'manufactures'), could be considered as of direct importance for the success of the 'external trade' category. Hoppit and Innes are wisely cautious concerning rigid categorization, including a secondary code of identification to cover inevitable cross-referencing, but it is still very difficult to isolate the real aims of mercantile lobbying in the period.

Although these methodological problems must be acknowledged, the commanding sweep of the Hoppit–Innes survey has provided a general legislative framework in which more specific issues can be addressed. In particular, their analysis of the subcategories of external and internal trade reveals a major discrepancy between commercial sectors, with the former emerging as by far the more successful of the two in the 1660–1800 period. Legislative initiatives relating to 'external trade' (which accounted for 15 per cent of all economic initiatives) suffered a failure rate of some 33 per cent in that period, while

---

[30] For governmental use of the clerks of the House to speed revenue bills, see O. C. Williams, *The Clerical Organization of the House of Commons, 1661–1850* (Oxford, 1954), 43–7.

'internal trade' (19 per cent of all economic measures) encountered a much bleaker 69 per cent. Hoppit and Innes speculated that these intriguing trends might be linked to the superior organization of the overseas commercial lobbies, and to their manipulation of the parliamentary system. These considerations undoubtedly help to explain the apparent efficiency of mercantile legislation, although many trading lobbies actually impeded the progress of commercial legislation in order to defend vested interests. Clearly, research must be directed to the specific objectives of these groups, and to the services which were provided by the increasingly prized parliamentary statute. Most pertinently of all, the success of commercial campaigners must be assessed in the light of the arguments being put forward by such lobbies, since changes in the presentation of mercantile issues could strongly influence their legislative improvement. Thus, we still need to know more about the *interaction* of commercial groups with their representatives at Westminster in order to measure governing attitudes towards overseas trade.[31]

In order to delineate the character and extent of mercantile contributions to political life, a survey has been taken of all petitioning to the House of Commons concerning overseas trade in the 1660–1714 period.[32] As Hoppit and Innes have shown, the Upper House does not appear to have been the key arena for commercial conflict, and even though battles fought in the Lower House might well have continued in the Lords, in general they merely represented a re-enactment of well-rehearsed positions. The inadequacies of the Commons Journals, especially in the pre-Revolution period have to be acknowledged, and no claim is made that the following analysis supplies comprehensive coverage for all mercantile initiatives at Westminster.[33] Nevertheless, while targeting a specific sector of parliamentary activity, this survey will highlight the breadth of interest in Westminster politicking, and the variable activity of several categories of lobbyist. Table 5.6 thus examines those petitions which were promoted by mercantile associations or had a direct bearing on overseas trade, and categorizes the lobbyists by economic or institutional criteria.

The most significant development revealed here is clearly the massive increase in the number of petitions submitted concerning overseas trade in the post-1690 period. Closer analysis of the incidence of petitioning suggests that this increment was non-linear in character, with spectacular bursts of lobbying

---

[31] Hoppit, *Failed Legislation*, 9–10.

[32] This sample broadens the scope of the Hoppit–Innes study, since it will include petitions which did not call for a specific legislative initiative.

[33] Even without the fire of 1834, it is doubtful whether the Commons archive would be complete. From the 1680s remedial action to organize parliamentary record-keeping had to be taken by the clerk of the House—S. Lambert, *Bills and Acts: Legislative Procedure in Eighteenth-Century England* (Cambridge, 1971), 22–3. For discussion of the compilation of the Journals, see D. Menhennet, *The Journal of the House of Commons* (London, 1971). For contemporary concern over the accuracy of the Journals, see *The Parliamentary Diary of Sir Edward Dering, 1670–3*, ed. B. D. Henning, (New Haven, 1940), 92; *CJ*, xii. 254.

TABLE 5.6 *Groups petitioning on mercantile issues, 1660–1714*

Group	1660–90	1690–1702	1702–14
Chartered merchant company	12	45 (8%)	34 (6%)
Unchartered merchants (with/without planters)	28	146 (25%)	110 (19%)
Merchants and other commercial groups	17	72 (12%)	55 (9%)
Chartered manufacturing or retailing company	4	49 (8%)	19 (3%)
Unchartered wholesalers, retailers, and manufacturers	20	168 (28%)	119 (21%)
Civic corporation	0	47 (8%)	98 (17%)
Others	19	68 (11%)	144 (25%)
TOTAL	100	595	579
Proportion of petitions with direct merchant involvement (%)	57	45	34

Sources: The table is compiled from *CJ*, viii–xviii. Clearly, the Journals can only supply minimum figures, for many petitions were never submitted to the House, their promoters deeming their presentation inopportune.

occurring in 1693–1700 and 1708–14. Thus, there appears a comparative sluggishness in commercial lobbying in the early stages of the great wars of the period, only for the rate of petitioning to rise significantly as wartime hardship became more unbearable, which increase was maintained on the immediate onset of peace. This pattern in general accords with the observations of Hoppit and Innes concerning the recurrent nature of vigorous legislative activity in post-war periods, and in the context of overseas trade this trend can be attributed in part to the frustrations engendered by high taxation and dangerous sea routes. Their persistence is all the more significant given the adverse affect which war generally had on levels of legislative activity. However, on its own conflict cannot account for several interesting developments in mercantile petitioning, most notably the significant decrease in the proportion of petitions originating directly from merchants or mercantile organizations, which suggests a much wider constituency of interest on issues relating to overseas trade. Thus, the identity of the commercial lobby requires closer inspection, and the general upsurge in campaigning on mercantile issues demands more fundamental causation.[34]

Although Table 5.6 suggests a declining importance for merchants and mercantile organizations, their general prominence within the politics of overseas trade should not be questioned. The table cannot be regarded as a comprehensive record of mercantile politicking, and the parliamentary

[34] Hoppit, *Failed Legislation*, 11.

activism of the overseas trader varied according to circumstance. In particular, the mercantile companies were apt to rely on less formal channels of influence than the petition.[35] Lacking the sophisticated machinery of the great companies, the unincorporated overseas traders resorted to petitioning on a much more regular basis than their regulated colleagues. Their campaigns also reflected the nature of the key commercial debates of the age, when traders formed organized lobbies to seize the privileges jealously guarded by the great companies. Beyond the ranks of the anti-monopolists, the table highlights the potential coordination and energy of several important unincorporated groups, most notably the colonial traders and planters, who increasingly used the Commons as a means to influence policy. It also demonstrates that unregulated merchants were prepared to align themselves with other commercial sectors to support their case, recognizing that such a united lobby would answer parliamentary concern to placate general economic interests. Given the lack of direct mercantile experience in the House, it was imperative that lobbyists reassure Members that a wide constituency of subjects would benefit by their proposals. This flexibility was crucial to the continuing prominence of the overseas trader on the parliamentary stage, and although overt mercantile lobbying in all its forms was proportionately reduced, a third of the petitions of Anne's reign could still be directly traced to those closest to the daily workings of international trade.[36]

While mercantile leadership remained significant, the table also demonstrates that wholesalers, retailers, and manufacturers were well aware of the importance of international trade for their own livelihoods, and were increasingly prepared to air their views. Of course, not even the most unreconstructed landed gentleman could doubt the interdependence of domestic and overseas trade, but the readiness of non-mercantile traders to comment on the international perspective of their grievances was very marked. The most voluble of these commentators were the clothiers from the leading woollen manufacturing regions of the north and west of England, who were apt to join with local merchants to advance the cause of their industry. Although historians have rightly questioned the homogeneity of the great 'wool interest', these campaigns betrayed sophisticated organization, and even an element of interregional coordination at critical moments. In part these collective efforts were promoted by the existing structure of wholesale trading in exported cloth, which required dealers to conduct their business via Blackwell Hall in London, and several petitions boasted subscriptions from provincial traders

[35] See Ch. 3, section i. McHattie's analysis of the 1710–13 Parliament suggested that the companies were far from uniform in their attitude to parliamentary petitioning, with the East India Company more prepared to lobby Westminster than the others. However, it too could recognize the imprudence of petitioning at particular junctures—MA thesis, 245–6, 297.

[36] For the political organization of the unregulated trades, see Ch. 3. For significant studies, see A. Olson, *Making the Empire Work: London and American Interest Groups, 1690–1790* (Cambridge, Mass. 1992); L. M. Penson, *The Colonial Agents of the British West Indies* (London, 1924).

assembled in the capital.[37] Retailers and manufacturers were in general more infrequent lobbyists, and less consistent in their demands, usually reacting to perceived threats caused by ministerial policy or events overseas. However, the noticeable decline in the petitioning of incorporated manufacturers under Anne should not be interpreted as the death knell of the domestic trading company, for surviving London records suggest that they remained active spokesmen for their trades, both informally and on the public stage.[38]

Perhaps the most interesting of the changes in commercial lobbying centres on the rise of the borough corporations as active commentators on overseas trade. Of course, town governors, particularly in the seaports, had been far from ignorant or disinterested in mercantile affairs prior to 1690, but the readiness of local magistrates to back commercial initiatives in the parliamentary arena is a significant development.[39] Often the town council was simply lending its weight to the views of the local trading elite, many of whom were councillors themselves. However, increasing importance appears to have been attached to gaining the respectable support of local governors as a means to influence the Commons. A concern to dispel suspicions of private or group self-interest was probably the principal motivation behind this trend, particularly in a Commons in which the competition for commercial favour was becoming ever fiercer. As we have seen with both declining York and expanding Liverpool, the town hall could prove vital for the advancement of commercial causes. Less certainly, civic involvement may also reflect an increased awareness on the part of local rulers that Parliament, and not the executive, was now the most important determinant of national policy with regard to overseas trade.[40]

These developments can be further illuminated by study of geographical differences, and Table 5.7 has been designed to identify broad changes in the origin of petitions.

The table clearly highlights the importance of the provinces in increasing pressure on Parliament for commercial change after 1690. London was far from bypassed as a source of political agitation, and its impressive lobby would undoubtedly have been swollen by a substantial number of the petitions of unspecified origin. However, the twenty-fold increment in provincial petitioning in the reign of William is unmistakable proof that extra-London forces

---

[37] T. Keirn, 'Parliament, Legislation, and the Regulation of the English Textile Industries', in L. Davison et al., *Stilling the Grumbling Hive*, 1–18; G. D. Ramsay, *The English Woollen Industry, 1500–1750* (Basingstoke, 1982), 65–72; Julian, M.Phil thesis, ch. 3; McHattie, MA thesis, 16.

[38] Brewer, *Sinews of Power*, 23–42. For discussion of livery company politics, see ch. 3.

[39] For discussion of the resourcefulness of the Augustan corporation, see Sweet, *The English Town*, *passim*; P. Gauci, 'For Want of Smooth Language: Parliament as a Point of Contact in the Augustan Age', *Parliamentary History* (1998), 12–22.

[40] For the corporate activism of York and Liverpool, see ch. 3, section iv. The importance of borough representations was echoed in the advice of Andrew Marvell to his Hull constituents, and that of Paul Shakerly to Chester leaders. Both urged their constituents to supply as many 'independent' petitions as possible—Julian, M.Phil. thesis, 57–8.

TABLE 5.7 *Geographical origin of petitions on mercantile issues, 1660–1714*

	1660–90	1690–1702	1702–14
London	29	148 (25%)	132 (23%)
London and provinces	3	6 (1%)	1
English provinces	17	334 (56%)	317 (55%)
Wales	0	3 (1%)	1
Scotland	0	0	26 (4%)
Ireland	0	1	3 (1%)
Colonies	0	9 (2%)	13 (2%)
Unspecified	51	94 (16%)	86 (15%)
TOTAL	100	595	579

Sources: See Table 5.6.

were striving hard to influence policy in the Commons, and this momentum was maintained in the succeeding reign. Many of these addresses were concerned to right the injustices felt by provincial traders at the monopolies of London-based companies, and these campaigns could generate up to fifty petitions in some instances, thereby sustaining a lobby over several parliamentary sessions. Predictably, the most prominent of provincial campaigners were the leading outports, with Bristol and Exeter noticeably active throughout the period, as befitting their size and long-term interest in maritime affairs. More significantly, their lead was taken up by the rising towns of Liverpool, Whitehaven, and Leeds, all with voluble mercantile groups, as well as by nascent manufacturing centres at Birmingham and Manchester. This evidence suggests that economic change was leading to increasing pressure on the political machinery of the state, as new commercial interests demanded that their concerns be respected. However, it would be premature to suggest that the economy was stoking the fires of parliamentary reform. Nearly 200 provincial petitions in 1690–1714 originated from boroughs without an MP, but not one alluded to its lack of direct representation. Furthermore, enfranchised provincial towns evidently felt that the testimony of their MPs was insufficient, since they applied even more parliamentary pressure than non-Member boroughs, submitting some 350 petitions. The readiness of the Commons to hear the grievances of any interest was an effective bar to fundamental constitutional reform, and all commercial groups learnt to work within the idiosyncratic framework of the unreformed political system.[41]

The mercantile lobby was far from purely urban in origin, and several of the western and northern counties submitted petitions as frequently as the

[41] The other petitions come from London, county groups (about 90 petitions), and a handful of regional interests. This petitioning further endorses P. Langford's argument that direct representation was merely one avenue for local interests—'Property and Virtual Representation in Eighteenth-Century England', *HJ*, 31 (1988), 83–115.

most active of provincial towns. It is particularly frustrating that the original county petitions on overseas trade do not survive, for they could illuminate the workings of commercial lobbying on a regional basis. Campaigns could even cross county boundaries, especially in the case of small towns and villages with mutual economic interest. Ministers were well aware of the influence which powerful alliances could bring to bear on the Commons, with the 'West Country' interest widely respected and feared. Even when on diplomatic service in Vienna, George Stepney warned the government to beware of regional campaigns for a retaliatory ban on trade with the Habsburg territories in 1704, observing that 'the votes of the western parts . . . are known to be numerous and powerful in the House of Commons, and to have great influence in all resolutions, especially in the granting of money for carrying on the war'. Even with little direct evidence of how these networks were maintained, it does appear that the great upsurge in mercantile petitioning had an impact on rural and semi-rural England, for an increasing number of commercial addresses boasted gentlemanly support. During the reign of Anne even farmers openly supported campaigns concerning the regulation of overseas trade. Of course, these petitions cannot conclusively prove that the landowning classes were adopting new economic priorities and interests, but it is significant that the 'natural' leaders of English society were keen to direct policy on overseas trade.[42]

The contents of the petitions, and the demands which they put forward suggest that commercial lobbyists were increasingly adept at presenting their case to the gentry-dominated Commons, which improvement may well have had an important influence on the success rate of their legislative initiatives. In particular, in the course of the period the arguments of the lobbyists betray much greater sophistication in their appeal to the public interest, evidently in an effort to win over the landed MPs. Eschewing economic theory, which would probably serve to alienate a gentry audience, they adopted the commercial self-justifications of Malynes, Roberts, and more recent mercantile apologists to equate mercantile with national power.[43] In this vein, the clothworkers of Gloucestershire celebrated their exports to the Levant as 'so national a trade' in 1710, while a year later the merchants and planters of Carolina proclaimed their imported goods to be 'matters of great weight in the balance of power and trade'. Over and over again, the Lower House was assailed by arguments stressing the value of trade as a means for national self-enrichment, and as a nursery for mariners. Whether it be millions of pounds of

---

[42] CO389/19, p. 4. In 1711 the Board of Trade were informed that the western counties had successfully manipulated the order of Commons' business so that they could press for the imposition of a duty on Irish yarn—CO389/21, fo. 404.

[43] Several Bristol petitions attempted to lecture the Commons on principles of economic theory in the 1690s, one boldly opening with the pronouncement that 'the wealth of this nation doth chiefly arise from the labour of its people'. They probably reflect the exceptional influence of John Cary—CJ, xi. 396; xiii. 84.

imperilled goods, or thousands of potential seafarers, no opportunity was lost to highlight the advantages which commercial reforms would bring to a country undergoing the greatest wars it had ever faced.[44]

These claims did not go uncontested. Although an interest group would be accorded respect for their peculiar expertise in the issue at hand, their partiality would be suspect, especially as rivals were keen to expose any bias. Petitions often attested to the priority of proving oneself before the House, a petition from Barnstaple in January 1706 insisting that the Newfoundland trade 'has been allowed amidst the cavils about foreign trade to be of the greatest importance to the kingdom'. Therefore, beyond the need to demonstrate the reality of a particular grievance, petitioners had to justify their claim for special consideration within a broad national context. Despite growing interest in political arithmetic, reliable statistics were rarely available to substantiate the claims of the petitioners, thus ensuring plenty of opportunity for local interests to profess themselves a 'not inconsiderable branch' of a country-wide trade. This was especially the case with the cloth industry, its output universally praised as Britain's 'greatest manufacture' or its 'staple commodity'. As a Leeds address of January 1700 succinctly put it, the fate of the nation's woollen manufacture was 'worthy the consideration of a Parliament of England'. Concerned observers such as John Cary duly complained that interest groups were 'perplexing the Parliament with notions fitted for their private interests under the splendid name of the public good'. However, even though conscientious Members would find it hard to resist local lobbies using this patriotic currency, its validity would be thoroughly tested by the rigours of the parliamentary process.[45]

Beyond the appeal to the nation, for the benefit of their landed audience lobbyists had to spell out the direct contribution of overseas trade to domestic prosperity. Thus, petitioners were not only keen to outline the international dynamics of their proposed reforms, but also to show how they would answer traditional gentry concerns, in particular the employment of the poor, and the maintenance of landed rents. For instance, in 1713 Whitehaven merchants endeavoured to protect their Iberian wine trade by pointing out that any favouritism towards their French rivals could threaten the export of English cloth 'on which the landed interest depends'. These overt calls to gentle self-regard could be even more pronounced in the House of Lords, which was reminded by a petition on the silver bill of December 1690 that the supplicant merchants were 'far less concerned in this affair than the nobility and gentry that have great estates in lands and money'.[46] The frequency with which these claims were made suggests that lobbyists copied the methods employed by successful petitioners, although their familiarity almost certainly worked to

---

[44] *CJ*, xvi. 288, 550.
[45] Add. MSS 5540, fos. 72–3; *CJ*, xii. 527; xiii. 99; xv. 101, 472; xvi. 124.
[46] *CJ*, xvii. 408; House of Lords MSS, main paper series 353, fo. 3.

harden parliamentarians against such appeals. However, it is significant that only 3 per cent of all mercantile petitions were rejected by the Lower House, and these failures mainly related to proposed tax measures, over which the House demonstrated understandable sensitivity in a time of national hardship. As a merchant group were curtly reminded in February 1693 after the rejection of one such petition for special consideration, your 'representatives are here and their consent is sufficient'. The arguments of the patriotic trader did have an impact at Westminster, but there were limits to parliamentary patience.[47]

While petitioners sought to engage Members in a common discourse of national improvement, the actual objectives of these lobbies varied enormously, as did their success at Westminster, and thus it is difficult to generalize about the Commons' response to commercial issues over the 1690–1714 period. Nevertheless, in broad terms the lobbyists attempted to secure the favour of Parliament in two ways.[48] First, Parliament was used to attack monopolies, and the great onslaughts against the London overseas trading companies accounted for nearly a third of all petitions considered here. This colossal wave of anti-company sentiment demonstrated that Parliament, and not the Crown, was regarded as the national arbiter on commerce, and its enhanced post-Revolutionary authority was sought as a weapon to undermine the royal authority of the company charters. Even more frequently, the Commons was asked to impose or remove restrictions on the movement of commodities, the lobbyists thus acknowledging the Lower House's supremacy over the Crown on revenue matters. The all-encompassing influence of the woollen industry was crucial here, its leaders being able to draw support from all over the country to crush Irish rivals or to bemoan the impact of imported Oriental textiles. Increasingly, commercial groups felt sufficiently emboldened to make direct pleas for the removal or increase of duties, although several learnt to their cost that a hard-pressed government would be less than generous to such appeals when the whole country was burdened by wartime taxation. Commercial groups had to be sensitive to the general climate of grievance at Westminster or else risk exposure for their lack of public spirit.[49]

---

[47] *The Parliamentary Diary of Narcissus Luttrell, 1691–3* ed. H. Horwitz (Oxford, 1972), 425. Earlier examples of trade-lobby rebuffs over taxation can be found in March 1671 and March 1677—*Grey Debates*, i. 401, iv. 224–5. A merchant-vintner petition against the raising of duties on wine was also rejected in April 1668 because it was unsigned and deemed 'only a design to put off the King's business and to retard the raising of money'—*The Diary of John Milward*, ed. C. Robbins (Cambridge, 1938), 244.

[48] It was very rare for a petition to seek the remedy of more than one specific grievance. A rare exception remains the Taunton agenda of January 1700, which demanded an end to monopolies, a cut in interest rates, a repeal of the ban on Flemish bone-lace, and a free market for 'all buyers' within England—*CJ*, xiii. 113–14.

[49] T. Keirn in L. Davison et al., *Stilling the Grumbling Hive*, 1–18; G. L. Cherry, *JMH*, 25 (1953), 103–19. The declining influence of the Crown in commercial affairs was also reflected in the way that petitioners sought to enlist ministerial and royal support as a means to influence Parliament—Add. MSS 61623, fo. 105.

Although heartened by the general receptiveness of the Commons to their addresses, certain merchant groups were clearly impatient to see Westminster take even further responsibility for the regulation of overseas trade. The growing authority of the statute ensured a steady stream of petitioners to Parliament's door, but many supplicants regarded Westminster as purely a means to an end. Even in the 1660s it was not uncommon for merchants to petition the House in the hope of putting extra pressure on the executive to change policy, but with the continuing decline of the Privy Council as an arbiter in commercial affairs, the post-Revolution era saw a marked increase in this tactic.[50] During the 1690s devastating shipping losses sparked major protests to the Commons over the Admiralty's protection of trade, and the House duly responded with inquiries into the activities of the fleet as well as remedial legislation. In the next war, mercantile petitioners urged the Commons to obtain ministerial approval for extra land and maritime defences to secure Newfoundland against French attack. On several occasions, interest groups railed against the injustices of foreign princes, including wartime allies, and expected MPs to aid their efforts in asserting British claims abroad. The great commerce treaty debates of 1713–14, detailed in the next chapter, saw economic debate at the heart of delicate international negotiations, with interest groups keen to lecture Members and ministers on the importance of trade for the future balance of power in Europe. Such outbursts were comparatively rare, but it is clear that commercial lobbies did not regard the Commons as a clearing-house for mundane trading issues, and that they increasingly saw it as a means to influence the direction of state policy.[51]

In this manner, the parliamentary activity of commercial groups demonstrated ready awareness of the profound constitutional changes of the time, and the Augustan period saw a transformation in their relationship with Westminster. Of course, the massive increase in their petitioning was not unreservedly welcomed in parliamentary circles, and even mercantile MPs could be heard to complain about the strain of representing the interests of their colleagues. Furthermore, increasing familiarity with the commercial lobbyist could have easily bred a contempt among Members for their factiousness and self-regard. Already burdened by requests from other groups for favour, the Commons discovered that the introduction of annual sessions was still inadequate to answer all matters of state, and thus traders faced a major challenge to gain sufficient parliamentary attention to champion their cause. For certain, no interest group could take for granted the response of a Lower

[50] For example, note the support given by the Commons to petitioning merchants over impounded goods in January 1667—*CJ*, viii. 678–81. D. Gardiner notes that after the Restoration ministers tried to reduce the number of petitions submitted to the Privy Council—'The Work of the English Privy Council, 1660–79', D.Phil. thesis (Oxford, 1992), 85–7.

[51] Of particular interest and contemporary significance were the campaigns against the Emperor's ban on British cloth in 1707, and against Commander Kerr the following year for having extorted payments for convoy protection.

House experiencing such major readjustment. Therefore, analysis of the Commons' treatment of mercantile legislation should reveal whether there was any change in the attitude of the gentry-dominated House to this persistent commercial lobby.

iii. Parliament and the passage of commercial legislation

Members could not have failed to note the growing sophistication of the commercial lobby, but there was no guarantee that they would endorse its appeal for parliamentary attention, or dedicate precious time to answering specific grievances. Although the post-1660 Commons might appear in general a more assertive institution, its relationship with the populace at large remained ambivalent. Its representative role ensured that it respected the views of its constituents, but it could not permit itself to become the puppet of particular interests. Moreover, although conscious of their responsibilities of office, Members did not regard themselves as mere delegates of their electorates, and could be most suspicious of the claims emanating from petitions to the House. Nevertheless, after the Revolution the Commons demonstrated concern to reform its organization in order to deal with a great increase in its accustomed workload. As Hoppit, Innes, and others have suggested, the lengthening of sessions, and their improved regularity, were fundamental preconditions for increased efficiency, but there were other important parliamentary initiatives taken to accelerate the legislative process, and several of them were taken in response to the growing demands of the commercial lobbies.[52]

In order to gauge the general response of the Commons to a more insistent commercial world, Table 5.8 analyses the success rate of legislation which was predominantly concerned with the regulation of overseas trade in the 1660–1714 period. Thus, it deliberately excludes measures which may have had only tangential relevance to foreign commerce, and it does not include revenue bills whose sole stated aim was to raise supplies for the crown. However, bills which reduced duties with the overt aim of stimulating overseas commerce have been counted.[53]

While in general endorsing the Hoppit–Innes thesis on the improved legislative performance of Parliament, the table suggests that the passage of

---

[52] Hoppit, *Failed Legislation*, 5. For analysis of the key procedural changes of the late seventeenth and early eighteenth centuries, see B. Kemp, *The Votes and Standing Orders of the House of Commons: The Beginning* (London, 1971); O. C. Williams, *The Historical Development of Private Bill Procedure and Standing Orders in the House of Commons* (London, 1948–9), i. 23–40.

[53] It is difficult to bring precision to the definition of a 'trade' bill, and here analysis has simply sought to prioritize measures of direct concern to overseas traders. Inclusion within the table does not simply reflect the title of bills, although in certain cases we know little about their contents. Hopefully, future research will build upon the Hoppit–Innes scheme to produce a systematic typology of legislative initiatives.

TABLE 5.8 *Success of mercantile legislation, 1660–1714*

	1660–90	1690–1697	1697–1702	1702–14
Bills introduced	95	44	43	58
Acts passed	32	12	15	29
Overall success rates	34%	27%	35%	50%
Number of sessions	24	8	5	14
Bills per session	4.0	5.5	8.6	4.1

Sources: The table has been compiled from *CJ*, *LJ*, and the *Statutes of the Realm*. The reign of William III has been divided in order to compare legislative performance in peace and war.

foreign trade legislation was not an especially easy task in the period.[54] Even under Anne, controversial measures such as the settlement of the Africa trade could founder in the face of severe opposition sustained over several sessions. More generally, the perennial influence of war appears to have acted as a deterrent for legislative initiatives.[55] In addition, the overall rise in success rates must be attributed in part to the passage of privately sponsored legislation in the sphere of overseas commerce, with merchants exploiting parliamentary powers to gain special dispensation for the import or export of their goods, or for the naturalization of foreign-built ships. The adaptability of Parliament was clearly attractive to the commercial classes, but even lobbyists with modest objectives could attest that Westminster was no easy short-cut to achieving influence. The considerable obstacles which lay in the path of any bill must be recognized, and there were particular pressures working on legislators when considering commercial matters, especially those of a wide potential impact. However, the significance of these limited gains in parliamentary efficiency will be magnified by closer analysis of the perils of the legislative process for the economic lobbyist.[56]

By 1660 the Commons had evolved several standard procedures for processing the demands of commercial groups at a pre-legislative stage.[57] As with

[54] Given the high success rate (67%) for overseas trade bills in the Hoppit–Innes survey for 1660–1800, the improvement of Anne's reign must have been further enhanced in the remainder of the eighteenth century—*Failed Legislation*, 9–10.

[55] K. G. Davies, *The Royal African Company* (London, 1957), 140–52; T. Keirn, in Brewer and Staves, *Early Modern Conceptions of Property*, 427–66. The Africa controversy is a good example of the way in which increased parliamentary organization could actually frustrate legislative success, rather than secure it.

[56] Following the passage of several acts to naturalize ships, the Commons received a petition from London shipowners against this 'growing' evil—*CJ*, xvi. 148. The success rate of such measures declined thereafter.

[57] For discussion of the important developments in Commons procedure in the Augustan period, see Lambert, *Bills and Acts*, chs. 4 and 5; Williams, *Historical Development of Private Bill Procedure*, i. 26–40. For subsequent developments, see P. D. G. Thomas, *The House of Commons in the Eighteenth Century* (Oxford, 1971), 45–64. Mercantile issues could easily recommend themselves as public measures, and thus avoid the fees and procedural incumbrances of private legislation.

all its multifarious business, any petition for redress could be transmitted to a specially appointed committee of inquiry, which would report back to the House and propose further action concerning the particular matter. The Commons, if sufficiently motivated by a petition, could even proceed direct to legislation, and appoint a committee to draft a bill to answer the ends of the lobby in question. Such precipitous haste was unlikely in the case of important affairs, unless the matter had been raised in a previous session. The House could also refer commercial issues to its grand committee of trade, which was appointed at the start of each session and scheduled to sit on one afternoon each week. Historians have concluded that this committee was wholly redundant by the Restoration, and that the ritualistic appointment at the opening of a session was a mere formality.[58] However, the House sometimes sought to activate this moribund institution, such as in January 1662 when it was ordered to sit twice a week to consider the decay of the woollen industry and the export of bullion. Moreover, the importance of this move was signalled by the concomitant order for all other committees to refrain from sitting at the same time. Only two years later, the Commons appointed a specific committee on 'the general decay of trade' to advocate measures on a wide spectrum of commercial issues, and a similar all-purpose committee of inquiry was chosen in the session of 1667. General committees clearly ran the risk of being overwhelmed by the business before them, and were always in danger of running out of parliamentary time. For instance, in the session of 1675, a committee investigating the balance of Anglo-French trade and several other controversial issues made its report on the very day that Parliament was prorogued. The House's appointment of general committees suggests a willingness to experiment with the ordering of its business, but these innovations clearly did not work. Instead, the Lower House preferred to use select committees to assess the veracity of grievances and the likely success of reforms before allowing measures to pass to the actual legislative process.[59]

The evidence of the Journals suggests that the Commons was creaking under the pressure of its workload well before the Revolution. Research into the early Stuart period has raised serious questions about the efficiency of the Commons, when irregular sessions did not aid professionalism in the matter of passing bills.[60] In the case of trade legislation, which would almost inevitably involve Members in a lengthy consultation process with experienced business-

[58] D. L. Smith, *The Stuart Parliaments, 1603–89* (London, 1999), 73–4. The committee for trade dated back to 1621, created at the height of a major economic crisis. Other such grand committees included those for law and religion, as well as the high-profile committee of privileges and elections, whose importance was enhanced amid the increased electioneering of the post-Revolutionary period.

[59] *CJ*, viii. 340–1, 537; ix. 15, 356. Lambert, *Bills and Acts*, 52–5, notes subsequent attempts by the Commons to group private business, but these experiments had ceased by the early eighteenth century. A motion of November 1703 appeared to revive the 'grand' committee on trade, but to little apparent effect (see below).

[60] Smith, *The Stuart Parliaments*, 42–3, notes only a 22% success rate for bills in 1603–25. The corresponding figures for 1660–85 and 1689–1714 were 34% and 51% respectively.

men, these inefficiencies could be very serious obstacles. The haphazard pattern of sessions under Charles II and James II did not help to cure the House of its fumbling, or encourage a more systematic approach to commercial issues. In May 1663, in an alarming instance of indecision, a committee on a petition of English clothiers refused to give opinion on the custom of foreign bought and sold, 'judging it to be a point of great concern, as well to the clothiers of England, as to the City of London'. This overt reticence was unusual, but on major issues, which might attract many petitions to the House, non-mercantile Members inevitably found difficulties in reaching a quick and satisfactory resolution. The appointment of generically experienced groups to select committees, such as 'all merchants', the Members for the seaports, or the MPs for specific boroughs and counties, highlighted the Commons' dilemma in ensuring an impartial yet informed decision on complex trade issues. However, it did not shrink from its responsibilities, and endeavoured to rise to the concerns of the commercial interests clamouring at the door. Of course, the increased efficiency in parliamentary legislation after 1660 was not merely occasioned by trade affairs, but commercial lobbyists can be identified as an important consideration behind developments affecting procedure and the activities of Members.[61]

The clearest sign that the Commons was responsive to commercial pressure groups was its concern to process the increasing number of petitions submitted. In particular, Members were alarmed by the pushiness of certain economic interests, and on several occasions these lobbyists were deemed to threaten accepted parliamentary procedures. For instance, in March 1671 a furious debate arose over a petition against proposed rates on imported sugar, during which Members queried whether the requirement for petitions to be presented by MPs was a sufficient protection against 'unfit' or 'scandalous' addresses. Although the House recorded its content with existing safeguards, the anxiety of Members still lingered, for in May 1678 a committee was appointed to examine why printed papers concerning the wool trade were circulated to Members at the door of the Commons when no petition against a current bill had been submitted to the House. Many contemporaries commented upon the scrum of petitioners haunting the lobby in the hope of finding a sympathetic MP, and surviving commercial records suggest that trading interests were in the thick of these mêlées. Such was the perceived importance of this antechamber for the success of any particular measure that the Commons had to intervene to prevent improper practice. For instance, in December 1667 a petition concerning exported leather prompted a motion (only narrowly defeated) 'that no printed papers of any kind should be licensed to be printed and delivered to the Members at the Parliament door, as was too frequently done'. More worryingly, a select committee was appointed in June 1689 to investigate a charge that an East India Company Member had

[61] *CJ*, viii. 492–3.

'spoken some threatening words to the petitioners' at the door of the House. The complaint was subsequently dropped, but given the fiscal importance of certain trade issues, such passions were bound to be engendered.[62]

The Commons was even more vigilant when trying to prevent violence from erupting in its precincts. Trade posed a particular hazard in this regard, since petitioners often claimed that the travails of overseas commerce were threatening to impoverish thousands of desperate workers. Any insensitive response on the part of the Commons could result in an angry mob of unemployed manufacturers coming to Westminster to vent their fury at the Membership. The passage of the Act against Tumultuous Petitioning in 1661, which cut the number of addressers to a mere ten, was clearly a political move to banish memories of the 1640s, but it also served to keep commercial interests in check, and to a certain extent pre-empted any direct appeal to the common multitude. As Sir John Birkenhead reminded his colleagues in the aforementioned debate on imported sugar duties in March 1671, 'your people in numbers should not come to disturb the councils; you yourselves are the petitioners'. Several instances reminded the Commons to be on their guard, and the House maintained a tough stance against intimidation, thereby lending no credence to the potential efficacy of mob rule. Although prepared to pressurize Members by raising the spectre of mass unemployment, merchants were also keen to distance themselves from disorder, Sir Francis Brewster piously observing in 1695 that artisans 'seldom determine disputes in other men's trades but with a club and broken head'. Nevertheless, the views of the masses could not be totally ignored, and Parliament had to show even-handedness if a genuine grievance arose. For instance, in November 1689 the rumour of a bill to allow the import and re-export of silk manufactures sparked a near riot among groups of London artisans, who, although they later petitioned the Commons for pardon, only did so after learning of the 'care that was taken therein for them'. Much more serious was the invasion of Westminster by a mob of weavers in January 1697, who entered the lobby to register their protest at the import of East Indian silks. The Commons ruled this action a high crime and misdemeanour, but also sought to assuage such discontent with a measure to protect domestic cloth manufacture. All Members concurred that violence should never be tolerated in the legislative process, but the threat of disorder was never far from their minds, especially in the midst of wartime hardship, when petitioning groups were eager to remind them of the dangers of poverty and despair.[63]

While violence remained a lingering concern for legislators studying commercial issues, a more immediate problem rested with the use of covert influence to support commercial interests. Political commentators were all-

---

[62] *Dering Diary*, 91; *Grey Debates*, i. 401–3; *CJ*, ix. 484–5, x. 167; *Milward Diary*, 152.

[63] *Grey Debates*, i. 402; *CJ*, x. 285–6; Olson, *Making the Empire Work*, 36–7; Julian, M.Phil. thesis, 51–2; F. Brewster, *Essays on Trade and Navigation* (London, 1695), 38.

too-aware that Members of both Houses maintained direct commercial connections, and indeed expected that MPs would speak on behalf of trades with which they had intimacy. However, the bribery of MPs to advance legislation remained a worrying concern, and in the increasingly competitive commercial environment of Westminster, the House was forced to confront the issue on several occasions. In 1667 John Ashburnham was expelled from the House for having received some £500 to seek favours for French wine merchants, his opponents castigating the trade lobby as 'like the Devil, both tempters and accusers'. The general resolve against corruption was highlighted by the appointment in October 1675 of a select committee to probe the influencing of Members for 'giving their votes and promoting bills', but it is clear that commercial corruption only became more of a problem after the Revolution. In January 1693 the House ruled that no Member was 'to accept of any entertainment at any public house for the carrying on any matter under the consideration of the House', a move which Sir John Guise, chair of the committee of the whole House on the East India bill, saw as a personal slander.[64] Only two sessions later, the most celebrated case of corruption was discovered, when a Commons inquiry revealed that the East India Company had invested some £160,000 in an effort to gain the support of MPs for its monopoly. Such notoriety was earned only a few years later by its rivals, the New East India Company, whose leaders fought a coordinated campaign to return sympathetic MPs from a number of small borough constituencies. Five Members were subsequently expelled, and the controversy excited the anti-mercantile distaste with which Davenant opened this chapter.[65] These scandals did not aid the cause of commercial groups in general, and fed growing unease over the moral impact of City wealth. The readiness of parliamentarians to commence impeachment proceedings against commercial figures after 1690 highlighted this concern. However, the House could do little more than respond with severity to cases of blatant corruption, which continued to embarrass its proceedings in trading matters. It was all-too-obvious to contemporaries that secret influence pervaded every aspect of a system which nominally relied on the independence of Members to ensure fair and open debate. Thus, in the absence of draconian reform, the House could only strive to ensure that the commercial affiliations of MPs were well publicized, and trust that rival interests would not permit Members to be misled over the partiality of the arguments put forward in parliamentary debate.[66]

If unable to stem the menace of the douceur, the House did take effective measures to ensure that the petitions submitted were genuine representations of subject opinion. In part, the House's hand was forced by external pressure,

[64] *Grey Debates*, i. 46; *Milward Diary*, 131–7; *Luttrell Diary*, 351.

[65] H. Horwitz, *JBS* 17 (1978), 1–18.

[66] Impeachment proceedings were commenced against twenty-two investors in the Scottish Darien Company in 1696, and two years later against several merchants who had partaken in covert Anglo-French trade—*CJ*, xi. 401–6; *HMC Lords*, NS iii. 225–34.

in that the waves of petitions and counter-petitions saw an increasingly competitive battle for popular support, with opponents claiming widespread backing for their respective positions. For instance, in March 1677 City MP William Love suggested that a mercantile petition concerning ship passes was 'contrary to all the opinions of the merchants upon the Exchange', and that several signatories had since disowned it. Likewise, in November 1689 the silk-throwsters were eager to refute claims that the import of raw silk was a threat to the clothing industry, and insisted that the signatures on a rival petition of weavers were bogus. Claims were made that a scrivener had merely collected names without showing the signatories the petition, and the Commons responded by resolving that in future 'all petitions presented to the House be signed by the petitioners with their own hands, by their names or marks'. This stance did not end concerns for the authenticity of petitions, which rival interests continued to voice, but petitioners appear to have adhered to this parliamentary requirement.[67]

Beyond periodic concerns for violence or corruption, the acid test of the House's attitude towards the mercantile lobby lay in its ability to process commercial demands in an equitable and efficient manner. In accordance with the Hoppit–Innes general survey, Table 5.8 demonstrates that overseas commerce had benefited from increased legislative success by the end of our period. This improvement is all the more impressive given the rise in the rate of mercantile bills entering the House in the sessions after 1690.[68] This efficiency clearly cannot be attributed to any one factor, although Hoppit and Innes are surely right to identify the regularity and length of sessions as crucial. Credit must also be given to extra-parliamentary changes within the state which significantly aided the Commons' treatment of trade. As John Brewer has observed, an increasing interest in statistics may have helped certain groups to secure the support of Members confronted by difficult points of commercial dispute, even though such data could be the basis for prolonged confusion.[69] More directly, overseas trade may have gained disproportionate encouragement from the improved efficiency of ministerial management, which Hoppit and Innes regard as a significant force behind the higher success rate for all types of legislation. The Journals reveal that government departments were increasingly in touch with the Commons on commercial issues, relaying both data and informed opinion. The industriousness of the Board of Trade was particularly significant after its reorganization in 1696, its hard-pressed staff supplying the Commons' demand for information on a much more regular basis. This fruitful relationship between the executive and the legislature

---

[67] *Grey Debates*, iv. 214–5; *CJ*, x. 285. Exeter petitioners twice attempted to cast doubt on the authenticity of their rivals' support—March 1696 and January 1700.

[68] The deflationary effect of the great wars can be measured against the impressive 8.6 bills per session introduced in the inter-war years.

[69] Brewer, *Sinews of Power*, 228–30; Hoppit in *EcHR* 49 (1996), 521–5.

suggests that the nation's rulers were prepared to accord commercial matters greater recognition as true affairs of state.[70]

It is most tempting to link these developments to other changes outlined in this chapter, especially the increasing number of overseas traders in the Lower House after 1690. However, this correlation cannot be made without closer analysis of the activity of merchant Members in the Commons. For these purposes a database has been constructed of all significant appointments concerning mercantile legislation in the Lower House in the 1690–1714 period. The resultant survey incorporates over 1,800 records of parliamentary activity relating to 145 bills, and thus provides a direct insight into the promotion of commerce in the Lower House. The Commons Journals are a difficult source to use, and historians have demonstrated increasing caution when interpreting the appointments contained therein. In particular, lists of committee members cannot be regarded as a reliable guide to those Members directly interested in a bill, nor even as evidence that they served on the committee. Nevertheless, certain key appointments can be taken as important indicators of legislative influence, especially those relating to the drafting of bills, their presentation, the chairmanship of the second-reading committee, tellerships, and the transmission of bills to the Lords. Analysis of these responsibilities cannot pretend to supply a comprehensive account of Members' interest in mercantile affairs, but this survey will illuminate the management of commercial legislation in the face of increasing demand for Westminster's statutory services.[71]

Before analysing the role of specific Members, it is important to note several interesting developments in procedure with regard to mercantile affairs which appear to indicate an increasing regard for commercial issues. Most importantly, a growing proportion of mercantile matters were referred to committees of the whole House, particularly towards the end of the reign of Queen Anne. This was a conscious policy on the Commons' part, since it resolved on 9 November 1703 that 'no bill relating to trade or the alteration of laws concerning trade be brought into the House until the proposition shall have been first examined and debated in the grand committee for trade, and agreed unto by the House'. There is no evidence to suggest that the grand committee appointed at the start of the session was ever resuscitated, but in its absence, the committee of the whole became an accustomed arena for mercantile legislation. In the period 1690–1702 only seventeen of our eighty-seven (20 per cent) commercial bills were heard by a committee of the whole,

---

[70] For discussion of the strengths and weaknesses of this line of communication when under pressure, see Ch. 6.

[71] The Commons Journals for the 1660–90 period are simply too inconsistent in their recording of appointments to attempt any meaningful analysis of Member activity. For a discussion of the listing of committees, see Henning, *House of Commons, 1660–90*, i. 79–82; Williams, *Historical Development of Private Bill Procedure*, 30–4.

whereas the corresponding ratio for Anne's reign was thirty-three from fifty-eight (57 per cent).[72] This change was no doubt linked to the fact that many mercantile issues raised revenue issues, which the Commons expected to be discussed only at 'a grand committee, where everyone has freedom of debate and might speak as often as they pleased'. However, fiscal concerns only partially explain this development, and other evidence suggests that this procedural change reflected the enhanced status of trade in parliamentary circles. Since its appearance in the early seventeenth century, the committee of the whole had been reserved for matters of general importance, because its more liberal laws of debate could promote fuller discussion among Members. Evidently, trade was increasingly deemed to be worthy of that audience, and as early as 1667 the diarist John Milward remarked that delicate Anglo-Scottish trade negotiations had been referred to a 'grand' committee, as it was 'a business of great consequence'. By February 1693 Narcissus Luttrell could remark that a similar referral of a bill to encourage privateers reflected its status as 'a matter of great import'. Significantly, in February 1709 a select committee requested the House to discharge them of a Levant Company issue, it being of 'too public a nature for them to give any opinion upon till they receive further instructions from the House'. The accordance of such respect to commercial measures did not always result in legislative success, but no less than twenty-eight of the thirty-three mercantile bills to go before a committee of the whole under Anne managed to pass the House, and nineteen reached the statute book.[73]

A more equivocal sign of Commons interest is suggested by the rising number of tellerships in connection with mercantile bills, with the eighty-seven bills of 1690–1702 producing thirty-six divisions (0.4 per bill), while the fifty-eight measures of Anne's reign saw forty-six (0.8 per bill). Given the vast increase in commercial petitioning, it is tempting to see this increment as further proof of the pressures which trade was imposing on the Commons, as rival interest groups fought out their battles at Westminster. The great debates over the East India trade or the French commerce treaty, which bore party political overtones, could arouse great passions and see divisions involving over 350 MPs. However, the average of votes cast in commercial divisions was actually lower than the general mean, and if trade issues were increasingly capable of splitting the House, their resonance was evidently lost on many Members. The tellerships thus provide a sensitive guide to the ambivalent response of the Commons, which, finding itself under great pressure to con-

[72] *CJ*, xiv. 210–11. This is an especially interesting finding, given that M. R. Julian's broader analysis of trends in legislation suggests that most 'economic' bills were discussed in select committee. He also observes that it was only after 1689 that committees of the whole were used for non-revenue issues, thus suggesting that mercantile issues were very much at the forefront of Commons business—Julian, M.Phil. thesis, 66–7.

[73] *Milward Diary*, 127; *Luttrell Diary*, 424; *CJ*, xvi. 127.

sider trade, acted with increasing alacrity and divisiveness, but not necessarily with wholehearted interest and support.[74]

Recognition of the House's equivocal attitude towards trade must also be acknowledged when turning from these general procedural trends to individual activity. As we have noted, the number of overseas traders in the House may have risen, but they remained vastly outnumbered by their gentle colleagues, and any increase in the general contribution of mercantile MPs to the passage of legislation would be significant indeed. However, their role appears limited, with gentry MPs far more prominent in the overt management of commercial measures.[75] Mercantile Members were active sponsors in matters of direct personal interest, but in general they were inconspicuous in the Journals. Nevertheless, this impression has to be tempered by awareness of the partiality of the Commons records regarding the management of legislation, and much behind-the-scenes activity remains obscure. The committee reports demonstrate that the House relied upon merchant testimony as a regular source of experience and knowledge on the matters before them, and other records suggest that commercial Members gave informal advice to managers of bills. Of course, the actual passage of legislation was not merely a question of insider expertise in commercial affairs, but a matter of legalistic precision, and thus it is no surprise that a major role was played by lawyers. Even more significant than the expertise of lawyers appears the contribution of ministerial agents, who carefully watched over the progress of commercial bills which had a direct bearing on the revenue, or international relations. Their involvement suggests a high governmental priority to the passage of mercantile legislation, epitomized by the coalescence of commercial advancement and public finance in such measures as the East India Act of 1698 and the South Sea Act of 1711.[76]

Closer inspection of merchant Member activity further illuminates the motivations and abilities of overseas traders entering the House. Although only a few merchants played a prominent role in the management of legislation, these exceptions proved that businessmen could operate effectively in the gentry-dominated Commons. Under William and Anne the most active legislators among the overseas traders fell into two categories. First in importance were the more experienced mercantile Members, most notably Sir Samuel Barnardiston, Sir Matthew Andrews, and Thomas Papillon, whose service

---

[74] Hoppit and Innes record mean divisions of 174 for 1660–88, and 212.8 for 1688–1714; the mercantile figure for 1690–1714 is 197.8—*Failed Legislation*, 17. Of course, these figures do not cover divisions within the committee of the whole House, which were not recorded by the Journals. Judging by private sources, these could be very stormy indeed.

[75] Industrious exemplars of non-mercantile MPs who were active in commercial affairs include Peter Shakerly, Chester MP, and Andrew Marvell, Member for Hull—McHattie, MA thesis, 150–3; Julian, M.Phil. thesis, 60.

[76] The government did pay the clerks' fees for ensuring the passage of revenue legislation—Williams, *Clerical Organization of the House of Commons*, 43–7. For an excellent example of the industrious ministerial agent, see Roseveare, in Coleman and Mathias, *Enterprise and History*, 135–50.

both inside the House and in government equipped them well for the demands of parliamentary management. Just as importantly, at their advanced ages they were probably much less heavily involved in the daily workload of trade. The other most significant group of active merchants were the representatives of the leading provincial towns, such as Robert Yate of Bristol, or Thomas Blofield of Norwich. The heavy pressure which the outports could impose upon a Member is becoming increasingly recognized, and their Members could prove particularly industrious, although usually in a local or regional cause.[77]

Apart from these traders, the only noticeably active Members with business backgrounds were the likes of Arthur Moore, one of the precious few who managed to span the divide between the City and Whitehall, and could recommend himself to government as an informed and well-connected agent. Most of the overseas traders seldom appear in the Journals, only occasionally gaining appointments to bills of particular concern to self or constituency. The principal reasons for this apparent reticence must rest with their lack of familiarity with the procedures of the House and the distractions of business during the sessions. Even the fearless Thomas 'Diamond' Pitt was prepared to acknowledge mercantile difficulties at Westminster, warning his son against 'prating in Parliament till he is master of the orders of the House, and knows who and who is together, and that he can speak to the purpose'. Although there was an obvious advantage in having a parliamentary sponsor well acquainted with the commercial background of a legislative initiative, lobbyists would often prefer a 'professional' politician at the helm of their campaign, who would be able to dedicate time to their cause, and anticipate the potential obstacles which parliamentary custom and their opponents might throw in the way. In the absence of an obvious candidate among sympathetic MPs, the onus of tactical leadership would rest with the expanding breed of parliamentary solicitors, whose specialist skills could make the difference between success and failure. Although lacking the organization and prominence of their Hanoverian successors, these agents were clearly seeking to capitalize on the rise in legislative activity in the Augustan period, and certain individuals, for instance the 'solicitor' James Allen, were in great demand among commercial lobbyists.[78]

Other sources do not suggest that the merchant MP was the quiescent backbencher, content with the prestige of a seat and unconcerned with the legislation of the House. In particular, surviving parliamentary debates indicate that traders were very keen to contribute to the House's discussion of

[77] Gauci in *Parliamentary History* (1998), 12–22.

[78] *HMC Fortescue*, i. 27. The name of 'solicitor Allen' can be linked to the parliamentary lobbies of the Eastland Company, the New East India Company, the Brewers' Company, the Pewterers' Company, the Vintners' Company, the Tallowchandlers' Company, and the Gunmakers' Company—Guildhall Lib. MSS 11,982, fo. 89'; 5442/8; 22188/4 (Dec. 1698); 15333/6 (1703/4); 6152/3 (1692/3); 5219/1 (1707/8); Bodl. Rawlinson MSS C449.

trade, particularly when vested interests were affected. Although these records supply a very patchy impression of Commons debate, it is significant that merchant Members were invariably prominent when commercial matters were aired, and would often make claims to particular expertise therein.[79] For instance, in order to highlight the commercial impossibilities of Tangier in 1680, William Love asserted his credentials in the following manner: 'I am a merchant, and all my trade has moved in the Mediterranean Sea. I was bred there and so are my children.' Even country gentlemen were ready to call upon their commercial expertise in order to resolve issues, Sir Edward Seymour reminding the Commons in a debate on customs duties in December 1692 that 'you have merchants and others in the House that understand these matters very well'. Thus, far from being embarrassed by their possible vested interest, merchant Members made a virtue of their experience, lecturing their gentry colleagues on the merits of the economic issue at hand. Their informed opinion could be tested by the rival case of commercial opponents, and the parliamentary diarists themselves appear to have been edified, and not necessarily alienated, by the cut and thrust of commercial debate.[80]

Merchant claims to special competence in commercial affairs did not go unchallenged, and accusations of self-interest were directed at them amid heated debates. In November 1670 London MP Jones warned that trade could be affected by duty rises, only to be tersely rebuffed by Sir Charles Harbord, who ventured that he 'would never have the farmer of customs, or the merchant, your counsellor only, but [only] your informer . . . we may quickly make a rich merchant but a beggarly kingdom'. Forty years later William Bromley queried the veracity of wartime news from Amsterdam simply on the basis that it had been 'brought into the House by a merchant from another merchant'. For such presumption he received a stinging rebuke from City magnate Sir Gilbert Heathcote, who claimed that in the nation's current calamity 'he had a greater stake to lose and paid more taxes than that gentleman'. It was such mistrust that the patriotic refrain of the mercantile petition sought to overcome, and although commercial interests were finding the Commons a more receptive audience, gentry suspicions still lingered. For instance, in November 1692, one Member pointed out that the fearsome losses to the enemy at sea were only harmful to the state, rather than to the

---

[79] Given the paucity of surviving diaries in this period, any conclusions concerning mercantile contributions to debates must remain impressionistic. The two most important diarists of the period (Grey and Luttrell) together record about sixty debates concerning the regulation of overseas trade, although several are very brief in outline. Mercantile Members are invariably active in these debates, and also feature prominently in discussions concerning the supply.

[80] Grey Debates, viii. 14; Luttrell Diary, 326. Note, in particular, how the Gloucestershire gentleman Sir Richard Cocks sought to deconstruct the source of the nation's economic malaise—The Parliamentary Diary of Sir Richard Cocks, 1698–1702, ed. D. Hayton (Oxford, 1996), p. xxxii. Also note Luttrell's explanatory notes (for himself) concerning the source and movement of foreign commodities—Luttrell Diary, 327, 334, 384–5.

overseas trader, since 'if the ship be lost, they have their loss of[f] the insurer, so the merchant has no prejudice, but the kingdom [has]'. On occasion social prejudices would rise to the surface, the caustic John Birch using discussion of the Merchant Adventurers' Company to opine in January 1671 that 'if your trade be worse, it is because the merchant must have his London and country house, and his wife must go as fine as his neighbour John's'. Fortunately for all concerned, such unhelpful commentary was the exception rather than the rule in even the bitterest of commercial debates, but there remained an onus on all interest groups to prove a national benefit.[81]

In this regard the merchant was only being asked to provide the assurances required of any other initiator of public business, but there remained a natural suspicion of the complex and potentially lucrative world of inter-national trade. However, lingering mistrust did not intimidate the merchant from contributing fully to the business of the House which fell in his particular field, and there can be little doubt that mercantile Members were ever-alert for debates concerning matters of direct business import. Even a suspicious Sir Edward Seymour recognized the sensitive parliamentary antennae of the commercial interest in February 1693, arguing against a bill to increase access to cloth exports with the observation that 'if the bill were really for the benefit thereof [the cloth trade], I doubt not but I should have heard from my corpo-ration in the matter'. The apparent forthrightness of the mercantile Members in commercial debate stands in some contrast to their recorded intervention in other Commons matters, and only with regard to constituency affairs could merchants be said to have made a more general impact. Nevertheless, although suspect in the eyes of their country colleagues, inexperienced as legislators, and oft distracted by other pressing concerns, there can be little doubt that the small minority of mercantile representatives played a dis-proportionate role in improving the efficiency of the Commons on trading matters. Merchants could not control the Lower House, but they could ensure that commercial issues would be given a full and effective hearing in the corridors of landed power.[82]

Although often too busy and green in the ways of Parliament to make a serious impact at Westminster, the merchant Member reflects the qualified success of the commercial classes in late Stuart England. This chapter has demonstrated that Davenant's fears of a militant bourgeoisie were unfounded, and that the increasing number of merchant MPs in the House was not the product of a desperate search for power and public status. The massive rise in commercial petitioning acknowledged the Commons' role as the key arena for initiating economic change, and merchants fully recognized the importance of political leverage in effecting their business objectives. However, even though personal

---

[81] *Grey Debates*, i. 275–6, 360, *Luttrell Diary*, 247; *Wentworth Papers*, 110.
[82] *Luttrell Diary*, 429.

honour may have been served by election to the House, patterns of parliamentary tenure suggest that the merchant Member was not trying to encroach on the preserve of gentlemanly power. In fact, election to Westminster was more valuable to the overseas trader as a means to preserve influence within his own urban world, rather than as a stepping-stone into a more genteel orbit. Both constituents and ministers could be impressed by the elevated status of the mercantile parliamentarian, and seek to promote legislation with his support. Such aid was sometimes achieved secretly and by dubious means, and it is clear that a great deal of mercantile activity never found its way into the Journals. However, even if the merchant Member did not figure as a manager of a bill, he could still hope to influence legislation in the open forum of debate, hoping that his experienced arguments might carry weight among those unfamiliar with trading matters.

There can be little doubt that the Augustan period was an important stage in the changing relationship between the merchant classes and Parliament, with evidence of a rise in the number of merchant MPs, increased petitioning, growing sophistication in economic debate, and improved success rates for commercial bills. However, it was not a revolutionary era, and with every advance there was a check to balance the impact of these innovations. Moreover, against these novelties must be juxtaposed the broad continuities of the political system, especially the continuing dominance of the gentry Member. As his other writings suggest, Davenant knew he was only playing to the gentrified gallery when creating the nightmarish character of Double, and commercial lobbies preferred to adapt to, rather than challenge the realities of landed hegemony. Some traders employed notorious methods to secure their objectives, but their impatience should not obscure the more significant efforts of commercial leaders to influence the Commons by argument and an appeal to the national interest. These general trends need to be studied through particular examples, for specific contexts provide a more subtle appreciation of their true impact. The next chapter will therefore analyse the debates surrounding the French commerce treaty of 1713, which conveniently falls towards the end of our study. Its importance has been recognized by many historians, and will be examined here to test the ideas put forward in the book, thereby emulating the many contemporary authors who took it as a suitable vantage-point from which to judge the impact of overseas commerce over a much longer period.

CHAPTER SIX

The Politics of Trade: The French
Commerce Bill of 1713

The greatest debate which happened in the last Parliament and perhaps a
debate of the greatest consequence that ever happened in any
Parliament.[1]

THE hyperbole of the political propagandist must always be tempered by the
more sober priorities of the historian, but there can be no doubt concerning
the profound resonance of the French commerce bill of 1713. This measure
was crucial to the government's attempt to settle Anglo-French trade at the
conclusion of the War of the Spanish Succession, and was considered vital for
re-establishing relations between Europe's leading rivals. Like so many of the
most enlightening episodes in history, the bill was a failure, finding defeat in
the House of Commons on 18 June by a mere nine votes. The division sent
shock-waves through the political world of its day, and has animated both economic and political historians ever since. Analysts of the early parliamentary
party have seen it as a set-piece of expert political sabotage and recovery, as a
ministry was ambushed by an alliance of opponents and dissidents, only to
emerge triumphant at the polls. Economic historians, most notably in the
shape of Donald Coleman, have used the controversy to explore the relationship between early economic theory and political practice, and to demonstrate
the faltering steps which commerce took upon the parliamentary stage at that
time. Most interestingly for this study, Coleman argued that contemporaries
perceived trade in 'quasi-political' terms, as an adjunct of international relations, and he stressed that the impact of commercial issues could not be
properly assessed without such broader perspectives. The preceding chapters
amply demonstrate my concurrence with this view, but this chapter will seek
to build on Coleman's work by further exploration of several key themes
raised by this study.[2]

[1] *The History and Defence of the Last Parliament* (London, 1713), 224–5.

[2] For the most detailed accounts of the controversy, see D. Coleman, 'Politics and Economics in the
Age of Anne: The Case of the Anglo-French Trade Treaty of 1713', in *idem* and A. H. John (eds.), *Trade,
Government, and Economy in Pre-Industrial England* (London, 1976), 187–211; G. S. Holmes and
C. Jones, 'Trade, the Scots, and the Parliamentary Crisis of 1713', *Parliamentary History*, 1 (1982), 47–77;
D. A. E. Harkness, 'The Opposition to the Eighth and Ninth Articles of the Commercial Treaty
of Utrecht', *Scottish History Review*, 21 (1924), 219–26. For analysis of its electoral consequences, see
J. O. Richards, *Party Propaganda under Queen Anne* (Athens, Ga., 1972), 129–53.

In particular, thanks to his groundwork, closer inspection will be made of the 'political' rhetoric of commercial debate, to see whether contemporaries had consciously accorded trade a greater priority on the agenda of state interests. As Coleman notes, there remains a vast contemporary literature on this debate, and much of it is influenced by party polemic, but many of the writers used the occasion to pose fundamental questions concerning the relationship between the state and trade.[3] It is imperative that these debates are followed, however fraudulent or partisan the statistics and arguments therein, for they can reveal how deeply trade had embedded itself as a truly 'national' issue. To this end, much greater emphasis will be laid on politics beyond the confines of Westminster and Whitehall, especially at the time of the 1713 general election which took place within weeks of the great vote of 18 June. Coleman did not scrutinize that campaign in any detail, leaving the issue of popular response largely unaddressed. Moreover, while he rightly exploded the myth of coherent party positions between mercantilist Whigs and free-trade Tories, he made little attempt to trace the complex political manœuvring which attended this controversy. Nevertheless, by outlining the importance of Anglo-French commercial relations since 1660, and by highlighting the continuing resonance of the issue during the succeeding century, he ably demonstrated the potential potency of commercial controversy. Unavoidably, this chapter is as much concerned with the retrospection of the protagonists of 1713 as their vision of Britain's commercial future. Amid the multifarious pressures of post-war Britain, political observers took the opportunity to reassess the development of trade over the previous half-century, seeking to understand the roots of the current dispute, and to achieve an informed perspective on such a thorny commercial matter. Thus, while the affair cannot be represented as the 'triumph' of the trader in any teleological sense, it remains a most convenient perch from which to analyse the development of commercial politics across the Augustan period.[4]

In order to address a complex and lengthy political battle, it is necessary to break down this chapter into four sections. First, we will turn to the origins of the debate, in order to ask why a commercial matter could become a national issue of such momentous importance. Then the key debates of the contending groups will be examined via a wide range of media, from sophisticated economic discussion to the chanting of the mobs. In turn, the great vote of 18 June will be analysed and the electoral response to this novel crisis. Finally,

---

[3] At least twenty-nine tracts gave extensive coverage to the French commerce treaty in 1713–14, and some of them ran to several editions. These figures do not include the extensive periodical coverage of the crisis (the *British Merchant* and *Mercator* supplying 284 issues on their own), nor the petitions submitted to national authorities on the subject.

[4] Despite the aforementioned studies, historians of Hanoverian Britain still look to the excise crisis of 1733 as the first occasion on which commerce played a significant role as a 'patriotic' political issue— K. Wilson, *The Sense of the People: Politics, Culture, and Imperialism in England, 1715–1785* (Cambridge, 1995), 129–32.

a concluding section will study the consequences of intensive commercial campaigning in the immediate and longer term. Unlike the privileged historian, contemporary politicians rarely enjoy the luxury of a single issue in their Westminster in-tray, and through all this discussion I have been keenly aware of the historian's duty not to overemphasize the particular significance of his favoured theme. Thus analysis of wine imports and cloth tariffs must take its place alongside the great party debates over religion, the succession, and the Union, and the success of economic issues judged against the less certain criteria of political opportunism and partisanship. However, given the great matters of state facing Britain's rulers, it is all the more significant that the commercial aspects of the controversy can still be credited as of importance to the combatants involved.

i. Origins and novelties

While it was clear that the end of the War of Spanish Succession would see Britain reassess relations with other European powers, there was no guarantee that trade would be very high on the agenda. Britain had entered the war with two overriding objectives: to secure the Hanoverian succession threatened by French support for the exiled Stuart court, and to ensure that the Bourbon monarchy did not control both France and the Spanish Empire. The trading classes certainly had a vested interest in political stability at home, and a more direct concern to maintain a balance of power within Europe and the New World, but it would be hard to portray the 1702–13 war as a commercial conflict per se. Historians have rightly drawn attention to the Tory preference for a 'blue water strategy' of fighting the enemy at sea rather than on land, but such concern should be attributed to party advantage and wartime taxation rather than to anxiety for Britain's maritime empire.[5] Moreover, even though a few hardline City merchants still argued for a crushing victory over French imperial pretensions after final peace negotiations had commenced at Utrecht in late 1711, the war had largely exhausted the patience of active traders. Having experienced only a brief interlude of peace in 1697–1702, overseas and domestic traders found it extremely difficult to make money while their foreign markets and commercial communications were disrupted by war, and their customers burdened by heavy taxation. The war had proved a bonus for some commercial groups, thanks to the aggressive extension of Britain's colonial territories and the huge demands of the allied war machine, but the

---

[5] Significantly, a study of the controversy over the African trade in 1689–1714 concluded that party divisions on this issue were determined by 'socio-political postures toward France or Holland, or in attitudes towards the royal prerogative, [rather] than by differences in economic theory or ideology'— T. Keirn, 'Monopoly, Economic Thought, and the Royal African Company', in J. Brewer and S. Staves (eds.), *Early Modern Conceptions of Property* (London, 1995), 427–66. In his forthcoming work, Steve Pincus will argue for a polarization of Whig and Tory views on political economy in the 1690s.

simple promise of peace received an enthusiastic welcome from all sections of society. Traders were thankful that a return to normality seemed on the horizon, and the conflict had certainly not given ministers any clear or broad mandate in the commercial arena. Both Whig and Tory leaders recognized the financial power of the City, and had sought to harness it for the purposes of political stability, but neither had established a clear party position on the question of trade.[6]

On the other hand, the peace offered an excellent opportunity for Britain to resolve long-running commercial disputes, both with its enemies and its allies. At the conclusion of the Nine Years' War in 1697, the reformed Board of Trade had been in favour of a commercial treaty with the French, but negotiations foundered, and only the Dutch managed to come to a trade agreement with Louis XIV. This diplomatic activity was not completely in vain, for when Britain embarked on abortive peace talks with France in 1709, the commercial treaty was revived as a desirable objective, and the Whig ministry ordered the Board of Trade to undertake a review of all such agreements with the French over the past sixty years. The board duly invited thirty leading merchants to comment on the likely form of a new agreement, and received responses from a wide variety of domestic and overseas traders. A draft treaty had been drawn up by October 1709, but the resumption of hostilities once again put trade negotiations on hold. Certain economic interests, such as the Levant Company, endeavoured to keep the issue alive, petitioning in April 1710 for a return to the Anglo-French trade relations of the 1660s, but there was no general lobby for such a treaty. Only with the change of administration later that year, which ushered in a Tory ministry dedicated to securing peace, was the prospect revived.[7]

Predictably, it was the mercantile sector which led the campaign for a commercial settlement with the French. The Levant Company petitioned again with similar demands, while the Hudson's Bay Company, perhaps the chief victim of French imperial expansion over the previous thirty years, eagerly sought confirmation of its territorial rights and reparations for its losses. Ministers reacted favourably to their demands, and by March 1712 a revamped commercial treaty had been submitted to the Board of Trade, and the process of mercantile consultation was under way once more. It is important to note at this stage that there was no chorus of petitions seeking to

---

[6] For the ambivalence of Augustan views on trade and credit, see J. G. A. Pocock, *The Machiavellian Moment* (Princeton, 1975), 423–61. It is significant that there is little discussion of party positions on trade issues in the secondary literature of the late Stuart period, historians preferring to concentrate on broader social tensions between land and the newly created 'monied' interest. For an expert summary of the latter see, G. S. Holmes, *British Politics in the Age of Anne*, 2nd edn. (London, 1987), pp. xliii–lxii; idem, *The Making of a Great Power* (London, 1993), 287–91.

[7] CO389/16, pp. 265–82, 289–98; CO389/20, fos. 375–6, 377–84, 391, 397–9, 413–31, 487. For a survey of the Board of Trade's role throughout the controversy, see I. K. Steele, *Politics of Colonial Policy* (Oxford, 1968), 135–9. For analysis of diplomatic manœuvres, see B. W. Hill, 'Oxford, Bolingbroke, and the Peace of Utrecht', *HJ* 16 (1973), 241–63.

exert pressure on the ministry and their diplomatic team. Such reticence on the part of the commercial lobbies is curious, for knowledge of the ministry's proceedings could not have been confined to the 'several merchants skilled in the trade to France' who were directly consulted by the Board. The most plausible reason for mercantile inactivity was the universal recognition that the resolution of international relations, especially matters of war and peace, lay within the prerogative of the Crown, and it was not even becoming for Parliament itself to dictate the course of diplomatic negotiation. It is vital to our general understanding of the controversy that we realize that the commercial 'ball' was very much in the ministerial court.[8]

The crucial move which elevated these commercial debates from a familiar round of ministerially led, *in camera* discussions in Whitehall to a full-blown parliamentary crisis must be credited to the Oxford administration. Previous analysts have usually viewed the Whigs as the catalysts for trade's transformation into a party matter, and there is much foundation for seeing them as partisan opportunists on commercial issues, particularly in the spring of 1713. However, this version of events ignores the fact that it was the Oxford ministry which first played the trade 'card' as early as June 1712, when the announcement of peace overtures was used to rally support for the ministry. At this time the Tory administration was finding particular difficulty in keeping its followers in line, with damaging fractures appearing over the peace negotiations and the succession. Earlier in the session the March Club of 'Hanoverian Tories' had emerged to put pressure on Oxford to safeguard the succession, adding to his established concerns for the loyalty of the much larger October Club, a group of Tory gentlemen dedicated to peace and supportive of aggressive anti-Whig policies. The timing of the preliminary Utrecht agreements was thus a sorely needed boost to ministerial authority within the Lower House, but the significance of Oxford's initiative should not be simply seen in terms of party manœuvre.[9]

The Queen's speech of 6 June 1712 was the most startling Crown pronouncement on trade to any Parliament since 1660. While due prominence was given to the progress of peace negotiations, a full report was given on the commercial treaty, including the difficulties which diplomats were finding in adjusting the duties of France and Britain to mutual satisfaction and advantage. In the same context, Britain's expected territorial gains of Gibraltar and Minorca were heralded as the security of Mediterranean trade, while the demolition of Dunkirk sought to assuage mercantile fears of French

---

[8] CO389/23, pp. 1–82, 102–6, 128. The lobbying of the Hudson's Bay Company is analysed in E. E. Rich, 'The Hudson's Bay Company and the Treaty of Utrecht', *Cambridge Historical Journal*, 9 (1954), 188–203. Significantly, serious divisions within the Levant Company over the settlement with the French surfaced the following year, but in 1712 the company appeared united in its appeal for the ministry to act—Bodl. Fol. Theta 665, fos. 189–90.

[9] For a discussion of the influence of the October and March clubs, see Holmes, *British Politics*, 251–2, 279–84, 342–4.

privateers. However, greatest pride was reserved for the gains expected in Hudson's Bay, Newfoundland, and the West Indies, with the oration concluding that 'our interest is so deeply concerned in the trade of North America that I have used my utmost endeavours to adjust that article in the most beneficial manner'. The final sweetener was the promised reward of the asiento contract to supply the Spanish West Indies with slaves, a privilege which the French Crown had enjoyed for the previous decade. Events would prove the ministry over-optimistic concerning French readiness to compromise, but the speech undoubtedly served the administration's immediate purpose, of giving renewed heart to its loyal majority in the Commons. Another royal speech that month, shortly before the prorogation, again stressed the opportunities within the nation's grasp, including that of 'improving our own commerce', and it was evidently this message which the ministry wished the departing Members to take to their constituents.[10]

The flood of addresses to the Queen during the parliamentary summer recess of 1712 suggested a positive response to the ministry's lead. Their predominant theme was to give thanks to the Queen for her promise to communicate the final peace terms, and to echo their support for the Church and the Hanoverian succession. However, the very fact that many of the addresses sought to rejoin the ministry on the question of trade is very significant, and novel. In general, loyal constituents of either party were all too willing to adopt the strategy set down by their political masters, but in this case the Tories were attempting to encourage their supporters by untested means, and were doubtless delighted to receive a good response. For instance, it might well have been expected that cloth-manufacturing Colchester would remind the Queen that it was trade 'upon which we of these parts so very much depend', or the burgesses of Sheffield lament how their iron masters had 'long wanted those free passages of commerce' which were now opening up. However, it was less predictable that the county of Merionethshire would insist that the destruction of Dunkirk 'must of course make the trade of Great Britain flourish', or that the gentle folk of Surrey would declare commerce to be now 'upon a better foot than it has been in any age'. Most interestingly, the belated address of the chiefs of the 'loyal clans of Scotland' confessed that 'though the trade does not so much concern us, we cannot but gratefully observe the regard your Majesty hath to the British commerce', and commended the recently formed South Sea Company for its commitment to the improvement of the fishery. Ministerial propaganda had served its ends well.[11]

It cannot be said that Lord Oxford was taking much of a gamble in employ-

[10] *CJ*, xvii. 258, 275. B. W. Hill notes that Oxford kept close supervision of diplomatic proceedings until late 1712, but probably had less direct influence thereafter, leaving primary control of the negotiation of the commercial treaty to Lord Bolingbroke—*HJ* 16 (1973), 261–2.

[11] *London Gazette*, June 1712–Feb. 1713, *passim*. Oxford's skill in manipulating the press to serve his political purposes has been highlighted by J. A. Downie, *Robert Harley and the Press* (Cambridge, 1979).

ing trade as a means of garnering support, for there was no clear party position on commerce per se, and thus little prospect of losing allies on account of this stance. Tactically, trade presented a good platform for his administration, since it echoed previous Tory attacks on the warlike stance of his Whig rivals, which they had decried as inimical to British interests. He could also reasonably expect that the oncoming of peace promised some recovery in the country's economic health, and was evidently keen to take the credit for any signs of commercial improvement. It was also clear that the peace dividend would more than compensate for the discontent of those economic interests for whom warfare had proved a positive benefit. In fact, hundreds of wartime petitions from the hard-pressed business sector had lectured Westminster in the patriotic language which the ministry now belatedly embraced. However, by portraying his ministry as the worthy custodians of national commerce, Oxford had lumbered his administration with the weighty obligation of ensuring that the French lived up to their promises. Even without the Queen's speech of 6 June, the peace negotiations would have dominated column inches and men's minds, but the ministry had now directed all subjects to consider their progress in a new light, thereby creating an 'economic constituency' far beyond the manufacturing, retail, and mercantile classes.[12]

ii. The rage of party and the politicization of trade

In the months immediately prior to the signing of the French commercial treaty, there were few signs that the ministry was in danger of losing support over economic policy. Those exerting pressure on the ministry over the treaty were exclusively of a commercial background, and while Parliament remained out of session, their efforts were centred on the Privy Council and the Board of Trade. In January 1713 a delegation of West Indian planters worriedly petitioned about a reported French ban on their sugars, which was 'the common discourse among the French here and upon the Exchange'. Similar concerns over French protectionism led the East India Company to address the Queen the following month, and due reassurance was given that diplomats at Utrecht had specific orders to uphold the company's interests. However, this message was accompanied with the mild rebuke that the Queen was 'surprised' to entertain petitions some fourteen months into the treaty process. Ministerial irritation turned to open anger following several representations from various groups of woollen and silk manufacturers, which, retorted Secretary of State Lord Dartmouth, 'did not seem designed for gaining any real advantages'. At this point there is little evidence to suggest that his Whig rivals were attempting to usurp the ministry's triumph on trade, but his

---

[12] For Oxford's pragmatic (and successful) management of the City's leading financiers, see B. W. Hill, 'The Change of the Government and the Loss of the City, 1710–11', EcHR NS, 24 (1971), 395–411.

observation serves to demonstrate that the ministry was resolved to maximize the political value of its commercial initiative.[13]

Of course, the ministry anticipated that the actual signing of the treaties of peace and commerce would present its rivals with the best opportunity to launch an offensive on its new citadel. The cessation of hostilities would be popular, but the terms of accord promised great debate. Thus, after the signing of the treaties on 31 March 1713, the administration once again tried to make all the political running, immediately recalling Parliament so that a triumphant ministry could trumpet its achievement at Westminster. On 9 April the Queen's speech duly elaborated on the success of Oxford and his ministers in bringing the French to terms, emphasizing the energy of the administration. The speech also exhorted Members to build on the peace, demanding that they ensure 'the easing of our foreign trade, as far as is consistent with national credit', and advocating the revival of domestic industries, especially the fishery. As yet the French commerce treaty remained outside the remit of Parliament, but it is clear that the ministry was confident that trade was an issue over which it could comfortably outmanœuvre its opponents.[14]

Tory triumphalism resounded from the press following the signing of the peace. By the end of May the *London Gazette* had recorded nearly 100 loyal addresses from all over the country, praising the Queen for her support for the Protestant succession, the Church, and the balance of power within Europe. About a quarter of them also made specific reference to the Queen's support for commerce, several of them claiming that their trade had already begun to recover thanks to the peace talks. Newsmen sympathetic to the ministry were also eager to herald the new dawn of Tory prosperity, taking full opportunity of the authorized publication of the articles of both treaties. In particular, the Tory *Post Boy* reported allegedly spontaneous celebrations for the announcement of peace in May, in which many manufacturers gave vivid demonstrations of their delight at the signing of the peace. In Alton, Hampshire silkworkers paraded in 'Indian habits' to display their confidence in their economic future, while in South Halstead, Essex, local woollens adorned 'even the most obscure lanes and corners'. Most evocatively, in Cambridgeshire and Kent processions took place in which 'Bishop Blaze [Blaise]', the patron saint of wool-workers, was accorded pride of place. The government-backed *Review*, which under Defoe had proved the paper most committed to trading matters, predictably dwelt on commerce from the time of the signing of the peace, lauding the treaties as an achievement worthy of the praise of generations to come. Nevertheless, amid his hyperbole of praise for the ministry, in

---

[13] CO 389/23, pp. 194, 215, 219, 221–2, 249.

[14] *CJ*, xvii. 278. For full transcripts of the treaties, see *CJ*, xvii. 331–40. Holmes and Jones note that at the outset of the session Oxford was most worried by a possible Whig attack on the issue of the succession, not the commercial treaty—*Parliamentary History*, 1 (1982), 48.

early May he was also the first to address a wave of criticism levelled against the much-acclaimed accord reached at Utrecht, remarking that he had erred in thinking that trade would prove 'a safe retreat from the noise and clamour of politics'.[15]

As in the preceding year, it was a ministerial move which raised the profile of trade as a political issue, and as a national cause. By the terms of the commercial treaty, certain issues could only be resolved with parliamentary consent, since several key articles related to the mutual adjustment of customs duties. The ministry probably made its first tactical mistake by not in the first instance submitting the commercial treaty to both Houses, but instead favoured a more indirect means.[16] On 2 May a proposal was made to introduce a bill to suspend duties levied on imported French wine since 1696, which measure was in effect the first test of the practical implications of the commerce treaty. This move immediately sparked strong opposition, with the motion to put the question to order such a bill only passing by 134 votes to 105, and the order itself then succeeding 144 to 105. The identity of the tellers suggest that this initiative enjoyed government backing, but the struggle continued only two days later when over 100 MPs opposed the second reading of the bill and then tried to adjourn debate. Another two divisions on the issue followed on 6 May, and the following day the ministry struggled to control the Lower House as it proceeded to address the Queen for a copy of the Anglo-Portuguese treaty of 1703, which had stipulated concessionary duties for imported port wines in exchange for favourable treatment towards English cloth exports. This move suggested fears that the wines bill might seriously affect the market for English woollens, and presaged many obstacles for the greater commercial bill itself. These concerns were amplified by a memorial submitted by the Portuguese ambassador to the Queen, warning of the possible reintroduction of a ban on imported English woollens. Even more worryingly, there were already signs of public anxiety, for eight petitions were submitted against the bill, all of them expressing concern that French wines would directly undermine their precious woollen manufactures.[17]

On 9 May the commercial treaty itself was formally submitted to parliamentary consideration, thereby relegating the wines bill to oblivion. A week is a long time in politics, and so it had proved disastrously for the Oxford camp.

---

[15] A steady stream of addresses appeared in the *London Gazette* from mid-April to late August, when electoral preparations intervened. See also *Post Boy*, 19–21, 21–3, 23–6, 26–8, 28–30 May, 30 May–2 June 1713; *The Review*, 26 May 1713. For a brief life of Bishop Blaise, reportedly tortured with woolcombs before his martyrdom, see D. H. Farmer, *The Oxford Dictionary of Saints* (Oxford, 1978), 44.

[16] Holmes and Jones suggest that the ministry introduced this limited measure due to a perceived lack of parliamentary time—*Parliamentary History*, 1 (1982), 49.

[17] *CJ*, xvii. 310, 314–16. A. Boyer, *Political State of Great Britain*, v. 300, 303. Boyer noted concerns that the wines bill was merely to serve the interests of a few wine merchants. For an account of the trade in Iberian wines, see H. E. Fisher, *The Portugal Trade* (London, 1971), esp. 24–8. For the genesis of the 1703 treaty, see A. D. Francis, *The Methuens and Portugal* (Cambridge, 1966); *idem*, 'John Methuen and the Anglo-Portuguese Treaties of 1703', *HJ* 3 (1960), 103–24.

Nevertheless, there was little prospect that the ministry would concede defeat on such an important issue, a fact reflected by the domination of Oxford allies on the committee appointed on 14 May to draft a bill to confirm the eighth and ninth articles of the commercial treaty. These two key clauses would effectively decide the fate of the whole treaty, and provided the focus for discussion of the political and economic uncertainties engendered by the peace. These two articles encapsulated the essence of the deal struck at Utrecht, since their stated objective was to open trading channels between the two countries, which since the Restoration had been clogged by increasingly high tolls on both sides. From the English perspective, a promised reversion to the French import tariff of 1664 was most desirable, and the ministry could expect to earn plaudits for efforts to reduce French tolls. However, this French concession was not granted to four exempted classes of goods, including the all-important export of English woollens. Moreover, restrictions on British access to French ports was also a key bone of contention, and these major grievances threatened to overshadow the other advantages gained at Utrecht. Evidently, there was much to debate in the fine print of the agreement, and even a dominant ministry would have anticipated serious questioning of its diplomatic endeavours.[18]

Despite the body-blows taken over the wines bill, there still did not appear any reason for panic in ministerial ranks. However, it soon discovered that its commercial propaganda of the preceding twelve months could be turned against itself. Within a week of the submission of the French commercial treaty to Parliament, there appeared *The Trade with France, Italy, Spain, and Portugal Considered*, a tract roundly critical of the apparent sell-out of British economic interests at Utrecht. This was the first of a veritable snowstorm of pamphlets which threatened the government's plans, as both Whig opponents and anxious traders questioned the commercial management of the administration. Such was the pressure on the government to justify its actions, that on 26 May there appeared the *Mercator*, a thrice-weekly government oracle dedicated to upholding the propriety of the French commerce treaty. More than any other event, its appearance suggested that trade was now very much on the political agenda, as the ministry struggled to convince a public of the sagacity of its much-publicized commercial policies. Of course, Oxford and his ministers channelled most of their energy into marshalling their supporters within the two Houses, as the key battleground for the passage of legislation. Nevertheless, having declared its commercial competence, and encouraged its supporters to glory in it too, the administration had to conduct a public debate

---

[18] *CJ*, xvii. 319, 354. For an account of the debate on 14 May, see *The Wentworth Papers, 1705–39*, ed. J. J. Cartwright (London, 1883), 334–6. For the development of the French tariff, see C. W. Cole, *French Mercantilism, 1683–1700* (New York, 1965), 9–18. The French were also critical of the 1664 tariff—W. C. Scoville, 'The French Economy in 1700–1: An Appraisal by the Deputies of Trade', *Journal of Economic History*, 22 (1962), 231–52.

over an issue with which the political nation was largely ill-informed, and had proven little interested in the immediate past. The campaign would thus retain many traditional political elements of faction-fighting and patronage, but, by necessity it would involve something of a learning process for both politicians and voters.[19]

As a sign of the novelty of this particular political controversy, the initial battle was for information which would sustain the arguments of the competing factions. Contemporaries had long been familiar with the ways in which specific interest groups had manipulated patchy economic data to prove their case, and Coleman has ably demonstrated how the French commerce bill occasioned a mad scramble for reliable statistical evidence which could establish whether Anglo-French trade could be managed to the benefit of British subjects. As he pointed out, despite the creation of the inspectorship of imports and exports in 1696, the government was far from able to supply acceptable accounts of prior economic trends, and customs commissioners in particular found the matter a cause for deep embarrassment. On the other hand, their rivals had an even tougher time of justifying their position, having to rely on scarce materials such as the famed Scheme of 1674, which argued that England suffered an annual deficit of over £1,000,000 in its trade with France. Quite simply, neither side could provide a satisfactory case to disprove the claims of their rivals, and the few statistics produced only gave politicians a thirst for better and more reliable sources on which to form economic opinion.[20] This quest for the 'truth' of the matter had an important impact on the course of the controversy. Most importantly, it placed an onus on both camps to educate a public audience about the realities of international commerce as fully and clearly as possible. The battle for the support of Members was their chief priority, whose voracious demand for information was supplied by the Customs Commission and the Board of Trade. However, such departmental aid did not always work to the ministry's advantage. For instance, on 14 May the Board submitted a formidable batch of papers relating to Anglo-French commercial negotiations over the previous four years, only for opponents of the treaty to move that they be read straight away, a delaying tactic which would have frustrated governmental plans for a quick resolution of the affair. The administration scored 'a thumping victory on this particular division, but it could not prevent both Houses from calling for a huge array of

---

[19] Downie, Harley and the Press, 171–6, stresses that Oxford retained direct control of Defoe's output. Boyer reported that Arthur Moore, a commissioner of trade, and Charles Davenant were suspected of penning the Mercator, only for Defoe to be later acknowledged as author—Political State, v. 323. On 11 June, in the last issue of his Review, Defoe conceded that the 'whore' of trade had been 'ravished out of my hands by the Mercator'.

[20] Coleman, Trade, Government, and Economy, 196–8. For a discussion of the 1674 Scheme of Trade, see M. Priestly, 'London Merchants and Opposition Politics in Charles II's Reign', BIHR 29 (1956), 205–19; and idem, 'Anglo-French Trade and the Unfavourable Balance Controversy', EcHR 2nd ser., 4 (1951), 37–52.

evidence, some of which found its way into print, thus sparking more wide-spread debate concerning the reliability of the port books and other sources.[21]

Beyond the question of mere statistics, opponents of the bill could bring forward an arsenal of mercantile experience to demonstrate how the treaty would work to the detriment of all sections of British society. It would be highly inaccurate to suggest that the ministry had failed to retain any commercial support, but the coordination of its rivals' campaign was impressive nonetheless. Westminster was bombarded with expositions of Britain's commercial plight, most directly in the form of thirty-eight petitions to the Commons, and another ten to the Upper House.[22] They came from all over the country, and purported to speak for a wide variety of traders, although the silk and woollen manufactures boasted overwhelming attention. In essence, they attempted to demonstrate how an adjustment of duties between Britain and France might ruin several fledgling industries, and alter the general course of trade not only across the Channel, but also throughout the Mediterranean, Northern Europe, and the Americas. Although there was an almost obsessive interest with the state of the balance of trade between France and Britain, it is important to note that the commerce bill debates were multi-linear in economic concern, and that one of the major aims of the bill's enemies was to instruct public opinion in the far-flung consequences of this agreement. In this manner they were continuing the campaign of many trading groups over the previous half-century, although no controversy had threatened to alter Britain's world trade on this scale. MPs were thus entertained to many skilful demonstrations of the complexities of world trade, as Levant merchants endeavoured to show how the woollen market was dependent on the control of French silk, while Bristol merchants extolled how French brandy threatened the rhythms of colonial trade. It is also significant that these lectures were specifically aimed at the ill-informed country gentleman, with continual reminders of the links between overseas trade and domestic prosperity, and warnings of the impending nightmare of reduced rents and an increase in the poor. The government press fumed at this campaign, and dismissed the petitions as the fraudulent creation of political rivals, but their importance was recognized by orders for the petitioners to appear before both Houses to give expert testimony.[23]

The government was not slow to recognize that it would have to win the battle for commercial credibility outside Parliament as well as within. There-

---

[21] *CJ*, xvii. 353. For a recent discussion of the continuing value of statistics in eighteenth-century political debate, see J. Hoppit, 'Political Arithmetic in Eighteenth-Century England', *EcHR* 49 (1996), 516–40.

[22] *CJ*, xvii. 354–430 *passim*; *LJ*, xix. 557–62. Political influence may have deterred the submission of other petitions, since Boyer reported that the ministry gave reassurances to the East India Company to forestall their address—*Political State*, v. 364.

[23] Some of these petitions were published for wider consumption—*A Collection of Petitions to the Hon. House of Commons against the Trade with France* (London, 1713); *The State of the Silk and Woollen Manufacture Considered in Relation to the French Trade* (London, 1713).

fore, its principal initiative, the *Mercator*, advertised itself as 'being founded on just authorities, faithfully collected from authentic papers and now made public for general information', and its very first issue promised to 'inform and explain to the people those things which were difficult'. By issue six, this objective had been clarified 'to level account of these things to the meanest heads, (viz.) of the tradesmen, manufacturers, and labouring poor of this kingdom' who had been deceived by party-inspired propaganda. This strategy was clearly aimed to combat the flood of petitions submitted to Parliament, and subsequent editions sought to cast doubt on their authenticity, attacking claims to the decay of trade as an 'old and exploded practice', to which anyone 'conversant either in Parliament or in trade' could bear witness. The ministry could still count on support within the commercial world, and recognized the need to cultivate the support of sympathetic traders, who could be found even within the ranks of anti-treaty petitioners such as the Levant Company.[24] As this study has stressed, merchants within the same trades could heartily disagree over economic policy, and the profound importance of the treaty controversy inevitably divided opinion within the commercial sector. The ministry naturally sought to exploit these rifts, and the *Mercator* was crucial for maintaining its commercial creditability under heavy pressure. Tory supporters welcomed the opportunity to go on the offensive in the public debate, with one MP urging his correspondent at Oxford to ensure that *Mercators* 'be constantly sent to some of your booksellers'. The ministry's distribution of thousands of copies of the new periodical throughout the country sparked bitter complaints from anti-treaty campaigners, and in the course of the year it would become the basis for several publications in Scotland and Ireland.[25]

While these discussions reverberated throughout the country, the capital remained the main centre of debate, and of tension. In late May the London militia was called out amid fears that unemployed silk-workers might riot in protest at the commercial treaty, which many declared would condemn them to continued misery. No disturbance took place, but Swift's *Examiner* and other Tory organs were quick to label their opponents as mob politicians who wished to back up the petitions with the activities of 'the unrepresented multitude'. Perhaps as a sign of government concern that its own policy of

[24] *Mercator*, 26 May, 4–6, 6–9 June 1713. The papers of Charles Cooke suggest that at a general court of the Levant Company on 28 May 1713 the motion to petition against the treaty was passed by 55 votes against 11 (with 8 abstentions). Interestingly, Cooke (an anti-treaty voter) computed how many cloths the rival interests had exported the previous year, in order to refute claims that the petitioners had not won over the greater dealers within the company—Bodl. Fol. Theta 665, fos. 189–90.

[25] Bodl. Ballard MSS 31, fo. 73; *Remarks on a Scandalous Libel* (1713), 5; *Extracts from Several Mercators* (Dublin, 1713); *The Trade of Scotland with France Considered* (Edinburgh, 1713). Stamp duty returns suggest that in June/July 1713 the print-run of the *Mercator* was 1,920—J. M. Price, 'A Note on the Circulation of the London Press, 1702–14', *BIHR* 31 (1958), 215–24. Downie argued that Oxford's propaganda machine was 'at its best in 1712 and 1713'—*Harley and the Press*, 162.

popularizing debate was backfiring, on 30 May a motion to print the French commerce bill was defeated by 148 votes to 86. Significantly, within a few days the leading Whig newspaper, the *Flying Post*, issued the first of a series of articles on the French commerce issue, lambasting French duplicity, and portraying itself as the patriotic defender of British trade. It was eager to cross swords with the *Mercator*, offering to supply 'a true British prospective-glass', and ingenuously claiming that 'no party division can be to a good man a bar against a true national interest'. Moreover, pointing to the example of the Dukes of Tuscany, it expressed hope that 'our nobility and members of the Hon. House of Commons [may] be continually prepared to make the most suitable laws for the facilitating of trade, and preserving the balance of it'. At last, the ministry's opponents had found a voice to sow discord within enemy ranks, even though their stance was merely adopting a nationalistic theme first championed by the Tories.[26]

Passions within Westminster were hardly less animated, as it became clear that the Whigs had found a weak spot in the Tory armour. Moreover, whether purely partisan posturing or not, the debates of June retain an immense interest for their insight into the attitudes of the ruling orders towards commerce. In particular, the ministry revealed incredible insensitivity to the mood of Westminster, channelling too much effort into convincing Members that the controversy was a Whig ruse, rather than address the central economic questions then troubling the two Houses. This high-handedness was exemplified on 10 June when the merchant Nathaniel Toriano was upbraided by government spokesmen for criticizing the Utrecht settlement at the bar of the House. Secretary of War Wyndham scoffed that Toriano's professed concern for a declining trade was merely anxiety for a declining party, but ministerial moves to censure the merchant were unsuccessful. Several days earlier it was reported that Bolingbroke had personally intervened in the Lords in a vain attempt to block the delivery of several petitions from London against the commerce bill.[27] Ironically, when the ministry did concentrate its efforts on commercial issues, it scored some important successes, most notably on 15 June, when the report of the Customs Commission threw serious doubt on the reliability of the Scheme of 1674, one of their opponents' most vaunted authorities. However, the personal advocacy of Oxford and Bolingbroke in the Upper House the following day only served to indicate the panic that had set into ministerial ranks. The elevation of two such important figures to the Lords in the course of the Parliament had already proved a blow to the

---

[26] Add. MSS 17677GGG, fo. 190; *Examiner*, 5–8 June 1713; *CJ*, xvii. 386; *Flying Post*, 4–6 June 1713. As early as January 1713 Defoe had warned the ministry that its rivals had incited an anti-French mob in Spittalfields, the centre of London's silk manufacture—*HMC Portland*, v. 264.

[27] Add. MSS 17677GGG, fos. 220–1, 229; Kreienberg dispatch 5 June 1713. For accounts of the Lords' proceedings on the bill, and the speeches of several merchants against the measure, see *HMC Lords*, NS, x. 95–162.

government's management of the Lower House, and from the outset they had misjudged the mood of their followers. Overconfidence, and a misunderstanding of the resonance of the issue of commerce had permitted their enemies to outmanœuvre them at virtually every turn, and on 18 June their bungling received its just reward.[28]

iii. The great vote and trade on the hustings

Despite profound and stormy debate over the French commerce treaty, it would have been a bold man to predict that the ministry would fall to defeat in the Lower House on this issue. There was widespread support for the end to the war, and amid tricky political times Oxford had proved extremely adept at warding off the spectre of failure by skilful manipulation of both men and measures. In fact, in the midst of the commerce bill controversy he had managed to overcome a revolt by Scottish MPs over a proposed duty on malt.[29] These attacks undoubtedly weakened his position, encouraging his political enemies to hope that a union of dissident groups might yet topple the administration. Nevertheless, despite these difficulties, divisions on the bill to enforce the eighth and ninth articles had not proved alarmingly close. In one of its biggest tests, the bill had been committed on 4 June by 202 votes to 135, and five days later an opposition motion to recommit a report on the commerce treaty negotiations of 1674 had been defeated by over eighty votes. If the ministry could maintain the discipline of its supporters, then there appeared little prospect of defeat. The Lords appeared a more troublesome hurdle, where Lord Halifax, the greatest 'City' minister of the 1690s, was orchestrating a carefully planned patriotic campaign against the treaty. What then happened for such a turnaround on 18 June, when the motion for the engrossment of the bill failed by 185 votes to 194?[30]

Historians and contemporaries alike have tended to centre on the partisan manœuvrings which contributed to the disaster of 18 June. The desertion of some seventy Tories over the bill was immediately linked to the great internecine struggles within ministerial ranks over the preceding two years, which had been principally fuelled by concern for the Hanoverian succession. Tory observers duly castigated their erstwhile allies as traitors, but also underwent

---

[28] CJ, xvii. 422–3.

[29] See Jones and Holmes, Parliamentary History, 1 (1982), 52–61, 65–8; C. Jones, '"The Scheme Lords, the Necessitous Lords, and the Scots Lords": The Earl of Oxford's Management and the Party of the Crown in the House of Lords, 1711–14', in idem (ed.), Party and Management in Parliament, 1660–84 (Leicester, 1984), 123–67.

[30] CJ, xvii. 402, 430; Add. MSS 17677GGG, fos. 208–9, 225. Halifax was later celebrated as the 'very spirit' of the subsequent anti-bill periodical—King, British Merchant, i. p. xvii. A surviving forecast made by Oxford for a division on the commerce bill in the Lords suggested that the Tories could only expect a very slim majority—Holmes, British Politics, 36–7, 422–3.

anguished self-assessment, and they did not spare their leaders from blame for this calamitous reverse.[31] However, while such politicking is essential to understand the division of 18 June, the events of that day, and most importantly the ministry's ability to weather the crisis, cannot be merely explained by the machinations of party brokers. In the cauldron of Westminster ministers were primarily concerned with these tactical considerations, but an issue of such public debate could not be entirely settled by the appeasement of a few rebel leaders. The great vote, and the elections which followed it, were animated by trade as a key theme of contention, and those events can reveal much about the resilience of commerce as an issue competing for political attention alongside other matters of state. It must be recognized that the vote of 18 June was merely the catalyst for an even more thorough analysis of Britain's economic future, as politicians continued their education in the politics of trade.[32]

Surviving accounts of the debate which preceded the vote suggest that it was a true trial of strength, with the House spending nearly eight hours on the matter before the division. No less than thirty-five speakers were listed on this occasion, seventeen for the bill and eighteen against. The identity of the opponents of the bill highlighted the bitter rifts within the Tories, for their ranks included Commissioner of the Admiralty Aislabie, and Francis Annesley, Commissioner of Public Accounts. However, all observers agreed that the crucial speech was that of Sir Thomas Hanmer, a leading figure among the Hanoverian Tories. He acknowledged that he had voted for the introduction of the bill, but, 'having maturely weighed and considered the allegations of the merchants, traders, and manufacturers . . . he was convinced that the passing of this bill will be of great prejudice to the woollen and silk manufacturers of this kingdom, consequently increase the number of the poor, and so, in the end, affect the land'. Declaring his independence from ministerial coercion, or indeed from that of the electorate, he declared his opposition to the measure on the grounds of 'the interest of his country and the conviction of his judgement'. Whig observers rejoiced in his Pauline conversion to their patriotic arguments, while the Tories suspected his motives, seeing only spite and ambition in his stance. Without further evidence, controversy over his motives will never be entirely resolved, and in all likelihood his politics will remain as enigmatic to historians as they did to many of his contemporaries. However, whatever the sincerity behind those words, the fact remains that a commercial campaign had succeeded in persuading a quintessential country gentleman to pay lip-service to arguments upholding the importance of overseas trade for all orders of society. Hanmer's speech was thus a major success

[31] D. Sczechi, *Jacobitism and Tory Politics, 1710–14* (Edinburgh, 1984), 136–8. Although Jones and Holmes see trade as influencing the 'extraordinary' desertion of Tories on 18 June, they do not consider the commercial consequences of the defeat—*Parliamentary History*, 1 (1982), 64–5. For contemporary commentary, see *HMC Portland*, v. 311–12; Bodl. Ballard MSS 31, fos. 98–108; Bodl. Carte MSS 211, fo. 133.

[32] Significantly, Coleman did not study the elections in any detail.

for opponents of the commerce bill, even though suspicion of his motives must remain.[33]

The survival of several lists of the Members voting on 18 June, and contemporary analysis of their motivations, permits a more informed understanding of the importance of trade in that division. Donald Coleman, in an effort to gauge the impact of popular pressure on Members in that vote, emphasized that the constituencies of the MPs voting against the bill did not correlate with the trading areas which petitioned against the measure. Focusing on the five woollen-manufacturing counties which were said to account for 'a majority of all those places named as likely sufferers in the petitions', he stressed that they only produced the negligible figure of twelve defectors. Moreover, Surrey and Cambridgeshire, which produced no petitions, had eleven Tory defectors, and thus a question mark remains over the impact of the preceding weeks of extra-parliamentary agitation. However, these bald statistics cannot be taken as proof that commerce had failed to make an impact as a political weapon. As Coleman wisely observes, such analysis does not take into account the third of MPs who did not vote on 18 June, and only speculation can be brought to their reasons for non-attendance.[34] More vaguely, Coleman also suggests that 'the nature of Parliamentary representation at the time' has to be taken into account, presumably in reference to the principle of virtual representation, which stressed the MP's duty to respect the common interest against that of his particular constituency. These caveats are serious and highlight the need for more work on this crucial division, particularly against the results of the subsequent elections, which can shine further light on the relationship between Members and constituents on this issue.[35]

Closer analysis suggests that Coleman's reading of the division lists is too narrowly focused, and results from his primary interest in the key issue of the woollen manufacture, whose supporters feared the competition of French rivals and possible exclusion from the lucrative Portuguese market. In fact, the five 'clothing' counties he lists accounted for less than a third (11.25 ex 38) of the petitions submitted to the Lower House concerning the French commerce bill, and a slightly greater proportion (20.25 ex 56) of all representations on the commerce treaty issue in that session. These figures suggest that they formed a significant core of opposition, but were not overwhelmingly important. It is

[33] Add. MSS 17677GGG, fos. 229–30; *Wentworth Papers*, 337–8. For a list of the speakers, see Boyer, *Political State*, v. 388–9. For a discussion of Hanmer's motives, see History of Parliament, 1690–1715 section, draft biographical article; Holmes and Jones, *Parliamentary History*, 1 (1982), 62.

[34] Holmes and Jones argue that the absentees *were* influenced by commercial pressure groups, noting that fifteen Tory MPs from petitioning constituencies failed to turn up. However, no direct evidence has been discovered to link non-attendance with extra-parliamentary lobbying—*Parliamentary History*, 1 (1982), 64.

[35] Coleman, *Trade, Government, and Economy*, 195–6. For an account of surviving lists on the French commerce bill, see G. M. Ditchfield, D. Hayton, and C. Jones, *British Parliamentary Lists 1660–1800: A Register* (London, 1995), 111. On the vote itself, there are four main lists, each with minor, but important discrepancies.

perhaps more significant to note that representations came from twelve other counties, thus indicating the widespread concern felt by an array of British merchants and manufacturers. Most significantly of all, his table ignores the seventeen petitions emanating from the metropolis, whose impact can be measured by the fact that three of the City MPs rebelled, as well as one of the Middlesex MPs. After Hanmer, it was the apostasy of the three Londoners which received most column inches in both Whig and Tory papers, reflecting the perceived importance of the City's voice on trading issues. More generally, the readiness with which election propaganda dwelt on the voting predilections of certain manufacturing counties suggests that, whether rightly or wrongly, it was believed that Members should speak for their regional trading interests.[36]

Although the apparent success of such extra-parliamentary pressure is significant, more fundamental political realities, especially party pressures, worked against any simple correlation between petitioning and the voting of MPs. Contemporary analysis of the waverers within Tory ranks was intense on both sides, and the ensuing election ensured much generalized debate on the loyalty of Members to their constituencies. Opponents of the commerce bill predictably rejoiced in the political anxieties of the Tory defectors, but the ministerialists did not shrink from the fight, and dissected the defeat in order to discover the means by which they could reunite the party. The Tory *Letter from a Member of the House to His Friend in the Country* made the most interesting insights, dividing the bill's opponents threefold into 121 Whigs, thirty-five 'Whimsical' or Hanoverian Tories, and forty 'lost sheep' whom the ministry could hope to win back. In the context of assessing voting preferences on 18 June, this last category is particularly significant, for it suggests that, unlike the two other groups, their opposition to the ministry was not based on political principle. Significantly, two-thirds of these lost sheep came from counties which had submitted petitions on the French commerce treaty, and thus the agitation over the issue can still be credited with an important impact. Only six of these lost sheep can be identified as businessmen, so the pressure to divert from the party line on this occasion, if non-partisan or non-professional, must presumably have come from their observation on the debate itself.[37]

There can be little doubt that the forthcoming summer elections played heavily on the minds of MPs on 18 June, but, before considering those contests, it is vital to analyse the immediate parliamentary aftermath of the great vote, since it has a most significant bearing on our understanding of

---

[36] *CJ*, xvii. 354–430 *passim*. The anti-ministerial *Remarks on a Scandalous Libel* annotated its division lists with several observations on county voting patterns, such as that not one MP from Gloucestershire, 'this clothing county', voted for the bill. This county provides one of the most suggestive examples of a link between extra-parliamentary agitation and absenteeism in the House, since five of its eight Members did not vote in the division of 18 June.

[37] For a summary of the *Letter*, see Boyer, *Political State*, vi. 88–97.

the whole controversy. Within days of the disaster of 18 June, a remarkable damage limitation exercise had been launched by the ministry, which in effect largely neutralized the shock victory of Oxford's opponents. Following feverish ministerial overtures to Hanmer, on 23 June it was Sir Thomas himself who proposed a Commons address to the Queen to thank her for efforts in establishing 'so good a foundation' for the national interest in the French commerce treaty. Yet his motion also implored her to appoint commissioners to treat with the French so that the treaty might be 'explained and perfected' in the interest of her people. In a much thinner House, the ministry's opponents appear to have been caught cold, for a motion to instruct the committee on the address to ensure that the French allowed free access to all ports was lost by 156 to 72. Whig observers subsequently attacked Hanmer for a complete volte-face, but his allies could simply retort that he was maintaining his patriotic principles by striving to secure the best agreement for the nation's trade, which might languish without an accord. Whatever his motives, however, his stance was crucial for rehabilitating the ministry's shaky hold over backbench opinion, and in a stroke redirected policy on an issue over which it had lost control. Emanating renewed vigour, the Queen's response to the address was most bullish, fixing on its more positive aspects to declare satisfaction that Members approved of both the commercial and the peace treaties. With an election coming up, the taste of defeat on a major ministerial issue would have proved a serious blow both to party unity and its standing in the provinces, but Hanmer had given them a lifeline, permitting them once again to go on the offensive.[38]

Although very late in the session, the ministry appeared most anxious to prove its commercial credentials. On the day Hanmer made his momentous address, the *London Gazette* announced that the government would soon publish details of the asiento contract granted to Britain by the Spanish, which worked to rebuff charges that Britain would allow Louis XIV to control the imperial power of his weakened Iberian neighbour. At Westminster itself, a committee of the whole House was appointed on 25 June to study the improvement of British fisheries, one of the controversial 'four species' exempted from the benefits of the commercial treaty. A dispute over the chairmanship of this committee highlighted how divisive trade issues had become, but the ministry prevailed on this occasion. Moreover, on 14 July, only two days before the prorogation of Parliament, the Commons agreed to address the Queen to issue a proclamation to suppress the export of wool, a demand cleverly designed to assuage the economic concerns of disgruntled Tory squires in the provinces and at Westminster. Simply reiterating a policy which had been maintained for centuries, this move reassured their supporters that ministers understood their worries, and remained a gesture which avoided

[38] *CJ*, xvii. 435–6; Ballard MSS 31, fo. 105. The fishery inquiry belatedly addressed a proposal made in the Queen's speech in April.

any of the serious problems raised by the eighth and ninth articles. Most importantly, the ministry could still boast the Queen's support for the French commerce bill itself, and her speech announcing the prorogation expressed hope that the next Parliament would understand the benefits of the treaty. Few could now doubt that the ensuing election campaign would see both the ministry and its adversaries square up over the question of trade.[39]

Although the dissolution of the Parliament was not formally declared until 8 August, electioneering had been under way for some time before, with Whig supporters very keen to turn the great vote into electoral advantage. The *Flying Post* in particular was keen to worry divisions within Tory ranks, calling for 'a *finalis concordia* among all the honest Whigs and Tories that wish well to the landed interest of our country', thereby echoing the observations made by Hanmer on 18 June. In response, ministerial allies did not shrink from the great issue, and rallied to Oxford's counter-offensive of the last weeks of the session. The addresses printed in the *London Gazette* continued their praise of the ministry's economic competence, and gave reassurance that the Tory gentry had not been alienated from its cause. For instance, in mid-July the Bedfordshire grand jury professed its intention of electing loyal MPs who would 'cheerfully concur in ratifying such well-designed schemes of commerce as have rendered your Majesty's endeavours for the prosperity of your people effectual'. These sentiments underlined the importance of the government's accord with Hanmer, and registered its determination to take the commercial fight to its rivals.[40] Further evidence of the Tory resurgence was given by the *Post Boy*, which delighted in reporting the widespread celebrations on 7 July, the official thanksgiving day for the peace. Festivities at Leicester revealed the Whigs could not monopolize the commercial platform, for local Tories staged a procession in honour of the woollen industry. The parade included 100 framework knitters wearing sashes of white yarn and 'making music on their main springs'; wool-combers attended by eighty pages wearing white woollen caps; then 300 combers with hats adorned with 'white and blue wool in imitation of a cinquefoil (the town arms)'; all of whom escorted a pageant to display 'the whole manufacture of stocking-making'. Following behind was Bishop Blaise, and then the corporation in support. A toast to the Queen was drunk with 'good Port-wine', and the day ended with a mayoral treat for an assembly of noblemen, gentlemen, and over 700 tradesmen. An observer could indeed have been forgiven for thinking that this was a Whig triumph, but the town was a solid Tory bastion, and the parade winded its way through streets decorated with green boughs, a Tory symbol of allegiance to the monarchy.

[39] *London Gazette*, 20–3 June 1713; *CJ*, xvii. 441, 465. Holmes and Jones note that the hardline Whigs concentrated their efforts on the succession, pressing the Queen to expel the Pretender from Lorraine—*Parliamentary History*, 1 (1982), 66.

[40] *Flying Post*, 16–18 Sept. 1713. The *London Gazette* reflected the shock of the ministry at the defeat of 18 June, including no addresses in the two editions following the vote, only to resume with a barrage of eleven remonstrances in the subsequent issue.

Thus, here was proof that the ministry's supporters were trying to maintain the initiative on commercial issues, and gain the political benefits of commercial patriotism. Significantly, their MPs had split over the commerce bill vote, and there were rumours of a campaign against the Member who had remained loyal to the ministry, but Tory unity was preserved. Furthermore, Leicester was a town that had made no overt contribution to the parliamentary controversy of the preceding session, but was evidently extremely familiar with the nuances of those debates, and concerned that their interests should be protected.[41]

Tory resilience on the question of trade presented their rivals with formidable obstacles, exacerbating the perennial problems experienced by all opposition groups when trying to sustain a disciplined campaign against the ministry of the day. On thanksgiving day, the anti-treaty camp was heartened by the sermon of the Bishop of Bath and Wells, who exhorted his parliamentary audience 'to look to our own balance, and merchant-like, to consider in what end a long ceasing of profit and vast increase of loss must necessarily determine'. Yet, only a day after the prorogation, the Hanoverian envoy noted the despondency of the Whigs at the Queen's continued support for the Oxford administration, which was already cited as a major electoral hurdle for them to overcome. More encouragingly, the Dutch envoy detected understandable nervousness among the Tories as they debated the timing of the impending dissolution, most thinking it best to delay in the hope that the controversy would blow over. Given the fact that the ministry had publicly committed itself to framing a new commercial treaty, this appeared a most forlorn hope, especially since the prorogation served to intensify the efforts of all interested groups to win over public opinion. Several historians have erred in thinking that the run-up to the vote of 18 June saw the key debate, for most of the literature on the commercial treaty was concentrated on the electoral campaign, which saw several interesting developments in the discussion of commercial themes.[42]

In the weeks between the prorogation and the dissolution, rival parties concentrated on the vote of 18 June, seeking to influence electors by publishing division lists to ensure that they knew how their Members had voted. Such lists had been a feature of the intensive politicking since the Revolution, but this was the first commercial issue to have merited this publicity. The ministerialists were first into the field again, issuing *A Letter from a Member of the House of Commons to his Friend in the Country*, which included the first list of Members who voted for and against the bill. This pamphlet sought to expose the fallacy and self-interest of the merchants and traders who had been examined at Westminster, as a prelude to blaming the defeat of 18 June on the apostasy of

---

[41] *Post Boy*, 16–18 July 1713; Bodl. Carte MSS 117, fos. 441–2.
[42] Boyer, *Political State*, vi. 15–16; Kreienberg dispatch 17 July 1713; Add. MSS 17677GGG, fo. 284. Neither Coleman nor Holmes and Jones studied the post-dissolution debate in any detail.

two unnamed peers, evidently Lords Abingdon and Anglesey.[43] In keeping with ministerial strategy, the address of 23 June was represented as Hanmer's 'best and earliest retreat', the self-declared patriot having been misled by the two peers. The perceived importance of clearing the ministry's name was also highlighted by the increasing space given to the issue in Swift's *Examiner*, which forecast that the controversy would soon end since the *Mercator* had given sufficient reassurances for 'the generality of those who wish well to their country'. The *Mercator* had duly peddled the ministerial line that the commerce bill was a victim of party sabotage, and, in a notable show of confidence, was the first to publish the bill itself in early August. Although this move did not promise to diffuse the situation, it suggested that Tory leaders had accepted their commitment to public debate, and were prepared to take risks to win over the doubters among their supporters.[44]

The publication of the *Letter* predictably led to a furious counter-assault by ministerial rivals, with the appearance in rapid succession of *A Letter to a West-Country Freeholder*, *Trade and Tor[y]ism Can Never Agree*, *Remarks on a Scandalous Libel*, and the *Caution to those Choosing MPs*. All of them highlighted the experienced mercantile voices which had spoken out against the commerce bill, and attempted to concentrate debate on the economic issues which were regarded as the ministry's weak spot. The *Letter to a West-Country Freeholder* was most acute in this regard, challenging head-on the notion that the ministry was actually a skilled and attentive guardian of national trade. In particular, it dwelt on the failure to remove the French from Newfoundland, the continuing uncertainties surrounding the proposed trade agreements with Spain, and the need to establish British trading rights within Flanders. *Trade and Tor[y]ism* went much further, identifying a deep antipathy within Tory ranks to the commercial classes, which was traced back to the Reformation! Addressed to the leading City Whig magnate Sir Gilbert Heathcote, 'a patriot and a merchant', it championed commerce as a bulwark against tyranny, and as a source of national prestige, reminding its readers that 'wealth is the child of trade, and parent of power'. The other two pamphlets sought to clarify the significance of the vote of 18 June, supplying corrected lists of the great division, and scoffing at suggestions that the victory was merely a result of the pique of a few Tory leaders. However, the author of the *Remarks* was also keen to stress that religious differences were no longer an immediate cause for concern, thereby signalling Whig unease that the ministry would relegate the commercial issue to a secondary importance behind traditional party battle-lines on the Church and the Crown. In particular, they feared that the Tories

[43] Boyer, *Political State*, vi. 88–97. For analysis of the careers of these two unpredictable High Church figures, see Holmes, *British Politics in the Age of Anne*, 273–4, 278–9.

[44] *Examiner*, 27–31 July 1713; *Mercator*, 1–4 Aug. 1713. In its urgency to combat rival commercial arguments, the Oxford administration may have shelved plans to publish Swift's great opus, *History of the Four Last Years of the Queen*, regarding it as unsuitable for their current needs—F. P. Lock, *Swift's Tory Politics* (London, 1983), 46–9.

would attempt to recreate their great triumph at the 1710 election, when the cry of 'the Church in danger' had helped to establish them in power.[45]

While this flurry of publications indicated the thoroughness of Whig preparations for the elections, their significance pales in comparison with the appearance in early August of Henry Martin's *British Merchant* as a direct rival to the *Mercator*. A twice-weekly publication, it may well have been prompted by the first issue in late July of the pro-government monthly *The General History of Trade*, which threatened to give the ministerialists a vital advantage in the press war. The very title of the *British Merchant* spelt out its determination to wrest the laurels of patriotism from the administration, and challenge the *Mercator*'s recent claims that opposition to the commerce bill was merely the result of party vindictiveness. Only two weeks previously, the *Mercator* had scoffed that 'to bar up trade with a nation because we differ in state matters and politic interests is the greatest absurdity that a nation can be guilty of', and had insisted that 'trade is no way concerned in such disputes as these'. Conscious that a party stance would not gain widespread support, the *British Merchant* rejoined that its opposition to the commerce bill was not a pre-meditated affront to ministers, but that it could 'without any derogation to their wisdom deny that they are so conversant in trade as to foresee all the ill consequences of every particular branch of it'. The experience of Oxford and his colleagues was seen as 'of a superior kind', and 'neither by their education or employments' had they gained knowledge of trading matters. Thus, for both their benefit and that of the reading public, the paper communicated the views of experienced traders, most . notably Sir Theodore Janssen and Nathaniel Toriano, who had already figured prominently at Westminster in the course of the dispute. Combined with the patronage of Lord Halifax, the anti-treaty campaign was provided with a champion in the weekly battle for readers. Of more general significance, its appearance suggested that the public arena had very much taken commerce to heart as the issue of the moment, and that, as the *Mercator* observed, 'affairs of trade have now taken a new turn'.[46]

The dissolution of Parliament on 8 August saw no radical change in the position of the contending parties. The Whig papers concentrated on the perfidy of the French in Newfoundland and the imperilled Portugal trade, while the *Mercator* stressed the gain which the Dutch would make in the

---

[45] G. S. Holmes, *The Trial of Dr. Sacheverell* (London, 1973). The timing of all the pamphlets cited here has been deduced from press advertisements and internal evidence. Authorship remains a problem, although the teams responsible for the *British Merchant* and the *Mercator* may well have played a important role in coordinating publication.

[46] For an account of the team behind the *British Merchant*, see Charles King, *British Merchant*, i. pp. x–xv; *Mercator*, 20–3 June 1713. The career and ideas of essayist Henry Martin are summarized in I. Hont, 'Free Trade and the Economic Limits to National Politics: Neo-Machiavellian Political Economy Reconsidered' in J. Dunn (ed.), *The Economic Limits to Modern Politics* (Cambridge, 1990), 101–13.

absence of an Anglo-French commercial accord, attacked the Scheme of 1674, and recalled the danger to Scottish interests. Nevertheless, the presentation of economic debate continued to evolve as rival supporters sought to gain converts to their cause. A month before the dissolution the *Trial and Conviction of Count Tariff* had transformed the dry statistics of commercial debate into an altogether more entertaining allegory of how the plain-speaking patriot Goodman Fact rebuffed the libels of the dandified Tariff, despite the testimony of his dissembling accomplices Don Asiento and the Mercator. In mid-August, *The Memoirs of Count Tariff* offered an alternative government response, in which the Anglophile Count's plans were frustrated by the machinations of the cunning Dutch broker Mynheer Coopmanschap and a (Whig) club in London, who overruled the pro-treaty arguments of the sage Alderman Traffic by encouraging provincial clothiers such as Harry Woolpack and the Yorkshireman Joshua Doubledozen to influence their MPs. That the biting wit of Grub Street had been bestowed on commerce was as significant a demonstration of popular interest in the controversy as any of the more learned expositions on the subject. Further proof of its appeal came in mid-September, when advertisements appeared for the sale of wall charts 'worth putting up in any gentleman's apartment' bearing the full text of the commerce treaty, together with 'the emblem of peace and traffic'. It also bore depictions of the places in which the treaty had been negotiated and signed at Utrecht, as well as of the declaration of peace at the Royal Exchange. As the elections would also prove, the treaty controversy had now transcended the province of the ministry, Parliament, and commercial interest groups.[47]

While economic debate thus matured, the intervention of a full-blown election campaign presented a stern test for lobbyists to maintain the attention of their audience against the distractions of other great affairs of state. The security of the Hanoverian succession, and the maintenance of a balance of power within Europe were undeniably at the top of the political agenda, and, as already noted, religion threatened to raise passions in the manner of 1710. Of course, the French commerce treaty was considered very much as a test of the trustworthiness of the belligerent Louis XIV, and during the campaign ministerial opponents were able to make much political capital of his delays in demolishing the fortifications at Dunkirk, which was regarded as a key danger to British shipping. On the other hand, the Tories could still vaunt their achievement in having brought peace to most of Europe after years of war, which would be appreciated by many trading interests whatever the details of the commercial settlement.[48] Most reassuringly of all, their ministers

---

[47] *Post Boy*, 12–15 Sept. 1713. No copy of the wall chart has been traced, although it may well have resembled the foreign publications to be found at the British Museum, most notably Abraham Allard's *L'Idée de la paix conclue entre les Hauts Alliés et les François* (1713). For discussion of the development of print media, see T. Clayton, *The English Print, 1688–1802* (New Haven, 1997).

[48] For the impact of the Dunkirk crisis, see Downie, *Harley and the Press*, 178–9.

continued to enjoy the support of the monarch, which would be vital in maintaining fragile party unity over crucial issues such as the succession. As sitting tenants in Whitehall, they could exert a vast range of electoral patronage to secure the loyalty of Members, and sway voters in the provinces. Nevertheless, in the previous election they had learnt that popular slogans such as the cry of the 'Church in danger' could prove instrumental in securing dominance in the Commons, and thus had to be wary of the impact of their rivals' new attack, even though it had no electoral pedigree. Their care in answering critics of their economic policies was indicative of such concern, but independent observers still predicted that they would win the election with some ease. As the hundreds of addresses over the preceding eighteen months had chorused, the country wanted peace, and with a Whig party heavily burdened with the stigma of war-profiteering, the ministry could expect to reap the reward of the peace dividend. These considerations must be borne in mind when coming to assess the evidence of the elections themselves.[49]

In short, the 1713 general election was a disaster for the Whigs, even for those partisans who endeavoured to employ the French commerce treaty as a means to win over votes. By its end, commentators thought that the Tories had secured some 400 of the 558 seats, with the Whigs reduced to a mere 120. To add insult to injury, the Tory papers took great pleasure in mocking the failure of their rivals to secure an advantage from playing the trade card, particularly when it involved a contest with a large electorate and could thus be represented as a reflection of public opinion. The Buckinghamshire county poll was one of these more celebrated examples, where several Whig peers, including the great electoral magnate Lord Wharton, appeared wearing wool about their hats, only to be 'baa'd out of the field' by the Tories, who secured a close 100–vote majority. After another close contest at Norwich, in which sheep were driven through the streets, the *Post Boy* crowed that Whig mourning would see encouragement given to the manufacture of black and white crapes, and even printed what was purported to be a rival's election 'hymn' :

> We'll call 'em French and Jacobites
> That trade and us make prize
> By voting all the wool to France
> Tho' all men know they're lies.

Most significantly of all, the Tories managed to take both seats at the Wiltshire election with some ease, which was heralded as proof that this 'great clothing county' had approved of the vote given by one of its incumbents for the French commerce bill. In neighbouring Gloucestershire, the support of the clothiers helped to give the Whigs a share of the seats, but in general trade did not prove to be a winning formula for them.[50]

[49] Holmes, *British Politics*, 350–66, provides a masterly discussion of the formidable electoral interest of the Crown.   [50] *Wentworth Papers*, 351; *Post Boy*, 12–15, 24–6 Sept. 1713.

The significance of the commerce bill should not be simply assessed by the performance of the Whigs at the polls. Coming in the wake of a controversy in which some thirty counties and ninety parliamentary boroughs had revealed a direct concern for commerce, it would be highly improbable that trade was not an important electoral factor.[51] At the height of the elections impartial observers clearly perceived its impact, the Dutch envoy observing that trade remained high on the political agenda, while his Hanoverian counterpart noted growing expectations that the commerce bill would be reintroduced. However, the Whigs could not make their new cause tell as successfully as it had within the Lower House, and in only a handful of contests did a woollen hat prove a decisive support.[52] As one historian has pointed out, Whig MPs who had voted against the bill were even less successful than Tories who had split from their party on that issue. Whig observers were left to bemoan the strength of government patronage, but the real key to the Tory success was their swiftness to neutralize the trade threat by the deal which they had struck in the dying months of the last session. The evident concern of the Tory 'sheep', both at Westminster and beyond, had been temporarily assuaged by the Queen's addresses before the prorogation, which had allowed ministerial supporters to stand toe-to-toe with their rivals on the hustings. Oxford had not allowed his enemies to monopolize the issue, and at the right moment had given heart to his grassroots support. Nevertheless, although the elections appeared a general vote of confidence in the ministry, the Tory electoral triumph only increased pressure on the ministry to fulfil those commercial expectations. Significantly, even in the mire of defeat, Whig observers could distinguish between their failure as a party, and their success 'on the court test, which is for or against the bill of commerce'. In their view, 'the bill has lost ground', which perception could only encourage further campaigning on that issue.[53]

This point is brought out by the best-documented contest of the election, which also happened to be the very last return to be decided, and thus took place when all political parties knew that the succeeding Parliament would be overwhelmingly Tory in character. The London poll only decided the fate of four seats, but, given their prestige and the City's status as Europe's premier trading port, the result was widely regarded as a crucial test of the ministry's

[51] These figures cover the addresses of 1712 and 1713, combined with petitioning to Parliament and evidence of local activity on commercial issues.

[52] History of Parliament: 1690–1715 section, draft constituency articles. Constituencies in which there were clear demonstrations of 'trade' allegiance include Buckinghamshire, Kent, Surrey, Wiltshire, London, Liverpool, Norwich, Minehead, Southwark, and Hindon. Other indications of the direct relevance of the issue can be found at Gloucestershire, Great Yarmouth, Leicester, and New Sarum.

[53] Cumbria RO (Carlisle), D/Lons/W2/3/13, Nicholas Lechmere to James Lowther, 17 Sept. 1713. Richards, *Party Propaganda*, 149–50, cites trade as the reason why there was not an even greater rout for the Whigs at the polls, and attributes the electoral success of the Tory MPs who had voted against the bill (79% re-elected) to the depth of Tory support for the 'Whig' issue of trade.

credibility. The City Whigs in fact made the administration's task all the more difficult by including three moderate Tories among their candidates, thereby hoping to split the rival vote. Most emphatically their platform was mercantile, since all four were leading overseas traders, and therefore would present a contrast to the sitting Tory Members, who included a banker and a scrivener. These tactics had proved unsuccessful for the Whigs at the shrieval election of the preceding June, and the Tory press bullishly celebrated the commercial credentials of their candidates, who were 'of experienced abilities and qualifications to promote the woollen, silk, and other manufactures of Great Britain in general, and of this honourable City in particular'. The fact that the London Tories were prepared to back three of the 'sheep' who had voted against the party on 18 June demonstrates that Tory campaigners were all-too-sensitive to the importance of commerce for their electoral fortunes. 'The shibboleth of trade' was duly heralded as the main point at issue, although Tory High Church mobs endeavoured to rekindle the religious fervour of the previous election, and Whigs taunted their rivals with accusations of Jacobitism. This agitation, and no little violence, did not prevent a high turnout, with at least 6,800 votes cast. After a poor start the Tories rallied to take all four seats, although less than 200 votes covered all eight candidates. Whigs bemoaned the advantage enjoyed by their rivals by dint of government influence over various City institutions, but the question remains whether their defeat was caused by the insidious workings of patronage, or by a failure to convince non-partisan liverymen that trade would be more secure in their hands.[54]

Fortunately, the 1710 and 1713 City polls survive, thus enabling closer scrutiny of the impact of trade on the early eighteenth-century electorate. Previous analysis of these poll books has fixed most readily upon the partisan consistency of the eighteenth-century voter, with some 85 per cent of voters sticking to the party platforms. The most authoritative account of London politics attributes the roots of Tory success to their support among the City's manufacturing and smaller traders, with the 'Whig' candidates performing strongly among the City elite. Analysis of this study's London mercantile sample also suggests that it was the Whigs who had managed to secure the support of the greater traders. Of the eighty-five members of our merchant sample who voted in 1713, sixty backed all four Whig candidates, and only nineteen supported their rivals, with the remaining six mixing or registering partial votes. While according with De Krey's general thesis, it is significant that *both* parties had made gains since 1710, their campaigning having enticed twenty-nine previously non- or mixed-voters to adopt partisan positions. This turnout of high-profile merchants highlights the importance of the issues at hand, and amid electoral fervour the Whig message was clearly more

[54] *Post Boy*, 22–24 Sept. 1713; *Letters of Daniel Defoe*, ed. G. H. Healey (Oxford, 1955), 416.

receptive to overseas traders. Without further evidence, it is impossible to say how decisive an issue trade was in the minds of these liverymen, but it is clear that the events of 1713 had successfully rallied opposition to the ministry. Although seriously outclassed in this particular aspect of the contest, the Tories could still congratulate themselves on having maintained the discipline of their own mercantile supporters, even among the Iberian and Mediterranean traders most directly threatened by the commerce treaty. Thus, even if it was the lower orders of London society which brought the Tories overall victory, their campaign to convince the country of the ministry's commercial competence had not been in vain. For certain, Sir William Withers, the only sitting City Member to have voted for the commerce bill, would have acknowledged the importance of the government campaign after his thirty-three vote majority over his fifth-placed rival John Ward.[55]

The City election had proved a close call for the Tories, and, despite the thumping majority achieved by the ministry in the country, the Whigs were generally acknowledged to have made some ground on them at the 1713 elections, particularly on account of trade. Even amid the euphoria of electoral triumph, government supporters still betrayed anxieties that the ministry would have to deliver on its promises, one of whom reminded Hanmer that Britain had still not secured a commercial accord with Spain, had not sent any ships to the South Seas despite the licences offered by Spain, and had not appointed commissioners to settle matters with the French over the commerce bill. As he reminded Sir Thomas Hanmer, 'some of these things must be done . . . before you meet at Westminster', thereby serving notice of his continuing responsibility for resolving the current controversy. The ministry itself needed little prompting, and during the elections had been working flat out to prepare their defences for the next session, most notably by seeking a commercial agreement with the Portuguese. They were also applying diplomatic pressure to recommence negotiations with the French on the basis of the discredited commerce treaty, believing that a modified accord would yet gain them widespread approval. Electoral victory had signified a broad welcome for the achievement of peace, but there was still very real pressure on the ministry to prove themselves the true guardians of the nation's trade.[56]

[55] G. S. De Krey, *A Fractured Society: The Politics of London* (Oxford, 1985), 244–9; W. A. Speck and W. A. Gray (eds.), 'London Poll-Books 1713', *London Record Society*, 17 (1981). Judging by Charles Cooke's analysis of divisions within the Levant Company, there was no significant swing between May and November 1713, with only three desertions to the 'Whig' slate at the parliamentary election—Bodl. Folio. Theta 665, fos. 189–90.

[56] *The Correspondence of Sir Thomas Hanmer*, ed. H. Bunbury (London, 1838), 151–4.

iv. Consequences and recrimination 1713–1714

The government's attempts to revive the commerce treaty in the finals months of Anne's reign have merited little attention, principally because of their ultimate failure. With the death of the Queen all efforts to secure the accord came to an abrupt halt, and the ensuing Whig administration only regarded the negotiations as a potential means to discredit their predecessors as Francophile traitors. However, the determination with which the Oxford ministry pursued the matter retains great significance, particularly as it had every opportunity to kill the issue if it so wished. The reassessment of the treaty after October 1713 lacks the high drama of the great vote and the election hustings, but the continuing debate on trade suggested that the controversy was not simply a party ruse of a desperate political faction. The intensive pamphleteering of the summer was not repeated, but political commentators did not feel ready to drop the issue of commerce, even once the election had seemingly endorsed the ministry's policies. The persistence of 'commercial' politics can largely be attributed to the government itself, with ministers determined to answer their critics, and maintain firm control of an issue which had caused them great embarrassment. Trade had to be on the agenda, and the Tories were resolved to ensure that this time it would work to their advantage.[57]

Discussions concerning the possible reintroduction of the commerce bill into Parliament had begun even before the elections were over. In mid-October Defoe addressed Oxford on this topic, perceiving that the bill would be necessary to foil the plans of anti-ministerialists. However, concerned that 'the clamour of the rabble. . . may prevail to prepossess the Members' against the bill, he advised that the ministry could not simply reintroduce it for fear of another uproar. Instead, he suggested that Oxford appear indifferent to the fate of the treaty, and use the accustomed proceeding of the House to the settlement of ways and means as an opportunity to put pressure on anti-treaty rivals. In particular, he thought that if the duties on imported foreign silks and wines were raised with the exception of French produce (which were already heavily loaded), then the commerce treaty would have a greater appeal to the Iberian and Mediterranean merchants. By this method Defoe thought he was 'bringing the trade up to the bill', although he did concede that 'clamours' might 'grow so loud as to make it reasonable not to hazard the debate in Parliament'. His comments highlighted the strategic control enjoyed by a dominant ministry within Westminster, but also its dilemma when tackling an issue over which extra-parliamentary opinion was acknowledged to have an important influence. There is no evidence to signify that Defoe's plan was ever seriously contemplated by ministers, but their subsequent actions suggest

[57] For discussion of the impact of ministerial divisions on the conduct of British diplomacy, see D. McKay, 'Bolingbroke, Oxford, and the Defence of the Utrecht Settlement in Southern Europe', *EHR* 86 (1971), 264–84.

that they heeded his caution on the potential political resonance of the issue. Significantly, Defoe's *Mercator* made no comment on the scheme, and by the time Parliament met the ministry had already embarked on another, equally hazardous track.[58]

Ministerial efforts centred on securing clarification from the French over the most controversial clauses of the existing treaty, in preparation for the re-submission of the accord before Parliament. The plan was relatively straight-forward, but the response of the French to these overtures could not be gauged with any certainty. In the wake of the failure of the commerce bill, they had aired ominous reservations about the viability of the treaty without the eighth and ninth clauses, thereby increasing doubts about the advantageousness of the whole treaty. British diplomatic efforts were led by Matthew Prior and the Duke of Shrewsbury, who testily rejected any idea that the treaty had rested on the two articles, and stressed that the settlement had directed the appointment of commissioners to resolve such difficulties. By late October it was reported that the French were ready to name their intermediaries, thus initiating preliminary discussions to clear obstacles for the conference. However, the ministry did not rest content with this progress, urging the French to enforce certain clauses of the commercial treaty to maintain momentum on the issue. In particular, the reciprocal removal of heavy duties on the shipping of the two nations was urgently pressed by the British, mindful no doubt of the political capital which such a move would yield at home. The French showed a readi-ness to do so, and gave encouraging signs of support on other trade issues, which helped to give credence to reports in mid-November that the commerce bill would be reintroduced in the next parliamentary session.[59]

At this stage the ministry was in a strong position to press for the revival of the commerce treaty. The election had re-established its authority, and it was under no pressure to hasten the calling of Parliament, which did not meet until the following February. Without a parliamentary focus, its opponents found it difficult to build on their uncertain gains at the preceding election, or to challenge the ministry on the promising issue of trade. Keen to maintain the initiative, in November 1713 the government attempted to mollify some of its severest mercantile critics by inviting their views on a newly drafted com-mercial treaty with the Portuguese. The ministry still had to act circumspectly, for in the following month anti-ministerialists reportedly made gains over the Tories at the London common council elections by championing opposition to the treaty. Moreover, this result was seen to have forced the City Tories to shelve plans to address the Queen in the hope of securing her renewed backing for the commerce treaty. With an election petition almost certain to

---

[58] *Letters of Daniel Defoe*, 417–24.

[59] Diplomatic activity concerning the commerce bill can be followed in PRO, SP 78/157–8 and SP105/27–9, 275; also note *HMC Portland*, v. 341–2. Shrewsbury, like Bolingbroke, could be brutally frank concerning his ignorance of trade—Hill in *HJ* 16 (1973), 261–2; *Camden Miscellany*, 31 (1992), 358.

be delivered by the City Whigs in the next session, the ministry could not mistake the continuing pressure it was under to secure real advantages for traders.[60]

The continuing battle of the *British Merchant* and the *Mercator* was the most direct manifestation of the importance of commerce as a trial of strength between politicians, and this newspaper war appears to have intensified in the course of 1714. The very fact that this weekly contest outlasted the election disputes of 1713 is in itself significant, but it was the development of the arguments put forward by both sides which really marks out the more fundamental importance of the controversy. Defoe and Martin maintained their interest in certain commercial issues in order to undermine each other's authority, focusing on the reliability of trade statistics in particular, but they also broadened the debate to encompass issues relating to the status of trade as a political issue. Both sides had examined the relationship of trade and party politics before, and both had denounced the workings of faction in commerce, and these arguments were the foundations for a more penetrating analysis of the workings of interest within trade and the state. *The British Merchant* was most illuminating in this regard, admitting that merchants did not always have the public interest at heart if it clashed with their pursuit of profit, and that 'our legislators therefore have had the wisdom in every age to guard the nation from the detrimental gain of the merchants'. Its authors thus highlighted the need for national institutions which could impartially consider the true common interest, across the claims of both traders and the landed. In the same breadth they were censorious of past governmental neglect of trade, pointing to the example of Louis XIV to prove that trade should be actively advanced by the state. These observations went far beyond the immediate controversy at hand, while also serving to maintain pressure on the ministry.[61]

The *Mercator* appeared less concerned to broaden the scope of the conflict, and displayed a partisan delight in denigrating its opponents as the creatures of a rival party, or as Dutch agents. Defoe adhered to the patriotic line that there should be no party in commercial matters, insisting that 'the business of trade is to get money . . . we know no Whig or Tory in trade'. Nevertheless, although more of a political beast, he also paid lip-service to the fundamental issues raised by the debate. In particular, he continually attacked the credentials of his rival Henry Martin as a spokesman on trade, and dismissed the views of his mercantile advisers as self-interested and unpatriotic. Sir Theodore Janssen came in for especial criticism in this regard, lampooned as 'an illiterate knighted foreigner turned pamphleteer', which status under-

[60] CO389/23, fos. 479, 482; Add. MSS 70070, newsletter 24 Dec. 1713; Add. MSS 17677HHH, fos. 3–4, 6, 10.
[61] *British Merchant*, 15–19 Jan., 4–7 May 1714. For circulation figures of these papers in 1713–14, see J. M. Price in *BIHR* 31 (1958), 221–2. The *British Merchant* peaked at 7,000 copies per week (i.e. 3,500 copies per issue) in April 1714. The *Mercator* briefly peaked at 14,400 per week (4,800 per edition) just before the great vote of 1713, but still kept a healthy 1,600 per issue in March 1714.

mined his expertise in matters of French trade. Thus, in common with his adversary Martin, Defoe called for informed and impartial discussion of commercial issues. The *Mercator* also managed to rise above the party slogans to question whether the controversy could be ever resolved, identifying *all* the statistics produced as 'but amusements, appearances without any foundation, and from which no true scheme of the trade can be drawn'. This enlightenment did not lead to any proposal for rectifying this state of affairs, but it again suggested that the conflict had raised serious questions concerning the formulation of trade policy. A journalist of Defoe's considerable skill recognized all too well that the manipulation of trade figures was far from a pointless exercise if it could affect public opinion, and he offered a range of illuminating comments on the increased pressure to tailor economic arguments to a wide audience. For instance, he was prepared to criticize his own government supporters over the presentation of their case, observing that the decision to publish the whole of the French commerce treaty was a mistake, as its length ensured that 'all that saw it had not either time or patience to read it'. Defoe again offered no real solution to improve public understanding of commercial debate, and kept his faith in the brick-bat warfare with which his readership was well accustomed. However, there can be little doubt that the sustained intensity of the commerce battle had familiarized a wide audience with the potential impact of overseas trade, and that these publications had played a key role in sustaining public interest in the controversy.[62]

Intense diplomatic activity in the winter of 1713–14 gave all interested parties continuing grounds for speculation concerning the fate of the commerce treaty. In late December the government announced the names of four commissioners to negotiate with the French on matters of trade, two of whom had acted as expert witnesses for the commerce bill at Westminster. Frederick Herne was a member of one of the leading families in Mediterranean trade, while Sir Joseph Martin, MP, was one of the few who could claim the title of universal merchant, with trading interests stretching from the West Indies to the Baltic.[63] They were joined by Charles Whitworth, an experienced diplomat who had worked closely with the Russia Company, and Hon. James Murray, doubtless included to acknowledge keen Scottish interest in the fate of French commerce.[64] As a team they were well suited to the task ahead, and were, as importantly, likely to gain the government credit for the seriousness with which they approached these negotiations. Interestingly, not one of them

---

[62] *Mercator*, 13–16 Feb., 6–8 Apr., 8–11 May 1714.

[63] CO389/24, fos. 63–4. Herne was the son of the great merchant and government financier Sir Joseph. Frederick had shown his support for the commerce treaty by sponsoring a celebratory treat in his Dartmouth constituency in May 1713—*Post Boy*, 23–6 May 1713.

[64] For Whitworth's dealings with the Russia Company, during which he may well have come into contact with Sir Joseph Martin, see Guildhall Library MSS 11741/4, pp. 83, 88. Scottish concern at the treaty was signalled by the Earl of Findlater in October 1713, when he proposed the establishment of a Scottish council of trade—*HMC Portland*, v. 351. The Scottish convention of burghs had sought to maintain pressure on the government since the summer of 1713—CO389/24, fos. 149–52.

had been mentioned when Lord Bolingbroke discussed likely candidates three months before at the height of the elections. At that stage only three nominations were considered, and the most significant name put forward was Sir William Withers, the sole City MP in favour of the commerce bill. Despite his loyalty to the ministry, after nearly losing his seat in the intervening general election he was evidently considered as too controversial a figure to represent British commercial interests. Important changes had thus been made to the commission, and the expertise of the final selection indicated that the ministry was sensitive to accusations of incompetence levelled at its past commercial diplomacy. Ministerial caution was further suggested by its decision to entrust the Board of Trade with the administration of the conference, although the board had to report to the Privy Council on its progress. As if there was any need, Bolingbroke stressed to the commissioners that these talks were of the 'utmost importance'.[65]

The French commissioners did not arrive until mid-February, by which time the ministry had already several commercial achievements to declare. In late January it was announced that Britain and France were to remove shipping duties in line with the stipulations of the commerce treaty, and that the French had also agreed to crack down on the notorious trade in smuggling English wool across the Channel. These positive signs of entente probably lay behind the *Mercator's* confident prediction in February that the commerce treaty would be discussed in the new Parliament. A letter from Matthew Prior to the newly elected Speaker Hanmer a few weeks later gave further indications that Westminster would soon hear the issue, with the diplomat airing his satisfaction that a patriot of Hanmer's standing would oversee debate on 'the commerce, or any other article'. However, it was not until the Queen's speech on 2 March that the assembled Members were given formal notice of the ministry's plans for the coming session. The speech was again notable for the prominence given to trade, with its opening paragraph reporting the recent signing of treaties of peace and commerce with Spain. Moreover, it went on to insist that 'our situation points out to us our true interest; for this country can flourish only by trade, and will be most formidable by the right application of our naval force'. No mention of the French commerce treaty was made, nor of the talks currently under way; a sure demonstration of the ministry's trepidation on the issue. It may well have had immediate cause to remain tentative, for just over a week later the *Mercator* reported that petitions were being prepared in readiness for the resubmission of the commerce bill. Until the conference of commissioners had settled matters afresh, the only likely con-

[65] *Letters and Correspondence, Public and Private of the Rt. Hon. Henry St. John, Lord Viscount Bolingbroke*, ed. G. Parke (London, 1798), 295, 408–11. The other nominees in October 1713 had been 'Mr Pitts' and 'Mr Sharp', neither of whom can be identified with certainty. At this time, John Drummond, Oxford's agent in the Netherlands, implored the Lord Treasurer to heed expert advice in ongoing talks over the Spanish commerce treaty, insisting that chief negotiator Arthur Moore 'cannot be a competent judge of all that concerns it'—*HMC Portland*, v. 336–7.

sequence of its revival was further confusion and disunity, an unappealing scenario for any ministry.[66]

While the administration dithered, several attempts were made to raise the commerce issue in the Commons. On 24 March the Queen was addressed to supply details of all commissions granted by the Crown since 1660 for the negotiation of trade treaties with France and other countries. A week later, the Commons requested an account of the customs paid on imported French goods since 1711, presumably to address allegations that the country would be deluged with luxury items as soon as hostilities ended. The figures produced suggested an impressive increase in French imports, principally to the benefit of the wine merchant, but still only totalling some £150,000. Despite these evident signs of interest in the French commerce issue, no decisive move was made either by the ministry or its opponents. By early May the Dutch envoy was convinced that the commerce bill would not be introduced this session, and suggested that this could be attributed to warnings given by some Members that they would never assent to it. Almost certainly he was referring to continuing divisions within the Tory camp over the matter, for the ministry had little to fear from its Whig enemies on their own. Nevertheless, having made strenuous efforts to reassure its allies of the wisdom of their commercial policies, the government could only have felt extremely frustrated at this continuing impasse.[67]

Although tentative in the Commons, the ministry derived much encouragement from the negotiations between the British and French commissioners, which appear to have proceeded extremely well in their opening weeks. Britain had begun by tabling three preliminary articles for clarification on key points of difference, without which there appeared little hope for any efforts to revive the treaty. In particular, Britain insisted that the French concede that the treaty did not rest on the eighth and ninth articles, and that British goods exempted by the 'four species' rule would be treated as favourably as those of other nations. France had expressed reluctance to enter into talks in this manner, but eventually relented, and by early April Prior could delight in their acceptance of Britain's demands on all these points. If France could be held to these conditions, the ministry's position would be considerably enhanced, for in effect the bulk of the treaty could be enforced without reference to Parliament, and the commercial competitiveness of certain British manufacturers would be automatically advanced, including the crucial woollens trade. The conference duly proceeded to debate other matters of international tension, especially colonial disputes, and within ministerial circles there was increasing expectation that the treaty might yet be saved. By late May the Dutch envoy was prepared to share Prior's enthusiasm, remark-

---

[66] Add. MSS 17677HHH, fo. 49; *Mercator*, 6–9 Feb., 9–11 Mar. 1714; *Hanmer Correspondence*, 154–5; *CJ*, xvii. 474.

[67] *CJ*, xvii. 525, 554; Add. MSS 17677HHH, fo. 214.

ing that the success of the trade talks suggested that Westminster might yet hear the matter this session.[68]

This optimism was sadly misplaced, and the events of June conspired to end any hope of a full commercial agreement between France and Britain. Cruelly for the ministry, after all its efforts to establish its reputation as a friend to British trade, it was to be an old-fashioned case of ministerial corruption that would undermine its efforts over the French commerce treaty. From mid-June onwards Arthur Moore, jocularly reviled by his enemies as 'the Prime Minister of Trade', was arraigned in both Houses for having exacted significant financial rewards for himself and several of his associates in the course of the negotiation of the Spanish commerce treaty. The evidence of malpractice was compelling, and it was only the prorogation on 7 July which saved Moore from official censure. In itself, this issue had no immediate relevance to the French commerce treaty, but the scandal cast a long shadow over the ministry's international dealings over the preceding three years, and seemingly vindicated the charges made in 1713 that the government was prepared to sell out the country for its own interests. Most embarrassingly, Moore had been one of the government's leading spokesmen for the French commerce bill the preceding summer, and his disgrace was a bitter blow to the ministry's commercial credibility.[69]

While this controversy raged, the progress achieved at the French trade talks faltered amid a resurgence of colonial tension. In particular, increasing concern that the French would not keep to their agreement to quit the Newfoundland fisheries was met by French counter-claims that British merchants had embarked on illegal trade with the Spanish West Indies. More worryingly for prospects of an agreement on reducing duties, negotiation of a commercial agreement with Portugal had run into trouble in early June when ministers encountered the thorny question of how to settle British import duties for wines from Portugal and France. Furthermore, with the future of the commercial treaty still uncertain British traders were becoming increasingly annoyed by the seizure of their vessels in French ports. As an exasperated Prior lamented to Bolingbroke on 18 June, the first anniversary of the great vote, British traders were making the 'real or pretended' mistake of believing that the two countries had commenced full trading relations again, and 'neither you nor I can help it'. This disillusionment was not shared by the *Mercator*, which defiantly insisted that the ministry was not afraid to bring the commerce treaty before the House, and that French prevarication was to blame for the failure to reach a settlement. However, the Queen's death on 1 August, and the rapid consolidation of a Whig ministry effectively sealed its fate. The overwhelming priority of establishing a new dynasty relegated trade

---

[68] CO 389/24, fo. 161 and ff.; SP78/158, fo. 85; Add. MSS 17677HHH, fo. 227.

[69] *A Letter to the Hon. A——r M——re* (London, 1714). The Moore crisis can be followed in Steele, *Politics of Colonial Policy*, 139–42.

to its more traditional back seat, and in this emergency there was little chance that as complex and controversial an issue as the commerce treaty would be resolved.[70]

Under George I no serious attempt was made to revive the French commerce treaty, but the matter was far from forgotten, and it would be wrong to see its disappearance as the simple result of the party revolution ushered in by the Hanoverian regime. The treaty had been closely identified with the Oxford administration, but ideological differences cannot account for Whig reluctance to resume negotiations with the French. Much more realistically, the difficulties which the agreement had caused the Tories were a powerful argument for leaving the issue well alone, even after the death of Louis XIV had put Britain in a particularly strong position to dictate terms. It is important to note that grassroots agitation on the treaty issue was forthcoming after the death of Anne, but Whig ministers spurned the opportunity to seek a favourable commercial accord with the French. Although hesitant, they had clearly learned several lessons from the controversy, since the King's first speech to Parliament in March 1715 accorded commerce creditable importance. In particular, the Crown promised to address the failure to enforce peace agreements 'essential to the security and trade of Great Britain', which at present rendered 'a great part of our trade' impracticable. Significantly, this pronouncement did not go unchallenged from the Tory benches, but the great merchant Sir Gilbert Heathcote rose to rebuff claims that peace had brought about a thriving and equitable trade between France and Britain. The new government and its allies were thus just as sensitive over their commercial credentials as their predecessors, and from the outset the ministers of the Whig oligarchy recognized that they had to be wary of the cry of the patriot trader.[71]

Therefore, if it is hard to espy any direct commercial consequence of the great debate of 1713–14, then it is all too easy to observe its ramifications for the politics of trade. This account has taken pains to convey the profound influence of the controversy on the development of economic debate in the public sphere, since general political accounts do not do justice to its wider significance. That is not to say that every commercial issue was suddenly of earth-shattering importance for the political nation, or that trade had taken its place alongside the succession and religion as matters of ideological dispute, for that would be to misrepresent the impact of this contest. However, the controversy had shown how commercial and landed interests could respond to trade issues in the new polity of post-Revolutionary Britain, and from that perspective alone the contest merits great significance. For centuries trading

---

[70] CO389/24, fos. 259, 262, 316; SP 78/158, fos. 195–6; *Mercator*, 17–20 July 1714.

[71] *CJ*, xviii. 18; Boyer, *Political State*, x. 216–17. In the run-up to the general election of 1715 some Whigs sought to make political capital over that 'felonious treaty of commerce'—*A Tender and Hearty Address to all the Freeholders* (London, 1714), 13–14. London was predictably animated on the issue— Boyer, *Political State*, ix. 82–7, 166–70.

interests had put pressure on MPs to represent their grievances at Westminster, but before 1713 there had never been such coordinated pressure at the electoral hustings over a commercial issue. Before 1689 it had been common for tracts and periodicals to direct government policy on commerce, but before 1713 none had done so on a sustained weekly basis with a view to garnering widespread extra-parliamentary support. Moreover, before 1713 no ministry had taken such exhaustive efforts to champion the economy as a matter of national concern, and emphasized its patriotic credentials on the basis of the defence of trade. On all these counts the French treaty controversy was a novelty, and, as has been stressed here, was by necessity an educative process for all the sides involved. The learning curve would continue after 1715, but the lessons of previous unrest would not be forgotten.

The subsequent history of the *British Merchant* can be taken as a measure of the importance of the controversy for the development of commercial politics in the eighteenth century. Within a mere six years a weekly periodical of the same name had appeared to champion the import of Indian calicoes, and met stiff resistance from the rival *Manufacturer* and *Weaver*. This trio of self-styled patriotic journals ran for only four months, the duration of the parliamentary contest, but this campaign highlighted the determination of trade lobbies to solicit a public audience for the resolution of specific commercial issues.[72] Even more significantly, in 1721 the merchant-turned-civil servant Charles King published a three-volume summary of arguments from the original *British Merchant*, distilling the series into a fluent treatise dedicated to exposing the true interest of the nation's commerce. At its end he included a 'very copious' index for the benefit of peers, MPs, merchants, and others, so that the work could be 'of constant use' when trade matters came before the legislature. The Whig grandee Lord Sunderland had no doubts as to its value, ordering King to issue a copy to every constituency in preparation for the general election of 1722.[73] The popularity and utility of these tomes was attested by further editions in 1743 and 1748, and it was fitting that at the outset of the negotiations which ultimately led to the Anglo-French commerce treaty of 1786 Lord Shelburne donated a copy to his French counterpart, commending it as 'a book which has formed the principles of nine tenths of the public since it was first written'. The 1713–14 dispute had thus acted as an aide-mémoire of the importance of mercantile power for Georgian statesmen, and we too should study it to understand the evolution of commercial debate in a key era of political change and economic expansion.[74]

[72] Defoe has been tentatively identified as the author of the *Manufacturer*, which successfully supported the passage in March 1720 of an act against the wearing of calicoes.

[73] King, *British Merchant*. A host of ministers, officials, peers, and merchants figured among its subscribers. For its circulation in 1722, see *CTP* 1720–28, p. 155; PRO, T1/240/32.

[74] *The Correspondence of King George III*, ed. J. B. Fortescue (London, 1927–8), vi. 136–7. Also note David McPherson's 1805 critique of Adam Anderson's account of the French commerce treaty— D. C. Coleman, *History and the Economic Past* (Oxford, 1987), 25–6.

Conclusion

A SIMPLE contrast between the marauding sheep of the Norwich election and the quiet reflection of Pepys's boat trip would suggest that the Augustan period had seen a significant development in the politics of trade. It is indeed tempting to interpret the great French commerce debate as a definitive watershed in the political development of the British commercial classes. It retains an indisputable significance as the first economic controversy to bring about a serious reverse for a ministry in the modern party era, but it cannot be portrayed as a conflict which changed the face of British politics and society. Whatever their claims to be the party of the commercial classes, the Whigs could not have established their ascendancy over Georgian Britain solely on the defence of trade, and successive Hanoverian ministries did not find themselves threatened by wave upon wave of commercial crises. Equally, the demise of the Tories under the first two Georges was not hastened by their supposed commercial antipathies, for their leaders had worked hard in the cause of trade, and were in fact instrumental in focusing national attention on economic issues. Nevertheless, the debates of 1713–14 ensured that the King's servants did pay close attention to trading matters, if only from an anxiety that no campaign could gather the momentum attained by the anti-French bandwagon. The salutary experience of Walpole's failure to control the patriotic furore over the excise reforms of 1733 or war with Spain in 1739 highlighted the potential resonance of commercial issues in an increasingly imperial era.[1]

Ministerial caution was well advised, for the French commerce debate had revealed that many economic groups had learnt to master the changing institutions of the British polity in order to achieve their goals. This process cannot be represented as a mercantile 'winning of the initiative' in any teleological sense, for the merchant politicians revealed no desire to challenge the supremacy of the landed for control of the state. A political equilibrium between the landed and the monied had been achieved without revolutionary upheaval, but this Georgian accommodation should not obscure the pressure for more fundamental reforms which could be espied at the heart of the controversy of 1713. In the Augustan era there had been calls for radical changes in the relationship between the business world and the state, most notably for the creation of a quasi-parliamentary assembly of traders, but the political system was sufficiently flexible to avoid dramatic innovation. There were still

[1] K. Wilson, *The Sense of the People: Politics, Culture, and Imperialism in England, 1715–1785* (Cambridge, 1995); P. Langford, *The Excise Crisis* (Oxford, 1975); J. Price, 'The Excise Affair Revisited: the Administration and Colonial Dimensions of a Parliamentary Crisis', in S. B. Baxter (ed.), *England's Rise to Greatness, 1660–1763* (Berkeley, Calif., 1983), 257–321; N. Rogers, *Whigs and Cities* (Oxford, 1989), 48–55.

few mercantile figures in the corridors of power, but the trader could seek to influence government policy in matters of essential importance to his profession, and eighteenth-century businessmen would prove themselves endlessly resourceful in exploiting political opportunities. The social fence was still very much intact, but the socio-political structures of the British state were sufficiently malleable to ensure that neither side saw much need to dramatically reposition themselves. These basic harmonies should not mask what was clearly a dynamic social tension, but the system proved that it could work in the interests of the broad propertied elite. In this way Britain had managed to emulate the political efficiency of the Dutch state in the seventeenth century, and avoided the problems inherent in the autocratic French system. This delicate balance of interests would be tested by periodic crises, but the political accessibility of Parliament remained a sure foundation for British economic growth.[2]

It is important to acknowledge that this political transition was far from a linear process, and that the specific crisis of 1713–14 was the cumulative result of commercial and political developments across the Augustan period as a whole. In fact, the most promising signs of state support for commerce came in the 1660s, when the restored Charles II established a mercantile advisory council, upheld and strengthened the Navigation Laws, and was prepared to tussle with the Dutch for control of the seas. These policies did not reflect a coordinated programme of economic expansion, and by the 1680s, when commerce made its most significant advances, the state had resumed a more traditional desultoriness in the promotion of overseas trade. As in so many other fields of English development, it took the massive wars of William and Anne to reactivate governmental interest in trade, and there can be no doubt that fiscal needs, rather than commercial acuity, promoted greater coordination between merchant and state. Whatever the ministerial motivation, however, the elevation of trade to party issue owed much to the sustained pressure of the commercial classes, who fully exploited the transition of power from Crown to Parliament to secure their particular interests. As historians have recently stressed, the early modern English state was largely a reactive mechanism, which left the initiative for reform and innovation to others. Commercial leaders were just as conservative in outlook, but in an increasingly competitive business world, they could not refrain from reminding ministers of their broader responsibilities for the economic development of the state.[3]

[2] For instructive foreign comparisons, see J. I. Israel, *Dutch Primacy in World Trade, 1585–1740* (Oxford, 1989); M. N. Pearson, 'Merchants and States' in J. D. Tracey (ed.), *The Political Economy of Merchant Empires* (Cambridge, 1991), 41–116. As a priority, analysis of British development should investigate commercial interest groups along the lines of Olson's work on Hanoverian transatlantic traders—*Making the Empire Work: London and American Interest Groups, 1690–1790* (Cambridge, Mass. 1992), chs. 8–11.

[3] J. Barry and C. Brooks (eds.), *The Middling Sort of People: Culture, Society, and Politics in England,*

This book has given great credit to the merchant classes for their contribution towards making the system work. As one of the richest and most innovative sectors of society, whose commercial and urban leadership required constant interaction with individuals from all walks of life, they can be represented as important intermediaries of social and political change. The structure of this book has been fashioned to demonstrate the manifold ways in which mercantile influence was felt, and to show how the world of the overseas trader was very much a public stage. In particular, their prominence in the government of England's port towns, and their connections across regional and national economies rendered them key agencies for developments which went far beyond the mercantile sphere. London merchants have figured most readily in this account, for their outstanding wealth and connections placed them in the vanguard of commercial change. Their influence and riches earned them the suspicion of their social betters, who recognized the potential impact of these magnates. Qualifying legislation highlighted fears that new wealth could overwhelm the existing landed elite, and a loss of political control was not a price which the aristocracy and gentry were prepared to pay for national economic strength. However, such measures did not characterize the ultimately productive relationship between the forces of land and commerce. Attention should instead be directed to the positive incentives to traders yielded by a more efficient, though still gentry-dominated Parliament. Due acknowledgement should also be given to the reliance of the governing classes on the trader for information and other services. Their inherent importance did not necessarily give overseas traders privileged access to power, and merchants had to justify their claims, and adjust their political strategies to secure the approval of state authorities. They were not alone in this regard, and the intense competitiveness of the commercial world, more than any other factor, helped to ensure a certain degree of even-handedness in the relationship between trade and state. Business motivation would remain suspect, but it is clear that mercantile issues gained much greater publicity, and the traders themselves proved particularly resourceful when tailoring their demands to address a changing polity.[4]

· This study has suggested that political adaptability was the key to the preservation of tolerable domestic relations, rather than any supposed social mobility. Certain traders rose dramatically, were fêted for their success, and gained the attributes of a gentry lifestyle without ever acquiring gentility per se. A general survey of mercantile life indicates that modest business success was by far the more common experience of overseas traders, accompanied by

1550–1800 (London, 1994), 1–27; L. Davison et al. (eds.), *Stilling the Grumbling Hive: The Response to Social and Economic Problems in England, 1689–1750* (Stroud, 1992), pp. xi–xli.

[4] In particular, John Brewer's work has highlighted the need for future research to integrate a more traditional form of 'institutional' history into broader studies of public life and political culture—*The Sinews of Power: War, Money, and the English State, 1688–1783* (Oxford, 1989).

the rewards of a comfortable and reputable life within their natural urban environment. Moreover, surviving evidence suggests that for most this was more than sufficient, and that there was no desperate pursuit of a gentle pedigree or other social accoutrements. The respect of one's contemporaries was universally sought, but it was doubtful whether traders desired, or even could afford the time to court the upper classes to advance their reputation. In the urban world, wealth and influence did count, but in the very direct sense that they could be used to improve the inherently unstable world of international business. For a businessman, the maintenance of reputation was undoubtedly important, but more immediately as a means to secure his credit, which would be essential for the maintenance of his trade. In this regard, a certain amount of public display would be a prudent investment to achieve credit-worthiness, but such repute could not be won merely by reference to a coat of arms or a gentle connection. Reputations were primarily built on local activity and achievement, and eminence in trade was not handed from father to son without proof of personal merit. In a most uncertain urban environment, even the most successful of traders were continually put on their mettle to prove their credentials, for reasons of honour as well as for profit. As the respective leaders of town and countryside, gentlemen and merchants did share common perceptions of the requirements for success in public life, but the means by which they sought that goal were necessarily different. These continuing realities of commercial life suggest that by 1720 there was no obvious rift within the middling orders of society between those oriented towards a genteel metropolitan culture and those who revealed a more traditional localism.[5]

Recognition of the inherent professional difficulties faced by the merchant classes must condition our appreciation of the impact of Britain's bourgeoisie. In particular, this study has endeavoured to highlight the uncertainties of business life as a corrective to seeing the upper middle classes as forever upwardly mobile. On close inspection, the London merchants of 1692 appear a wealthy and distinguished elite within the metropolis, but their careers and associations do not betray an inherent confidence in the stability of the upper strata of the commercial society. As scores of mercantile petitions testify, it would be difficult to contend that any section of the commercial world experienced inexorable growth in the Augustan period, and even the most successful branches could be undermined by war. In an era of general transition, the merchant classes underwent a variety of profound changes, and some

---

[5] C. Muldrew, *The Economy of Obligation: The Culture of Credit and Social Relations in Early Modern England* (Basingstoke, 1998), esp. 148–95. For stimulating discussion of the relationship between the 'national' and 'communal' orientation of the middling classes see, D. Wahrman, 'National Society, Communal Culture: An Argument about the Recent Historiography of Eighteenth-Century Britain', *Social History*, 17 (1992), 43–72; idem, *Imagining the Middle Classes: The Political Representation of Class in Britain, c.1780–1840* (Cambridge, 1995). For criticism of this dichotomy, see R. Sweet, *The Writing of Urban Histories in Eighteenth-Century England* (Oxford, 1997).

sectors did see their markets increase dramatically, but recent research has wisely conditioned the extent of the commercial 'revolution'. The wide disparity of experiences represented by our chosen samples endorses such caution, and argues for closer inspection of the social and political consequences of Britain's expanding economy. In particular, the essential cosmopolitanism of the City merchant raises many questions concerning the feasible impact of commercial leaders in the Hanoverian period. Further research is also needed on the organization of eighteenth-century trade to see if larger firms came to dominate all of Britain's rapidly expanding markets, for this change would have had profound repercussions for both the workings of mercantile politics, and for attitudes towards the commercial classes as a whole.[6]

Recent emphasis on the 'concentration' of trade into the hands of a small number of super-rich dealers poses very interesting questions concerning the development of the merchant classes, and this study has acknowledged that the inequalities of international commerce affected contemporary perceptions of the overseas trader. If they considered commerce at all, most outsiders would have been dazzled by the glittering success of a Hearne, Heathcote, or Houblon, but the typicality of these traders must be questioned. These prominent individuals gained notice for their role as government advisers and financiers, rather than as traders, and their success did not reflect the fortunes of the vast majority of their mercantile colleagues. City-based observers would have been more aware of the fragility of mercantile wealth, and thus would more readily appreciate the scale of the achievement of the honest trader, and accord him the respect which commercial success deserved. Such was the patience and luck required for the accumulation of a trading fortune, that social mobility would be a generational, rather than an individual process. Moreover, commercial gain by itself was insufficient to win lasting praise, and the magnate had to be ready to accept his responsibilities as a leading figure within urban society. This practical limitation on the advancement of individuals undoubtedly reined in the ambition of the commercial classes, and helped to ensure their commitment to their urban environment, rather than to the orientation of a national genteel code. There is evidence to suggest that the financial 'revolution' may have permitted an elite tier of merchants to gravitate into more rarefied national circles, and that many merchants may have evaded traditional urban responsibilities in favour of other routes to respectability. However, in general this study has highlighted the continuities within the mercantile classes, and stressed that there was little in the way of 'elite withdrawal' from the urban hierarchy by Augustan merchants.

---

[6] D. Hancock's absorbing *Citizens of the World* (Cambridge, 1995) should inspire much greater interest in the Hanoverian merchant, although it may in fact question the typicality of his group of 'outsiders'. The dearth of work on the eighteenth-century London bourgeoisie was noted with concern by a recent bibliographic survey—L. Schwarz, 'London 1700 1850', *London Journal*, 20 (1995), 46–52.

Ambitious traders could not afford to isolate themselves from their colleagues and neighbours, and continued to gain vital connections and respect on account of their non-commercial activities. Indeed, a certain degree of 'snobbery' existed on both sides of the gentry–merchant divide, and the development of such middle-class 'consciousness' or culture remains a key area for future research.[7]

This study has concentrated on the celebration of the patriot merchant as a defining theme of the 'public' overseas trader in this period. The concept was by no means novel in 1660, with arguments for the utility of the overseas trader having been aired for decades before, but the popularization of the patriot ideal, and the way in which political parties fought for the mantle in 1713–14, marks out the period as crucial for popular perceptions of the merchant. Just as the more acceptable professions of the law and medicine acquired increasing respect in this period, so overseas trade underwent a similar process of reassessment and rehabilitation. In particular, the celebration of the merchant as a useful subject, empowered by special knowledge, fitted neatly with the arguments forwarded on behalf of other professions. There remained plenty of detractors of all these occupations, and the merchant could never escape the basic social stigma associated with the pursuit of wealth. Nevertheless, patriotic arguments ensured that overseas traders were not bracketed with such rapacious City caricatures as the jobbers and brokers of Exchange Alley. It cannot be assumed that a gentry-dominated polity would have readily appreciated the difference between merchant and jobber within a broad 'monied elite', particularly given the continuing dependence of overseas trade on joint-stock investment. The resilience of the patriotic trader following the South Sea Bubble in 1720 suggests that changing attitudes towards commerce cannot be dismissed as an insignificant shift in contemporary taste.[8] For commercial issues to have been given the priority which they received in the eighteenth-century Parliament, there had to be a common recognition of the value of trade among the gentle hordes assembled there. The urgency with which mercantile petitioners lectured them on this theme suggested that they did not take their task for granted, but traditional suspicions of commercial self-interest could be overcome by a well-supported claim to the public good.[9]

On its own, the occurrence of debate on the patriotic credentials of

[7] R. Grassby, *The Business Community of Seventeenth-Century England* (Cambridge, 1995), ch. 8. Margaret Hunt has conclusively argued that emulation was only one of many social impulses discernible among the middling classes—*The Middling Sort: Commerce, Gender, and Family in England, 1680–1780* (Berkeley, Calif., 1996).

[8] As a sign of post-Bubble confidence, Defoe's *Complete English Tradesman* of 1726–7 elevated the retailer or artisan to patriotic status. However, it is significant that he continually invoked mercantile examples to substantiate his claims.

[9] John Brewer has argued that an appeal to the public good was more commonly employed in eighteenth-century Westminster—*Sinews of Power*, 246. For stress on the continuing diversity of middling 'patriotism' in the eighteenth century, see L. Colley, *Britons: Forging the Nation 1707–1837* (New Haven, 1992), esp. ch. 2.

commerce at Westminster cannot suggest that a sea-change had taken place in the public profile of the merchant. However, arguments which stressed the national benefit of economic change were significantly refined in this period, and can be traced from the pocket handbooks of the trader, to the floor of the House of Commons, and finally to the fashionable folios of Addison and Steele. Traders undoubtedly gained more by stressing the enlightened self-interest which their landed betters would secure by commercial innovation, but patriotic arguments formed a central and positive element to discussion of overseas trade. Analysts of literary developments have recently confirmed the strength of this trend in the fictional works of the eighteenth century, but it is important to see that the real proving-ground of contemporary attitudes was in the political world. For merchants, it was in Westminster and Whitehall that they sought respect and influence, rather than in Grub Street or Drury Lane, and there is plenty of evidence to suggest that they had made considerable headway by the accession of George I. Beyond the number of merchants and tradesmen in the Commons, recognition should be given to the arguments of the commercial classes, and to the success which their claims to national service enjoyed, which lay enshrined in the preambles to the statutes of the period. As studies of the aristocracy and gentry have stressed, no social group can irradiate negative satire, but the merchant politician had evolved a coherent and assertive plea for particular consideration within the state, and had found a receptive audience in the parliamentary home of landed privilege. Snobbery would persist, but the message had got home to the people who really mattered.[10]

Hopefully, this work will encourage others to produce the kind of 'useful' work on trade lauded by Pepys at the outset of this book. Here, greatest interest has centred on the practitioners of overseas trade, but the attitudes and activities of the commercial classes in general must be further illuminated by research, as historians bemoan the relative dearth of such studies compared to the world of the nobility and gentry. In particular, analysis of the development of commercial attitudes to empire would be most illuminating, particularly within a domestic contest. More provincial work would also be of great benefit, especially if it could establish the significance of political connections within commercial 'regions' and across various sectors of the economy. Without such analysis we will continue to ignore the breadth and diversity of England's singular political culture, which was fashioned to suit the needs of a far wider constituency than the landed elites alone. Focus on the merchant has highlighted the vibrancy of the Augustan state, and work on his urban brethren can only further refine our understanding of a changing society, modernizing within the straight-jacket of its deeply conservative hierarchy. It can be no mere coincidence that this peculiar brand of polity has been widely regarded as Britain's greatest export.

[10] J. Raven, *Judging New Wealth* (Oxford, 1992).

Bibliography

MANUSCRIPT SOURCES

1. Bodleian Library, Oxford

Ashurst papers
Ballard MSS
Carte MSS
Dashwood papers
Folio.Theta 665 (miscellaneous papers)
Rawlinson MSS and letters

2. Borthwick Institute, York

Prerogative Court of York wills

3. British Library, London

Additional MSS

5540   Cary papers
17677 De L'Hermitage diplomatic reports
24120 Wotton's notes on baronets
28079 Merchant Adventurers' Company papers
45538 Henry papers
70070 newsletters

Harleian MSS

7497–8   South Sea Company minute books

Oriental and India Office

East India Company minute books B36–50

4. Clothworkers' Hall, London

Apprenticeship and freeman records
Courtbooks

5. College of Arms, London

I.30 funeral orders
K.9 visitation of 1687

6. Corporation of London Records Office

Assessment boxes	1690 and 1692 poll taxes
BR/P	brokers bonds
CF1	freemen admissions
MCD38	mayoral court records
CSB	inventories

7. Drapers' Hall, London

Apprenticeship and freeman records
Courtbooks

8. Guildhall Library, London

Parish and vestry records
Livery company records
Transcripts, 1695 assessments for parishes without the walls
2480 Jewer monumental transcriptions
10823 Boddington papers
11471 Russia Company minute books
11892 Eastland Company account books

9. History of Parliament Trust, London

Manuscript transcripts	Kreienberg dispatches
	Lonsdale MSS
	Devonshire MSS at Chatsworth
	Strathmore MSS at Glamis Castle

Draft biographical and constituency articles

10. House of Lords Record Office, London

Main papers series

11. Lambeth Palace, London

Marriage licences, Faculty Office and Vicar-General

12. Lancashire Record Office, Preston

Diocese of Cheshire probate records

13. Leathersellers' Hall, London

Company minute books

14. Liverpool Record Office, Liverpool

MF2/2–5	corporation minute books
352/CLE/REG/2/1	Liverpool freeman register
920 NOR	Norris papers
Glasgow notes	
Wakefield notes	

15. Merchant Adventurers' Hall, York

Company of Merchant Adventurers minute book 1677–1736
Eastland Company, York residence minute book 1645–97
Merchant Adventurers, York residence minute book (Hamburg court book) 1693–1815

16. Mercers' Hall, London

Courtbooks
Index of freemen and apprenticeships

17. Morden College, Blackheath, London

College records
Morden papers

18. The Public Records Office, Kew, London

A	Hudson's Bay Company records
C24	Chancery court depositions
CO1, 388–9	Board of Trade papers
E179	hearth taxes
E190	port books
HCA13	Admiralty court deposition records
PC2	Privy Council registers
PCC	Prerogative Court of Canterbury wills
SP78	State papers, foreign
SP105	Levant Company records
T1	Treasury papers
T70	Royal African Company records

19. Quakers' Library, London

Monthly meeting books

20. Society of Genealogists, London

Boyd index of Londoners

21. York City Archives, York

B34–44   corporation books
E85   letters concerning city affairs 1663–1718
F8   quarter sessions records
E73   poor rate records
K96   window tax returns
Ms.30   poll tax returns

22. York City Library, York

Skaife notes concerning civic officials

PRINTED PRIMARY SOURCES

1. National Series

Calendar of State Papers, Domestic
Calendar of State Papers, Colonial
Calendar of Treasury Books
Calendar of Treasury Papers
Commons Journals
Historical Manuscripts Commission: Buccleuch
                                        Fortescue
                                        House of Lords
                                        Portland
Lords Journals
Statutes of the Realm

2. Periodicals

ADDISON, J. and STEELE, R., *The Spectator*, ed. D. F. Bond (London, 1965).
BOYER, A., *The Political State of Great Britain*
The British Merchant
The City Mercury
DEFOE, D., *The Review*, ed. A. W. Seard (New York, 1938).
The Examiner
The Flying Post
The General History of Trade
The General Remark on Trade
The Gentleman's Magazine
HOUGHTON, J., *A Collection of Letters for the Improvement of Husbandry and Trade* (1681–5).
——*A Collection for Improvement of Husbandry and Trade* (1692–1703).
The London Gazette

The Manufacturer
The Mercator
The Post Boy
The Weaver
The Whitehall Evening Post

3. Other

ALLARD, A., *L'Idée de la paix conclue entre les Hauts Alliés et les François* (1713).

A to Z of Restoration London (London, 1992).

B., J., *The Interest of England Considered* (London, 1707).

BARBON, N., *A Discourse of Trade* (London, 1690).

BENNETT, J. (ed.), 'The Rolls of the Freemen of the City of Chester', *Record Society of Lancashire and Cheshire*, 51 (1906), 55 (1908).

BISSET, A. B. (ed.), 'The Eastland Company Residence, Register of Admissions to the Freedom, 1646–89', *Borthwick Lists and Indexes*, 17 (1996).

BLUNDELL, B., 'Journal of a Liverpool Merchant', *Lancashire Record Office Report, 1967–8*.

BLUNDELL, N., 'Diary', *Transactions of the Historical Society of Lancashire and Cheshire*, 110, 112, 114 (1968–72).

BOLINGBROKE, Viscount, *Letters and Correspondence, Public and Private of the Rt. Hon. Henry St. John, Lord Viscount Bolingbroke*, ed. G. Parke (London, 1798).

BREWSTER, F., *Essays on Trade and Navigation* (London, 1695).

——*New Essays on Trade* (London, 1702).

A Brief History of Trade in England (London, 1702).

BURNET, G., *Bishop Burnet's History of His Own Time*, ed. T. Burnet and M. J. Routh (Oxford, 1823).

C., S., *A Dialogue between a Country Gentleman and a Merchant Concerning the Falling of Guineas* (London, 1696).

Calendar of the Court Minutes of the East India Company, ed. E. B. Sainsbury, W. Foster, and W. T. Ottewill (Oxford, 1907–38).

CARR, C. T., 'Select Charters of Trading Companies, 1530–1707', *Selden Society*, 28 (1913).

CARY, J., *An Essay on the State of England in Relation to its Trade* (Bristol, 1695).

——*An Essay on the Coin and Credit of England* (Bristol, 1696).

Caution to those Choosing MPs (1713).

The Character and Qualifications of an Honest, Loyal Merchant (1686).

CHILD, J., *A New Discourse of Trade* (London, 1693).

CLAY, J. W. (ed.), 'Paver's Marriage Licences', *York Archaeological Society*, 40 (1909), 43 (1911), 46 (1912).

CLEMENT, S., *The Interest of England as it Stands with Relation to the Trade of Ireland* (London, 1698).

COBBETT, W. (ed.), *Parliamentary History of England* (London, 1806–20).

COCKS, R., *The Parliamentary Diary of Sir Richard Cocks, 1698–1702*, ed. D. Hayton (Oxford, 1996).

COKE, R., *A Discourse of Trade* (1670).

——*Reflections on the East India and Africa Companies* (London, 1695).

A Collection of Petitions to the Hon. House of Commons against the Trade with France (London, 1713).

Considerations upon Corrupt Elections of Members to Serve in Parliament (1701).

DAFFORNE, R., *The Merchant's Mirror* (London, 1635).

DAVENANT, C., *The Political and Commercial Works*, ed. C. Whitworth (London, 1771).

DEFOE, D., *The Complete English Tradesman in Familiar Letters* (London, 1726–7).

——*A Plan of the English Commerce* (London, 1731).

——*A Tour throughout the Whole Island of Great Britain*, ed. G. D. Cole (London, 1927).

——*Letters*, ed. G. H. Healey (Oxford, 1955).

DE LA PRYME, A., 'Diary', *Surtees Society*, 54 (1869).

DE MONCONYS, B. (ed.), *Journal des voyages de Monsieur de Monconys* (Lyon, 1966).

DERING, E., *The Parliamentary Diary of Sir Edward Dering, 1670–3*, ed. B. D. Henning (New Haven, 1940).

——*The Diaries and Papers of Sir Edward Dering, Second Baronet, 1644–84* (London, 1976).

DICKINSON, H. T. (ed.), 'Letters of Bolingbroke to the Earl of Orrey, 1712–13', *Camden Miscellany*, 31 (1992), 349–71.

DRAKE, F., *Eboracum: Or the History and Antiquities of the City of York* (London, 1736).

ENFIELD, W., *An Essay towards the History of Leverpool* (Warrington, 1773).

EVELYN, J., *Navigation and Commerce: Their Original and Progress* (London, 1674).

——*The Diary*, ed. E. S. De Beer (Oxford, 1955).

Extracts from Several Mercators (Dublin, 1713).

FIENNES, C., *The Journeys*, ed. C. Morris (London, 1949).

FORTREY, S., *England's Interest and Improvement, Consisting in the Increase and the Store and Trade of this Kingdom* (Cambridge, 1663).

The Freemen of London's Necessary and Useful Companion, or the Citizen's Birthright with the Foreigners' and Aliens' Best Instructor (London, 1707).

GENT, T., *The Ancient and Modern History of the Famous City of York* (London, 1730).

——*Annales Regioduni Hullini* (1735).

GEORGE III, King, *The Correspondence*, ed. J. B. Fortescue (London, 1927–8).

GLASS, D. V. (ed.), 'London Inhabitants within the Walls, 1695', *London Record Society*, 2 (1966).

GREY, A., *Debates of the House of Commons, 1667–94* (London, 1769).

Guildhall Library Staff, 'Supplement to the London Inhabitant List of 1695', *Guildhall Studies in London History*, 2 (1976), 77–104, 136–57.

GWYNNE, R., 'Minutes of the Consistory of the French Church of London, Threadneedle Street', *Huguenot Society*, 58 (1994).

HANDSON, R., *Analysis or Resolution of Merchant's Accounts* (1669).

HANMER, T., *Correspondence*, ed. H. Bunbury (London, 1838).

HATTON, E., *The New View of London* (London, 1708).

——*Comes Commercii* (London, 1716).

——*The Merchant's Magazine* (London, 1721).

HESSELS, J. H. (ed.), *Ecclesiae Londino-Batavae Archivum: Epistulae et Tractatus* (London, 1882).

HEYWOOD, T. (ed.), 'The Norris Papers', *Chetham Society*, 9 (1846).

The History and Defence of the Last Parliament (London, 1713).

Honest Advice to the Electors of Great Britain on the Present Choice of their Representatives (London, ?1708).

HORWITZ, H. (ed.), 'Minutes of a Whig Club', *London Record Society*, 17 (1981).

HOWELL, E. (ed.), *Ye Ugly Face Clubb, Leverpoole, 1743–53* (Liverpool, 1912).

HUGHES, T. C. (ed.), 'Rolls of the Freemen of the Borough of Lancaster', *Record Society of Lancashire and Cheshire*, 87 (1935), 90 (1938).

IRVINE, W. F. (ed.), 'Marriage Licences Granted within the Archdeaconry of Chester', *Record Society of Lancashire and Cheshire*, 65 (1912), 69 (1914), 73 (1918), 77 (1924).

KEYMER, J., *Observations* (1696).

KING, C., *The British Merchant* (London, 1721).

KING, G., *Two Tracts*, ed. J. H. Hollander (Baltimore, 1936).

Lancashire Parish Record Society, 35 (1909), 101 (1963).

LEE, S., *The Little London Directory* (London, 1677).

LE NEVE, J., *Monumenta Anglicana* (London, 1719).

A Letter from a Member of the House of Commons to his Friend in the Country (1713).

A Letter to a West-Country Freeholder (1713).

A Letter to the Hon. A[rthu]r M[oo]re (London, 1714).

LEYBOURN, W., *Panarithmologia* (London, 1693).

The Linen and Woollen Manufactory Discoursed, with the Nature of Companies and Trade in General (London, 1691).

LISET, A., *Amphithalami* (1660).

A List of the Names of the Subscribers to a Loan of Two Millions (1698).

LUPTON, D., *London and the Countrey Carbonadoed and Quartered* (1638).

LUTTRELL, N., *A Brief Historical Relation of State Affairs* (Oxford, 1857).

—— *The Parliamentary Diary of Narcissus Luttrell, 1691–3*, ed. H. Horwitz (Oxford, 1972).

MACKY, J., *A Journey through England in Familiar Letters* (1714).

MALYNES, G. DE, *Consuetudo: vel Lex Mercatoria* (1622).

MARIUS, J., *Advice Concerning Bills of Exchange* (1670).

MARSHALL, G. W., 'Le Neve's Pedigrees of the Knights', *Harleian Society*, 8 (1873).

MILWARD, J., *The Diary of John Milward*, ed. C. Robbins (Cambridge, 1938).

MOENS, W. J. C. (ed.), *The Marriage, Baptismal, and Burial Registers, 1571–1874 . . . of the Dutch Reformed Church, Austin Friars, London* (London, 1884).

MONTEAGE, S., *Debtor and Creditor Made Easy* (1682).

MORTIMER, T., *The Elements of Commerce, Politics, and Finance* (1772).

MUN, T., *England's Treasure by Foreign Trade* (London, 1664).

PEET, H., 'Liverpool in the Reign of Queen Anne, 1705 and 1708', *Transactions of the Historical Society of Lancashire and Cheshire*, 59 (1908).

PEPYS, S., *The Private Correspondence and Miscellaneous Papers of Samuel Pepys*, ed. J. R. Tanner (London, 1926).

—— *The Diary*, ed. R. Latham and W. Matthews (London, 1983).

PETTY, W., *A Treatise of Taxes and Contributions* (1662).

PETYT, W., *Britannia Languens* (1680).

Poll books: Essex 1715; London 1710, 1713, 1722; Middlesex 1705; Surrey 1705.

PUCKLE, J., *England's Way to Wealth and Honour* (London, 1699).

QUARRELL, W. H., and Mare, M. (eds.), *London in 1710* (London, 1934).

'Register of the Freemen of York, 1559–1759', *Surtees Society*, 102 (1900).

Remarks on a Scandalous Libel (1713).

RICH, E. E. (ed.), 'Minutes of the Hudson's Bay Company, 1671–4', *Hudson's Bay Company Series*, 5 (1942).

—— 'Minutes of the Hudson's Bay Company, 1679–82', *Hudson's Bay Company Series*, 8 (1945). ˈ

ROBERTS, L., *The Merchant's Map of Commerce* (London, 1638).

SELLERS, M. (ed.), 'Acts and Ordinances of the Eastland Company', *Camden Society*, 3rd ser., 11 (1906).

SHAW, W. A., 'Naturalizations and Denizations of Aliens in England and Ireland', *Huguenot Society*, 18 (1911) and 27 (1923).

The Six Distinguishing Characters of a Parliament Man (London, 1700).

SMITH, A., *An Inquiry into the Nature and Causes of the Wealth of Nations*, ed. E. Cannon (London, 1904).

SMITH, D. (ed.), 'The Company of Merchant Adventurers of York, Register of Admissions, 1581–1835', *Borthwick List and Indexes*, 18 (1996).

SMITH, S., *The Golden Fleece, or the Trade, Interest, and Well-Being of Great Britain Considered* (London, 1736).

SPECK, W., and GRAY, W. A. (eds.), 'London Poll-books, 1713', *London Record Society*, 17 (1981).

The State of the Silk and Woollen Manufacture Considered in Relation to the French Trade (London, 1713).

STRYPE, J., *A Survey of the Cities of London and Westminster* (London, 1720).

A Tender and Hearty Address to all the Freeholders (London, 1714).

THOMAS, D., *An Historical Account of the Rise and Growth of the West India Colonies* (London, 1690).

TOLAND, J., *The Art of Governing by Parties* (1701).

Trade and Tor[y]ism Can Never Agree (1713).

The Trade of Scotland with France Considered (Edinburgh, 1713).

A Treatise [Concerning the East India Company] (London, 1681).

TRYON, T., *England's Grandeur and Way to Get Wealth* (London, 1699).

—— *Some Memoirs of the Life of Thomas Tryon* (London, 1705).

Usury at Six Per Cent Examined (London, 1669).

VAN MUYDEN, Madame (ed.), *A Foreign View of England, 1725–9: The Letters of Monsieur Cesar de Saussure to his Family* (London, 1995).

VERNON, J., *The Complete Comptinghouse* (London, 1678).

WENGER, M. R. (ed.), *The English Travels of Sir John Percival and William Byrd II* (Columbia, NY, 1989).

WENTWORTH, T., *The Wentworth Papers, 1705–39*, ed. J. J. Cartwright (London, 1883).

WHISTON, J., *A Discourse on the Decay of Trade* (London, 1693).

—— *To the King's Most Excellent Majesty* (?1693).

—— *The Causes of our Present Calamities* (1696).

—— *The Mismanagements in Trade Discovered* (1704).

WIDDRINGTON, T., *Analecta Eboracensia: Some Remains of the Ancient City of York*, ed. C. Caine (London, 1897).

SELECT SECONDARY SOURCES

AGNEW, J. H., *Belfast Merchant Families in the Seventeenth Century* (Blackrock, 1996).

AGNEW, J.-C., *Worlds Apart* (Cambridge, 1986).

ALEXANDER, J. M. B., 'The Economic Structure of the City of London at the End of the Seventeenth Century', *Urban History Yearbook*, (1989), 47–62.

ALLEN, D., 'Political Clubs in Restoration London', *HJ* 19 (1976), 561–80.

ANDERSON, G., and TOLLINSON, R. D., 'Apologiae for Chartered Monopolies in Foreign Trade', *History of Political Economy*, 15 (1983), 549–66.

ANDERSON, S., *An English Consul in Turkey* (Oxford, 1989).

ANDREWS, C. M., *British Committees, Commissions, and Councils of Trade and Plantations, 1622–75* (Baltimore, 1908).

ANDREWS, K. R., *Trade, Plunder, and Settlement: Maritime Enterprise and the Genesis of the British Empire, 1485–1630* (Cambridge, 1984).

APPLEBY, J., *Economic Thought and Ideology in Seventeenth-Century England* (Princeton, 1978).

ARCHER, I., *In Pursuit of Stability* (Cambridge, 1991).

ASHLEY, M., *Financial and Commercial Policy under the Cromwellian Protectorate* (Oxford, 1934).

ASHTON, R., *The City and the Court, 1603–43* (Cambridge, 1979).

BAILYN, B., and MORGAN, P. D. (eds.), *Strangers Within the Realm* (Chapel Hill, NC, 1991).

BARRY, J., and BROOKS, C. (eds.), *The Middling Sort of People: Culture, Society, and Politics in England, 1550–1800* (London, 1994).

BAXTER, S. B. (ed.), *England's Rise to Greatness, 1660–1763* (Berkeley, Calif., 1983).

BEER, A. R., *Sir Walter Raleigh and His Readers in the Seventeenth Century* (Basingstoke, 1997).

BEIER, A. L., and FINLAY, R. (eds.), *London, 1500–1700* (London, 1986).

BEIER, A. L., CANNADINE, D., and ROSENHEIM, J. M. (eds.), *The First Modern Society* (Cambridge, 1989).

BERLIN, M., 'Civic Ceremony in Early Modern London', *Urban History Yearbook* (1986), 15–27.

BLACK, J., *A System of Ambition? British Foreign Policy, 1660–1793* (London, 1991).

——and GREGORY, J. (eds.), *Culture, Politics, and Society in Britain, 1660–1800* (Manchester, 1991).

BOLD, J., and CHANEY, E. (eds.), *English Architecture Public and Private* (London, 1993).

BOWEN, M. V., *Elites, Enterprise, and the Making of the British Overseas Empire, 1688–1775* (London, 1996).

BOYLE, J. R., and DENDY, F. W., 'Extracts from the Records of the Merchant Adventurers of Newcastle-upon-Tyne', *Surtees Society*, 93 (1895), 101 (1899).

BRADDICK, M., *The Nerves of State: Taxation and the Financing of the English State, 1558–1714* (Manchester, 1996).

BRENNER, R., *Merchants and Revolution* (Princeton, 1993).

BREWER, J., *The Sinews of Power: War, Money, and the English State, 1688–1783* (Oxford, 1989).

BURTON, I. F., RILEY, P. W. J., and ROWLANDS, T., 'Political Parties in the Reigns of William III and Anne', *BIHR* special supplement 7 (1968).

BYWATER, M. F., and YAMEY, B. S., *Historic Accounting Literature: A Companion Guide* (London, 1982).

CANNY, N. (ed.), *The Oxford History of the British Empire: The Origins of Empire* (Oxford, 1998).

CARLOS, J. M., KEY, J., and DUPREE, J. C., 'Learning and the Creation of Stock-Market Institutions: Evidence from the Royal African and Hudson's Bay Companies, 1670–1700', *Journal of Economic History*, 58 (1998), 318–44.

CARRUTHERS, B. G., *City of Capital: Politics and Markets in the English Financial Revolution* (Princeton, 1996).

CARSWELL, J., *The South Sea Bubble* (London, 1960).

CHALKLIN, C. W., and WORDIE, J. R. (eds.), *Town and Countryside* (London, 1989).

CHANDAMAN, C. D., *The English Public Revenue, 1660–88* (Oxford, 1975).

CHAPMAN, S., *Merchant Enterprise in Britain from the Industrial Revolution to World War One* (Cambridge, 1992).

CHAUDHURI, K. N., *The Trading World of Asia and the English East India Company* (Cambridge, 1978).

CHERRY, G. L., 'The Development of the English Free Trade Movement in Parliament, 1689–1702', *JMH* 25 (1953), 103–19.

CHRISTIE, I., *British Non-elite MPs, 1715–1820* (Oxford, 1995).

CLARK, G. N., *Guide to English Commercial Statistics, 1696–1782* (London, 1938).

CLARK, P., *British Clubs and Societies, 1580–1800: The Origins of an Associational World* (Oxford, 2000).

CLARKE, J. C. D., *English Society, 1688–1832* (Cambridge, 1985).

CLAYTON, T., *The English Print, 1688–1802* (New Haven, 1997).

CLEMENS, P. G. E., 'The Rise of Liverpool, 1665–1750', *EcHR* 29 (1976), 211–25.

CLUTTERBUCK, R., *The History and Antiquities of Hertfordshire* (London, 1815).

COKAYNE, G. E., *Complete Baronetage* (Gloucester, 1983 repr.).

COLE, C. W., *Colbert and a Century of French Mercantilism* (New York, 1939).

—— *French Mercantilism, 1683–1700* (New York, 1965).

COLEMAN, D. C., *Sir John Banks* (Oxford, 1963).

—— *History and the Economic Past* (Oxford, 1987).

—— and JOHN, A. H. (eds.), *Trade, Government, and Economy in Pre-Industrial England* (London, 1976).

—— and MATHIAS, P. (eds.), *Enterprise and History* (Cambridge, 1984).

COLLEY, L., *Britons: Forging the Nation, 1707–1837* (New Haven, 1992).

CORFIELD, P., *The Impact of English Towns* (Oxford, 1982).

—— (ed.), *Language, History, and Class* (Oxford, 1991).

—— *Power and the Professions in Britain, 1700–1850* (London, 1995).

CRESSY, D., *Birth, Marriage, and Death: Ritual Religion and the Life-Cycle in Tudor and Stuart England* (Oxford, 1997).

CROFT, P., 'Free Trade and the Commons, 1605–6', *EcHR* 2nd ser., 28 (1975), 17–27.

CROWHURST, P., *The Defence of British Trade* (Folkestone, 1977).

CULLEN, L. M., *Anglo-Irish Trade, 1660–1800* (Manchester, 1968).

CUSSANS, J. E., *History of Hertfordshire* (London, 1870–81).

DAVIES, K. G., *The Royal African Company* (London, 1957).

DAVIS, R., *The Rise of the English Shipping Industry* (London, 1962).

DAVIS, R., 'The Rise of Protection in England, 1689–1786', *EcHR* 2nd ser., 19 (1966), 306–17.

——*Aleppo and Devonshire Square* (London, 1967).

——*A Commercial Revolution* (London, 1967).

——*English Overseas Trade, 1500–1700* (London, 1973).

DAVISON, L., HITCHCOCK, T., KEIRN, T., and SHOEMAKER, R. B. (eds.), *Stilling the Grumbling Hive: The Response to Social and Economic Problems in England, 1689–1750* (Stroud, 1992).

DE KREY, G. S., *A Fractured Society: The Politics of London* (Oxford, 1985).

DEVINE, T. M., *The Tobacco Lords: The Merchants of Glasgow, 1740–90* (Edinburgh, 1975).

DICKSON, P. G. M., *The Financial Revolution in England*, 2nd edn. (Oxford, 1993).

DITCHFIELD, G. M., HAYTON, D., and JONES, C., *British Parliamentary Lists, 1660–1800: A Register* (London, 1995).

DOOLITTLE, I., *The City of London and its Livery Companies* (Dorchester, 1982).

——*The Mercers' Company, 1579–1959* (London, 1994).

DOWNIE, J. A., *Robert Harley and the Press* (Cambridge, 1979).

DUFFY, M., *The Englishman and the Foreigner* (Cambridge, 1986).

DUNN, R. S., and DUNN, M. M. (eds.), *The World of William Penn* (Philadelphia, 1986).

EARLE, P., *The Making of the English Middle Class* (London, 1989).

——*A City Full of People* (London, 1994).

——*Sailors: English Merchant Seamen, 1650–1775* (London, 1998).

EHRMAN, J., *The Navy under William III* (Cambridge, 1953).

ELLIS, F. H. (ed.), *Poems on the Affairs of State: Volume 6* (New Haven, 1970).

FARMER, D. H., *The Oxford Dictionary of Saints* (Oxford, 1978).

FERET, C. J., *Fulham Old and New* (London, 1900).

FISHER, H. E., *The Portugal Trade* (London, 1971).

FOSTER, W., *A Short History of the Worshipful Company of Coopers of London* (Cambridge, 1944).

FRANCIS, A. D., 'John Methuen and the Anglo-Portuguese Treaties of 1703', *HJ* 3 (1960), 103–24.

——*The Methuens and Portugal, 1691–1708* (Cambridge, 1966).

FRENCH, C. J., 'Crowded with Great Traders and a Great Commerce: London's Domination of English Overseas Trade, 1700–75', *London Journal*, 17 (1992), 27–35.

GALLEY, C., *The Demography of Early Modern Towns: York in the Sixteenth and Seventeenth Centuries* (Liverpool, 1998).

GAUCI, P., *Politics and Society in Great Yarmouth, 1660–1722* (Oxford, 1996).

——'For Want of Smooth Language: Parliament as a Point of Contact in the Augustan Age', *Parliamentary History* (1998), 12–22.

GOSS, C. W. F., *The London Directories* (London, 1932).

GRASSBY, R., *The English Gentleman in Trade: The Life and Works of Sir Dudley North, 1641–91* (Oxford, 1994).

——*The Business Community of Seventeenth-Century England* (Cambridge, 1995).

GRELL, P., ISRAEL, J. I., and TYACKE, N. (eds.), *From Persecution to Toleration* (Oxford, 1991).

GWYNNE, R., *Huguenot Heritage* (London, 1985).

HABAKKUK, J., *Marriage, Debt, and the Estates System: English Landownership, 1650–1950* (Oxford, 1994).

HANCOCK, D., *Citizens of the World* (Cambridge, 1995).

HANDLEY, S., 'Local Legislative Initiatives for Economic and Social Development in Lancashire, 1689–1731', *Parliamentary History*, 9 (1990), 231–49.

——'Provincial Influence on General Legislation: The Case of Lancashire, 1689–1731', *Parliamentary History*, 16 (1997), 171–84.

HARKNESS, D. A. E., 'The Opposition to the Eighth and Ninth Articles of the Commercial Treaty of Utrecht', *Scottish History Review*, 21 (1924), 219–26.

HARRIS, R., 'American Idols: Empire, War, and the Middling Ranks in Mid-eighteenth Century Britain', *Past and Present*, 150 (1996), 111–41.

——*Politics and the Rise of the Press: Britain and France, 1620–1800* (London, 1996).

HARTE, N., and QUINAULT, R. (eds.), *Land and Society in Britain, 1700–1914* (Manchester, 1996).

HASLER, P. W. (ed.), *The History of Parliament: The House of Commons, 1558–1603* (London, 1981).

HEATHCOTE, E. D., *Account of Some of the Family Bearing the Name of Heathcote* (Winchester, 1899).

HENNING, B. D. (ed.), *The History of Parliament: The House of Commons, 1660–90* (London, 1983).

HILL, B., 'The Change of Government and the Loss of the City, 1710–11', *EcHR* NS, 24 (1971), 395–411.

——'Oxford, Bolingbroke, and the Peace of Utrecht', *HJ* 16 (1973), 241–63.

HINTON, R. W. K., *The Eastland Trade and the Commonweal* (Cambridge, 1959).

HOLLAENDER, A. E. J., and KELLAWAY, W., *Studies in London History* (London, 1969).

HOLMES, C., and HEAL, F., *The Gentry in England and Wales* (Basingstoke, 1994).

HOLMES, G. S., *The Trial of Dr. Sacheverell* (London, 1973).

——*Augustan Society* (London, 1982).

——*British Politics in the Age of Anne*, 2nd edn. (London, 1987).

——*The Making of a Great Power* (London, 1993).

——and JONES, C., 'Trade, the Scots, and the Parliamentary Crisis of 1713', *Parliamentary History*, 1 (1982), 47–77.

HONT, I., 'Free Trade and the Economic Limits to National Politics: Neo-Machiavellian Political Economy Reconsidered', in J. Dunn (ed.), *The Economic Limits to Modern Politics* (Cambridge, 1990), 41–120.

HOOCK, J., and JEANNIN, P., *Ars Mercatoria* (Paderborn, 1991).

HOPPIT, J., *Risk and Failure in English Business, 1700–1800* (Cambridge, 1987).

——'Political Arithmetic in Eighteenth-Century England', *EcHR* 49 (1996), 516–40.

——(ed.), *Failed Legislation, 1660–1800* (London, 1997).

HORN, D. B., *The British Diplomatic Service, 1689–1789* (Oxford, 1961).

HORNSTEIN, S. R., *The Restoration Navy and English Foreign Trade, 1674–88* (Aldershot, 1991).

HORWITZ, H., *Parliament, Policy, and Politics in the Reign of William III* (Manchester, 1977).

——'The East India Trade, the Politicians, and the Constitution, 1689–1702', *JBS* 17 (1978), 1–18.

——'Testamentary Practice, Family Strategies, and the Last Phases of the Custom of

London, 1660–1725', *Law and History Review*, 2 (1984), 223–39.

HORWITZ, H., 'The Mess of the Middle Classes Revisited', *Continuity and Change*, 2 (1987), 263–96.

HOUGHTON, W. E., 'The History of Trades: Its Relation to Seventeenth-Century Thought', *Journal of the History of Ideas*, 2 (1941), 33–60.

HUNT, M., *The Middling Sort: Commerce, Gender, and Family in England, 1680–1780* (Berkeley, Calif., 1996).

HUNTER, M., *The Royal Society and its Fellows* (Chalfont St Giles, 1982).

IMRAY, J., *The Mercers' Hall* (London, 1991).

IRVINE, W. F., *Liverpool in the Reign of Charles II* (Liverpool, 1889).

ISRAEL, J. I., *European Jewry in the Age of Mercantilism, 1550–1750* (Oxford, 1985).

—— *Dutch Primacy in World Trade, 1585–1740* (Oxford, 1989).

JACKSON, G., *Hull in the Eighteenth Century* (Oxford, 1972).

JOHN, A. H. (ed.), *Trade, Government, and Economy in Pre-Industrial England* (London, 1976).

JOHNSON, B., *The Last of the Old Hanse* (York, 1949).

JONES, C. (ed.), *Party and Management in Parliament, 1660–1784* (Leicester, 1984).

—— (ed.), *Britain in the First Age of Party* (London, 1987).

JONES, D. W., 'London Merchants and the Crisis of the 1690s', in P. Clark and P. Slack (eds.), *Crisis and Order in English Towns, 1500–1700* (London, 1972), 311–55.

—— *War and Economy in the Age of William III* (Oxford, 1988).

KEIRN, T., 'Monopoly, Economic Thought, and the Royal African Company', in J. Brewer and S. Staves (eds.), *Early Modern Conceptions of Property* (London, 1995), 427–66.

KELLET, J. R., 'The Breakdown of Guild and Corporation Control over the Handicraft and Retail Trade in London', *EcHR* 2nd ser., 10 (1957–8), 381–94.

KEMP, B., *The Votes and Standing Orders of the House of Commons: The Beginning* (London, 1971).

KERMODE, J. (ed.), *Enterprise and Individuals in Fifteenth-Century England* (Stroud, 1991).

—— *Medieval Merchants: York, Beverley, and Hull in the Later Middle Ages* (Cambridge, 1998).

KEY, N. E., 'The Political Culture and Political Rhetoric of County Feasts and Feast Sermons, 1654–1714', *JBS* 33 (1994), 223–56.

—— 'The Localism of the County Feasts and Feast in Late Stuart Political Culture', *Huntington Library Quarterly*, 58 (1996), 211–37.

KNIGHTS, M., 'A City Revolution: The Remodelling of the London Livery Companies in the 1680s', *EHR* 112 (1997), 1141–78.

KOEHN, N., *The Power of Commerce* (Ithaca, NY, 1994).

LAMBERT, S., *Bills and Acts: Legislative Procedure in Eighteenth-Century England* (Cambridge, 1971).

LANDAU, N., *The Justices of the Peace, 1679–1760* (Berkeley, Calif., 1984).

LANG, R. G., 'The Social Origins and Social Aspirations of Jacobean London Merchants', *EcHR* 2nd ser., 27 (1974), 28–47.

LANGFORD, P., *The Excise Crisis* (Oxford, 1975).

—— 'Property and Virtual Representation in Eighteenth-Century England', *HJ* 31 (1988), 83–115.

—— *A Polite and Commercial People* (Oxford, 1989).

—— *Public Life and the Propertied Englishman, 1689–1798* (Oxford, 1991).

LANGTON, J., 'Residential Patterns in Pre-Industrial Cities: Some Case Studies from Seventeenth-Century Britain', *Transactions of the Institute of British Geographers*, 65 (1975), 1–27.

LASLETT, P., 'John Locke, The Great Recoinage, and the Origins of the Board of Trade, 1695–8', *William and Mary Quarterly*, 3rd ser., 14 (1957), 370–402.

—— *The World We Have Lost: Further Explorations* (New York, 1965).

LEES, R. M., 'Parliament and the Proposal for a Council of Trade, 1695–6', *EHR* 54 (1939), 38–66.

LESGER, C., and NOORDEGRAAF, L., (eds.), *Entrepreneurs and Entrepreneurship in Early Modern Times* (Haarlem, 1995).

LETWIN, W., *The Origins of Scientific Economics: English Economic Thought, 1660–1776* (London, 1963).

LI, M.-H., *The Great Recoinage of 1696–9* (London, 1963).

LINDERT, P. H., 'English Occupations, 1670–1811', *Journal of Economic History*, 40 (1980), 685–712.

LINGELBACH, W. E., 'The Internal Organization of the Merchant Adventurers of England', *TRHS* NS, 16 (1902), 19–67.

—— *The Merchant Adventurers of England: their Laws and Ordinances with Other Documents* (New York, 1971).

LOCK, F. P., *Swift's Tory Politics* (London, 1983).

LOFTIS, J., *Comedy and Society from Congreve to Fielding* (Stamford, 1959).

LOUNSBURY, R. G., *The British Fishery at Newfoundland* (New Haven, 1934).

McCUSKER, J. J., and GRAVESTEIJN, C. (eds.), *The Beginnings of Commercial and Financial Journalism* (Amsterdam, 1991).

McGRATH, P., 'Merchants and Merchandise in Seventeenth-Century Bristol', *Bristol Record Society*, 29 (1955).

—— *The Merchant Venturers of Bristol* (Bristol, 1975).

McKAY, D., 'Bolingbroke, Oxford, and The Defence of the Utrecht Settlement in Southern Europe', *EHR* 86 (1971), 264–84.

McKENDRICK, N., and OUTHWAITE, R. B. (eds.), *Business Life and Public Policy* (Cambridge, 1986).

McVEAGH, J., *Tradefull Merchants: The Portrayal of the Capitalist in Literature* (London, 1981).

MARSHALL, P. (ed.), *The Oxford History of the British Empire: The Eighteenth Century* (Oxford, 1998).

MENHENNET, D., *The Journal of the House of Commons* (London, 1971).

MILLER, H. K., ROTHSTEIN, E., and ROUSSEAU, G. S. (eds.), *The Augustan Milieu* (Oxford, 1970).

MINCHINGTON, W. E. (ed.), *The Growth of English Overseas Trade in the Seventeenth and Eighteenth Centuries* (London, 1969).

MORGAN, K., *Bristol and the Atlantic Trade in the Eighteenth Century* (Cambridge, 1993).

MULDREW, C., *The Economy of Obligation: The Culture of Credit and Social Relations in Early Modern England* (Basingstoke, 1998).

MULLET, M., 'The Politics of Liverpool, 1660–88', *Transactions of the Historical Society of Lancashire and Cheshire*, 124 (1972), 31–56.

MURPHY, J., 'The Old Quaker Meeting-House in Hackins Hey, Liverpool', *Transactions of the Historical Society of Lancashire and Cheshire*, 106 (1954), 79–98.

MURRAY, H., *Scarborough, York, and Leeds: The Town Plans of John Cossins, 1697–1743* (York, 1997).

NAMIER, L., and BROOKE, J. (eds.), *The History of Parliament: The House of Commons, 1754–90* (London, 1985).

NEAL, L., *The Rise of Financial Capitalism* (Cambridge, 1990).

NEWTON, R., *Eighteenth-Century Exeter* (Exeter, 1984).

NICHOLSON, S., and BLACK, A., *The Changing Face of Liverpool, 1207–1727* (Liverpool, 1981).

NIGHTINGALE, B., *Lancashire Nonconformity* (Manchester, 1893).

NORMAN, P., 'Notes on the Later History of the Steelyard in London', *Archaelogia*, 61 (1909), 389–426.

OLSON, A. G., 'The Board of Trade and London Interest Groups in the Eighteenth Century', *Journal of Imperial and Commonwealth History*, 8 (1980), 35–50.

—— 'The Virginia Merchants of London: A Study in Eighteenth-Century Interest-Group Politics', *William and Mary Quarterly*, 3rd ser., 40 (1983), 363–88.

—— *Making the Empire Work: London and American Interest Groups, 1690–1790* (Cambridge, Mass., 1992).

PALLISER, D., *The Company of Merchant Adventurers of the City of York* (York, 1985).

PEARL, V., *London and the Outbreak of the Puritan Revolution* (Oxford, 1961).

—— 'Change and Stability in Seventeenth-Century London', *London Journal*, 5 (1979), 3–34.

PENNINGTON, D., and THOMAS, K. (eds.), *Puritans and Revolutionaries* (Oxford, 1978).

PENSON, L. M., *The Colonial Agents of the British West Indies* (London, 1924).

PICTON, J., *Selections from the Municipal Archives and Records* (Liverpool, 1883).

PINCUS, S., *Protestantism and Patriotism* (Cambridge, 1994).

—— 'Coffee Politicians Does Create: Coffee-houses and Restoration Political Culture', *JMH* 67 (1995), 807–34.

—— 'Neither Machiavellian Moment Nor Possessive Individualism: Commercial Society and the Defenders of the English Commonwealth', *American Historical Review*, 103 (1998), 705–36.

POCOCK, J. G. A., *The Machiavellian Moment* (Princeton, 1975).

POLLINS, H., *Economic History of the Jews in England* (East Brunswick, 1982).

POWER, M., 'Councillors and Commerce in Liverpool, 1650–1750', *Urban History*, 24 (1997), 310–23.

PREST, W. (ed.), *The Professions in Early Modern England* (Beckenham, 1987).

PRICE, J. M., 'Notes on some London Price Currents', *EcHR* 2nd ser., 7 (1954–5), 240–50.

—— 'A Note on the Circulation of the London Press, 1704–14', *BIHR* 31 (1958), 215–24.

—— 'The Tobacco Adventure to Russia', *Transactions of the American Philosophical Society*, NS 51 (1961), 1–120.

—— *France and the Chesapeake* (Ann Arbor, 1973).

—— *Capital and Credit in British Overseas Trade: The View from the Chesapeake, 1700–76* (Cambridge, Mass, 1980).

—— *Perry of London: A Family and a Firm on the Seaborne Frontier, 1615–1753* (Cambridge, Mass., 1992).

—— and CLEMENS, P. G. E., ' A Revolution in Overseas Trade: British Firms in the Chesapeake Trade, 1675–1775', *Journal of Economic History*, 47 (1987), 1–43.

PRIESTLY, M., 'Anglo-French Trade and the Unfavourable Balance Controversy', *EcHR* 2nd ser., 4 (1951), 37–52.

—— 'London Merchants and Oppositional Politics in Charles II's Reign', *BIHR* 29 (1956), 205–19.

QUINN, J. F., 'York Elections in the Age of Walpole', *Northern History*, 22 (1986), 175–97.

RABB, T., *Enterprise and Empire* (Cambridge, Mass., 1967).

RAMSAY, G. D., *The English Woollen Industry, 1500–1750* (Basingstoke, 1982).

RAPPARPORT, S., *Worlds within Worlds* (Cambridge, 1989).

RAVEN, J., *Judging New Wealth* (Oxford, 1992).

REDDAWAY, T., *The Rebuilding of London after the Great Fire* (London, 1940).

REYNOLDS, W. H., 'Grantees of Arms, 1687–1898', *Harleian Society*, 67–8 (1916–17).

RICH, E. E., 'The Hudson's Bay Company and the Treaty of Utrecht', *Cambridge Historical Journal*, 9 (1954), 188–203.

—— *The History of the Hudson's Bay Company, 1670–1870* (London, 1958–9).

RICH, E. E., and WILSON, C. (eds.), *The Cambridge Economic History of Europe* (Cambridge, 1977).

RICHARDS, J. O., *Party Propaganda under Queen Anne* (Athens, Ga., 1972).

RICHARDSON, R. C., *The Debate on the English Revolution* (London, 1977).

ROGERS, N., 'Money, Land and Lineage: The Big Bourgeoisie of Georgian London', *Social History*, 4 (1979), 437–54.

—— 'Clubs and Politics in Eighteenth-Century London: The Centenary Club of Cheapside', *London Journal*, 11 (1985), 51–8.

—— *Whigs and Cities* (Oxford, 1989).

ROSENHEIM, J. M., *The Emergence of a Ruling Order: English Landed Society, 1650–1750* (Harlow, 1998).

ROSEVEARE, H., *Markets and Merchants of the Late Seventeenth Century* (Oxford, 1987).

ROTH, C., *The Great Synagogue, London* (London, 1950).

—— *A History of the Jews in England*, 3rd edn. (London, 1964).

Royal Commission on Historical Monuments, *City of York* (London, 1972).

SACKS, D. H., *The Widening Gate: Bristol and the Atlantic Economy, 1450–1700* (Berkeley, Calif., 1987).

SAUNDERS, A., *The Royal Exchange* (London, 1991).

—— (ed.), *The Royal Exchange* (London, 1997).

SCHAMA, S., *The Embarrassment of Riches* (London, 1987).

SCHUMPETER, E. B., *English Overseas Statistics, 1697–1808* (Oxford, 1960).

SCHURER, K., and ARKELL, T. (eds.), *Surveying the People* (Oxford, 1992).

SCHWARZ, L., *London in the Age of Industrialization* (Cambridge, 1992).

—— 'London, 1700–1850', *London Journal*, 20 (1995), 46–52.

SCOTT, W. R., *The Constitution and Finance of English, Scottish, and Irish Joint-Stock Companies to 1720* (Cambridge, 1919).

SCOVILLE, W. C., 'The French Economy on 1700–1: An Appraisal by the Deputies of Trade', *Journal of Economic History*, 22 (1962), 231–52.

SEDGWICK, R. (ed.), *The History of Parliament: The House of Commons, 1715–54* (London, 1970).

SELLERS, M., 'The York Mercers and Merchant Adventurers, 1356–1917', *Surtees Society*, 129 (1917).

SHAW, W., *The Knights of England* (London, 1906).

SHOEMAKER, R. B., *Gender in English Society, 1650–1850* (Harlow, 1998).

SKEEL, C. A. J., 'The Canary Company', *EHR* 31 (1916), 529–44.

SMAIL, J., *The Origins of Middle-Class Culture: Halifax, Yorkshire, 1660–1780* (Ithaca, NY, 1994).

—— *Merchants, Markets, and Manufacturers* (Basingstoke, 1999).

SMITH, D. L., *The Stuart Parliaments, 1603–89* (London, 1999).

SMOUT, T. C., *Scottish Trade on the Eve of the Union, 1660–1707* (Edinburgh, 1963).

STATT, D., *Foreigners and Englishmen* (Newark, NJ, 1995).

STEELE, I. K., *Politics of Colonial Policy* (Oxford, 1968).

STEELE, R., *A Bibliography of Royal Proclamations of the Tudor and Stuart Sovereigns, 1485–1714* (Oxford, 1910).

STEVENSON, L. C., *Praise and Paradox* (Cambridge, 1984).

STONE, L., and STONE, J. C. F., *An Open Elite? England, 1540–1880* (Oxford, 1984).

SUPPLE, B., *Commercial Crisis and Change in England, 1600–42* (Cambridge, 1959).

SUTHERLAND, J., *The Restoration Newspaper* (Cambridge, 1986).

SUTHERLAND, L. S., *The East India Company in Eighteenth-Century Politics* (Oxford, 1972).

SWEET, R., *The Writing of Urban Histories in Eighteenth-Century England* (Oxford, 1997).

—— *The English Town, 1680–1840* (Harlow, 1999).

SZECHI, D., *Jacobitism and Tory Politics, 1710–14* (Edinburgh, 1984).

THIRSK, J., and COOPER, J. P. (eds.), *Seventeenth-Century Economic Documents* (Oxford, 1972).

THORTON, A. P., *West India Policy under the Restoration* (Oxford, 1956).

THRUPP, S., *The Merchant Classes of Medieval London, 1300–1500* (Chicago, 1948).

TOUZEAU, J., *The Rise and Progress of Liverpool from 1551 to 1835* (Liverpool, 1910).

TRACEY, J. D. (ed.), *The Political Economy of Merchant Empires* (Cambridge, 1991).

Victoria County Histories: *Lancashire: Volume 4* (London, 1911); *Yorkshire: The City of York* (London, 1961).

WAHRMAN, D., 'National Society, Communal Culture: An Argument about the Recent Historiography of Eighteenth-Century Britain', *Social History*, 17 (1992), 43–72.

—— *Imagining the Middle Classes: The Political Representation of Class in Britain, c.1780–1840* (Cambridge, 1995).

WALCOTT, R., 'The East India Interest and the General Election of 1700–1', *EHR* 71 (1956), 223–39.

WALKER, J. W., 'Yorkshire Pedigrees', *Harleian Society*, 94–6 (1942–4).

WARD, J. P., *Metropolitan Communities* (Stanford, Calif., 1997).

WEATHERILL, L., *Consumer Behaviour and Material Culture in Britain, 1660–1760* (London, 1988).

WHYMAN, S., 'Land and Trade Revisited: The Case of John Verney, London Merchant and Baronet', *London Journal*, 22 (1997), 16–32.

—— *Sociability and Power in Late-Stuart England* (Oxford, 1999).

WILLAN, T. S., 'The Navigation of the River Weaver in the Eighteenth Century', *Chetham Society*, 3rd ser., 3 (1951).

WILLIAMS, O. C., *The Historical Development of Private Bill Procedure and Standing Orders in the House of Commons* (London, 1948–9).

—— *The Clerical Organization of the House of Commons, 1661–1850* (Oxford, 1954).

WILSON, C., *Anglo-Dutch Commerce and Finance in the Eighteenth Century* (Cambridge, 1966).

—— *England's Apprenticeship, 1603–1763*, 2nd edn. (London, 1984).

WILSON, K., 'Empire, Trade, and Popular Politics in Mid-Hanoverian Britain: The Case of Admiral Vernon', *Past and Present*, 121 (1988), 74–109.

—— *The Sense of the People: Politics, Culture, and Imperialism in England, 1715–1785* (Cambridge, 1995).

WITMER, H. E., *The Property Qualifications of Members of Parliament* (New York, 1943).

WOOD, A. C., *A History of the Levant Company* (Oxford, 1935).

WUNDERLI, R. M., 'Evasion of the Office of Alderman in London, 1523–1672', *London Journal*, 15 (1990), 3–18.

ZAHEDIEH, N., 'Making Mercantilism Work: London Merchants and Atlantic Trade in the Seventeenth Century', *TRHS* 6th ser., 9 (1999), 143–58.

UNPUBLISHED THESES

ALEXANDER, J. M. B., 'The Economic and Social Structure of the City of London, c.1700', Ph.D. thesis (London School of Economics, 1989).

AMBROSE, G. P., 'The Levant Company, mainly from 1640–1753', B.Litt. thesis (Oxford, 1933).

ASCOTT, D. E., 'Wealth and Community: Liverpool 1660–1760', Ph.D. thesis (Liverpool, 1996).

BROWN, S., 'Politics, Commerce, and Social Policy in the City of London, 1782–1802, D.Phil. thesis (Oxford, 1992).

DE KREY, G. S., 'Trade, Religion, and Politics in London in the Reign of William III', Ph.D. thesis (Princeton, 1978).

DICKIE, T. M., 'Commerce and Experience in the Seventeenth-Century Mediterranean: The Market Dynamics, Commercial Culture, and Naval Protection of English Trade to Aleppo', D.Phil. thesis (Oxford, 1997).

DOOLITTLE, I., 'The Government of the City of London, 1694–1767', D.Phil. thesis (Oxford, 1979).

FORSHAW, D. M., 'An Economic and Social History of Liverpool, 1540–1680', BA thesis (Nottingham, 1953).

GARDINER, D., 'The Work of the English Privy Council, 1660–79', D.Phil. thesis (Oxford, 1992).

GLAISYER, N. A. F., 'The Culture of Commerce in England, 1660–1720', Ph.D. thesis (Cambridge, 1999).

HIBBERD, D. J., 'Urban Inequalities: Social Geography and Demography in Seventeenth-Century York', Ph.D. thesis (Liverpool, 1981).

HUNNEYBALL, P., 'Status, Display, and Dissemination: Social Expression and Stylistic

Change in the Architecture of Seventeenth-Century Hertfordshire', D.Phil. thesis (Oxford, 1994).

JONES, D. W., 'London Overseas Merchant Groups at the End of the Seventeenth Century and the Move against the East India Company', D.Phil. thesis (Oxford, 1970).

JULIAN, M. R., 'English Economic Legislation, 1660–1714', M.Phil. thesis (London School of Economics, 1979).

LEWIS, F., 'The Demographic and Occupational Structure of Liverpool: A Study of the Parish Registers, 1660–1750', Ph.D. thesis (Liverpool, 1993).

LOUGHEAD, P., 'The East India Company in English Domestic Politics, 1657–88', D.Phil. thesis (Oxford, 1981).

McHATTIE, M. D., 'Mercantile Interests in the House of Commons, 1710–13', MA thesis (Manchester, 1949).

NEWMAN, E. K., 'Anglo-Hamburg Trade in the Late Seventeenth and Early Eighteenth Centuries', Ph.D. thesis (London School of Economics, 1979).

SCOTT, D. A., 'Politics, Dissent, and Quakerism in York, 1640–1700', D.Phil. thesis (York, 1990).

WITHINGTON, P., 'Urban Political Culture in Late Seventeenth-Century England: York 1649–88', Ph.D. thesis (Cambridge, 1998).

WOODHEAD, J. R., 'The Rulers of London: The Composition of the Courts of Aldermen and Common Council of the City of London, 1660–89', MA thesis (London, 1961).

Index